P9-CDT-656

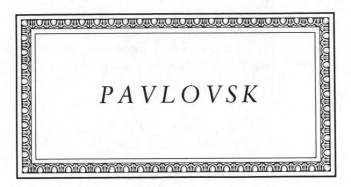

PAVLOVSK

Also by Suzanne Massie

THE LIVING MIRROR
Five Young Poets from Leningrad

JOURNEY
(with Robert K. Massie)

LAND OF THE FIREBIRD
The Beauty of Old Russia

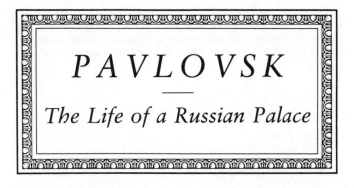

PAVLOVSK

The Life of a Russian Palace

BY

SUZANNE MASSIE

LITTLE, BROWN AND COMPANY

BOSTON   TORONTO   LONDON

Copyright © 1990 by Suzanne Massie

All rights reserved. No part of this book may be reproduced in any form or by any electronic or mechanical means, including information storage and retrieval systems, without permission in writing from the publisher, except by a reviewer who may quote brief passages in a review.

First Edition

Library of Congress Cataloging-in-Publication Data

Massie, Suzanne.
    Pavlovsk : the life of a palace / by Suzanne Massie. — 1st ed.
       p.   cm.
    Includes bibliographical references (p.   ).
    ISBN 0-316-54970-3
    1. Pavlovskiĭ dvorets-muzeĭ — History.   2. Neoclassicism
(Architecture) — Russian S.F.S.R. — Pavlovsk (Leningradskaia oblast')
3. Pavlovsk (Leningradskaia oblast', R.S.F.S.R.) — Buildings,
structures, etc. I. Title.
NA7771.P3M37 1990
725'.17'0947453—dc20

90-6023
CIP

Photograph credits:

First color section: All photographs by Boris Smelov except for page 5 (right), Vladimir Terebenin; pages 5 (top left, bottom left), 8 (top), 10 (bottom) and 11, M. Velichko, *Pavlovsk Palace* (Aurora Art Publishers, 1973).

Black and white section: All photographs from Pavlovsk Palace Photographic Archives except pages 12 and 13, courtesy Princess Vera of Russia; page 14, courtesy A. M. Kuchumov.

Second color section: All photographs by Boris Smelov except pages 12 (top), 13 (bottom), and 14, Pavlovsk Palace Photographic Archives; pages 12 (bottom) and 15, M. Velichko.

10 9 8 7 6 5 4 3 2 1

MV NY

BOOK DESIGN BY ROBERT G. LOWE

*Published simultaneously in Canada
by Little, Brown & Company (Canada) Limited*

Printed in the United States of America

For all those who created — and re-created —
the beauty of Pavlovsk

Ignore the past — you lose an eye
Forget the past — you lose two eyes

— Russian proverb

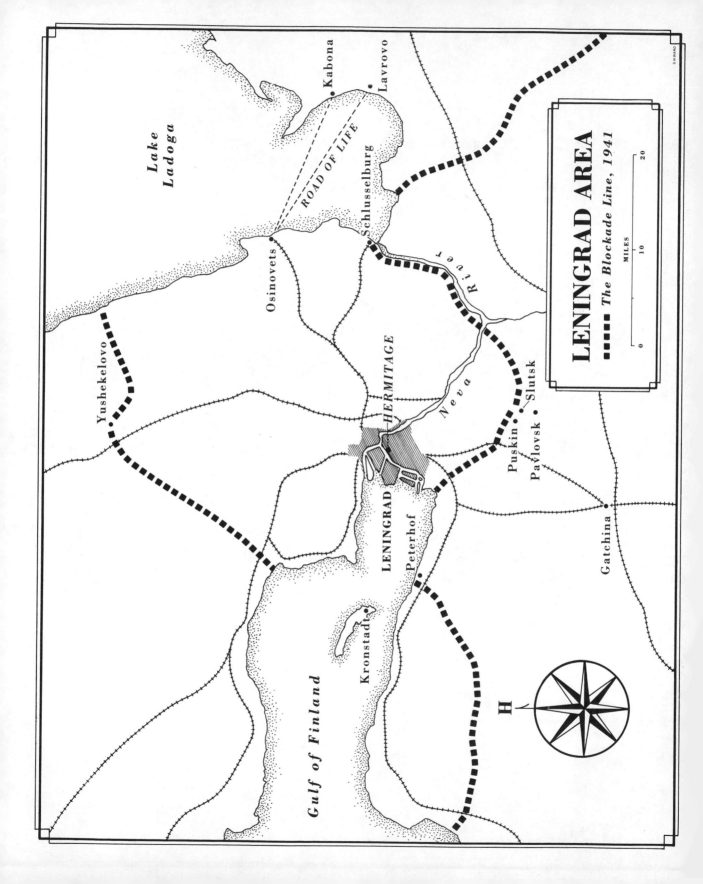

LENINGRAD AREA

The Blockade Line, 1941

■■■■

MILES

0   10   20

Lake Ladoga

Kabona

Lavrovo

ROAD OF LIFE

Schlusselburg

Osinovets

Neva River

HERMITAGE

Yushekelovo

Puskin · · Slutsk

Pavlovsk

Gatchina

LENINGRAD

Peterhof

Kronstadt

Gulf of Finland

N

G.W.WARD

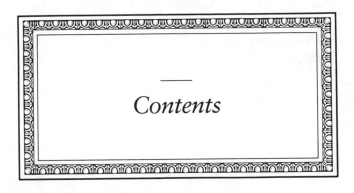

Contents

x   *Contents*

Acknowledgments

*T*HE WRITING of this book was accomplished at the Harvard Russian Research Center where, since 1985, I have been privileged to be a Fellow. The center is directed by Professor Adam Ulam, a preeminent scholar of Soviet history at Harvard University and a man of exceptional civilization and humanity. Professor Ulam and his deputy director, Marshall Goldman, have created at the center an inimitable atmosphere of scholarship, professional support, inspiration, and human warmth, for which I am profoundly grateful. Throughout the course of my work, my colleagues at the center shared their special insights and expertise with me, and always gave me their cheer and support. I thank them for their interest in and encouragement of my work. Most especially I wish to thank my dear friend Carol Leonard, who saw me through many difficult hours both personal and professional, as did Sanford Leiberman, Anthony Jones, John Le-Donne, Christine Porto, and Cathy Reed. My deep thanks, too, to Mary Towle, the guardian angel of the center, who efficiently handles the myriad details of organization that make it possible for us to work in peace.

I am greatly indebted to Professor Hugh Ragsdale of the University of Alabama who generously shared his knowledge of the personality and reign of Paul I and permitted me to read his *Tsar Paul and the Question of Madness* in manuscript. I drew much valuable material from this work. I am indebted to Professor Ulam for taking time to read my entire manuscript, to Professor Erich Goldhagen of Harvard for reading the chapter "We Are Barbarians," and to Professor Alan Fletcher of the New England Conservatory of Music who read the chapter

"Musical Pavlovsk." Their suggestions and comments were invaluable. Any errors are mine alone.

One phase of my research, from September to December 1985, was accomplished as a Senior Exchange Scholar in Leningrad thanks to a grant from IREX (International Research and Exchanges Board). The final six months of writing this book was supported by a grant from the Brown Foundation, Texas. My thanks to them and to Louisa Serafim.

At the time I began this book, few saw its possibilities. I remember gratefully William Loverd, who believed in it from the beginning. I am very grateful to Little, Brown, and in particular to Roger Donald, whose enthusiasm for this story came at a time of great personal discouragement, and to Robert Hyde, Director of Foreign Sales at Little, Brown, whose faith in this book and my ability to write it helped me greatly. My thanks also to my editor, Jennifer Josephy, Michael Mattil, copyeditor extraordinaire, and my agent, Anne Sibbald.

This book was researched and written during an extremely difficult period in my life. That it has now finally been accomplished is thanks to the faith, support, and help of devoted friends from many countries. There is no way for me to express to them how vital their friendship was to me. Each, I hope, knows the immense contribution that he or she made to this work.

I thank Leslie Kitchell Bullock and Ridgely Bullock, precious friends of many years who came to my rescue in a desperate time, and I am deeply grateful for the continuing friendship and extraordinarily generous support of Juan de Beistegui at a time when, without it, I would most certainly have been overcome by financial difficulties.

My thanks to my dear friends Wren and Timothy Wirth and Teresa and John Heinz, who, during the years of writing this book, sustained me with their humor, hospitality, wisdom, and affection. Also to Marilyn Swezey, Bishop Basil Rodzianko, Phyllis and Henri Glaeser, Johanna Hoerler, Janet Kellock, Louis Martinz, Martha and Charles Humpstone, Michael Capozzi, and Charles Remington.

I am also most indebted to Raymond and Shirley Benson of the United States Embassy in Moscow, who extended their help, advice, and the warm hospitality of their home in Moscow, as well as to Anton and Ines Kassonof of the same embassy, and, in Leningrad, to United States Consul General Charles Magee and his wife, Maida, and Lyndon and Mary Ann Allin.

A special *merci* to Ambassador Guy de Muyser of Luxembourg, one of the most charming and capable diplomats it has been my pleasure to know, and to his wife, Dominique, who extended to me their friendship and the haven of their charming embassy in Moscow during several visits. During the past two years I owe a special debt of gratitude to the current United States Consul General in Leningrad, Richard Miles, and his wonderful wife, Sharon, for their friendship, support, and generous hospitality of their residence on many occasions.

This book has been a true joint effort between Russians and Americans. Although the major research in the Soviet Union was accomplished in the years before *glasnost,* a time when friendship and cooperation with a foreign writer could present difficulties for Soviet citizens, help and friendship were always given to me in the astonishing abundance that is one of the glories of the Russian character. When I was in the Soviet Union, Russian friends fed me, cheered me, and opened their homes and hearts. It is impossible for me to list all those who helped me, but special thanks go to Kiril Ukraintsev and the late Mikhail Priveyantsev of VAAP (Soviet Copyright Agency) Moscow and to Sergei Zhitinsky of VAAP Leningrad for their help during all my trips to the Soviet Union throughout the writing of this book; to Radomir Bogdanov and Valentin Bereshkov of the Institute of USA and Canada Studies; and to Danil Granin and Alexander Bransky of the Leningrad Union of Writers.

I owe a great debt to many museum curators and specialists in Leningrad. My deepest gratitude is owed to Anatoly Mikhailovich Kuchumov, a remarkable man whom I revere, and to his wife, Anna Mikhailovna. I thank also Aleksandr Kedrinsky of the Catherine Palace, and Vitaly Suslov and Dmitry Warygin of the Hermitage.

To all at the Pavlovsk Palace Museum my heartfelt thanks for accepting this writer as one of their own through these many years, most especially curators Irina Alekseyeva, Valeriya Belanina, Irina Skopich, Ludmilla Koval, Marina Flit, and Sophia Jarasova, and to Evdokia Makhrova, former director. Also *bolshoe spacibo* to Galina Sautkina, museum specialist of both Pavlovsk and Gatchina, and Natalia Bondarachuk of Len Concert, Irina Kalinina and Mikhail Litviakov of Leningrad Documentary Films, and Boris Smelov, a great artist-photographer.

Vladimir Telemakov generously shared his knowledge and his research on the palace evacuations to Siberia, Kuchumov's search for lost objects, the children's restoration school, and Treskin's career, which were of enormous help to me.

During the most difficult year of writing this book, I was kept together and immeasurably helped by Erin McBurney, who was my research assistant in 1986/ 87. I am deeply indebted to her for outstanding research, knowledge of military matters, efficiency, and devotion. I thank also Ethan Feffer, who brought his cheerfulness and expertise at the computer to my aid, and Anita Bucknam for her help with the notes and meticulous work of incorporating my corrections into the final manuscript. In addition I am most indebted to Lynn Scheib for her exact, precise research help and for making available to me her excellent master's thesis, "No Longer a Memory," on the restoration of Pavlovsk. Thanks also to Elena Starenko, who transcribed many tapes of interviews, Nicholas Ohotin of the American Society for the Preservation of Russian Monuments and Culture Inc. in New York for his translations, and David Rivera and Jenny Bauer.

My family, as always, supported me faithfully. I thank my cousin Jean Flavien Lalive, my sisters Simone Dur and Jeannine Leavenworth and my brother-in-law Urs Dur for his help with German translations and for sharing his knowledge of Nazi history. My son, Robert Massie, and his wife, Dana, immeasurably gladdened my life during the writing of this book by presenting me with two grandsons. My daughter Susanna Massie Thomas brought me a new son-in-law and always inspired me by her outstanding example of true grit and determination. My daughter Elizabeth Massie shared her humor, imagination, and buoyant love of life, which can brighten even the darkest day.

Finally, I owe an enormous debt of gratitude to two remarkable friends, who, during the final difficult year of writing, never failed to sustain me. One is Karla Munger, whose enthusiasm, flow of comments and reactions, and total faith in me and this book kept me at my computer. The other is Seymour Papert, who abundantly gave his affection and the benefits of all his special talents. He read this manuscript several times, always offering valuable suggestions and insights, and, brilliantly gifted in mind and heart, always knew how to get me back on my horse when I fell off.

Preface

WITH THE SOUND of a cannon shot that reverberated through the city, the ice cracked and the Neva began to live again. Huge floes of gray-blue pushed by the swift currents of the newly liberated river rushed toward the Baltic Sea.

In the life of every human being there is a moment when everything that has gone before seems to have been leading to a single awakening. This happened to me in the spring of 1967. My first trip to Leningrad was the beginning of a voyage of personal discovery that changed the course of my life.

I had come with my former husband to put the final touches on the research for a book, *Nicholas and Alexandra,* into which we both had poured our creative energy for many years. It was the late Marvin Ross, then curator at Washington's Hillwood Museum, who pointed the way. Ross, a cultivated gentleman of the old school, was one of the rare Westerners who, in those days, had managed to maintain contact with Soviet museum specialists. He told me an intriguing tale: there was a palace outside Leningrad where the curator at the time of the Nazi invasion had supposedly saved uniforms of the last Tsar. The palace was a place that Ross called "the finest restoration in the world." I was determined to go there, and despite the fact that Intourist was sullenly uncooperative, we managed to secure a car. Contemplating the burly back of our uncommunicative driver, we set forth into the countryside to find it. Pavlovsk turned out to be the wrong palace for our research, but the right one for me.

We had refused a guide, only to find when we arrived that no one at the palace spoke English. At that time my Russian, which is now fluent, consisted of a knowledge of the Cyrillic alphabet and a few verses from great Russian poets, which I had memorized. Nevertheless, we somehow made our quest for the curator understood and were told to wait. Time passed. We had almost given up hope when a tall, bearded young man approached us. "Can I help you?" he asked in accented English. "I am a poet of St. Petersburg." He then went on to explain politely that the curator was being sought; in the meantime we were to consider ourselves guests and tour the palace. It was the first time I glimpsed the rooms that have now become so familiar. I did not suspect that the beauty of Pavlovsk was to capture me as it had so many others.

It did not occur to me then to wonder what a poet was doing as a tour guide in a palace. I learned later that in those bleak days there was a "parasite law" in the Soviet Union, which meant that those with no regular work risked being sent to labor camps. To avoid this danger, unofficial poets and artists, excluded from official unions and hard-pressed to do their creative work, took all manner of lowly jobs. Sometimes sympathetic curators of museums managed to provide them with minimal employment, and the result was that the museums of Leningrad numbered among their janitors, snow clearers — and occasionally guides (only for Soviet citizens, never for foreigners) — some of the greatest artists of the city.

The curator we sought was absent that day, and we decided to leave. The poet had disappeared with his group, but just as we were about to rejoin our car, he ran up, took my arm, and said the words that the voice of the palace has never stopped repeating, "Will you come back?"

That night, in Leningrad, we went to one of his poetry readings and met our first Russian friends. During the next few days, they took us for long rambles through the streets of the city. I fell in love with its magnificent architecture and incomparable sky, and I did come back — not once but many times. During the next five years, communicating their knowledge and passion for their city and its history, the poet and his friends took me through the looking glass that separated foreigners from Soviet citizens in an odyssey that led me to write several books, and now, eighteen years since I conceived the desire to write it, this one.

For Pavlovsk kept drawing me back, and I never made a trip to Leningrad without making a pilgrimage to the palace. I saw it in every season — in autumn, when falling leaves turn the earth to amber, in the diamond-bright frosts of winter, in the tender, green blossoming of spring, and the warm, lazy, flower-filled days of summer. At dusk I stood awestruck before the palace, majestic and silent, rich with its memories, watching the last molten rays of the sun gild the colonnaded dome and the silhouettes of swallows etching black crescents against the deep blue sky.

I met Anatoly Mikhailovich Kuchumov in 1968. The restoration was still in progress. Anna Zelenova was director; Anatoly Treskin was working on the Corner Salon. As chief curator, Kuchumov sometimes led tours himself. He was a short, energetic man with a compact body, square, practical hands, and eyes that twinkled with humor. When he spoke of the palace he loved, an infectious smile would often illuminate his face. When he laughed it took him entirely, like a mischievous schoolboy, crinkling his eyes nearly shut over his high Slavic cheekbones. He would surprise me by setting off the magnificent clocks, expectantly waiting for my expression of delight when I heard their tinkling chimes play eighteenth-century melodies. He would proudly lift up the white cloth coverings that protected the rare upholstery of French tapestry and delicate silk to hear my exclamations of admiration. Protective as a terrier about the rare objects under his care, he would, as he was talking, occasionally caress them fondly. In June, to brighten my Spartan hotel room, he would sometimes give me a branch of lilac from the thick bushes of the park or, from the Private Garden, a few fragrant white roses, which bear the poetic name Tsaritsa of the North.

Over the years, I grew to know intimately the paths, the ponds, the whisper of the birches in the park, and in that magical place, which celebrates the resilience of the human spirit and its eternal quest for beauty, I found inspiration and personal solace from the problems of my own life.

Because of my struggles raising a child with hemophilia, I knew something of despair, and as a writer, I came to be fascinated with the problem of how people faced the unconfrontable and what values they called on to sustain them in their struggles. The challenge the indomitable museum workers had faced after the war touched me profoundly. The restored palace stood as a living example that the unconfrontable could be faced — and vanquished. It was a palace created by a woman, and re-created by the determination of another; the more I saw it, the more determined I grew to try to tell its story.

The road to accomplishing this dream was to be long — eighteen years. For eleven of those years I was arbitrarily and mysteriously denied a visa to the Soviet Union. During that period of exile from the city I loved, I wrote *Journey* and *Land of the Firebird*, but I never forgot Pavlovsk. When, in 1983, I was able to return, I tried again. In order to do my research I needed official permission to stay in Leningrad and work in the archives at the palace for several months. *Glasnost* and its fresh gusts of air were still three years away, and bureaucrats, nervous about the efforts of an independent writer, barricaded my way with an impenetrable barrage of *nyets*. I persisted, borrowing money for two more unsuccessful trips. In 1985, almost ready to abandon hope, I was finally able to scale the obstacles in the Soviet Union, only to find to my dismay that in the United States the way was no easier. At home, I was greeted with yawns of indifference from several publishers. Stories of dissidence were the interest of the moment. I discovered that in the USA fashion and the dollar could exert as stern a censorship as the bureaucratic myopia and fear in the USSR. Luckily for me, in both countries there were a few people whose imagination led them to take risks, and to these I am immeasurably indebted.

The bulk of my research in the Soviet Union was accomplished during six months of work in Leningrad in 1985, made possible by both sides: in the spring of that year through an invitation from VAAP (the Soviet Copyright Agency) and the Writer's Union in Leningrad, and from September to December through a grant from IREX (International Research Exchange) in the United States. I lived in a hotel room provided by the Academy of Sciences and traveled to Pavlovsk — a one-and-a-half-hour trip from the city on subway, train, and bus — through the rain, sleet, and snow. At night, I often returned too weary to clamber on a crowded bus again to go to the generous friends who were always ready to share their meals with me, so I warmed *pirozhki* (filched from the hotel dining room at breakfast) on the radiator and used my little electric coil to boil water for packages of dried soup I had brought with me from the United States.

Then, in the spring of 1986, I was given the extraordinary chance — the first for a foreigner since the Revolution — to live for a time in a modest apartment in the town of Pavlovsk, a few minutes walking distance from the gates of the palace. Devoted Russian friends set me up in housekeeping by lending their dishes, pots, and sheets.

Those sunny summer days living and working at Pavlovsk were days of perfect contentment, which I count among the happiest of my existence. Inhaling the perfume of the green meadows and flowers, I walked every morning through the park to the palace, delighting in the fact that even the militiamen and the palace cats sunning themselves on the windowsills recognized me. I would climb the smooth stone steps that led to the second floor, there to work in a tiny wood-paneled library with the musty smell of old books and a single window that looked out over birches and the park. When my eyes were exhausted from reading, I would take a stroll, gaze at meadows full of wildflowers, the perfect symmetry of Cameron's Doric Temple of Friendship, and the beautiful parterres of Brenna, then return to my work renewed. The museum workers accepted me as a friend, sharing their lunches of hard-boiled eggs and homemade pickled cabbage. Water was boiled on a hot plate, and at four we would sit on a balcony overlooking the park in the back of the palace, chatting, sipping tea, and sampling delicious golden cloudberry jam that one of the curators had brought from home.

I spent long afternoons with Anatoly Mikhailovich. He lived with his wife of fifty years in a small apartment in Pavlovsk, surrounded by the objects and pictures he loved, working at a simple, white-painted desk that had once belonged to the Empress Alexandra, which he had found smashed on a trash heap after the German armies left. On it sat a bust of Apollo, above it hung an old gravure of the fountains of the Catherine Palace. On the wall at the foot of his modest couch bed, where he could see it when he woke, was a picture of the church in the village of his youth. Paralyzed on his right side by two strokes and a severe heart attack, his right hand immobilized, he was sometimes sad and tired when I arrived, but as soon as he began talking about his past, his work and experiences, new energy flowed. His eyes began to sparkle, his voice grew stronger. When his black-and-white cat obstreperously interrupted him by leaping about on the furniture, with his good hand Anatoly Mikhailovich would reach for a bottle of cheap cologne he kept on his desk and spray it vigorously in the cat's direction ("He hates the smell," he would say). I sat listening, entranced by this remarkable man's stories of the past, oblivious to the hours that always passed too quickly. And then, no matter how I demurred, he and his wife would always insist that before leaving I have a cup of tea brewed with boiling water poured from their old samovar, along with sweets and a slice of Russian torte smothered in thick whipped-cream icing they always managed to obtain and have ready on their little table set with their best porcelain.

How Pavlovsk grew from a royal residence to become the beloved patrimony of a people is a love story. Pavlovsk is the finest example of Russian neoclassicism, incorporating ideals of harmony and measure, antique forms and motifs, as well as the acceptance of the latest fashions of Europe. But the architecture and the ensemble that was created is Russian — with as different a look as branches from roots, and tied to the tumultuous blossoming of all Russian culture and literature. The modern story of the palace is the tale of a people's heroic efforts to save and preserve it through revolution and war for future generations.

Those who built Pavlovsk, saved it, restored it, were united by a love for this place that reaches across history. Faced with its beauty, all political boundaries faded away.

It is a sad fact that our ability to wage war greatly exceeds our capacity to heal its effects. Pavlovsk was destroyed in two and a half years. It took forty-five years to restore it, and the work continues. As I looked at the palace, I often wondered: What if such a calamity had happened to us in the United States? What buildings would we consider of such vital importance to our national spirit that we would work for almost half a century to restore them? The drive to restoration has a passion and force in the Soviet Union unknown to us in the West, where often beauty of the past is neglected and left to decay and ruin, perhaps because, having experienced no such violent break with the past, we take it for granted. For the dedicated group of museum specialists in Leningrad — helped by thousands of their fellow citizens, confronted with ruins and the threat of the total disappearance of their historical identity — the preservation of beauty and memory became more vital than their own lives.

Solzhenitsyn once wrote: "When a culture is taken away from a people it is like committing a lobotomy on them." Both Stalin and Hitler tried. The people of Leningrad refused to allow it. The restoration of their city and their palaces, a restoration not only of buildings, but of their country's memory and soul, is a startlingly human achievement accomplished against superhuman odds. No one has ever done anything like it. It is unique.

It is now twenty-three years since I first saw the Neva and Pavlovsk. They still stir me as they did that first time. The heady exhilaration of love at first sight, sharpened by adversity and enriched by familiarity and knowledge, has deepened into the passion of a lifetime. The book I dreamed of is finally finished, but the palace and its people will be a part of my life forever.

PART ONE

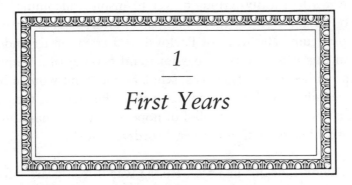

1

First Years

Les rois faisaient des folies sans pareilles
Ils depensaient notre argent sans compter
Mais lorsqu'ils construisaient de semblables merveilles
Ne nous mettaient-ils pas notre argent de cote? *

— French saying

UNDER THE MOTHER-OF-PEARL SKY of the northern Russian countryside, some seventeen miles south of the city once called St. Petersburg, the palace is set in a vast park full of silvery birches and dark firs. In the spring the tender green leaves and white blossoms of bird cherries cover the slopes like green waves crested with foam. Thick bushes of lilacs perfume the air. In summer, luxuriant rolling meadows are sprinkled with fields of lavender and white wild-flowers. Secret pools and lakes serenely disposed through the park reflect the passing clouds. The meandering little river Slavyanka invites the wanderer to plunge deep into the forest. Only the fresh wind blowing through the trees, the sound of the cuckoo and the nightingale, and the solitary cries of sea gulls break the perfect silence. In autumn, among the dark green firs, thousands of birch trees blaze yellow and the falling leaves turn the earth to amber. Then, rising like a dream at the end of an *allée* of burnished golden linden trees, the yellow and white Palladian colonnaded palace and its graceful neoclassical temples and stat-

---

* The extravagances of kings were beyond compare, / They spent our money without counting. / But when they constructed such marvels, / Were they not putting aside our money for us?

ues appear to their greatest advantage, blending the beauty of nature and art, of East and West, in a harmony which only the measure and refinement of the eighteenth century could conceive.

This palace has had a mysterious power to inspire uncommon love and devotion and so has survived for more than two hundred years through fire, war, and almost total ruin. The story of Pavlovsk is a story of art and architecture, but more than this it is a story of passions and people; of an emperor and an empress, grand dukes and serfs, artists, scholars, men and women high and low, who built it, rebuilt it, and would not let it die. They gave it their lives and the palace lives on beyond them, a symbol of hope and the eternal human quest for beauty, an oasis of serenity in a forever disordered world.

The story of Pavlovsk begins in 1777. Russia was fifteen years into the reign of Catherine the Great. Born a minor German princess, Sophia of Anhalt-Zerbst, she had come to Russia at the age of fourteen to marry the heir, and by her ambition, cunning, and intelligence had succeeded in becoming in 1762, at the age of thirty-three, Empress of Russia. Catherine ruled Russia for thirty-four years, a hard-driving woman of formidable will and political skill who, despite her celebrated love affairs, was at work by 5 A.M. each day.

By her own description, she had a mind "infinitely more masculine than feminine." She worked hard, and brilliantly knew how to use men to accomplish her political goals. She seized power by staging a coup with the help of a group of palace guardsmen led by Grigory Orlov, a man who was her lover for ten years. During her reign, she surrounded herself with a group of outstanding military men who became known as the Catherinian Eagles;* their conquests won her the title "Great." With their support and that of her great love and partner, the fiery Grigory Potemkin, Russia under Catherine acquired vast new territories, including the Crimea and Poland, and grew enormously in power and influence in Europe.

Catherine's reign saw the apotheosis of the aristocratic period in Russia. It was a time when Russia, having absorbed European culture, began to produce her first great artists of international fame — the painter Dmitry Levitsky, the poet Gavril Derzhavin, the sculptor Fedot Shubin. It was a time of extraordinary lavishness. With serf labor, Russian noblemen built and maintained houses with

---

* The Catherinian Eagles, who helped bring Catherine to the throne and supported her throughout her reign, included the five Orlov brothers (Alexis, Grigory, Feodor, Ivan, and Vladimir), Potemkin, the field marshals Suvorov and Rumyantsev, the generals Kutusov and Bibikov, and Prince Golitsyn.

hundreds of servants and kept their own serf orchestras and artists. Catherine wanted her court to rival the splendor and elegance of Versailles. She encouraged Western influences. Following Catherine's lead, Russian aristocracy spoke French rather than Russian. The Russian exuberance, the bright colors and gilt of Empress Elizabeth's time, passed into the grandeur of a neoclassical era that glittered with the cold light of diamonds. Skilled at public relations, Catherine spread her own fame and that of her court by carrying on an extensive correspondence with the great men of Europe, thus winning for herself a reputation as a brilliant intellect, the "Semiramis of the North."*

During the first years of her reign, Catherine was principally concerned with putting down rebellions and consolidating her power, but she then turned her enormous energy to the embellishment of the capital and her palaces. She collected art and bought Old Masters by the boatload, beginning the famed collections of the Hermitage. She had statues erected, including the famous "Bronze Horseman" statue of Peter the Great, which became one of the symbols of St. Petersburg. Lavishly, she commissioned buildings and once wrote "the mania for building is a diabolical thing, it consumes money, and the more one builds, the more one wants to build; it is a disease like drunkenness." Catherine was a powerful ruler with many talents, a woman of intellect and determination; she read widely, made laws, built an empire. But as a wife and mother she was an utter failure.

In order to become empress she had to remove her husband, Peter III, the grandson of Peter the Great and nephew of Empress Elizabeth. Royal history is full of enigmas; the true character of Peter and the circumstances of his death are among them. What is known is that eight days after Catherine had seized power, Peter was killed in what was said to be a drunken scuffle with a group of men led by Alexei Orlov, brother of her lover Grigory.

Ten years into the unhappy union of Catherine and Peter, on October 1, 1754, a son was born, his birth clouded in rumors that he was not the son of Peter but of a lover of Catherine's — another mystery never resolved. Paul was eight years old when his mother became empress. Despite the whispers of illegitimacy that surrounded him, Paul always chose to believe that he was the son of Peter III, and throughout his life harbored a deep resentment of his mother that affected and embittered his character and drove him to his tragic end. Mother was jealous

---

* Semiramis was a ninth-century-B.C. Assyrian queen, who founded the city of Babylon. She became a legendary figure, noted for her wisdom and beauty.

of son and son resented mother. Paul grew up without affection, brilliantly educated but never loved.

A French historian, Pierre Morane, has written: "Few princes have made such a painful beginning in life as the son of Catherine II, Paul Petrovich. He grew up in a family devoured by hate, among a tumult of vulgar passions and degrading quarrels, in an atmosphere of spies and informers." Paul never, in fact, had either a father or a mother. Immediately after his birth, he was taken away by his grandaunt, Empress Elizabeth, to be surrounded by nurses, wrapped in pink velvet blankets, and smothered in black fox furs, and raised as a ward and treasure of the state. Catherine next saw him forty days after his birth, then three more times during his first six months. Only after he was seven years old did she see him once a week. As for Elizabeth, Paul said at age eleven that he was accustomed to seeing her just once or twice a year. He was a lonely child, spoiled by nurses and raised by tutors, with no real tenderness in his life.* His father had been murdered. He was distrusted by his mother, who occasionally covered him with bursts of affection followed by cold indifference, and all his life attempted to discredit him. The fact that as the heir he was very popular with the Russian people, who often greeted him with warmer demonstrations of affection than they did his mother, only intensified the tension between them.

In the eighteenth century, there was an almost total conviction of the importance and value of education. Paul was drowned in mathematics, history, and modern languages, speaking and writing Russian, German, and flawless French. He was tutored in religion by Metropolitan Platon of Moscow, and became both tolerant and genuinely pious. Splendidly instructed, but deprived of secure affection and surrounded by intrigue, he grew up nervous, tense, and suspicious, perceiving the world as a threatening place with danger on every side. As a child he was willful, impatient, and restless. Pampered and treated obsequiously by servants and courtiers, he grew vain. Full of a sense of his own importance but often snubbed and ignored by his mother and her close circle of friends, the ones who really mattered, he was oversensitive to slights. Like many small boys, he loved stories of knights, especially of the Knights of Malta. (Unlike most small boys, as an adult he was able to indulge his whims, and when he became Tsar, in a curious twist of history, he became the Knights' protector.) Although he was

---

* Count Nikita Ivanovich Panin, a distinguished diplomat, became Paul's tutor in 1760 when Paul was six years old. Selected by Empress Elizabeth for the post, he quickly became an adviser and confidant to Catherine. Like her, he distrusted the sympathies and abilities of Paul's ostensible father, Peter. A strict disciplinarian, Panin gave Paul a remarkably enlightened and liberal education.

prohibited from playing with guns and toy soldiers, he grew up with a passion for the military and reviewing troops, which he ordered about and incessantly drilled as if they were mindless tin soldiers. With age, he became ever more rigid and tyrannical, compulsively seeking in rules and external order the inner security he lacked. He was a paradoxical man: often tender and paternal toward the Russian people, resentful and contemptuous of the privileged classes (who returned the sentiment and finally destroyed him).

As he grew up, Paul eagerly sought to be included in the councils of government, but to his vexation and chagrin, Catherine excluded him. In his notebooks he expressed a sensitive concern for the well-being of the Russian people and land, and condemned Catherine's foreign policy of aggrandizement and conquest. In 1774, when he was twenty, Paul proposed that all offensive war be repudiated and the entire armed forces of the country deployed only for self-defense. No one paid any attention to his ideas, least of all his mother.

When Paul was nineteen, Catherine invited the Landgravina of Hesse-Darmstadt to visit St. Petersburg along with her three daughters and suggested that Paul choose one as his bride.* He decided on Wilhelmina, the second, and in 1773, according to Orthodox tradition, Wilhelmina was rechristened Natalia Alekseevna and married Paul. Although his wife was self-centered and frivolous, Paul was madly in love and for once happy — only to have his young wife die three years later, in April 1776, after suffering horribly giving birth to their stillborn child. At her death Paul wept inconsolably and was plunged into despair. To help him overcome his grief, Catherine, who felt that for reasons of the succession a new marriage was essential — and as soon as possible — brutally presented him with irrefutable evidence that his wife had been having an affair with his best friend.

The second time, the choice proved happier. The brother of Frederick the Great, Prince Henry of Prussia, was in Petersburg at the time of the death of Paul's wife and had gained the confidence of Catherine. He suggested that his grandniece, seventeen-year-old Sophia-Dorothea of Württemberg, would be an excellent possibility. Although her family was not wealthy, her blue-blooded lineage was impeccable. She was from an ancient family, which combined the houses of Württemberg and Montbéliard. Her father was the youngest son of Duke Frederick-Eugene of Württemberg who had spent long years in Prussian service, and her mother, Princess Sophia-Dorothea, was a vivacious and charming

---

* Hesse-Darmstadt was a small area in central Germany. Many of Europe's royal families, including the Romanovs and the Windsors, trace their ancestry back to families from this region.

woman, the daughter of the Margrave of Brandenburg-Schwedt and niece of
Frederick the Great of Prussia, who was to become Paul's idol.*

Named after her mother, Sophia-Dorothea was born in Stettin on October 25,
1759, into a warm and happy family.† She was the eldest daughter of eight
children, five boys and three girls. In 1769, when she was ten years old, her
family took up residence in the ancestral castle at Montbéliard, forty miles from
Basel, then in the Duchy of Württemberg, in what is today Alsace.‡ The castle
was situated high above the town on the site of a former fortress, surrounded by
cedars of Lebanon, which legend said had been brought from the Holy Land in
1400 by one of their ancestors. In 1771, her father began building a summer
residence at Étupes, a pretty village some four miles from Montbéliard on the
road to Basel. Her father's great enthusiasm was gardening and landscaping, and
a plan of the garden he made at Étupes was published in Le Rouge's *Detail de
nouveaux jardins à la mode* in 1776. Gardening was a passion in the family.
Sophia-Dorothea and her brothers and sisters planned and executed gardens;
they had their own plots, which they spaded themselves. Taught by her father,
she gained experience in gardening that provided the basis for a lifelong interest
in horticulture and a near-professional knowledge of botany.

Étupes was a fairyland kingdom. It included an orangerie that was considered
one of the finest in Germany, as well as a dairy, built like a Swiss chalet and
decorated with vases of faenza pottery of the sixteenth century. Her mother, the
Duchess, had a Temple to Flora constructed, which was covered with climbing
roses trained up from the sides to the roof; there the Duchess loved to sit and
read. Situated on little islands in the middle of the river were many natural grottoes, and these grottoes, full of stalactites, sparkled magically when they were
illuminated at night. The islands were connected to the land by fantastic little
Chinese bridges. In the forest there was also a cottage, which had once been a
charcoal-burner's hut. The Duchess transformed the interior with simple and

---

* Frederick II, or Frederick the Great, King of Prussia from 1740 to 1786, made Prussia the greatest military
power of its day and vastly increased its territory. A benevolent despot, he favored French culture, filled his
court with intellectuals, and was a patron of the arts.
† Stettin, a small port town at the confluence of the Oder River and the Baltic in Prussian Pomerania, was the
birthplace of two empresses of Russia: Catherine the Great in 1729, and Maria Feodorovna in 1759.
‡ The Duchy and later Kingdom of Württemberg, located in the southwest corner of Germany, arose during
the fifteenth century. During Maria Feodorovna's (née Sophia-Dorothea) lifetime, Württemberg was ruled by
her uncle, Charles Eugene. Though a lesser duchy at the time, Württemberg was noted for its extremely grand
and formal court, a flowering of its arts and sciences, and one of the most modern universities of the day, the
Hohe Karlsschule.

rustic furnishings and turned it into a summer schoolroom for the children. Sophia-Dorothea loved this cottage and insisted on sleeping there one night despite the violent protestations of her straitlaced governess that this would lower the dignity of the House of Württemberg. Long after Sophia had left for Russia, when her governess passed the cottage she would still harrumph, "To think that the future Empress of All the Russias slept there!"

The children spent idyllic summers at Étupes. They would decorate the statue of Flora with garlands of flowers, milk cows in the dairy, turn the lawns into bowling greens, and feed and tame the birds in the aviary. Memories of this lovely estate of her youth stayed with Sophia-Dorothea all her life, and it later became the prototype for the palace of Pavlovsk.

Dorothea grew up to be a warm and loving young woman. Her uncle Louis-Eugène was a friend, disciple, and correspondent of Rousseau, and all the family was influenced by this association. By curious coincidence, a tutor of one of her brothers was married to a Swiss woman descended from a companion of Peter the Great, and the princesses often asked this tutor to tell them stories of Peter and Russia. It was later written of Dorothea that "she had a most ardent and almost prophetic curiosity about that country." Her closest friend and companion was a neighbor named Henriette de Waldner (nicknamed Lanele), who later became the Baroness d'Oberkirch. Together the two young girls pursued a daunting program of studies. Dorothea's favorite subjects were history and literature. Every morning the girls rose at 6 A.M. to read such heavy works as the *Histoire Universelle* by Abbé Millot and *Caractères* of La Bruyère. Then they played Schenkel quartets on the clavecin, followed by a brisk morning walk. Dorothea also learned to embroider beautifully and to paint watercolors and became a talented artist.

Growing up in a bilingual society, she spoke and wrote perfect French and German. When she and her friend Lanele were separated, she often wrote her three or four times a week, and on December 31, 1775, at age sixteen, Dorothea wrote her friend letters in four different languages — German, French, Italian, and Latin.

As she turned seventeen, Sophia-Dorothea was tall, buxom, and rosy-cheeked, with a lovely complexion and a sunny disposition. Strong and tender, thoughtful and naïve, she had been brought up with German reserve and a distrust of French "levity" and had been taught to believe that in a woman, family virtues were to be valued above all. At the time her name was suggested in St. Petersburg, she was nominally engaged to the Prince of Darmstadt (brother of Paul's ill-fated first wife), whose advances and proposals she had received with indifference. Before matters could proceed, the prince had to be convinced to give up his proposal. Her great-uncle Frederick the Great offered to handle the matter himself, and did so with such diplomacy that the young prince acquiesced and plans were drawn up for Paul and Princess Dorothea to meet in Berlin. Two months after the death of his first wife, Paul set off to meet his proposed new fiancée. It had been decided that if all went well, the wedding would be celebrated in St. Petersburg in the fall. All went very well indeed.

The first meeting took place at the home of the Queen of Prussia, Elizabeth-Christina. The Grand Duke made a favorable impression on all those he met. Despite being quite short in stature, Paul was well proportioned and had a serious, intelligent face with kind eyes. In the opinion of observers, his snub nose, inherited from his maternal grandfather Prince Anhalt-Zerbst (and about which Paul was always very sensitive), did not mar his appearance. In fact, wrote the Baron of Asseburg, the Danish ambassador, "any young girl would fall in love with the Grand Duke — he has a very handsome face and his conversation and manners are engaging. He is gentle, well educated, courteous and cheerful." The nervous, sharp-spoken, and irascible side of Paul, which grew more pronounced over the years, was then almost unnoticeable to outsiders.

Paul was attracted to the young princess from the first, and a few days after they met wrote to his mother: "I have found my fiancée . . . she is pretty, tall, well built, not shy: she answers questions intelligently and promptly and it is already clear to me that she has made herself felt in my heart and is not without feelings for me." On July 12, Prince Henry carried a letter from Catherine to his brother, Frederick, and Dorothea's parents with a formal marriage proposal, which was accepted the day it was received. On July 15, Sophia-Dorothea wrote to her friend Lanele: "I am quite pleased, more than pleased. I have never been so happy; the Grand Duke is extraordinarily kind and has all the right qualities. I flatter myself with the hope that my fiancé loves me; this makes me very, very happy." Paul wrote to Catherine: "My choice is made. Regarding her physical appearance, I am able to say that my choice will not disappoint you; regarding her heart, she is extremely sensitive and gentle. Her education is complete. Yesterday I was quite surprised to discuss geometry with her; her knowledge of science is very well grounded, she is greedy to study Russian." (Indeed, Dorothea mastered the Russian alphabet only a few days later.) "I am not able to describe either my bride or my pleasure." Paul remembered this visit to Berlin and Potsdam with pleasure all the rest of his life and developed a great admiration for Prussia and Frederick the Great, whom he sought to emulate forever after. On July 25, Paul left for Russia and shortly after his intended bride followed. Thanks to a 40,000-crown gift from Catherine, her family, always short of funds, were able to accompany her.

On August 31, Dorothea was at Tsarskoe Selo, where she met Catherine for the first time. Earlier she had confessed in a letter written to Lanele, "I am afraid of Catherine. . . . I know I shall be timid with her and she will think me a little fool. . . ." But she need not have worried. Her redoubtable future mother-in-law found her delightful. Catherine wrote in September: "I am attached to the charming princess . . . she is exactly what one would wish, with the figure of a nymph and a complexion of lilies and roses. Everyone is delighted with her . . . in a word, my princess is everything that I would wish for and I am quite happy." Although Dorothea's brothers had been raised as Lutherans, her father had not raised his daughters in any religion, in view of their future marriages. Dorothea took the Orthodox faith and with it, according to Orthodox practice, a new name: Maria Feodorovna. The wedding took place on October 13, 1776, a little over five months after the death of Paul's first wife.

At the time of their marriage the meticulously organized Paul composed an "Instruction" for his young bride to explain to her how she should behave and what was expected of her. Among his admonitions were that she should learn the Russian language, acquire a knowledge of Russian history, politics, and geography, and take her new religion seriously and practice it piously. As for dealing with Catherine, he urged Maria Feodorovna to be attentive and gentle and to get close to the Empress, gain her trust, and not express disappointment or complain to her about anyone at all. He specified that they would receive money every four months and she should manage the budget carefully (which she always did) so that they should not run short of funds. Any remaining sums were to be placed in a savings account. Her wardrobe should never be bought on credit and all purchases should be made through a single person to avoid flatterers. In fact, Maria Feodorovna was so thrifty that at the beginning of their marriage she wore Paul's first wife's dresses and even her shoes.

Their manner of life was to be strictly regulated, wrote Paul: "By subjecting ourselves to well-known rules, we protect ourselves from our own fantasies and give them as an example to others." There would be special days for lunches, receptions, and dinners; no changes — that would look like caprice. Two orders of etiquette were indicated — one for ordinary days and another for receptions and holidays. If receptions were boring, that was unfortunate but her duty, and "it would be even better to retire afterwards." Furthermore, he said, "We do not have the custom of seeing foreigners except on days appointed for receptions." She was to treat everyone alike, and she was to get up early (all her life Maria Feodorovna normally rose by 6 A.M.) so as to have time for her coiffure, to take an hour or two for her personal duties, and to be finished with these by noon — on Sundays and holidays by 10:30. After lunch there was to be reading, music, and an appointed time for study of the Russian language and other subjects. As to bedtime, he wrote: "I beg the princess to submit to my custom of regular schedule. I do not have the possibility in spite of my young years of staying up all night." And finally, "I will not speak of love or affection, for these depend entirely on good fortune; but so far as friendship and trust are concerned, these things depend on ourselves . . . it is appropriate for her above all to arm herself with patience and meekness in order to tolerate my ardor and volatile disposition and equally my impatience." Paul urged her to be completely candid with him and never to allow anyone to reproach him in a conversation with her and to accept indulgently all that he might express coldly, but with good intentions, in respect to her way of life, dress, and so on.

To all this Maria Feodorovna added only a gentle note, explaining that these rules were not as necessary as he thought, and that his anxieties about her conduct came largely from the bad experience of his first marriage.

Two months after her marriage, she wrote to Lanele: "The Grand Duke is a most adorable husband. My dear husband is a perfect angel and I love him to distraction." Maria Feodorovna never changed her feelings for Paul, and despite everything that happened later, despite his difficult and often tyrannical character, she truly loved him, perhaps the only person who ever really did.

On December 20, 1777, at the age of eighteen, in what was to be a pattern of difficult deliveries, the young Grand Duchess gave birth to a son who was named Alexander. Catherine, who at forty-eight had been concerned about the succession, was overjoyed. In a letter to Baron von Friedrich Melchior Grimm* in December 1777, she wrote: "Do you know Monsieur Alexandre? Not Alexander the Great but a tiny Alexander who was just born on the 12/20 of this

---

* Baron von Friedrich Melchior Grimm, a social and cultural critic in pre-Revolutionary France, began publication of a biweekly cultural newsletter for foreign nobles and sovereigns in May 1753. Catherine, an eager subscriber, entered into a regular correspondence with him. She met him in person in 1773, on the occasion of Paul's first wedding.

month at 10:45 in the morning. All this is to say that the Grand Duchess has just given birth to a son who, in honor of Saint Alexander Nevsky, has received the pompous name of Alexander and whom I call Monsieur Alexandre. It is a pity that fairies have gone out of fashion; they would have endowed an infant with whatever one desired. As for me, I would have given them beautiful presents and whispered in their ears, ladies, give him a good disposition, above all a good nature and experience will take care of the rest. . . ."

The baptism was a grand occasion attended by Joseph II, of Austria, and other dignitaries of Europe. During the ceremony Catherine wept with joy. That December, in America, George Washington and his Continental army were leaving to spend the cold winter at Valley Forge after the British defeat at Saratoga on October 17, 1777. Catherine, who had taken a great interest in the events in America and had once written Washington, offering to send the Cossacks to help, made allusion to the British state of mind when she wrote Grimm: "Monsieur Alexandre was baptized yesterday and everybody is well except the English who have dropped their heads to their stomachs ever since the deplorable adventure of General Burgoyne."

Almost immediately after his birth, Catherine took Alexander away from his parents to raise him according to her own ideas. She lavished attention on him. Every day the child spent hours in her room; she played with him and designed toys for him. She gave him his first lessons, carefully chose his tutors, and supervised his education. He grew up completely unafraid of her. Shortly after his birth she had written, "I am quite indifferent as to whether Alexander has sisters or not but he must have a younger brother." Maria Feodorovna obliged by giving birth to a second son in May 1779, named Constantine by his grandmother, who dreamed of making him King of Greece. He, too, was whisked away to be raised by her, along with the two granddaughters who followed. The rest of Catherine's granddaughters were educated under the wing of their parents, as were her third and fourth grandsons, Nicholas and Michael, born after her death. Ironically, despite all Catherine's efforts, Alexander and Constantine left no legitimate heirs and in the end it was a son educated by Maria Feodorovna who carried on the dynasty.

The new city of St. Petersburg, founded on the delta of the Gulf of Finland by Peter the Great in 1703, displaced Moscow as the new capital of Russia in 1711. During the years that followed, as the city began to grow, a series of splendid summer residences built by both tsars and aristocrats sprang up around it like a necklace of pearls. On the gulf, there was Peterhof, Peter the Great's "Versailles on the Sea," with its magnificent cascades, fountains, and formal French gardens designed by LeBlond, then Strelna and Orienbaum; and at Tsarskoe Selo, south of the city, the magnificent baroque Catherine Palace with its golden balconies and caryatids. The building of both city and palaces continued unceasingly through the eighteenth and early nineteenth centuries, resulting in a group of fairy-tale residences and estates of unparalleled beauty and sumptuousness, which reflected the growing power of Russia and the flowering of her art and civilization.

In her joy over the birth of her first grandson — one of the few times when she was entirely pleased with her son — Catherine in 1777 gave Paul and Maria Feodorovna a tract of land of 362 *desyatinas* (977 acres), together with "woods, ploughed lands and two small villages with peasants" along the little Slavyanka River, three miles away from Tsarskoe Selo, so that they could build a residence of their own.

Long before, the land had belonged to Lord Novgorod the Great, the powerful free merchant state that in the middle ages flourished in the north of Russia for several hundred years until weakened, and then conquered, by the tsars of Muscovy in the fifteenth and sixteenth centuries.* This land had fallen into the hands of the Swedes. In the early eighteenth century Peter the Great had wrested it back, along with a nearby town then called by the Finnish name Saari (meaning "island") because of its relatively high location on a plateau overlooking the delta plain below. When Saari, or Saarskoe as it was russified, became the summer home of the tsars of the new capital of St. Petersburg, it came to be called Tsarskoe Selo — the Tsar's Village. Gradually, Tsarskoe grew into a charming town where the dignitaries of the court built homes and dachas. Not far from Tsarskoe were the Slavyanka River and thick forests full of wild game where the emperors and empresses of Russia enjoyed hunting. As a young man Paul had loved to ride there, so this was the land that Catherine decided to give him and his young wife. From then on in documents it is called "the village of Pavlovsk."

When Catherine gave the land, there were two small rustic log buildings hidden

---

*Novgorod rejected princely rule in 1136 and became an independent city; its domain included a vast area of northern forest that extended to the Urals, and later even into Siberia. Novgorod was ruled by elected officials; princes were needed only for military defense and were hired, and fired, freely. Never conquered by the Mongols, Lord Novgorod the Great, as the inhabitants referred to their city-state, was able to maintain its contacts with the West and join the Hanseatic League. Its art, architecture, culture, and commerce prospered until it was subjugated by Ivan the Terrible in the late fifteenth century.

in the tangled forest, stopping places for the hunt, which were known by the German names of Krik and Krak, as such lodges were common on the estates of the German nobility. The small, well-lit rooms of Krik were simply furnished, and the original building of Krak was in the "Dutch" style, complete with a turret. Maria Feodorovna wrote that as young newlyweds she and Paul had enjoyed some of their happiest moments at Krik, where they spent their summers from 1777 to 1780, and which became known as "Their Highnesses' Dacha."

In the spring of 1778 soldiers from the garrison regiments began to clear the woods, open up roads, and prepare the ground for building; and in that year two simple wooden houses were built — Paullust (Paul's Delight) and Marienthal (Marie's Valley).* Paul and Maria Feodorovna selected the site for Paullust, which was built in the style of a manor house over the remains of an old Swedish fortress on the banks of the Slavyanka, which was dammed to make a pond. Paullust was a small wooden house, crowned by a cupola, with flower beds around it and small Chinese bridges nearby. Marienthal was a two-story house designed in the Dutch style with small gardens. In addition, there were a Chinese kiosk and some romantic "ruins."

However, Catherine kept firm hold of the purse strings. For the first four years of Paul and Maria Feodorovna's married life, she had to approve personally all expenditures at Pavlovsk, and she chastised them for using their personal funds, insisting that they use only monies issued by the Crown. Lavish with her lovers, Catherine was always niggardly with her son. Once when the young couple wrote her a humble request for funds, she replied tartly, "Dear Children, you can of course imagine how unpleasant it is for me to see you short of money; I can only assume that you are continually being robbed and that is why you are in need although you lack nothing."

In 1780, Catherine decided to "graciously loan" the young couple the services of her new favorite architect — a Scotsman named Charles Cameron.

In the eighteenth century in the midst of turmoil in their own land, many Scots emigrated to America and to Russia. General Patrick Gordon became a favorite adviser and general of Peter the Great, and the Tsar was attended by a Scottish doctor who briefly interested Peter in the Jacobite cause. Both Peter's daughter Elizabeth and Catherine also had Scottish doctors. A Scottish admiral won a famous victory over the Turks at Chesme Bay in 1769. Yet another of these adventurous Scots was Charles Cameron, who became the favorite architect of

---

* The architect[s] of Paullust and Marienthal is unknown but may in fact have been Cameron.

Catherine the Great, whose desires he executed for seventeen years. Like Francesco Bartolomeo Rastrelli, who in Peter the Great's time came to Russia at sixteen along with his sculptor father and became the Empress Elizabeth's favorite architect, Cameron spent his most creative years in Russia. Unrecognized in his own land, he became famous in Russia. Even today, relatively little is known of Charles Cameron; there are gaps in his life where he disappears entirely for years. Although he probably arrived in Russia sometime in 1778, it is not even certain exactly how he came or who invited him. What is certain is that on August 23, 1779, Catherine wrote to Grimm: "Now I have secured Mister Cameron, Scottish by nationality, Jacobite by persuasion, great designer nourished by antiquity, known for his book on the Roman baths."

Even this was incorrect, for it now appears that, perhaps to impress Catherine, Cameron created for himself a romantic and noble ancestry and even used a concocted coat of arms of the Lords of Cameron to which he had no right. He was in fact born in London, probably in 1740, and lived there until he was thirty, in a comfortable household loyal to King George, where he trained and apprenticed to his father Walter Cameron, a successful carpenter and builder. No one knows what schools he attended as a boy, but as his book later showed, he somehow became a good classical scholar and learned French. In 1767, amid rumors of scandal involving a daughter of Isaac Ware, a London architect whose pupil he had been, he left for Rome, where he lived for two years.

In Cameron's time there was a great interest in the work of Andrea Palladio, the great sixteenth-century Italian architect. In England Cameron had studied Palladio's drawings of Roman baths, and in Rome he obtained the permission of Pope Clement XIII to undertake research and excavations for his own illustrations of the Baths of Titus. In Rome he met Charles Louis Clérisseau, a famous French draftsman, architect, and painter of ruins, who had earlier taught both Robert and James Adam and was later hired by Thomas Jefferson. Although Cameron was probably not a pupil of Clérisseau, his later work shows that he was deeply influenced by the contact with this irascible, turbulent Frenchman, who later spent some time in Russia doing sketches for Catherine. A few years after he returned to England, Cameron's work resulted in a book, *The Baths of the Romans,* which was to attract Catherine's attention. The Empress was a great reader in several languages and kept informed of everything that was happening in Europe. When she was interested in an author, she often summoned him to her. The Scots were to have a profound influence on the architecture of their time — their combination of romanticism and realism suited the age perfectly. English houses were designed in the style of Roman temples and baths with pillared porticoes and Pantheon-like domes — a style introduced by the Scottish Adam brothers and, later, in America by Thomas Jefferson and brought to Russia by Cameron.

After he was taken on by Catherine, Cameron was given his own house in Tsarskoe Selo and later married one of the four daughters of John Busch, Catherine's English gardener, who lived with his family in apartments above the Orangerie.

In 1752, Empress Elizabeth had asked Rastrelli to design a grand summer palace for her in Tsarskoe Selo. Named the Catherine Palace, after her mother, the wife of Peter the Great, it has a façade twelve hundred feet long, one of the longest in the world. The entire palace was painted a bright blue, and decorated with a multitude of ornamentation — caryatids and balconies all gilded, which gave an exuberant, opulent effect.

Catherine loved Tsarskoe, and generally arrived in April, in time to celebrate her birthday on April 21, or in May, and spent the summer there. Accompanied by her favorite greyhound, Sir Tom Anderson, she loved to walk in the park, which was always open to the public, and mingle with her subjects. But she did not like the lavishly ornamented palace and decided to make changes. She allowed the gold to peel off and had everything covered in less gaudy paint.* She commissioned Cameron to design three suites of private apartments. For her he created charming intimate rooms, delicately decorated with opalescent milky white, blue, and green. Gone were the opulent colors of Elizabeth's time; instead Cameron used muted tones of bronze, lavender, olive, and pistachio. One of his masterpieces was a small blue room called "La Tabatière," because its interior resembled the enameled snuff boxes that Catherine loved to give as presents. Her bedroom was in lilac, with molded glass columns, and a ceiling of glass with a bronze circular pattern repeated in inlaid floors of many colored woods. Walls were covered in milky glass, lamps were made of rock crystal, and the white overmantel of the fireplace was decorated with white amethyst and gold studded with Wedgewood medallions imported from England.

In 1784–1785 Cameron also designed the opulent Agate Pavilion of jasper,

---

* At the time of the repainting, contractors offered Catherine nearly half a million silver rubles for permission to collect the fragments of gold that had peeled off. Haughtily, she refused, saying, "I am not in the habit of selling my old clothes."

malachite, lapis lazuli, alabaster, and porphyry, and the Cameron Gallery, which, in an unusual homage to an architect, was named for him. There Catherine loved to stroll among the busts of the great men of history she admired.*

Catherine was for Cameron the munificent and indulgent patron of which every artist dreams. She trusted him and gave him unlimited funds, which allowed him to work with no interference and use any materials he wished, however lavish. With her, he lived a favored life. This was not to be the case with Pavlovsk.

---

*Placed between the Ionic columns of the gallery were thirty busts of Catherine's favorite philosophers and statesmen. These included Demonsthenes, Cicero, and Charles James Fox, a contemporary British statesman whom she admired. In 1789, on the eve of the French Revolution, Catherine threw both Fox's and Voltaire's busts into the rubbish in a rage, banishing them from the gallery because their views of the Revolution opposed her own.

2

The Count and Countess of the North

*. . . un chez soi, une colonnade, un temple
à Pavlovsk me font plus de plaisir
que toutes les beautés d'Italie. . . .**

— Maria Feodorovna (1782)

*P*AVLOVSK is a woman's palace. The gift of an Empress delighted by the birth of her first grandson, it was to become the lifework of her daughter-in-law, Maria Feodorovna. It was the first house that was really hers, the place where she would live the happiest moments of her life. Maria Feodorovna was young, and unlike Catherine, her interests were domestic; not being empress, she had time to devote to it. She had much artistic talent and many ideas of her own, so from the start she interested herself in every detail.

At the outset, the young couple greeted their prestigious new architect happily, and following his instructions with fascination asked the thirty-four-year-old Cameron to draw up plans for the gardens, the beginning of a park, and to design several rooms and suites in Marienthal and Paullust, an Orangerie, and the first of a group of pavilions. In eighteenth-century gardens, such pavilions were not only common but considered as essential as the main house itself; and so, in 1780, Cameron began by designing two of the most important of the fifteen pavilions he was eventually to conceive for Pavlovsk.

* ". . . one's own home, a colonnade, a temple in Pavlovsk give me more joy than all the beauties of Italy. . . ."

The palace occupies a special place in the history of Russian art, for from its beginning it was a place of innovations. In a gesture that speaks eloquently of the young Maria Feodorovna's preoccupation with creating harmony for her husband, the first pavilion she requested from Cameron was to be the Temple of Friendship. In the hope that it might serve to improve the strained relations between mother and son, she dedicated it to Catherine the Great.

For Cameron, this temple was not only the first building that he constructed after his arrival, but his first, long-awaited chance to design a building according to his own dreams. And so it was that architecture born among olive trees under the blazing blue sky and hot sun of Greece was to find a graceful place in the fir and birch groves and pale, misty light of northern Russia. Conceived by Cameron, constructed by Russian craftsmen, the Temple of Friendship became the first Doric building in Russia. In a country accustomed to ornate carving, golden cupolas, and bursts of color, it was startlingly new. Nothing like it had ever been seen in Russia, and it was to have tremendous influence on the design of later Russian country houses.

Cameron's design was stark and simple. The pavilion was to resemble an ancient temple: sixteen columns supporting a low dome; windowless, with plain walls, a simple oak door, and an entablature decorated with friezes, classical garlands, and dolphins symbolizing friendship. Inside, sculptured plaster roses decorated the ceiling, and there was a frieze of dolphins; as furnishing, there were sixteen specially designed banquettes *à la grecque* with carved legs made to resemble the flames of love. In a special niche of honor stood a statue of Catherine as Ceres "Benefactress" with the inscription, "We dedicate this with love, respect, gratitude, and thankfulness."

Emperor Joseph II of Austria, a guest in Russia at the time, was present at the laying of the cornerstone, along with such leading figures of Catherine's court as Nikita Panin, Paul's former tutor, and Catherine's powerful favorite Prince Potemkin. When it was finished, Catherine found it beautiful — but too dark. So to please her, Cameron changed it. In 1780, the Empress, satisfied, wrote Maria Feodorovna and Paul: "I noticed with great pleasure that inside, with the doors closed, there is enough light from the upper windows to be able to read at 5 in the afternoon." But alas, despite Maria Feodorovna's effort, the Temple did not much improve Paul and Catherine's relations.

Cameron's great talent was his ability to integrate a building into its surroundings — sometimes allowing a part to emerge, sometimes hiding his structure completely in the trees. He placed his temple on a bend in the river and surrounded it with splendid northern trees — silver poplars, which were special favorites of Maria Feodorovna, and transplanted Siberian pines that had been sent to Peterhof at the time of Paul's birth and became the ancestors of all the other Siberian pines at Pavlovsk. Such was Cameron's sense of proportion and so perfectly did the temple fit into its setting that it did not appear large and only when approached more closely was it clear how monumental it was.*

Cameron next designed the Apollo Colonnade, placing it at the entrance to the park to proclaim it a sanctuary, protected by the muses and watched over by Apollo for those who sought poetry. The colonnade, a double row of columns supporting a heavy entablature, enclosed a statue of Apollo. Cameron cunningly constructed it of porous limestone with an intentionally coarse finish to give it the look of an antique monument ruined by time.

Recalling the happy days of her childhood, Maria Feodorovna wanted Pavlovsk to resemble Étupes as closely as possible and decided to re-create the Dairy, Chalet, and Charcoal Burner's Hut she had known in her childhood home. She called on Cameron to build them, although the great neoclassicist was probably not delighted with the assignment of such pastoral conceits.

Maria Feodorovna asked him first to design the Old Chalet. Tucked in the woods and built like a Swiss chalet, it was simply but cozily furnished with a small library and became for her a favorite place to retreat and read. At the chalet, her young children each had a little garden plot and a room for tools, and as she had done in her youth, each worked his or her own flower gardens and vegetable patches, the young Grand Dukes preparing the ground while the young Grand Duchesses watered and weeded until their mother would gaily summon them to breakfast by ringing a bell on the roof.

In the case of the Dairy, she chose the site and decided on the planting that Cameron was required to follow, using plants she arranged to have sent from Württemberg. The charm of these eighteenth-century pastoral buildings lay in the unexpected contrast between the plain exteriors and the refinement within. The Dairy was built of rough logs with a thatched roof. There was a milking shed with six stalls, rooms where milk products were kept and prepared, and a sitting room. The domed ceiling of the Dairy was covered with paintings and the walls lined with ceramic tiles. There were bright calico draperies at the windows, gilded furniture, and Dutch, Chinese, and Japanese vases arranged on marble

---

* In the early days the Temple of Friendship served as a concert hall; breakfast and supper were frequently taken there. A small kitchen designed by Cameron to resemble a hermit's hut was built on the opposite side of the river.

tables and shelves. Until well into the nineteenth century, fresh milk was always kept ready in a large Japanese vase with a silver tap; it stood at the center of the room on a tripod table. On hot summer days people would come in from their walks for a rest, a drink of cold milk or cream, and a slice of fragrant country bread. To provide dairy products, Maria Feodorovna later added a picturesque farm with a greater productive capacity on the edge of the park.

Early in 1784, Cameron designed an aviary, which was considered as essential in the eighteenth century as a fishpond. *Volière,* as it was called, became one of the most poetic corners of Pavlovsk. Cameron constructed a small classical temple, with metal netting embossed with the Imperial coat of arms stretched between the galleries and the Doric columns. There, among flowers and plants, nightingales, goldfinches, starlings, and quails fluttered, while quacking ducks and honking geese swam in the little pond in front. In a small central hall, windows were hung with white muslin draperies tied with blue ribbons. There were mirrors, stone vases, and a collection of ancient marbles, pottery, and small bronzes found in recent excavations in Rome and bought for the palace.

With all this building activity in the park, it was not very long before Maria Feodorovna and Paul decided that a more substantial main house was needed, and they asked Cameron to design a new stone palace. In 1781, they decided to build, and chose a site only a few yards away from the wooden palace of Paullust, which was eventually torn down. The palace of Pavlovsk is the first residence known to have been designed by Cameron. It was to be the summit of his career, for as things turned out, he was never to have another commission on such an extensive scale.

Cameron designed a palace that would have the feeling of an intimate country residence, taking his inspiration, it is believed, from Palladio, specifically from a woodcut in the *Quattro libri dell' architettura* of the unfinished Villa Tressino at Meledo in Italy, an illustration which Thomas Jefferson used later and followed even more closely in his design of the University of Virginia. The palace was composed of a cube-shaped central building three stories high crowned with a low dome encircled by sixty-four slender columns, flanked by two single-story colonnades of curved open-winged galleries that linked it to one-and-a-half-story service buildings. Each of the four façades presented a different appearance; they were given an air of great elegance by molded friezes and relief decorations, which were executed by the Russian sculptor Ivan Prokofiev.

Just as the project was getting under way, Paul and Maria Feodorovna obtained Catherine's permission to take an extended grand tour of the Continent.

They were anxious to see the famous palaces of Europe, and although Maria Feodorovna was unhappy and reluctant to leave her young children, she was very eager to visit Montbéliard, her family, and her bosom friend Lanele (now married and the Baroness d'Oberkirch), whom she had not seen for five years.

Of their future palace all they saw before they left were Cameron's sketches, poetic but not very precise. Never overly concerned with technical execution, Cameron imagined architecture not on paper but on the site, and would only later follow up his first dreamy sketches with structural drawings and precise instructions. This way of working left a great deal of room for misunderstanding with his clients, and problems were rapidly to appear when they left, for then Cameron had to submit everything not only by mail, but indirectly, through Maria Feodorovna's and Paul's newly appointed director, Karl Kuchelbecker, a meticulous and precise Baltic German.

On their European trip, the young Grand Duke and Duchess were to travel nominally disguised under the incognitos "The Count and Countess of the North." Accompanied by a large retinue, they left Russia in September 1781 and were gone for fourteen months, returning in early November 1782, several months after the first cornerstone of Pavlovsk had been laid and the building was well in progress.

Traveling first through Poland to Vienna, where Maria Feodorovna's overjoyed family came to meet her, they continued to Italy, visiting Turin, Rome, Venice, and Florence. They also later visited other European countries, but the highlight was their visit to France and their triumphal stay and reception in Paris and the court of Versailles. They were received in a sunburst of royal generosity by Louis XVI and Marie Antoinette and witnessed the apotheosis of French court life and the ultrarefined aristocracy, which only a few years later was to be swept away by the French Revolution.

Lanele traveled to Paris to meet her childhood friend, who on May 18, 1782, arrived amid a great clatter of carriages, gaily waving her handkerchief out of her coach window. At Maria Feodorovna's request, Baroness d'Oberkirch was to accompany her as lady-in-waiting, and she kept a detailed journal of the activities, dress, and festivities, leaving for posterity a lively description of a France in full glory before the Revolution. They all stayed at the Russian Embassy on the rue de Gramont, and there Maria Feodorovna presented her husband to her best friend, who had first met the Grand Duke at the time of their engagement, for the second time, saying, "He is another me and I pray you to love him because of your love for me." Lanele wrote, "The Grand Duke was then 28. At first glance, he did not seduce; he was small in stature, but upon looking at him longer one discovered in his physiognomy so much intelligence and finesse. His eyes were so bright, so witty, so animated and his smile so mischievous . . . yet with an expression of gentleness and dignity."

On the bright spring day of May 20, they were to make their first ceremonial visit to Versailles, the most glittering court of Europe, epicenter of all aristocratic elegance. It was a time of elaborate dresses with ruffles and panniers many yards wide. Fashion also dictated coiffures several feet high in which were tucked not only flowers but sometimes even small ships in full sail. Maria Feodorovna and Lanele had to rise at 6 A.M. in order to complete their hairdos and dressing in time for a midday dinner. ("*Grandes toilettes* are terrible and boring," wrote Lanele.) Meanwhile, in order to take an advance look unobserved, Paul slipped away incognito to attend Mass at Versailles. At church, he watched the cortege of the Chevaliers de Saint d'Esprit and came back much impressed with the elegance of what he had seen as well as the beauty of the Queen.

Later that day, grandly coiffed and attired, the Count and the Countess of the North along with their suite made their official grand entrance at Versailles. Maria Feodorovna wore magnificent jewels and a dress of silver brocade embroidered with pearls, whose skirt, draped over panniers, was twenty-one feet around.* They were introduced to their contemporaries, the twenty-eight-year-old King and twenty-seven-year-old Queen of France, Louis XVI and Marie Antoinette, as well as to thirteen members of the royal family and seventeen of their suite. Louis exhibited his habitual shyness in answering Paul's warm phrases, but Marie Antoinette, according to Baroness d'Oberkirch, was "charming," treating the Countess as if she had known her all her life, inquiring minutely as to her guest's tastes and what she could offer her that would be pleasing, and asking to see her often. As evening came, there was a splendid dinner. Versailles was lit by a thousand chandeliers and by girandoles with forty candles on all the tables ("Impossible to describe the splendor!" wrote Lanele). Dinner was followed by a concert and an opera, during which the Queen graciously said to Maria Feodorovna, "I know that you, as I am, are a little shortsighted. Please permit me to remedy this and keep this simple jewel in memory of me, would you permit this?" She presented her with a magnificent fan ornamented with diamonds in which was contained a lorgnette. Finally there was a supper, and the Russian visitors all returned to Paris, exhausted, at 3 A.M.

* Madame d'Oberkirch says "six aunes," which equals approximately seven meters.

During the seventeen days that followed, Paul and Maria Feodorovna, exhibiting admirable royal stamina, in a dizzying round of dinners, opera, theater, and balls, met all the leading aristocrats of France. Indefatigably they managed to visit every notable church, monument, and park in Paris, including the Tuileries gardens and the new promenades of the Champs-Élysées, as well as hospitals, prisons, and the factories of Gobelins and Sèvres.

During subsequent visits to Versailles, there were spectacles and splendid fireworks. On a bright May morning they visited the Petit Trianon — "a delightful sight," wrote Madame d'Oberkirch, "with the garden full of lilacs . . . we heard the nightingales." They saw the famous cascades and fountains, the ruins, the temples, the statues. As Marie Antoinette loved the opera and had been a pupil of Christoph Gluck, they attended several performances and heard Gluck's *Orfeo ed Euridice,* in which the great dancer Vestris performed. After the opera, at a private supper, Beaumarchais read them his controversial play *Le Mariage de Figaro,* banned from the stage because of its revolutionary tone. At the Comédie Française, they saw Collé's *Partie de chasse de Henri IV,* acted by the best French actors. As Henri was one of Paul's heroes, Paul was delighted and asked to see it again.

Twice, wearing a bat mask and leaving her cloak open to show a magnificent dress embroidered with jet and sequins, Maria Feodorovna slipped off with her friend Lanele to the public masked balls, which took place at the Opéra, where disguised aristocrats and commoners mingled. Although Lanele, a straitlaced Protestant, disapproved ("One is exposed to hear and see many things which can only make one blush"), and the Russian ambassador warned her that there would be ten spies watching her, plus ten more from the French police, Maria Feodorovna replied gaily: "That's too many! But they won't take away my pleasure!"

In a more serious vein, she also went to the Academy, where she astonished the academicians of France with her knowledge, dazzling them by being able to recite to almost all a passage from their most renowned works. At the invitation of the King, she spent several hours in his library examining the treasures of scientific and sacred books, medals, and antiquities, as well as two extraordinary globes of 1704.

They attended Mass twice at Notre Dame, where the pious Maria Feodorovna was very moved by the sight of the historic cathedral. They also insisted on visiting hospitals and the poor and made several visits to prisons, going down into the cells to see how the prisoners were treated. When he was asked why he was so determined to make these visits, Paul answered, "The farther away one is placed from the miseries of humanity, the closer one must approach them so as to know and receive them." Everywhere, they liberally distributed money. "Their charity was inexhaustible," wrote Baroness d'Oberkirch. "Never was a petition addressed to them in vain; they went out with purses full of gold and returned with them empty." After a Mass in Notre Dame, they distributed great sums to foundlings and to the poor. At one prison they left 18,000 livres, at another 10,000, to settle the debts of those incarcerated. In all, in an astonishing display of Russian royal largess, during their stay in France they gave away two million francs.

On May 30, they went to visit the Gobelins factory, where it was explained to them that the water of the small local river was the secret of the beauty of the wool dyes. In all the factories and ateliers they visited, they examined everything and surprised everyone with their extensive knowledge of all the arts and trades. "In our factories they enter into the tiniest details with the workers using technical words and employing artistic terms as well as the craftsmen," said a contemporary, the Chevalier du Coudray. Louis XVI presented them with four magnificent tapestries from a rare set of twenty-seven designed by Charles Antoine Coypel with varying backgrounds of crimson and rose, orange and straw colors.

On June 13, they went to the famous Sèvres factory where they ordered three hundred thousand livres' worth of porcelain. At the end of their visit, the King presented Paul with two pairs of fine monumental vases, cups, and other gifts. Maria Feodorovna was then shown a toilet set of extraordinary beauty. Made of lapis-blue porcelain, it was decorated with miniature paintings and borders of enamel, which imitated jewels and pearls mounted in gold, a technique which was considered to be the last word in the art of porcelain decoration. Two cupids, placed on the frame of the limpid oval mirror, played at the feet of the Three Graces. The gold and bronze decorations were the work of Jean Claude Duplessis, goldsmith to the French court, the jeweling by the enameler Joseph Coteau. It was a masterpiece, a never-to-be-repeated set of sixty pieces worth 60,000 gold livres. Maria Feodorovna exclaimed in admiration: "*Mon Dieu!* How beautiful it is! Without a doubt it is for the Queen!" At which time Count d'Angevilliers with a courtly bow replied, "The Queen offers it to Madame la Comtesse du Nord and hopes that it will please you and that you will keep it in memory of Her Majesty." It was only then that the nearsighted Maria Feodorovna noticed that her own coat of arms was placed on the set. Surprised and delighted, she cried: "The Queen is a hundred times too kind! . . . Oh, the magnificent gift!"

Afterward, Baroness d'Oberkirch wrote, Maria Feodorovna worried terribly that this priceless gift might be damaged during the long trip home and ordered that every precaution be taken with the packing.

In France, away from his mother and the intrigues of the Russian court, Paul was an entirely different person. Relaxed, charming, with his impeccable French and quick appreciation of his hosts' remarks, he made such a splendid impression on the French that they paid him their highest compliment by saying that it seemed as if he had been educated and brought up in France. He exhibited a gift for the *bon mot* at the right time and his comments were often repeated. He made an excellent impression on Benjamin Franklin, who was then in Paris as the first American minister to the Court of Versailles. In 1782, Franklin was seventy-seven years old, and with his simple clothes and manner, the darling of the French court. In his *Autobiographical Writings,* Franklin commented,

> The Comte du Nord came to M. de Vergennes while we were drinking coffee after dinner. He appears lively and active, with a sensible, spirited countenance. There was an opera that night for his entertainment. The house being richly furnished with an abundance of carving and gilding, well illuminated with wax tapers and the company all superbly dressed, many of the men in cloth of tissue and the ladies sparkling with diamonds, formed altogether the most splendid spectacle my eyes ever beheld.

At the end of their visit, there was a final gala evening at Versailles, with an opera, ballet, and a dinner for three hundred. Maria Feodorovna wore a superb necklace of chalcedonies — a stone unknown in Europe — which was much admired by the Queen, and they did not return to Paris until 4 A.M.

Finally, there was an extraordinary weekend hosted by the Prince de Condé at Chantilly. Five hundred people sat down for meals, served by three times as many servants, not counting the Prince's ample personal household staff. On the first day there were theatrical performances by the finest actors of France, followed by illuminations and a ball. Everyone stayed the night, and the Prince thoughtfully arranged that there be not a sound to disturb his guests in the morning. The next evening the entire park was illuminated, the company promenaded in their coaches, fished in the pools, visited balls in various pavilions, and were served a splendid dinner in a clearing in the woods, where, tucked in the forest, invisible musicians played. All this was topped off with a deer hunt by torchlight.

Maria Feodorovna and Paul were, understandably, enormously impressed. They were enchanted by the gardens, the fountains, the *allées sablées,* which they later tried to emulate at their palace of Gatchina. Only a few years after this grand affair, the Prince de Condé, forced to flee France at the time of the Revolution, was only too happy to accept the hospitality of Paul.

On June 6, Paul and Maria Feodorovna went to bid their final farewell to Marie Antoinette and Louis at Choisy. The royal couples parted, Madame d'Oberkirch wrote, "with tears and embraces." They were to correspond in the ensuing years, but never met again, for barely eleven years later the fairyland at Versailles disappeared and their hosts both perished under the guillotine of the French Revolution.

Paul and Maria Feodorovna's European trip was to have an enormous effect on the building and decoration of Pavlovsk. While abroad, the young couple were exposed to all the latest ideas of fashion and art of the Continent. With great enthusiasm, they visited ateliers and stores in every city, conversed with European architects, developed their own taste, and grew more independent. In Rome, they devoted every afternoon to visiting the studios of celebrated artists or to browsing in antique shops. A good number of the paintings by the masters of the hour — Pompeo Battoni, Angelica Kauffmann, Raphael Mungs, Hubert Robert, and Greuze — were chosen and bought in their studios. Like all enlightened travelers of their time, the royal couple brought back statues and busts, but such was their eye and taste that only one later turned out to be false, while some were of exceptional beauty. There was also a model in plaster of an antique bronze faun, which, Maria Feodorovna wrote in her travel journals, was the first such copy ever made, adding that Queen Caroline had allowed this reproduction to be made only after repeated entreaties on her part. A table with mosaic representing the Colosseum was given to them by Pope Pius VI. Most of the chimneys for the palace were ordered in Rome.

Everything that Maria Feodorovna acquired eventually came to rest at Pavlovsk, and the sentimental importance that she attached to these works of art collected during that wonderful trip when she traveled through Europe, fêted by everyone and discovering at each step an unknown marvel and new enchantment, was enormous. All this was bound to lead to troubles with the proud and strong-willed Cameron. He was accustomed, as late-eighteenth-century architects were, to planning the entire arrangement of an interior — designing and placing the furniture and all ornamentation down to the doorknobs as an inseparable part of an architectural scheme — and he did not like to be interfered with. While in Europe, Maria Feodorovna and Paul ordered great quantities of furniture and materials according to their own newly developing taste, without consulting him. For Cameron, this was heresy.

Throughout the trip, Maria Feodorovna kept a detailed journal and made voluminous notes about everything she saw. Yet, despite all the activities and new impressions, she never for a single day forgot Pavlovsk. "One's own home, a colonnade, a temple at Pavlovsk give me more joy than all the beauties of Italy," she wrote from Turin. She carried on an almost daily correspondence with Kuchelbecker, the palace director, minutely monitoring the progress of the work at the palace. This remarkable correspondence, preserved in the archives of Pavlovsk, provides a vivid glimpse of the building of an eighteenth-century palace from the ground up, and attests to the meticulous interest of Maria Feodorovna and Paul in every detail of their new house and the extent to which they participated in its planning.

These letters from Maria Feodorovna and Paul, sometimes directly, sometimes through their secretary Nikolai, were carried back and forth from the capitals of Europe by swift couriers who, amazingly, accomplished the long journey to Pavlovsk on the average in ten days, bringing back sketches, measurements, and plans.

Letters often crossed in the mail and disagreements multiplied. Cameron, who was working at both Tsarskoe Selo and Pavlovsk, trying to satisfy two sets of clients, was often slow, his sketches often unclear. One can see the growing unease at Cameron's tendency to use extravagant materials and the impatience with his delays.

> Turin, April 18 (from Maria Feodorovna):
> With the materials you now have on hand I think that the work can now proceed quickly. I am awaiting with impatience Mr. Cameron's answer about the facade on the garden about whether it must absolutely remain as he has projected it or whether he wishes to change it again. If the cherry trees about which you spoke are fine ones, I wish that they be planted around the chalet where the others are presently. If they are mediocre, place them near the new dairy. Has Cameron not yet given you anything on the subject of the new dairy about which I spoke to you in a letter dated from Rome?

> May 2:
> Where are you in respect to the cascade and water conduit? . . . I am afraid the two things cannot be separated . . . for to make the last before

the first would spoil the garden. I pray you to ask General Bauer what it will all cost.

Rome, May 15 (from Nikolai, the secretary):

The Grand Duchess has this morning received the plan of the third floor of her house. . . . Referring to our letter of yesterday we would like to know if the new plan requested for the facade facing the garden does not bother him [Cameron] or if he could imagine one which would give a more elegant form to the facade all the while conserving the same advantage for the third floor. . . .

I enclose a list of furniture ordered here by Her Imperial Highness for her house at Pavlovsk . . . in your reply please include an exact note of the height of the rooms, the quantity of curtains, armchairs and sofas needed for each.

Signed by the secretary Nikolai, the following letter from Paris, dated May 21, the day after Maria Feodorovna's and Paul's gala entrance to Versailles, demonstrates how closely Pavlovsk remained on their minds even in the midst of the glittering festivities at Versailles:

Enclosed you will find the plan of the facade approved by Their Imperial Highnesses with the following remarks: "We would wish that the three central windows would not have triangular cornices but a simpler decoration, as those of the two sides. One prefers the ornaments above the windows as they are in plan T rather than those in plan P. We consent that the three windows of the middle should be in the form of a balcony . . . the perron should not be semicircular, but square . . . the pilasters of the side of the windows should not be sculpted but plain. . . ."

As for the memorandum of M. Cameron about the fireplaces, furniture etc., I must warn you in general that he must give up all the grand projects of marbles which he wishes to obtain from Carrara to make a staircase, face the hall and to make columns 11–18 feet tall. The list of marbles bought in Italy will be sent to him. . . . The Grand Duchess will order here a few fireplaces of the height and width that M. Cameron requests but not for all the apartments and . . . simple stone should be used or stucco for those which she has not ordered marble. . . . You will see by the list of furniture ordered in Lyons which will be used and which will have only chairs and curtains. However as these will be of Pekin or tartar plain with figured borders, it is not enough to say that there should be so much material for the curtains. . . . The Grand Duchess has changed the *Paradnaya* into a boudoir. . . . It will be necessary to detail how many pairs of curtains, what height and width so that you will not be sent too much material or too little Pekin and borders. . . . Please request M. Cameron to follow these orders exactly and to send us the measurements as soon as possible. [One can imagine the difficulties in fulfilling such a request, as neither rooms nor windows were yet built.]

Although most of the correspondence was carried on by Maria Feodorovna, Paul occasionally added his own comments, supporting and pressing her case and asking for precise financial accounting of monies spent.

Their director, Kuchelbecker, scrupulous and honest, informed them of every detail, however humble, and also provided them with news of their children. His detailed letters during 1782 provide a unique historical record of the progress of the palace as it began to go up stone by stone.

Pavlovsk, March 19:
They are making the parquets and we have begun and are planting the *allée* of large trees . . . every day 30 sailors from the port come, principally to clean up the site around the palace.

Undated:
As soon as Monsieur Cameron can come here we will dig the foundation. As it will be filled with snow and perhaps water, we are thinking of making a ditch which will finish in the garden near the ruin and which, as it is covered during all the winter, will keep the excavation dry. I took M. Benkendorf a pineapple and flowers for Their Imperial Highnesses. [Little Alexander and Constantine were four and three years old respectively at the time and living with their grandmother, the Empress, at Tsarskoe.] . . . your gardener has transported the flowers which were in the large Orangerie and has changed all the pots.

St. Petersburg, January 16:
Your two sets of seeds have arrived. The second is still at the customs but I hope to have it tomorrow. . . . I have bought Linneaus' book for your garden. . . . I will enclose a list of the bushes and that of a case full of seed sent to Your Imperial Highness from Siberia.

February 20:
Your Imperial Highness will receive the catalogue of the plants at Pavlovsk and that of M. de Swatzfer . . . just arrived from Holland. The fowl have arrived from Holland and have to be sustained over the winter with the help of a stove . . . the duck and the red goose have managed to last out their

second winter. . . . We now have almost 3 million bricks on the site. . . . I
have contracted for 1,200 tons of lime. The plans of Mr. Cameron are done,
Thank God. . . . From time to time I send the Grand Dukes flowers from
Pavlovsk.

In the middle of the Russian winter, Kuchelbecker wrote the following letter,
dated March 2, which gives a startling idea of the sophisticated hothouse culti-
vation undertaken at Pavlovsk even in the early days before the main palace was
built.

Although Your Imperial Highness does not especially adore pineapples, I have
nevertheless accepted thirty plants and they did not cost us anything except
to go and get them at Peterhof. The gardener went to town to present a
flowering rosebush to Their Imperial Highnesses. . . . I would like to bring
them a cherry tree in bloom. There are several trees, a peach tree, an almond
tree and plum trees in flower. The violets have passed. If the snow and the
ice did not remind us of it, one could forget that this place is at 60 degrees
latitude. The grapevines and so many other trees are in flower, the daffodils,
the primroses, the hyacinths are already blossoming and soon to do so the
lilacs, the buttercups and the *oreilles d'ours* [aromatic primroses]. . . . the
rosebushes in bud in our greenhouses make us regret each day that the spring-
time in our hot houses is not seen by Your Highness.

March 12:
   The last oak wood requested by M. Cameron has been brought . . . as
well as several thousands of barrels of lime.

March 26:
   As of today we have here 3,500,000 bricks, approximately 4,000 barrels
of lime, 120 cubiques of luma, 50–60 of these of gravel and all the wood
for the scaffolding. They are bringing boards but I wish there were
more. . . . Twelve men have started their work again today breaking and
taking away the ice.
   The 20th of March has arrived . . . we are transporting 200 fruit trees
from Count Bumianov, all in good shape. The 27th, a case containing rho-
dodendron plants which M. Palace has had brought from Siberia arrived in
good shape. . . .
   Having received this month the last plans of M. Cameron for the new
house, . . . I came here yesterday to make the agreements with the masons
and the carpenters and to see if it would be possible to have a single contractor
for the entire work. I beg Your Imperial Highness to send back as quickly as

possible the plans and the order for the facades she wishes to see executed. . . . It is not too late to change. As the presence of Their Imperial Highnesses was announced I have taken measures to make the bridge over the house of Your Imperial Highness without risk. . . . The dry but very cold weather has made it impossible to proceed vigorously with the work in the garden. There are very beautiful flowers in the Orangerie of all kinds and the Grand Dukes are receiving them often. . . .

May 7:
    The Grand Dukes have asked for flowers for the birthday of Her Majesty [Catherine]. In consequence the gardener brought them everything that was most beautiful. . . .

On May 11, Catherine herself decided to come and cast her Imperial eye on the work at Pavlovsk, and Kuchelbecker described the occasion:

Her Majesty the Empress came to Pavlovsk around six o'clock with her suite. . . . Her Majesty was still in the house of Your Imperial Highness when I arrived, from which she emerged on the side of the garden taking the path toward the Ruin. From the Ruin Her Majesty wanted to go down to the right of the Temple where the paths are not yet made. . . . I prayed M. Nelidinsky to go by a better path but Her Majesty wished to continue, therefore Her Majesty was at the Temple and from there took the path toward the Cascade. Before arriving she asked several questions on the water, which I had to answer as no one could explain it sufficiently to Her Majesty. She stopped a moment at the Cascade, passed to the Chalet asking me questions from time to time. She sat a moment at the Chalet and asked me several questions about the Colonnade then took the path to the edge of the garden . . . and having ordered her carriages she returned by the same path and left by the place of the entrance. I would be too happy if Her Majesty was satisfied by what she saw at Pavlovsk during her presence, which was entirely unexpected.

At last, after all the crisscrossed letters and the misunderstandings, the great day finally came, and Kuchelbecker wrote on June 4:

The first stone was laid for the house of Your Imperial Highnesses along with the most ardent and sincere wishes for Your Imperial Highness and His Imperial Highness the Grand Duke for your happy return and that this house should long serve as a place of relaxation and pleasure. . . .
    I did not permit myself to invite anyone except Mr. Cameron who came with a few Englishmen. By accident, Colonel Strademan and Lieutenant

Chanov were also here. The masons had brought the priest from the Slavyanka at their own expense, which I nevertheless assumed as I also took it upon myself to offer them some vodka, beer, and pretzels. Since then the work on the foundation advances with diligence.

The next day at five o'clock in the afternoon Their Imperial Highnesses the Grand Dukes arrived with their suite. Their Imperial Highnesses stopped at the house of Your Imperial Highness to drink tea, eat strawberries and take a walk. They wanted to work on the house of their dear mother and they did and made a present of 100 rubles to the workers as they did to the soldiers of the guard of one ruble per man. Monseigneur Alexandre then asked to be taken to the house of the Grand Duke [Paullust], where the cannons are emplaced. Two cannons were brought out, which Their Imperial Highnesses wanted to be shot. They were told that according to the rules, they had to be far out of the way and they could fire and when I saw that they had gone down the mountain and climbed up the other, I then ordered the cannons to be fired. The Monseigneur stopped to see how they fired and then took the road back to Tsarskoe. I hope very much that Their Imperial Highnesses amused themselves enough to hope for their speedy return to Pavlovsk.

And so, with these simple ceremonies and the presence of young Alexander and his little brother Constantine, the actual building of the palace of Pavlovsk began.

As for Paul and Maria Feodorovna, after Paris they continued their tour through the Loire valley, seeing some of the famous castles, and then went to Brittany, sometimes staying in some very poor and rustic inns. In Brest the muddy streets were impassable, so they were carried about in sedan chairs. They visited Belgium and Holland and finally spent a joyous month at Montbéliard and Étupes with Maria Feodorovna's family. On September 27, mother and daughter, sobbing inconsolably, parted. Maria Feodorovna was never to see either her friend Lanele or her mother again.

They returned to Russia in early November, happy and full of the sights they had seen. But Paul, who occasionally had been indiscreet enough to criticize his mother in public and some of her policies in his letters came home to discover that he had been overheard and his comments read, and he found himself more isolated than ever.

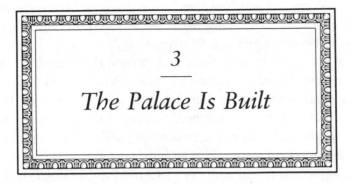

3

The Palace Is Built

Princesse de Württemberg, Grande Duchesse,
Imperatrice, elle ne sera qu'une femme et rien de plus. *

— Corberon, *La Cour de Russie*

SO WROTE A PATRONIZING FRENCH DIPLOMAT in 1778 when Maria Feodorovna was not quite twenty years old. Unlike Catherine, Maria Feodorovna did not have a mind "infinitely more masculine than feminine." Living as she did under the shadow of the Empress for nineteen years, chroniclers of her epoch paid scant attention to her. She reigned as Empress for five years only; she takes up little space in history books; no full biography of her exists. She lived the life of a woman — not a politician — but in this she was outstandingly successful, in many ways far more successful than her power-driven mother-in-law.

Over twenty-one years, she bore Paul ten children — four boys and six girls,† and assured the Romanov dynasty, which before her was faltering and during

* "Princess of Württemberg, Grand Duchess, Empress, she will always be a woman and nothing more."
† Maria Feodorovna's ten children were: Alexander I (1777–1825); married Louise of Baden, rebaptized as Elizaveta Alekseevna upon her marriage. Constantine (1778–1831); his first wife was Julia-Henrietta of Saxe-Coburg; his second, Johanna Grudzinska. Alexandra (1783–1801); married the Palatine of Hungary, the Austrian Archduke Joseph. Elena (Helena) (1784–1803); married Frederick of Mecklenburg. Maria (1786–1859); married Charles of Weimar. Ekaterina (Catherine) (1788–1819); her first husband was George of Oldenburg; her second, William I of Württemburg. Olga (1792–1795). Anna (1795–1865); married William II of the Netherlands. Nicholas I (1796–1855); married Charlotte of Prussia, rebaptized Alexandra Feodorovna upon her marriage. Michael (1798–1849); married Helene of Württemburg.

her lifetime reached its apogée. Maria Feodorovna is the only woman in Russian history, and perhaps in all history, to be the wife of an Emperor and the mother of two more. Two of her daughters became queens: Anna, who nearly became the wife of Napoleon and was prevented from doing so largely because of Maria Feodorovna's vehement objections, went on to become Queen of the Netherlands; Catherine became Queen of Württemberg.*

She was a good and loving mother, and despite the fact that Catherine took over her four oldest children in their early years, Maria Feodorovna managed to maintain close relationships with them, as with all her children. They remained genuinely attached to her, honored her, and minded her counsel all their lives. Her husband permitted himself relationships with other women, yet Maria Feodorovna remained always faithful to him, sustaining his liaisons with grace and even making a best friend and ally of Catherine Nelidova, with whom Paul had a passionate but platonic *amitie amoureuse*.

Four of her daughters and one of her sons died before her; her husband was brutally murdered. She bore her personal tragedies with courage and dignity. Not only did she put up with Paul's tyrannical behavior, but she sincerely loved this difficult and troubled man, and after his death honored and mourned him. Through everything, she never complained or became embittered, always calling herself "the happiest of women." As a widow she became a one-woman ministry of health and culture, the prototype of the public-spirited women of the nineteenth century. Her life epitomized the finest qualities of the aristocracy — a love of beauty, taste, a sense of responsibility, duty, compassion, and leadership.

Although Catherine once sneered that "she reads books she does not always understand," Maria Feodorovna had an impressive range of interests and knowledge, as her enormous and varied library attests. She entirely managed two huge domains, overseeing their budgets and every activity and taking a close personal interest in the health and welfare of their populations.

She was an accomplished artist, enough so to be mentioned in the encyclopedias of her time — skilled in watercolor, she also knew engraving, designed cameos, and created objects of ivory and amber, which she often presented as gifts. In addition she embroidered magnificently, was a gifted musician, and was a renowned specialist in horticulture, with a lifelong passion for flowers and plants.

Pavlovsk was the lifework of this talented, devoted, and energetic woman. It was her creation, to which she applied all her considerable artistic ability and

* The contemporary descendants of Maria Feodorovna include the present Queen of Holland, Prince Philip of England, and the late Marina of Kent.

tireless energy. No palace bears the stamp of its owner more. To it Maria Feodorovna gave forty years of her life, and there she left all that was best and most characteristic of herself. In a great collective effort, the work at Pavlovsk brought together many of the greatest artists and craftsmen of the time — both Russian and European. These artists gracefully encompassed the delicacy of the late eighteenth century and the full flowering of the elegant neoclassicism of the nineteenth century, creating a unique harmony between East and West.

For the first ten years of their marriage, Paul and Maria lived the ideal of eighteenth-century domestic bliss — a rosy-hued pastorale where shepherds and shepherdesses in silks and satins tended flocks that were always snowy white. Early in their marriage, Paul had written to Prince Henry of Prussia, Maria Feodorovna's granduncle, "Wherever my wife goes, she has the gift of spreading gaiety and ease and she has the art not only of dissipating my black moods but of giving me back the disposition I had almost lost."

After their two sons, during the next five years in quick succession came four daughters: Alexandra in 1783, Elena in 1784, Maria in 1786, and Catherine in 1788. At Pavlovsk, Maria Feodorovna created for Paul a serene family life. Paul had simple tastes. His favorite dishes were sausages and fruit compotes; he preferred mineral water to alcohol. He enjoyed company, and had a mischievous sense of humor. He enjoyed riding but not hunting, played chess, and loved the theater. During the long frustrating years of his wait for the throne, Maria Feodorovna organized and planned innocent amusements to cheer him. At Pavlovsk there were amateur theatricals, often staged in the open, picnics, long invigorating jaunts and walking games. Swallowing his gloomy thoughts and putting aside his military gear, Paul would often take part in these. In her letters Maria Feodorovna called him *"notre cher Grand Duc,"* writing, "I always love to be in unison with my husband." When at Pavlovsk, they usually had breakfast in the Dairy and took their evening tea at the Chalet. Evening concerts were performed at Krik or the Hunter's Cabin and other garden pavilions. There were *"parties de plaisir"* in distant corners of the park: the place to which participants were sent as a group or were to gather separately was determined by a lottery of tickets on which instructions were written. Once in 1798, when Paul had been away on a long trip, she arranged that while riding he be met in the woods by a peasant who directed him to Krik where his children were waiting for him with songs they had prepared for the occasion.

In the early years life was regular and calm, private rather than ceremonial. They rose early — sometimes as early as 4 A.M. On a rainy day in early September Maria Feodorovna wrote: "I read, write, study music and do a little work . . . in the evenings I play cards. . . ." In October: "We usually have supper at 4 or 5 o'clock . . . after supper we spend time reading and in the evening I play chess until 8 or 9 o'clock. . . . Then three or four of us make 100 circles of the room; at each turn Lafermier* pulls a seed from his hat and with each dozen he makes an announcement to the room in a loud voice. Sometimes in order to enliven our amusements and make things more varied M. Benckendorf and I try to run in leaps and bounds."

Paul, fascinated since childhood by the stories of knights, sometimes dressed his chamberlains in coats of mail, caparisoned their horses, and staged medieval tournaments. Maria Feodorovna devoted special attention to the theatrical performances that were Paul's favorite entertainment. These were acted by amateurs, their friends, and members of their court. French songs and operettas were preferred to tragedies, rehearsals on the small stage were jolly and spontaneous. When Maria Feodorovna wanted to surprise Paul she would put on a performance in complete secrecy.

Theatrical performances were always staged on Paul's name day (July 10), and on his birthday (October 1), accompanied by lightning and fireworks. In 1787, for his birthday, Maria Feodorovna organized a masquerade. The entire garden of Pavlovsk was illuminated with fireworks illustrating in the sky the themes of the celebration, finishing with a fiery representation of "The Temple of Marital Love." Maria Feodorovna thought out all of the details in advance, devised an intricate plan for the festivities, and wrote all the instructions herself.

For several years Pavlovsk was their only residence, and an enormous amount of time and attention was lavished on it. As his patrons were waiting to move in, Cameron built the Orangerie with two wings for Maria Feodorovna, while work on the palace continued unceasingly. Although far from finished, the palace was inhabitable by 1783; the interiors were not entirely finished until 1796, and work and improvements never stopped until Maria Feodorovna's death in 1828.

But in 1784, after the death of her former favorite, Count Orlov, Catherine gave his palace of Gatchina to Paul. Some mean tongues said that it was because no one wanted the huge, brooding castle. Commissioned by Catherine for Orlov in 1766, and built by Antonio Rinaldi, an Italian architect who had come to Russia during the reign of Elizabeth, Gatchina was an immense fortresslike structure with two octagonal towers and five hundred rooms. Strangely, despite the

---

* The Franco-German Franz Lafermier, who had been a teacher and elocutionist, became librarian to Paul.

fact that the palace had belonged to the man who had murdered his father and had been the lover of his mother, Paul loved Gatchina. With its military air, it could have been built for him, and it became his favorite residence.

Gatchina was located at the intersection of major roads that linked St. Petersburg, Warsaw, and Moscow, forty-two kilometers south of St. Petersburg, and seventeen kilometers southeast of Pavlovsk. It was a larger town than Pavlovsk, with some two thousand inhabitants, versus six hundred, and it gave Paul the illusion that he was solely in charge of a domain of his own. Paul's residence there also suited Catherine perfectly. It was isolated enough to keep Paul safely out of the way, for as he grew older, he was increasingly restive, impatient at being ignored and excluded from councils of state. Like many royal heirs before and since endlessly waiting for his time to reign, he was bored. In 1784 he lamented, "I am thirty years old and have nothing to do."

Paul turned Gatchina into a military camp with two thousand troops dressed in wigs and Prussian uniforms — a toy army of living men — and kept himself busy by rising at dawn and relentlessly drilling his men each day, clocking their movements with the aid of a special cane with a watch embedded in the handle, and meting out punishments for the slightest infraction of the rules. Following the paradoxical pattern that was his life, in 1793 Paul also attempted to reform and create a renaissance in the town. He built a wooden church where Catholic and Lutheran services were performed. He established a hospital and a school for local children, without any restrictions of sex or social class, and founded an orphanage for the children of the military, in addition to building glass, porcelain, and textile works, and other factories. He regulated rents and established measures of poor relief for peasants. Yet always suspicious and fearful, he surrounded Gatchina with barriers and sentries; everyone who came was interrogated, and houses could be searched on the slightest pretext.

This martial miniature kingdom was a far cry from the serene Rousseau-like country atmosphere at Pavlovsk, and was to become the first minor chord in the domestic harmony between Paul and Maria Feodorovna, for from then on they divided their time between the two. Pavlovsk remained the home and center of family life, the domain of Maria Feodorovna; in 1788 Paul gave it to her, while he began to spend more and more of his time at Gatchina, which seemed to exacerbate his tendency toward irascible and tyrannical behavior.

In the sumptuous and richly decorated palace of Gatchina, Paul and Maria Feodorovna set up their own private court. The Ambassador of France commented favorably: "Never did a family offer more ease, grace and simplicity in its home — dinners, balls, spectacles and celebrations — everything there is marked by the best tone and the most delicate taste. The Grand Duchess, dignified, affable and natural, beautiful without coquetry, amiable without pretense, gives the impression of virtue adorned." Others were less complimentary. A contemporary wrote that "Gatchina looked like a foreign court. Barracks, stables, all the buildings were Prussian . . . and as for the troops they looked as if they had just arrived, still warm, from Prussia." Many commented sourly on the rigid military tone, the barriers and sentinels who challenged everybody. Some of Catherine's elegant courtiers snickered at the social attempts of the young couple and their relatively modest receptions and theatricals. Many hesitated before accepting their invitations, as Catherine made it very clear that she did not look benignly on her favorite courtiers and ministers attending the soirées at Gatchina.

At twenty-five, Maria Feodorovna took over the large responsibility of running both households, with their myriads of servants, gardeners, and workmen. In this, her life was a sharp contrast to the life of Catherine's court with its Frenchified ladies of fashionable eighteenth-century society. Instead she became more like the Russian country noblewomen of the period who looked after all their estates and households in detail. She was brought into close contact with people of all classes of society, and this experience developed in her an unusual capacity for domestic affairs and social projects, which she accomplished with an energy that astonished her peers.

At Gatchina, Maria Feodorovna tried to make the gardens a modest copy of the grounds of the Prince de Condé's grand estate at Chantilly, which she had so admired during their trip to France, but it was Pavlovsk that was her love, and there she lavished her closest attentions.

Sensing correctly that Gatchina was to be the first breach in her domestic intimacy, she grew more and more impatient to have Pavlovsk finished and increasingly upset by Cameron's incessant delays. On September 14, 1785, one year after Paul had received Gatchina, she wrote to Kuchelbecker, "Gatchina is a very dangerous rival and it is imperative that you devote all of your abilities and diligence so that Pavlovsk can stand up to the comparison."

Things were not going well with Cameron. Between him and his employers there was a clash of both personality and taste. The owners of Pavlovsk were young, enthusiastic, and eager to express the new ideas and styles of their epoch. For Cameron, ancient Greece and Rome were the sole sources of beauty, and a copy of an ancient building was worth more than all modern creations. Utterly sure of himself and his taste, sometimes arrogant, with a stubborn Scottish character, he preferred to do nothing rather than change his opinions, even if this meant jeopardizing his own position.

As the favored architect of Empress Catherine, grandly installed at Tsarskoe Selo with a large staff of skilled assistants and draftsmen of various nationalities, his own foundry and sculpture studio, Cameron was used to demanding and being granted the best of everything — semiprecious stones, marble, and gold. He frightened Maria Feodorovna with his prodigality and extravagance, and it was hard for him to remember that while the Empress denied him nothing, she was not so generous with her son. Maria Feodorovna, always good and compassionate, gave the major part of her money away to those who asked for it, and as her parents still had two daughters and five sons, this little world often made appeal to the purse of the sister who had made a rich marriage. Under these conditions, it was not easy to erect the palace. Yet perhaps Pavlovsk owes some of its intimate charm to this enforced thriftiness, for it did not become the typical residence of a sovereign, a solemn frame for grand rituals, but rather the home of a person of taste, of a noblewoman disposed to live a wide and intelligent existence.

In 1784–1785 as work progressed, wherever she was, Petersburg or Moscow, she wrote to Kuchelbecker every day — sometimes several times a day — about every detail. In these letters, her worry about money is a constant thread and lament. September 6, 1784: "I am sending you, my dear Kuchelbecker, something to help the work. I won this money today at cards — there are 70 rubles." On May 15: "I am sending you 40 rubles, my good Kuchelbecker. I ask you especially to pay the laborers of the earth as much as is humanly possible. . . . Send me the measurements of the chimneys so I can have the closings made here — it will not cost money." On April 25: "I am sending you 500 rubles which I have borrowed. Reward those who have worked so well breaking the ice." And in 1786: "I am sending you all the money I have. I do not possess another *liard*. I allow myself to believe that it will accomplish miracles."

Cameron had not looked kindly when Maria Feodorovna and Paul had bought furniture from the best French *ébenistes,* silks, and even whole fireplaces abroad without consulting him. Maria Feodorovna did not care so much whether the ceiling of her room was inspired by ancient originals. She wanted to create her own environment, to set off to greatest advantage her French furniture, the splendid Savonnerie and Gobelins tapestries, and the priceless Sèvres toilet set that had been given by the King of France.

Maria Feodorovna did not like the polychrome decoration, the Pompeiian arabesques and medallions that Cameron had used so successfully at Tsarskoe Selo. In 1784 she wrote to Kuchelbecker: "The medallions, being part of the ornaments, ought to be all in white; to do the contrary is to ignore the rule of architecture. The background of the frieze, and the frieze itself ought to be in white; it is nobler that way."

Paul, of course, could be counted on to dislike everything his mother liked, and Maria Feodorovna, if one is to judge from the often pleading tone of many of her letters, was often caught between a difficult husband and a stubborn architect. On August 13 she wrote: "My husband consents, although regretfully, to having a vaulted ceiling in the bedroom, but on condition that it takes the least disagreeable form possible . . . so beg Cameron, in God's name, to do something good; above all that he takes care not to add any arabesque ornament."

With rising impatience, in 1785 she wrote:

> You must remember, my dear Kuchelbecker, that I had clearly indicated that you must hold yourself to light colors for the dining room. I do not want anything to clash and it seems to me that we had decided that the frieze should be a tender rose color, the backgrounds of the walls apple green, the background of the medallions in rose or light blue, and the other lilac. I remember that I had wanted the background of the two medallions of the same color, but that Cameron did not wish it. In God's name, my dear friend, please insure that all this should have a decent appearance. You already know from experience that gentleness does not help with Cameron, so tell him candidly that his procedures are unsupportable and he should take warning, as you are advising him as a friend that one will no longer address oneself to him.

In 1786 Cameron was called by Catherine to do work in the Crimea, and this provided the diplomatic opportunity his dissatisfied patrons were seeking. When Cameron left, his assistant Vincenzio Brenna took over. Paul and Maria Feodorovna had met the Florentine architect during their travels in Italy. He had previously worked in Poland, and in 1783, at Paul's invitation, arrived in Russia, where he was to spend the next nineteen years. Brenna had several advantages; he was slightly younger than Cameron, more pliant, and, perhaps most important, he was their man.

Cameron had managed to finish the Egyptian Vestibule and the five adjoining rooms of the Private Apartments. He had completed designs for many of the State Rooms including the Italian and Greek Halls. Yet because so much of the work was later carried on by Brenna, it is now difficult to distinguish rooms directly attributable to him, and authorities disagree. He left behind a superior artistic leadership to which Brenna, while responding more flexibly to his patrons' taste, adapted in a most inventive and harmonious way.

What the young couple yearned for was uncomplicated line, regularity, and discipline; in their own words, "noble simplicity and a calm greatness," a protest against the insincerity and sophistication of Catherine's court. Paul preferred Roman classicism. The Roman civic virtues of heroism and self-sacrifice, love for nation, and stoic self-control were qualities he admired and sought desperately to achieve.

Brenna, drawing on his knowledge of the interiors of Imperial Rome and the late Italian Renaissance, replaced the intimacy of Greece and the delicate sentimentality of the eighteenth-century pastorale with a richer, more austere classicism. Instead of Greek classical ornaments and bas-reliefs, Brenna introduced a stately and majestic style of Imperial cyphers, crowns, and Roman trophies, creating an atmosphere of martial splendor, which Paul loved. To work with him, Brenna assembled a great team of decorators and craftsmen. He gave a prominent place to sculpture and sumptuously painted ceilings, to rich color and lustrous silks, many of them ordered by Maria Feodorovna and woven in Lyons. Upholstery was of Lyons silk with drapery borders of delicate tints and colorful flower designs; the colors changed from room to room in a carefully thought-out pattern, which was in perfect harmony with the character of a summer palace set in nature and acres of flower beds.

In decorating the studies and libraries of the State Suites, Brenna gave a prominent place to the fine furniture and objects bought in France. He set off to greater advantage the rich crimson Gobelins tapestries from the King of France by curving the walls meant to receive them.

Taking his inspiration from the palace of Versailles, Brenna flanked the Greek Hall — with its beautiful colonnade of *faux marbre* green columns that gave the impression of a Greek temple — with the white and gold Halls of War and Peace, and made the adjoining Italian Hall a replica of a Roman temple. In 1792 he designed for Maria Feodorovna a magnificent State Bedroom in imitation of the state bedroom of the King of France (where, of course, kings never slept but received courtiers). The room was a flowery arbor. Wall panels of cream-colored silk painted in tempera with flowers, fruits, musical instruments, and gardening implements, were executed in brilliant and fresh colors by the German painter Johann Jacob Mettenleiter from the sketches of William Van Leen, who had worked for the court in Paris. The painted ceiling was trellised, and the room's centerpiece was a huge gilded bed with cupids at each corner and an altar of love where cupids held garlands of flowers. Brenna ordered the furniture, the couch, and armchairs from Henri Jacob in Paris, and a unique chandelier with a transparent white and ruby stem and a shimmering fountain of crystals was provided by St. Petersburg craftsmen. Brenna's great achievement is that although his interiors were highly individual, they harmonized perfectly with the architecture, developing and enriching Cameron's original scheme.

Despite their earlier problems, when Cameron came back to Pavlovsk, Paul and Maria Feodorovna were happy to see him. On September 8, 1787, she wrote: "Cameron's visit to Pavlovsk pleased me greatly. You will tell him in my name that I am sure his attention will embellish Pavlovsk greatly and I am waiting to see the effect of his attention. I approve his bridge and send it back to you for execution." They entrusted him with several more pavilions and constructions in the park, but they avoided his work in the interiors, and to Cameron's chagrin, it was Brenna who from then on dominated.

To help in their task of building and decorating the palace, Cameron, Brenna, and the architects who followed them were able to draw on an unusually rich panoply of artists and craftsmen who were gathered together at a unique moment in history.

In 1777, when Catherine gave the land along the Slavyanka to Paul, the new capital of St. Petersburg was only sixty-five years old. The building of this city by munificent rulers and aristocrats with unlimited resources and a passion for grand architecture and lavish decoration attracted attention all over Europe. Craftsmen, artists, and merchants from many nations streamed into the city — some summoned, and others simply coming on their own to look for work, opportunity, and excitement.

From its founding Peter had wanted a fruitful contact with the West, and in a tradition that was to be the glory of the city until the Revolution, foreigners were welcomed. During the eighteenth and the nineteenth centuries, they flocked to St. Petersburg as they did to the other new world of America across the ocean, to try their luck, make their fortunes, or simply to visit. These foreigners founded their own communities, churches, and newspapers, and helped to make St. Petersburg one of the most glamorous and exciting places on earth. Many of them found the atmosphere so congenial that they remained and became Russian themselves, leaving their echo in the many foreign names that exist there still.

The great water city erected on the marshy delta of the Gulf of Finland pulsed with life and activity. Ships of all nations docked in its port. Americans, Swedes, Dutch, and English sailed in triumphantly on tall-masted ships, while Russians and tribes from the interior arrived on riverboats and barges. Forests of masts clustered along the quays, which swarmed with skippers and sailors from every land. The streets buzzed with the sound of the languages of every nation in Europe and many of those of Asia. Its way of life, which poetically adapted the tastes of East and West to the northern latitudes, evoked for Europeans a special romance. Called the "Northern Palmyra," the "Venice of the North," and the "Babylon of the Snows," suspended between water and sky, illuminated by iridescent white nights in summer and sunk in inky darkness in winter, Petersburg became a European city that was nonetheless, in its own way, distinctively Russian, something very much its own.

The grand buildings and magnificent palaces of St. Petersburg were erected by teams of Russians and Europeans working in close cooperation, communicating in many languages, mingling their skills and knowledge. This marriage of talents produced unique and splendid effects. At Pavlovsk, created at the height of the aristocratic period in Russia, this ferment of artistic creation and outpouring of international talent came together in an exceptionally successful way, making the palace a symbol of this serendipitous meeting of East and West.

Russian and European artists nourished each other. Europeans took advantage of rich native materials: the vast stores of semiprecious stones from the Urals, and the extraordinary variety of woods available. Absorbing European taste, Russian craftsmen began to create their own distinctive decoration, furniture, and objects of art marked by the national love for sumptuous decoration and exuberant color. Many artists, like Cameron, who could not find sufficient outlets for their talents in their own countries were to find in Russia rich and appreciative patrons and a fertile ground for their creativity. Like him, artists of many nations were to spend most of their creative lives there.

From Italy came not only great architects like Rastrelli, Rinaldi, Quarenghi, and Brenna, but the great set designer and landscape architect Gonzaga, and whole families of painters like the Scotti family who, like Quarenghi and Gonzaga, came from the Lake Como region and the city of Lugano in what is present-day Switzerland. Finding insufficient opportunity for their talents in the Italy of their time, northern Italian artists and craftsmen set out to find work in Prague, Sweden, France, Spain, and even Constantinople. Over the centuries scores of talented architects, sculptors, stoneworkers, and painters who sprang from this small mountainous region made their way to Russia. From the fifteenth to the nineteenth century approximately ten thousand stoneworkers left, crossing the Alps and making their way to the Baltic on foot, taking their tools and their children with them. Domenico Trezzini, who came from Astono, twelve kilometers from Lugano, along with his brother and their sons and twelve artisans, came to Peter the Great by sailing around the North Cape and debarking in Archangelsk, there to make their way for hundreds of miles through desolate forests to reach St. Petersburg, where they built the Peter and Paul fortress and cathedral. Their compatriot, Pietro Solari, had come to Russia even earlier, in the fifteenth century, to help build the Kremlin.

Summoned by his compatriot Quarenghi, who was from Bergamo and had come to Russia five years before, Giovanni Scotti, along with his brother Carlo and their sons, arrived in Russia in 1784. Scotti was an artist-decorator who had worked in Württemberg for Maria Feodorovna's family. The sons began working as apprentices and then continued the work of their fathers in Russia. Three Scottis — Giovanni, his brother Carlo, and his nephew Pietro — all worked under both Cameron and Brenna painting the ceilings at Pavlovsk. Giovanni died in Russia in 1785; his brother Carlo never used the portion of his contract that stipulated payment for his return trip to Italy. He and his entire family remained in Russia, which he considered his second homeland.

Cameron brought 140 Scottish stoneworkers to work with him at Tsarskoe Selo. The English gardeners, John Busch at Tsarskoe Selo and Sparrow at Gatchina, helped to create and tend the elaborate flower gardens.* There were Germans, like the painter Johann Iakov Mettenleiter, who painted both walls and ceilings at Pavlovsk. David Roentgen, a famous German cabinetmaker well introduced to the Russian court by Grimm, who had written to Catherine about him, was also known to Maria Feodorovna and Paul, who had seen an exhibition of his work at Montbéliard during their European trip. Roentgen was to make six trips to Russia from 1783 to 1791, and executed commissions both for Catherine and at Pavlovsk. He was accompanied on his first visit in 1783 by his talented pupil Heinrich Gambs, who settled in Russia and whose two sons, born in Russia, also became cabinetmakers. Gambs formed a large group of Russian and foreign cabinetmakers who fulfilled court commissions, among them those of Maria Feodorovna, many of which were intended as gifts to Catherine from Paul and his wife.

In 1790, along with an Austrian merchant, Jonathan Ott, Gambs opened a

---

* English gardeners in Russia lived quite well. Potemkin's gardener, Gould, is noted to have lived in splendor, kept horses and carriages, and even given entertainments for the nobility.

workshop and eventually the famous furniture house of Gambs and Ott in St. Petersburg, which produced furniture in the Roentgen style until the Revolution.

There were scores of Frenchmen, beginning with the architect Peter the Great called "his treasure," Alexandre Le Blond. After him came Jean Baptiste Vallin de la Mothe, Thomas de Thomon, and the sculptor Étienne Falconet, who at Catherine's request worked for eleven years to create "The Bronze Horseman" statue of Peter the Great, one of the most famous equestrian statues in the world. At Pavlovsk, a protégé of Maria Feodorovna, Henri Gabriel Viollier, a miniaturist painter from Geneva, designed furniture for some pavilions and headed a group who designed sets of furniture for palace rooms. The French bronzesmith Pierre Agi carried out commissions for the state and taught students at the Academy of Arts until 1804. After the French Revolution, even more came. The famous French painter Elisabeth Vigée le Brun, who spent seven and a half years in Russia and painted the portraits of many of the notable aristocrats of the day, including Paul, Maria Feodorovna, and their children, remarked that she saw so many of her countrymen at parties that St. Petersburg seemed just like Paris.

These foreigners and many others combined their skills with those of gifted Russian artists. The talented gilder and sculptor Ivan Prokofiev began working with Cameron in 1786 at Pavlovsk, where he executed the bas-reliefs of the exterior façades and the original gilded statues of the Egyptian Hall.

The eighteenth-century discovery of rich deposits of semiprecious stones in the Urals and the Altai region resulted in the 1780s in the establishment of stone-polishing factories near the deposits. Russian jasper was outstanding for its great tonal variety. However, because of the slow transportation of the huge slabs by waterways to the factories and the complex process of production, the manufacture of a single large vase or bowl could take dozens of years. In 1793 the talented self-taught inventor Filip Strizhkov devised a machine for the mechanical working of stone, and one of the first bowls made by his method, of splendid pinkish-green jasper, came to decorate the Greek Hall at Pavlovsk. Lilac-gray vases of speckled jasper from the Altai region also were produced for Pavlovsk by Strizhkov. Vassily Kokovin, another master craftsman from the Urals region, produced two beautiful, perfectly polished vases of extremely hard gray-green Kalkin jasper for the palace. At the end of the eighteenth century, Russian stonemasons devised a technique known as "Russian mosaics," using thin slabs of green malachite and blue lapis lazuli to face columns and table tops, which gave the impression of being of solid stone.

Russia is a land of abundant and varied forests, and over many centuries Russian native skill in woodworking and love of carved decoration had produced master craftsmen. In 1711, Peter the Great closed the carving workshops in the Imperial Armory in Moscow, where during the seventeenth century, the finest workshops had been, and moved all the carvers to the Petersburg shipyards, where they were employed by the Admiralty to prepare parquetry for the palaces of Petersburg.

There was a particular aspect to Russian woodworking and cabinetmaking unique to Russian society — the serf. Every estate had its own carpentry work-shop, and serfs looked after all the carpentry needs of the estate to which they belonged. Serfs were the most prolific producers of furniture, and many were extremely talented artists. Using a profusion of colored woods, which made bright tinting superfluous, they created pieces distinguished by the rich flamboy-ant style of Russian decoration, characterized by detailed and elaborate work-manship and splendid inlaid effects. Many magnificent examples of their work are known, but unfortunately few of their names. One such serf master was Matvey Veretennikov, who in 1790 made Paul's desk, which is now in his library at Pavlovsk.

Among outstanding master Russian cabinetmakers was Christian Meyer, whose family, originally of German origin, was established for many generations in Russia before the arrival of Roentgen. Meyer, at Catherine's request, taught carpentry to both Alexander and Constantine. Between 1795 and 1800 he made two chests of drawers for Pavlovsk, which are unfortunately no longer at the palace today.

Using the extraordinary skill of Russian workmen, Cameron, Brenna, and Quarenghi designed floors from a whole palette of rare woods, which produced effects as rich as oriental rugs. In the beginning woods from local trees were used: birch, walnut, pine, as well as maple, oak, beech, hornbeam, ash, elm, and pear, apple, alder, juniper, and cherry. By the end of the eighteenth century, at the time of Pavlovsk, more and more rich and expensive wood, many from exotic and faraway places, were added, until fifty types of wood were used for floors. The tall ships that crowded the quays of St. Petersburg brought wood from the brazilwood family, rosewood, and mulberry. To make the intricate "colored" effects beloved in the later eighteenth century, parquetry makers used black ebony from Africa, violet rosewood, rose amaranth, yellow and red sandalwood from Asia, tobacco wood, lemon citron and wild orange trees, satinwood, palm, olive, and ironwood from Greece, the Mediterranean, and Egypt. Depending on the materials used, parquets were described as "colored" or "semicolored." For each room in the palaces architects devised a different design, which Russian master carvers executed with astonishing delicacy and skill. Cameron introduced a strong symmetry and a repetition of ornament, antique motifs of acanthus, palmettos, garlands of flowers, and depictions of musical instruments in keeping with his love for the classical. Quarenghi complemented his severe and monumental interior patterns with wood, which gave them warmth and life. For Brenna, wood motifs did not create a rhythm as they had for Cameron, but added magnificence to his martial motifs and interiors.

Many beautiful objects and furniture were created and bought in Europe especially for Pavlovsk. In 1783, the first shipment of antique marbles, purchased in Italy at Cameron's request — statues, Roman portrait busts, urns, and antique pottery discovered during the archaeological excavations at Pompeii — arrived at the palace. Between 1783 and 1785, for use in the State Rooms, sixteen sets of furniture, more than two hundred pieces, were ordered from Henri Jacob * in Paris; these were executed from detailed instructions and even designs done in Russia, the shape of many of the pieces determined by the place they were to occupy. Because of the destruction during the French Revolution, these pieces, along with others acquired earlier in France, made Pavlovsk, until World War II, the finest repository of Louis XVI furniture in the world.

Twelve paintings were commissioned for the palace from the fashionable French painter Hubert Robert in 1784. Bronze was an important element in Brenna's decorative designs and a great number of bronzes, often chosen personally by Maria Feodorovna, were brought to Russia from France, including some by the great masters Thomire and Gouthière.

The palace acquired a remarkable collection of clocks — ninety-six in all. Clocks were prized objects of luxury in the eighteenth century, and much attention was paid to their cases, which were made of ormolu,† mother-of-pearl, tortoiseshell, colored marble, and rare kinds of wood. Resounding through the halls at the striking of the hours was a symphony of tinkling silver bells and chimes.

In the second half of the eighteenth century, the Imperial Glass Factory began

---

* A talented French furniture maker not related to the renowned Georges Jacob and his sons Georges and François Honoré, he nevertheless took full advantage of the name, deliberately creating confusion between his own business and that of his namesake, even to setting up shop in the same neighborhood. No one knows how his connections with the Russian court began; perhaps the difference between Henri and Georges did not seem as great in Petersburg as in Paris.

† Ormolu, sometimes termed chased ormolu, is a gilded bronze made from a gold-colored alloy of copper, zinc, and tin.

producing crystal and colored glass, and Russian craftsmen created for Pavlovsk a large number of beautiful and distinctive lighting fixtures: chandeliers with stems of ruby, blue, dark green, and turquoise glass, whose bronze frames seemed to melt away among the rainbow prisms of almond-shaped crystals that shimmered like fountains at the slightest movement of air. Others were made of porcelain, forged steel, carved wood, and oriental alabaster. Ivan Petrovich Kulibin created special mirrored reflectors that illuminated long dark palace corridors both day and night. Quarenghi designed chandeliers for the Pavlovsk ballroom, which were executed by Johann Zeck, one of the finest chandelier-makers in Petersburg. Zeck made lanterns of tin and ormolu, of tin painted green, traced with delicate flowers, and candle pivots of flower-painted milk-white glass. Nikolai Lvov, a leading classical architect, poet, and student of geology, designed a chandelier that looked like a crystal basket. Formed by a garland of crystal ropes hanging in rows descending from a crystal fountain, with the candles mounted on pivots of colored glass, it was first created for Paul, and so became known as the "Gatchina Chandelier." They were also used at Pavlovsk, and the design then spread all over Russia.

From the sixteenth century onward, Russian steelworkers of Tula had developed unique metalworking skills. In the eighteenth and nineteenth centuries they turned from making fine weapons to objects of luxury, which were renowned throughout Europe. By heating metal in a special furnace, they achieved shades of burnishing from dark green to lilac to pale blue and pink. Blue was particularly striking in combination with light tones of unworked steel, and they added decorative details with gilt and bronze to achieve delicate effects of colors. They furnished Pavlovsk with fine steel worktables, footstools, and chandeliers. Once a year at Tsarskoe Selo, a famous fair was held at which the Tula masters exhibited their works; there, in 1789, from the Tula master Samarin, Catherine purchased for Maria Feodorovna an extraordinary toilet set, which consisted of twelve pieces: a table with elegant mirror and vases for hair powder, a chair, and a footstool. All were fashioned of steel and decorated with ormolu, silver damascening, and "steel diamonds" — thousands of steel drops elaborately wrought and faceted like diamonds.*

Russian craftsmen produced fine examples of bronze and silver work for the palace; the finest architects and artists took part in the work of the Imperial

---

* So renowned was the skill of the Tula workers that they figure in a famous story written by Nicholas Leskov in 1881. To prove their metalworking superiority, the English sent a tiny steel flea to Russia. A left-handed Tula worker surpassed them; he was able to put horseshoes on the flea.

porcelain factory, which provided Pavlovsk with many fine objects, including vases in a variety of shapes and sizes that were often presented as gifts from the factory to the Tsar's family on various festive occasions. The collection of ivory and amber work at Pavlovsk was unrivaled. Used for table decorations, trimming of bureaus and firescreens, writing sets and candelabra, some of the objects were made by Maria Feodorovna herself. In the village of Frianovo near Moscow, magnificent silks for the upholstery of the formal rooms were woven especially for the palace, made from designs based on those of Phillipe de la Salle, a famous French designer of Lyons.

Pavlovsk became a treasurehouse of all these artistic talents, capturing and preserving the beauty of a great epoch in Russian history, summing up all the ideas of beauty of Russian decoration and the best of the soul, spirit, and industry of a people and an age.

Paul's and Alexander's reigns saw the final flowering of the aristocratic arts in Russia. In the architecture and the decorative objects made for their courts, rulers and nobility turned to Western forms and, in a very Russian manner, tried to outdo them in splendor. Often they succeeded, leaving buildings and works of art whose opulence and beauty still amaze. But Pavlovsk, despite its richness, retained a warm intimacy and a sumptuous coziness, which it owes to its patroness and which enchants us still.

In 1795, a delighted Maria Feodorovna wrote a long letter to her mother taking her on a tour through each room of the palace, describing the furnishings and even the placement of objects in personal detail. In her *cabinet de toilette* she points out the "beautiful small chest made of mother-of-pearl which I owe to the goodness of my good and excellent mother"; in her boudoir, "the table which was given to me by the Emperor Joseph." In the library: "Under the arch there is a large writing table similar to that of Roentgen. It is supported by twelve columns of ivory which I turned on a lathe." She comments on the miniature ivory temple that sits on the table:

> on the pediment of the temple is a cameo of the Grand Duke mounted in clear glass on which I painted a trophy in grisaille. On the other side is the Grand Duke's monogram. . . . On the base of the temple are more paintings in grisaille; in the middle of the temple is an eight sided altar made of amber and ivory; on the central one my monogram in a medallion painted on glass and mounted in amber; on the other, medallions of my seven children beginning with Alexander whose monogram is linked with that of Elizabeth. (I made this present last year [1794] to the dear Grand Duke when our dear

Olinka was still alive and Annette was not yet born.) I painted all the children's monograms in roses and myrtle; mine is in small blue flowers. . . . The writing set is of amber in antique form, the penknife, the paperknife, the pencil and seal handle are all in amber and made by me; I even engraved the monogram of the Grand Duke in steel for the cachet.

This unique record, the only such detailed inventory of a palace ever made by an empress, was to prove invaluable one hundred fifty years later in the darkest days of the palace's future.

In just thirteen years, from a tangled wilderness a palace had risen that could hold its own with the most celebrated residences of Europe. Now the first phase of its life, the joyous years, were over and the shadows that had sometimes clouded the sunshine began to darken the sky.

The approaching storms and misfortunes were heralded in 1789 by the thunderclaps of the French Revolution. In August of that year the sad news was brought to Pavlovsk that French revolutionaries had seized Montbéliard and forced Maria Feodorovna's parents to leave their ancestral home. At Pavlovsk a liturgy was celebrated and that evening at a musical performance, a sad cantata composed for the occasion was sung, which began:

> What kind of fury has come from Hell
> Aflame with a ghastly light? . . .
> Liberty through violence they exclaim!

In 1795, Maria Feodorovna gave birth to her sixth and last daughter, Anna, and her fifth died, little Olga, born in 1792 and only three years old. Another son, Nicholas, was born in 1796 and finally, in 1798 a last son, Michael. After this especially arduous delivery, the doctor said there could be no more.

Family problems increased. Catherine made it extremely difficult for Paul and Maria Feodorovna to see their elder sons, permitting them to visit their parents at Pavlovsk or Gatchina only two or three times a year, specifying precisely the number of hours they could stay. Like a shadow, Catherine's own man Saltykov would accompany the Grand Dukes everywhere, strictly enforcing the Empress's commands, never allowing the children to remain a moment longer than their grandmother had decreed. The young Princes were not permitted to address their parents normally; Catherine did not want them to speak with frankness of their feelings nor to shed the artificial rules of etiquette. Father and mother were forced to address them as "Your Highness" and their children would respond in the same fashion. One can imagine the distress this caused the tenderhearted and maternal Maria Feodorovna.

Intrigue and discord between Paul and his mother grew worse; their meetings became increasingly rare. A contemporary reported that whenever Paul would take leave of his mother, the Empress would heave a sigh of relief and exclaim, "Thank God! That is a mountain off my shoulders!"

The year 1796 was a year full of turbulence and woe. Catherine was anxious to marry off her grandchildren as soon as possible. In 1793, Alexander, at age fifteen, was married to a young beauty, Louise of Baden, barely fourteen. The unhappy marriage produced two daughters, both of whom died. Constantine was married off, also unhappily, to Julia-Henrietta of Saxe-Coburg a few years later. In 1796 Catherine turned her attentions to her granddaughters and determined to betroth Alexandra, then only thirteen years old, to the young and handsome King Gustav IV of Sweden, who was just seventeen. The French portraitist Elisabeth Vigée le Brun, who painted young Alexandra and her sister Elena, writes that Alexandra had a Greek beauty, a "celestial face" and "such a fine and delicate complexion" that "one would have thought she was nourished by ambrosia." The King arrived in August and Madame Vigée le Brun noted that when young Gustav saw her portrait of his intended bride he was so taken that his hat fell unnoticed from his hands.

In the days that followed, the young couple fell in love. All were delighted until, unhappily, matters foundered on the rock of religion. Gustav refused to allow his bride the right to have her own chapel and Orthodox priest in the royal palace of Lutheran Sweden. In September, on the night their engagement was to be formally announced, with the priests and the entire court assembled and Alexandra dressed in her sparkling ballgown, the King did not appear. Finally, a mortified Catherine, her voice heavy with emotion, announced, "*Mesdames,* there will be no ball tonight." The Swedish King departed a few days later, leaving behind a heartbroken Alexandra, who never recovered entirely. She was married to Archduke Joseph, Palatine of Hungary,* but was not happy among the Austrians, who also made her suffer because of her religion, and after enduring many torments died in childbirth at eighteen.

During those years Paul's disposition grew worse. Portraits of the time show a great change in his face. He has a nervous, fearful look and his eyes are prom-

---

* The term *palatine* describes an administrative office in Hungary. At first just head of the judicial system, the palatine became the most important person in the realm after the king, serving as the head of the entire administrative system of the country.

inent and bulging. His manias grew ever more pronounced. Daily he grew more moody and withdrawn and his behavior more difficult. Less and less did he seem able to control his emotions. Any slight could cause an outburst of rage, and he sometimes grew so angry that his head swelled and he seemed close to apoplexy. He became obsessed with the idea that behind his back people scorned him. Everyone noticed this downward spiral. Little by little all of Paul's entourage began to look on him as a sick person in need of supervision and care. Hoping to restrain his choleric outbursts and to mitigate the severe punishments he meted out, Maria Feodorovna rose at dawn and went with Catherine Nelidova, Paul's *amie du coeur,* to his daily ruthless drilling of the troops. Sadly she wrote in 1798: "There is not one who does not daily remark on the disorder of his faculties."

By 1796 rumors flew that Catherine intended to dispossess her son in favor of her grandson. In June of that year, shortly after Maria Feodorovna had given birth to her third son, Nicholas, at Tsarskoe Selo, Catherine brusquely entered her bedroom, handed her a paper, and tried to persuade her to have Paul abdicate in favor of his oldest son. Despite all threats, Maria Feodorovna loyally refused to have anything to do with this scheme or any other like it. Alexander, approached a month later, also refused.

Before she could accomplish her aim of rearranging the succession, one cold November morning Catherine, at the age of sixty-seven, was unexpectedly seized by a stroke and fell into a coma. Seeing the special courier who arrived at Gatchina, Paul, sure that he had been disinherited, exclaimed to his wife, "We are lost!" Instead, the messenger had come to announce Catherine's second stroke. In a coach with eight horses, Paul and Maria Feodorovna raced to Tsarskoe Selo. At his dying mother's bedside, for a moment Paul was overcome with the sorrow of a son. He kissed Catherine's hand and shed a few tears. There were also reports that as the doctors attended Catherine's last moments, Paul and an aide frantically searched her drawers for a document about the succession and burned it. At nine o'clock in the evening of November 17, 1796, Catherine died. Paul ordered her cabinet sealed, and no paper changing the succession was ever found. After forty-two years of waiting, her unhappy and troubled son was Emperor at last.

There was a macabre epilogue. When Paul's father, Peter III, died, he had not yet been crowned, so he had not been buried in the cathedral in the Peter and Paul fortress, the official burying place of the emperors since Peter the Great. Paul had his father exhumed from his burial place in the Alexander Nevsky monastery, where nothing was found but some bones and the sleeve of a uniform. The Imperial crown brought especially from Moscow was laid on top of his father's coffin, which was placed next to Catherine's in the Church of Kazan.

From the window of her home, Madame Vigée le Brun witnessed the funeral procession. As she described it:

> The procession of Peter marched first with Alexei Orlov, the man who had killed him, leading the cortège holding the crown on a golden cloth. The coffin of the Emperor was preceded by a Chevalier of the Guard, clad from head to toe in heavy golden armor, while that of the Empress was in steel and the other assassins were forced to carry her mortuary shroud. Paul came behind on foot, followed by his wife and children and the entire court. All were forced to walk all the way across the Neva on foot to the fortress in bitter cold.

The chevalier in gold later died of exhaustion. The court wore mourning for six months. Separated in life, Catherine and Peter were to spend eternity together.

The vengeance of the thwarted son was swift. Paul closed Tsarskoe Selo and would allow no member of the Imperial family to live there. Three weeks after his mother's death, Paul dismissed Cameron and took away his Grace and Favor house. Two years later Cameron was in such straitened circumstances that he was reduced to selling his books. Catherine's favorites were banished, the mausoleum she had had built for Potemkin in the Crimea destroyed, and his remains exposed to the birds. The day of his coronation, April 5, 1797, Paul had the laws of succession changed; henceforth only males could rule Russia.

One of his first acts was to confer upon Pavlovsk the status of a town and officially turn it over to Maria Feodorovna. Now that it was proclaimed an official residence, the dimensions of the palace were no longer considered adequate. Brenna, appointed Chief Architect to the Court, was commissioned to make the necessary alterations to accommodate a larger Imperial household and to create new halls for the formal life of the court. Brenna enlarged the palace by adding a second enclosed story to the original wings and putting a new semicircular block at the end of each. As a result, although he designed light open loggias with arcades of trelliswork in the style of garden architecture over the galleries of the first story, the palace lost its airy country residence feeling and became a more imposing building. Inside he added a suite of large State Apartments and a new large hall to house the palace's art collection, which had grown to five hundred paintings. The deposed Cameron was called back briefly, in 1800, to design the white marble Pavilion of the Three Graces in Maria Feodorovna's

Private Garden. This pavilion, which provided a splendid view over the Slav-yanka, became a favorite of Paul's; there he would receive his ministers' reports and conduct affairs of state. Thereafter, poor Cameron spent lonely years designing a few houses for noblemen in the Russian provinces.

As Emperor, Paul, alternately reformer and tyrant, careened from decision to decision so capriciously that very soon in St. Petersburg a caricature circulated that showed him holding a paper in each hand; one marked "Order," the other marked "Counterorder," while written on his forehead was "Disorder." Characteristically, he also did many good things, founding schools and an orphanage for eight hundred children, and munificently supporting the arts. He acquired a reputation of being benign to the peasants, and took a special interest in the enlisted ranks of the army, but was extremely severe with the nobility, disregarding their traditional privileges and subjecting them to exile and corporal punishments. Not surprisingly, they hated him. He was generous and noble-minded at one moment, cruel the next; people lived in fear of his bizarre caprices: he decreed the color houses could be painted, clothing dyed, and forbade the wearing of colorful scarves and round hats. He was so morbidly sensitive about his appearance that he refused to have his likeness imprinted on the coin of the realm and banned the use of the word for "snub nose." He demanded that people once again bow whenever the Emperor approached — an old Muscovite practice that Peter the Great had hated and abolished. Even well-dressed ladies had to sink down in a low curtsey into the mud of the streets as the Emperor passed.

In a strange quirk of history, Paul fulfilled one of his childhood dreams. From the time he was a boy, Paul had been fascinated with the Catholic Order of the Knights of St. John of Malta founded in the eleventh century, which was seen as Christian Europe's last defense against the Turks and Moslems of the Barbary Coast. By the eighteenth century, the Order had become an anachronism and was looking for support. Within two months after Catherine's death, Paul established what had been the Polish Priory of the Order in Russia under his guidance, and guaranteed them a generous annual budget. To show their gratitude, in a lavish ceremony in St. Petersburg on December 10, 1797, the Polish Knights declared Paul a protector of the Knights. When Malta fell to Napoleon on June 23, 1798, St. Petersburg became the temporary headquarters of the Knights of the Order and in November 1798, a group of French émigrés, led by the Prince de Condé, who had hosted the fairytale weekend at Chantilly, made the Orthodox Paul the Grand Master, although this resulted in a dispute with the Vatican.

Paul was extremely proud of this honor and asked Brenna to prepare a hall at

Pavlovsk especially for the court receptions of the Order. Brenna created a subtle and cooly beautiful hall with pale green walls and white plaster bas-reliefs and friezes. The only decorations were noble Roman sculptures of the third and fourth centuries, some originals and some eighteenth-century copies brought from Italy. He also created a chapel with the Maltese falcon over the altar. In the park, Brenna constructed a metal Turkish tent of blue and white stripes for ceremonies of the Order and there the Knights gathered in full regalia.

Paul's foreign policy was as erratic as his domestic acts and he did many eccentric things, including issuing an invitation to the crowned heads of Europe, published in the press, to resolve the wars of the continent by personal combat in a series of duels, thus sparing their populations the curse of war. This bizarre suggestion made him the laughingstock of Europe.

In 1798, in St. Petersburg, at the end of the Summer Garden, Paul had the lovely wooden palace designed by Rastrelli, where he had been born, torn down. In its place he had Brenna erect the gloomy and martial Mikhailovsky Castle, surrounded by a moat and five drawbridges that were lowered twice a day. Paul was in such haste to move into this new fortified castle that he hurriedly had it filled with furniture from the homes of Catherine's former lovers, and in November of 1800 insisted on moving in before the walls had even dried. As a result, the paintings and wall hangings rotted and the entire place was so damp that some said the rooms were filled with fog. Yet even there, surrounded by eight thousand cyphers of his name, he was still haunted by nightmares and thought he saw ghosts in the halls. Only a few months earlier, in May 1800, Maria Feodorovna had written to Nelidova:

> . . . as to our train of life, it is not gay, for our master is anything but. He carries in his soul a core of sadness which undermines him. His appetite suffers, he does not eat as before and a smile is rarely seen on his lips. I scrutinize him often and my heart is constricted to see him in this state.

In a conversation with Paul before he became Emperor, the Comte de Ségur, the French Ambassador, had warned: "As for the misfortunes you fear, believe me, it is in dreading them that one calls them forth." Now this melancholy prediction was to come true. Paul, who imagined plots and conspiracies everywhere, was unable to discern a real one when it was actually upon him.

The leader of the conspiracy was Count Peter von Pahlen, Governor General of Petersburg, a man whom Paul had covered with honors and estates and trusted completely. Poisonous as Iago, Pahlen fed Paul's pathological suspicions and convinced him that a plot to take over the throne was being formed against him by his wife and children. Always obsessed by the fate of his father, Paul fell into the trap and believed these false confidences, and instructed the perfidious counselor to imprison his wife and sons. The wily Pahlen refused to obey without a signed order from the Emperor. Once obtained, he took it to Alexander, saying, "Your father is of unsound mind. You are all lost if you do not have him restrained." Reading the order and seeing the name of his mother, Alexander exclaimed: "This is too much!" No one knows what Alexander then said to Pahlen. It is believed that he received a promise from the conspirators that no harm would come to the Emperor and that his father would only be restrained. What Pahlen did not say was that he and his co-conspirators were prepared to go further.

On the night of March 24, 1801, despite his meticulously drilled guards, the moats, and the drawbridges of the Mikhailovsky Castle, that which Paul had most feared happened. At eleven that night five of the conspirators met and drank to the success of their enterprise. One was Platon Zubov, the last favorite of Catherine, whom Paul had recalled from exile and covered with favors. The loyal Semyonov Regiment, which had been on guard in the morning, had been replaced with the Preobranzhanksky, who were in on the plot, so without any difficulty the drawbridges were lowered and the gates silently swung open.

The Emperor had retired and the whole vast castle lay slumbering. Without opposition, the conspirators made their way to Paul's bedchamber. The two guards at the door defended him bravely; one was killed. Hearing the commotion at his door Paul leaped out of bed in his nightshirt and tried to hide behind a firescreen.* There are several versions of what then ensued. One says that in searching for him, half drunk, one of the assassins knocked down the screen and found the Emperor cowering behind it. When he recognized his assassins Paul cried pathetically, "Is it you, Zubov? I thought you were my friend!" Frantically he tried to run toward Maria Feodorovna's door, but because of his suspicions he had ordered it double-locked and barricaded. Paul fought desperately with his assassins. In the course of the struggle, the Emperor was hit over the head with a gold snuff box and then strangled with an officer's scarf.

Awakened by the noise and thinking Paul had been taken ill, Maria Feodorovna, unable to get through the barricaded door, ran down a long gallery in her nightgown and wrapped in a fur cloak. By the time she reached him, all was

---

* The firescreen behind which Paul attempted to hide from his assassins is now at Pavlovsk in Paul's library. From the workshop of Gambs, 1794, it is made of mahogany with gilt bronze mounts and amber and ivory decoration. It contains a medallion of mother and child thought to have been painted by Maria Feodorovna.

finished. One of the conspirators, Count Beningsen, barred the door. When told the Emperor was no more, she fell fainting to the floor.

An officer had been dispatched to inform Alexander. He was found distraught and sobbing in the arms of his wife. Roughly he was told, "Enough. Come now. Reign." At first he refused, until his wife Elizabeth threw herself at his feet and begged him to take up the reins of government. One account says that when he tried to approach his grieving mother some hours later, she cried, "Leave! Leave! I see you covered with the blood of your father!" Alexander, his face wet with tears, answered, "As God is my witness, my mother, I did not order this horrible crime!" Impressed with the ring of truth in his voice Maria Feodorovna listened and when told of the betrayal sank to her son's feet and said, "I salute my Emperor." Alexander raised her, then knelt before her expressing words of respect and tenderness.

Alexander bore his guilt for the rest of his life. The death of his father was to haunt him and profoundly affect his reign. His tenderness for his mother endured as long as he lived. He could never refuse her anything and held her in such respect that he not only preserved for her all her former honors at court, but gave her precedence over his own wife.

The official cause of death given was apoplexy. As the news spread in the city, there was general rejoicing. Madame Vigée le Brun, just returning from Moscow, says she found St. Petersburg in a delirium of happiness. "People were crazy with joy, danced in the streets. Some illuminated their houses. Many rushed up to my carriage and seized my hand crying, 'What a deliverance!' " But official Petersburg with its intrigues and sycophants was not all Russia, and in persistent popular legend the strange, tormented, paradoxical Paul has been remembered as a ruler who was killed by aristocrats because of his sympathy for the people.

During the ensuing days when Alexander appeared in the streets, people fell to the ground to kiss his feet. Alone in her grief, Maria Feodorovna with her young sons went every day to Paul's bier in the Church of Kazan to pray and to weep. At Alexander's coronation in September, she wrote Nelidova from the Kremlin: "I am alone in my study, there I can give myself up to my memories; I am together with the husband that has been taken away from me. . . . I can retrace the happy moments that I have passed here . . . and I lift my soul to God so that the Father of all Goodness may cover with blessings the one for whom I shall weep always and who was my benefactor." At twenty-five, her blond and handsome son who looked so much like her, was Emperor of Russia. That same sad year the unhappy Alexandra died. In the space of five years Maria

Feodorovna had lost her father, her mother, two of her daughters, and her husband.

After Paul's death, no member of the Imperial family ever set foot in the Mikhailovsky Castle again. Alexander permitted the staff to take whatever they wanted and had the doors to the bedroom walled up. In 1823 the castle was given to the School of Military Engineers. Maria Feodorovna ordered that a significant amount of furniture, bronze and marble, mirrors, and other objects that had belonged to her and Paul be moved from the Mikhailovsky Castle to Pavlovsk. From his study she took the writing table, bureau, clocks, and two paintings that Paul loved of the Archangel Michael and the Madonna. She also had the blanket on which Paul had spent the last moment of his life, as well as all of the furniture and pillows from his bedchamber, including the bloody sheets, transferred to Pavlovsk and kept in a large room next to her own bedroom, to which she alone had the key. For the rest of her life, when she was at Pavlovsk she never missed going into this room every day. His bloodstained nightshirt she enclosed in a casket, which, when Alexander came for official business, she placed on the table between them.

Pavlovsk became more important to her than ever. She would seclude herself there, coming early in spring and staying until late fall, living in Petersburg only in the winter. In quiet isolated corners of the park she had memorial monuments erected to her parents, her husband, and her daughters; there she went alone to pray and to weep.

Rising at dawn she would walk through the gardens and along the deep and rustling *allées* where she had first strolled with her husband in the happiness and brilliance of her youth, and then with her children, her joy and pride. Now she walked in sorrow, stopping in front of the trees, each of which had a history, lingering before those that had been planted at the birth of each child.* At forty-two, Maria Feodorovna was a widow, a woman alone, left without the difficult man whom, despite everything, she had loved so devotedly and to whom she had dedicated her life.

---

* Beginning in 1785 saplings commemorating the birth of each child were personally planted by the Imperial family in what came to be called "The Family Grove" near the Centaur Bridge. To each tree was affixed a brass name plate.

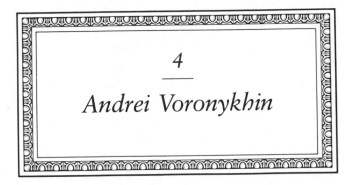

4

Andrei Voronykhin

FOR MARIA FEODOROVNA the disasters did not stop. In 1803 two more deaths followed in quick succession: she lost her childhood friend Lanele and her daughter Elena, aged nineteen, the wife of Frederick of Mecklenburg, who, like her sister, perished in childbirth. And then, during a freezing night at the beginning of January 1803, a defective chimney flue at Pavlovsk caused a fire in one of the palace rooms. The conflagration spread quickly, destroying a major part of the palace, the decor of the State Apartments and the living rooms of the central building. Soldiers of the garrison, helped by the townspeople and peasants from the neighboring villages, fought the fire for three days. Thanks to their devoted efforts, many of the furnishings of the palace were saved, as well as some door panels, fireplaces, and mirrors, but seared fragments of stucco moldings were all that were left of Cameron's and Brenna's beautiful interiors. The palace had to be done all over again.

The Empress was grief-stricken. She gave orders to find Brenna — who had left for Europe in 1802, taking along his assistant, young Carlo Rossi — to recover the sketches and designs he had taken with him, but Rossi arrived back in Petersburg with only a few. Cameron was also summoned. His fortunes had begun to prosper again in the years immediately following Paul's death. Alexander, who remembered the architect fondly from his youth at Tsarskoe Selo, appointed Cameron to the post of Architect in Chief to the Admiralty, gave him an apartment in the Mikhailovsky Castle, restored all his privileges, and granted him a handsome annual salary. At the time of the fire, Cameron, working on a hospital and barracks on the island naval base of Kronstadt, came to Pavlovsk again to help — but not to direct — the restoration. The man chosen, the fourth architect to work at Pavlovsk, was for the first time a Russian, one who would perfectly express the growing vigor and individuality of the new Russian culture, which was to flower in the nineteenth century.

This man was Andrei Nikiforovich Voronykhin, a serf* born on October 28, 1759 — only two weeks after Maria Feodorovna — in the little town of Novoe Usol'e far in the Urals in the Perm region, on the vast lands belonging to the Stroganov family. One of the most brilliant and original of the architects and artists of his nation, he rose to become a member of the Academy of Art in St. Petersburg, a professor of architecture, and Chief architect to the Dowager Empress.

On the village records a minor serf clerk was named as Voronykhin's father, but this man was almost surely not his real father. Andrei's unusual artistic talent was apparent from early childhood. By the age of six or even seven he was sent to the studio of the Stroganovs' master icon artist, Gavril Ushakov. By thirteen he had mastered icon painting and shown a great talent for architecture. He was sent to the icon workshop of the Pysorsky Monastery, and at age eighteen, in 1777, the year that Maria Feodorovna married Paul, to Moscow, where he lived in one of the Stroganov residences and studied under the great Russian architects Vassily Bazhenov† and Matvei Kazakov. The next year, he and his brother were invited to paint the refectory passages at the famous Troitse-Sergeevsky Monastery.‡

It was a peculiarity of the serf system that talented serfs were sometimes singled

* Serfdom in some form existed in almost every nation and did not finally end until the nineteenth century. It had come gradually to Russia, being unknown before the seventeenth century. In 1649, Tsar Alexis issued a decree that definitely bound a large portion of peasant farmers to hereditary labor. Remnants of serfdom were not abolished in the United States until 1833, when the patroon system in New York State finally ended. As for slavery, the British Empire abolished it in 1833, the United States in 1863.

† Vasily Bazhenov, designer of Paul I's imposing Mikhailovsky Castle in St. Petersburg, was one of Russia's most distinguished eighteenth-century architectural theoreticians. An exponent of classicism, he also valued medieval architecture. Constantly accentuating the historical significance and social mission of Russian architecture, Bazhenov was the first Russian architect to begin to consider a structure in relation to its surroundings, seeing architecture as a method of organizing the space of a city.

‡ The Troitse-Sergeevsky Monastery, located in the contemporary town of Zagorsk seventy-five kilometers north of Moscow, was founded by St. Sergius of Radonezh in 1345. When the district was laid waste by Tartars, the miraculous survival of the body of Saint Sergius made the monastery a place of pilgrimage. It became one of the most important monastic institutions of Russia, and Saint Sergius came to be the patron saint of Moscow.

out and given special education and possibilities. Through the slightly more than a century of serfdom in Russia, much magnificent work remains a mute testimonial to anonymous serf artists and artisans, but Voronykhin's life and career is unique. He had a powerful patron who was none other than Count Alexander Stroganov himself. And although the count was one of the most knowledgeable and munificent patrons of the arts of his time, such attention to one of his talented serfs implies something more personal. The persistent conjecture that the count, or perhaps the count's brother, was in fact Andrei Voronykhin's natural father, is supported by later portraits in which Andrei's noble bearing and resemblance to the count are unmistakable. Whatever the truth, Voronykhin was brought up in a special way, as if he were a member of a privileged class.

Count Alexander Sergeievich Stroganov, Voronykhin's lifelong mentor and protector, was the eighteenth-century scion of the powerful Stroganov family, whose immense wealth passed into legend in the pithy Russian proverb "Richer than the Stroganovs, you won't be."

In the sixteenth century the Stroganovs, a trading family from Novgorod, began a profitable salt-mining operation in northeast Russia. By the midcentury they had moved into the Perm region of the Urals, where Tsar Ivan the Terrible granted them vast territories in which they engaged in the salt, iron, fur, and timber trade. As if they were an independent nation, the family was permitted to attract settlers, build towns, and even maintain its own army. In 1578, in one of the famous exploits of Russian history, the Stroganovs hired a band of daring cossacks led by Yermak Timofeievich to defend their Siberian lands against the Tartar Khan of Siberia. In 1581 they equipped Yermak for a major military foray into the heart of Siberia. Thanks to gunpowder, a band of 840 men was able to defeat an army of many times that number and to occupy the capital city of Yashlyk.

Through the centuries the Stroganovs continued to support Russia's rulers. In 1613 they helped to bring Michael Romanov to the throne. A Stroganov supported Peter the Great financially and built and equipped two ships for Peter's navy. For this, to the Stroganovs' vast fortune were added titles — from Peter, that of baron, and in later years, from Paul, that of count.

In the eighteenth century, Alexander Sergeievich Stroganov became the trusted confidant and adviser of three Empresses and two Emperors. Born in 1733, educated in Paris and Geneva, he returned to Russia at the sudden death of his father and, at the insistence of his close friend Empress Elizabeth, he married the daughter of Count Vorontsov, one of her advisers. The marriage was unhappy and he was embroiled in divorce proceedings for many years — terminated only by the death of his wife in 1769.

On the night of her assumption of power, he rode with Catherine, and at court fell in love and married the vivacious and beautiful Princess Trubetskaya. The couple went to live abroad, primarily in Paris, where for the next ten years they maintained a lavish household and were leading members of the *beau monde*. Their only son, Paul, was born in Paris in 1772. In 1779 Catherine, wanting her friend back at her side, managed to block their funds and when the Princess was forced to pawn her diamonds, the Stroganovs decided to return home at last. When Stroganov returned from Paris, he immediately brought Voronykhin to St. Petersburg where he lived as a member of Stroganov's household, affectionately called "*notre peintre.*"

While in Paris, Stroganov had met Gilbert Romme, a brilliant ascetic young scholar educated by monks in his hometown of Riom in the Auvergne. Romme had arrived in Paris in late 1774, where he first lived in a poor neighborhood, eking out his living giving science and mathematics lessons, carefully rationing out his meager supply of wood to try to roast the chestnuts his mother sent him from home to keep him alive. His scholarship attracted the attention of Count Golovkin, an independent free-thinking Russian living in Paris, who hired him to tutor his son in mathematics. Golovkin introduced Romme to the world of French aristocrats, intellectuals, and *Philosophes*. At Golovkin's home, in early 1779 he met Stroganov and fortune smiled on the struggling scholar. The Encycopediste Denis Diderot suggested to Stroganov that Romme might be an excellent tutor for Paul, then almost eight years old, and Stroganov invited Romme to come to Russia, offering him a munificent salary to become his son's tutor for ten years.*

Stroganov maintained one of the most lavish households of a lavish epoch; his hospitality and splendid balls were legendary. In his Petersburg and Moscow establishments alone, he kept over a hundred servants; with the exception of a few Europeans personally attached either to him or to his son, all were serfs. Stroganov boasted his own museum of natural history and one of the finest private libraries of the day. During his lifetime he was Russia's greatest patron of artists and writers. An avid collector of coins, medals, stones, and paintings, his collections numbered over sixty thousand objects.

---

* Romme's pay from Stroganov for tutoring was 55,000 gold livres, which made him comfortable for life.

Romme arrived in St. Petersburg in December 1779. He was ascetic and highly moral (according to his friends, "a man who lived only to think"). Small, angular, and nearsighted, with an austere character reminiscent of Cromwell's Puritans or America's Quakers, he cut a strange figure in Stroganov's extravagant and sprawling household. Upon his arrival the gracious Stroganov showed Romme his fine library and museum full of curiosities, then, ushering him into a set of spacious apartments where personal servants had been provided for him, said: "Here is your kingdom, my friend. Fly here freely. I will do everything that depends on me so that you will be happy in my country."

The new tutor immediately wrote a stern assessment of his young charge; Paul, he said, was "stubborn, lazy, selfish and insensitive. . . . He has many sensations, more correct ideas than his age would indicate — but no sentiments." His pupil spoke nothing but French, so tutor and student had to learn Russian together, and the exacting and moralistic Romme set out to mold not only the mind, but the character of his young pupil.

Shortly after Romme's arrival there was a scandal in the Stroganov household that was to affect the course of Voronykhin's life and career. Empress Catherine's current favorite, young Ivan Rimsky-Korsakov,* then twenty-four years old, fell in love with the older Countess Stroganova, who passionately returned his affections, and the two ran away together. Although custom dictated that the lovers should have been beaten with birch rods, the count instead behaved in a nobly forgiving and generous fashion. He gave his wife splendid homes in Moscow and in the country, where she lived with Rimsky in great style until her death, while the count remained in Petersburg and raised their son with the help of the austere Romme and the companionship of Andrei Voronykhin.

The count, the ideal Russian aristocrat, generous, expansive, imaginative, and socially concerned, continued his distinguished career. Catherine made him a senator. He served on the commission that drafted her new laws and was insistent on the construction of schools for peasants. Under Paul he served as president of the Academy of Art, and during his tenure there was a tremendous flowering of Russian art. He also became director of the Public Library. Alexander made him a member of the Directorate of Schools, and in his older years he was very active in the good-works projects that occupied Maria Feodorovna as a widow. (She always referred to him as "*mon bon ami*" or "*mon bon vieillard.*")

For the next ten years, Voronykhin's, Paul's, and Romme's lives would be

---

*Ivan Rimsky-Korsakov was an ancestor of the famous nineteenth-century composer Nikolai Rimsky-Korsakov.

tightly joined. Romme was a true son of the Enlightenment — a geographer, astronomer, doctor, naturalist, mathematician, indefatigable traveler, moralist, and utterly conscientious mentor. A few years after he had arrived in Petersburg, he concluded that in order to develop the initiative and independence of his young pupil, travel would be necessary. He decided to start with Russia. Accompanied only by Voronykhin and Paul's Swiss valet, Clement, they were to travel under Spartan conditions in order, said Romme, to harden his pupil to hunger, thirst, heat, and cold. "With few provisions — we will find ways to live. The trip will fortify his temperament and make him sober and active, will perfect him in his own language, will instruct him as it instructs me, and conserve his innocence."

Beginning in 1781, thirteen-year-old Paul, twenty-three-year-old Voronykhin, and thirty-five-year-old Romme, along with Clement, traversed the Russian Empire in a series of travels that continued for more than five years. They visited the Stroganov domains in Siberia, learning mineralogy and inspecting factories. They went to the White Sea and to the Crimea and the southern regions, and spent long periods in Kiev, Smolensk, and Moscow. During these journeys, Voronykhin compiled an album of 125 drawings in pencil, charcoal, and watercolor called *Voyage Pittoresque de la Russie* for the count. When they returned to Petersburg in June of 1786, Stroganov gave Voronykhin his freedom; it is said at Romme's request, and in recognition of his exceptional talents.

One month later they left to spend four years in Europe. Traveling with a small entourage, which included Paul, Voronykhin, Paul's cousin Baron Grigory Stroganov, and his French tutor, de Michel, a friend of Romme's, and an adviser from the French embassy, plus the faithful Clement, they began by visiting Berlin and then went to Romme's home in France. In October of 1788 they moved to Geneva, where Paul and Grigory studied at the University of Geneva and Voronykhin continued to study and paint. They conducted a major tour of Switzerland and Alsace, with Voronykhin as "*dessinateur*," and arrived in Paris in the winter of 1788/89 as revolutionary clouds were gathering over France. The National Assembly had been proclaimed in June of that year, and the Bastille stormed on July 14. Just before their arrival, a mob had marched on Versailles and forced the royal family and the Assembly to Paris. Romme, a Montagnard with revolutionary sympathies, plunged into political activities. Young Paul, inspired by his tutor's enthusiasm, changed his name and joined the Jacobin Club. Only Voronykhin stayed aloof from the political ferment and diligently pursued his studies in modern and ancient architecture, physics, mechanics, anatomy, natural history, and complex mathematics.

In Russia, a watchful Catherine surveyed reports of the growing storm in France and by 1790, Stroganov, worried at the increasing revolutionary activity of his son, wrote a courteously firm letter to Romme, insisting that the young men return home immediately. A young kinsman was dispatched to bring them back; Voronykhin and Paul were spirited out of Paris in December 1790 just before the whirlwind.* Romme, a Jacobin deeply involved in political activities, refused to leave with his charges. Four years later, during the Terror, he was arrested and sentenced to the guillotine. As he was being taken from the courtroom the austere schoolmaster of passionate ideals exclaimed, "I would spill my blood for the Republic, but I will not give to my tyrants the satisfaction of scattering it!" Then entering the chamber where they were to be held, he pulled out a concealed kitchen knife, plunged it into his heart, and died.

When Paul returned home, Catherine, afraid that he might infect others with his revolutionary ideas, sent him to live in his Moscow estates, and he was not permitted to return to St. Petersburg until her death in 1796. During this period Voronykhin remained in charge of Paul's welfare.†

In the years immediately following his return from Paris, Voronykhin steadily continued his spectacular professional rise. In 1791 he was called on to restore the huge Stroganov palace on Nevsky Prospect, which had been heavily damaged by a fire. In this, his first major project, he masterfully incorporated his own style into the preexisting architecture and design, retaining the exterior façade of Rastrelli's magnificent green and white baroque palace, but transforming the wings and redecorating reception rooms. In late 1793, he submitted a watercolor to the Academy of Art, and at age thirty-five was accepted into the Academy as a painter. He continued working for the Stroganovs and their relatives, designing everything from furniture and interiors to entire buildings.

In 1800, in what was to be a decisive step in his career, his designs for a gallery, obelisk, and fountains at Peterhof received an award from the Academy of Arts and resulted in his first official commission — to build a colonnade and supervise major repairs of the Samson fountains. That same year the Academy

---

* Louis was imprisoned in 1792, and after a series of trials was guillotined on January 21, 1793. After months of imprisonment in solitary confinement, Marie Antoinette followed him to the scaffold on October 16, 1793.
† In later years Paul became a close friend of Alexander. He served as a senator and deputy minister of the interior, and distinguished himself as a hero at the Battle of Borodino, attaining the rank of lieutenant general.

recognized his architectural talents and awarded him the rank of architect, together with an annual stipend. He was to teach architecture at the Academy for many years. In 1801, at the age of forty-two, Voronykhin married an Englishwoman, Mary Lond, the daughter of an Anglican clergyman from North Wales, then working in St. Petersburg as a governess in the Stroganov household. They moved into a place of their own near the Church of Kazan, not far from the Stroganov palace, and had six sons; none inherited his father's artistic talent and only one survived to adulthood.

In that year of Emperor Paul's assassination, winning out against all other architects including Cameron, Voronykhin won the prestigious competition for the design of a new Kazan Cathedral.* Again Stroganov may have helped, for the count knew that Paul wanted something along the lines of St. Peter's in Rome and may have suggested this to Voronykhin as well as having him draw up plans before the commission became public. Voronykhin designed a splendid new stone cathedral, situated in the center of the city, which became the focus of a new architectural ensemble that threaded its way down the capital's main avenue, the Nevsky Prospect. Later the cathedral was to contain all the flags captured by the Russians in the war against Napoleon, as well as to be the final resting place for General Kutuzov, the brilliant military strategist of the war against Napoleon.

Generous and noble to the end, Count Stroganov devoted the last eleven years of his life to, he said, "atoning for the sins of his youth" — primarily overseeing the construction of the Kazan Cathedral. In 1811 on the day of the great cathedral's dedication, he held a last lavish ball. The next day he fell ill; twelve days later, he was dead.

When Voronykhin was called to Pavlovsk after the fire in 1803 and named Chief Architect of the Dowager Empress, he was simultaneously occupied with a myriad of other projects. An artist of prodigious creative energy, he designed several other important buildings, and in the last fourteen years of his life produced approximately four hundred plans and drawings. But it was in the salons and pavilions of Pavlovsk that Voronykhin's brilliant artistic and design talents achieved their fullest expression.

He began the reconstruction only a few days after the fire was extinguished;

---

* The original wood cathedral built in Peter's time houses an important icon of the Kazan Mother of God, known as the icon of the "Caesars of the North." Until the time of Paul the cathedral had been used for royal weddings. The cathedral, called the Kazan Cathedral (Kazansky Sobor), is shaped in a great arc 111 meters long, supported by ninety-six Corinthian columns. Since 1932 the cathedral has housed the Museum of the History of Religion and Atheism, which is primarily devoted to antireligious propaganda. Today this is being dismantled.

the great sum of two hundred and thirty thousand gold rubles was alloted for the repair and restoration. Using the surviving fragments of the original decor as his starting point, he summoned all the available drawings as well as the advice of those who knew how the original apartments had looked. He did so well and worked so quickly that on May 6, 1803, only a few months after he arrived, Maria Feodorovna wrote to Nelidova:

> Well, my dear friend, you are expecting exclamations of alas and endless lam-entations, but I will tell you: pass over the hideous first aspect, its sad impres-sion, and then one finds sweet and agreeable sensations again. Pavlovsk is like a lovely woman who has passed through a cruel sickness. The trances to which she has been subjected are frightening, but little by little, one finds again the same agreeable features, the same charm and one tells oneself: as soon as she is perfectly well again, it will not be noticeable, she will acquire freshness; *eh bien!* Thus will it be with Pavlovsk. I bless God for what has remained.

She also wrote to Count Semyon Vorontsov in London, and told him of the loss of statues, paintings, furniture, part of her library, and collection of engrav-ings. What upset her most was the loss of the fine poplar trees near the palace, which she had planted and tended and which had grown tall. To keep the fire from spreading these had been cut down. In a cry from the heart she exclaims that she could rebuild her house and have the objects restored, but that nothing could replace the beautiful trees which she admired from her window. She begs him to send her, "half a dozen of the tallest poplars you can possibly get."

Voronykhin tried to save all that was best and most typical of the Cameron and Brenna interiors. Based on the wishes of Maria Feodorovna, he tried to restore parts of the palace to their prefire state, but most of Cameron's papers consisted of architectural details, not overall plans, and the palace archives con-tained none of Brenna's plans or designs; so where items had been entirely de-stroyed he redesigned them according to his own ideas and materials. Sadly, very few of his original sketches and designs were preserved.

He called on the aging Quarenghi, who in 1800 had been invited by Paul to redecorate five principal rooms on the main floor, to help him; the fine wooden doors with inlaid decoration and bronzework were restored from Quarenghi's drawings. The fact that Voronykhin was very familiar with the palace, having worked there under Brenna in Paul's lifetime, no doubt helped him to work more quickly, and he was so conscientious that he was able to accomplish both the structural work and all the decorations in less than two years.

A unique feature of Pavlovsk, one that gives the palace its great artistic importance, is that throughout its history it was always a cutting edge, a place of cultural cross currents and innovations, where new crafts were developed and artists were free to express their own individuality. In his restoration Voronykhin introduced important changes, bringing to his work his unique gifts and experience. At Pavlovsk he was able to express all the artistic ideas he had absorbed from his upbringing and extensive travels with Romme through both Russia and Europe, ideas which combined his Russian taste and profound knowledge of Russian traditions and crafts with his superior European education.

His knowledge of mineralogy and his familiarity with the semiprecious stones of the Urals led him to design stone vases of jasper, agate, and rhodonite; these were executed by the master craftsmen of the region of his birth.* Using stone, he worked out entirely new types of lighting arrangements for the palace. In the Greek Hall, he designed twelve suspended lamps made of white marble in the Roman style; in the Empress's private rooms, hanging and standing lamps from which light glowed through agate and alabaster. Russian craftsmen of the Imperial Glass Factory executed his designs for objects, tables, and Roman tripods made entirely of glass.

Voronykhin gave a great deal of thought to the furniture. The original carved and gilded furniture by pre-Revolution Parisian cabinetmakers now seemed old-fashioned. In the beginning, for reasons of sentiment, Maria Feodorovna wanted to have the original decoration reproduced down to the smallest detail. Voronykhin bowed to her taste in the Tapestry Room and in the State Bedroom, restoring the gilded cupids and flowered silk panels, and retaining all the original furniture, but was able to convince the Empress that a new epoch called for a more contemporary decor, "*à l'antique*," with the result that all other State Apartments received new furniture according to his sketches.

After the French Revolution, artists and architects in France and, led by Voronykhin, in Russia, turned for inspiration to the art of republican and ancient Rome. Excavations at Pompeii and Herculaneum exercised strong influence on the interiors of the period. In France, the new trend was led by Louis David, the monumental painter, and by the architects Charles Percier and Pierre Fontaine.

---

*In 1800 Stroganov, then president of the Academy of Arts in St. Petersburg, led expeditions to search for deposits of colored stone, and was concerned to improve the tools and machinery used to manufacture hard stone pieces. He strengthened the links between craftsmen at Ekaterinburg and architects, notably Voronykhin, to whose designs they worked. He also created opportunities for their sons, sending them to the Academy of Arts in St. Petersburg.

In Russia, Voronykhin worked out a highly original style of his own, and this style made history in Russian applied and decorative arts.

Voronykhin restored and redesigned the Greek and Italian Halls, replacing the original molding on the walls of the Italian Hall with *faux marbre,* very much in fashion in Europe at the time. For the Greek Hall he had magnificent Russian-made monumental fireplaces faced with Russian lapis-lazuli and jasper brought from the Mikhailovsky Palace.

He determined the choice of forms for the furnishings according to the architecture and function of the various apartments. In the Italian Hall, couches were made to resemble the couches of Roman patricians; in the Halls of War and Peace, the curule chairs of Roman consuls. Using the great skill of Russian carvers, he designed a spectacular set of furnishings for the Greek Hall of gilt carved wood patinated in imitation of bronze. Exuberant Russian touches of color were added by upholstery of Beauvais tapestry or hand-embroidered fabric.

In the 1790s because of Napoleon's Egyptian campaign there was a great new interest in Egyptian art. Voronykhin was the first Russian artist to introduce Egyptian motifs into architecture and the applied arts. At Pavlovsk he replaced the original statues of the Twelve Months in the vestibule with imposing black Egyptian figures and signs of the zodiac.

He worked on plans for a large new addition to the palace, a semicircular library in one of the wings (which Rossi, employing Voronykhin's concept, later built) and he redesigned the personal apartments of the Empress, which included a library, boudoir, and bedroom. Voronykhin was the first Russian artist to incorporate French doors and large plate-glass windows that, in a very modern way and far ahead of his time, made the beauty of nature outside an element of the interior decoration.

The period from 1780 to 1840 is called the Golden Age of Russian furniture. With the Petersburg cabinetmaker Heinrich Gambs, Voronykhin created a style called "Russian Empire." This style, always decorated with brass strips or rosettes, is distinguished by clean geometrical lines whose simplicity is very modern. Beginning in 1803/04, Gambs, working to Voronykhin's designs, produced pieces for Pavlovsk. From 1805 to Voronykhin's death, he worked exclusively to the artist's designs, and some of the examples resulting from this collaboration reached a standard rarely surpassed. Voronykhin's furniture designs exhibited a superlative, and very Russian, imagination and fantasy. For Maria Feodorovna he designed *bureau-jardinières* that incorporated pots for flowers, and for her library a startling carved and gilded armchair, the uprights of which were made in the form of cornucopias to hold plants, so the Empress could sit always closely surrounded by the flowers she loved so much. On the legs and arms of his armchairs are carved griffons, sphinxes, heads of women, and eagles' claws. For the Empress's bedroom he designed armchairs whose backs are formed by a single giant anthemion * of ebonized wood, and whose arms represent snakes turning back on themselves.

For the apartments on the ground floor of the palace he created one of the most perfect specimens of Russian interior design of the early nineteenth century, a study called the Little Lantern Room. For this intimate study, to bring in nature, which Russians and the Empress loved so much, Voronykhin designed a rotunda of bow windows that looked out onto Maria Feodorovna's Private Garden, full of pansies and white roses; he also designed metal plant stands whose uncluttered classical lines look very clean and modern. The furniture is black and gold, the rugs scattered with flowers. There is in this room a remarkable sense of intimacy, serenity, and a sumptuous coziness that is essentially Russian.

The years of Voronykhin were the years later described by Tolstoy in *War and Peace*. In his diplomacy and his dealings with other nations, the charming Tsar Alexander was often enigmatic. In his relations with the new ruler of France, Napoleon Bonaparte, he behaved in a complicated and crafty manner. Russia and France fought in Austria and Prussia; then in a surprising about-face, on June 25, 1807, Alexander allied himself with Napoleon at Tilsit. Napoleon even proposed that he marry Alexander's sister Anna, and was ready to abandon Josephine to do it, but Maria Feodorovna vehemently objected, saying that she had already lost two daughters because of premature marriages. Alexander, citing his mother, resisted Napoleon's offer. In the end, relations between the two rulers were abruptly severed and on June 24, 1812, Napoleon crossed the Niemen River on the border of Lithuania and Poland and invaded Russia with his Grand Army of six hundred thousand men.

Arrogant and sure of victory, he confidently drove for Moscow. But the French, and indeed all of Europe, were astonished at the ferocious Russian resistance the mighty French army met. Led by their crafty commander in chief, one-eyed General Kutusov, "the Fox of the North," the Russians at first retreated, burning their lands as they went. Kutusov stood against the French on September 7 at Borodino, only ninety-five kilometers from Moscow, and after

---

* An anthemion in an ornament of floral forms in a flat radiating cluster. It is also called a honeysuckle ornament.

sustaining appalling losses retreated once again. Within a week, the French occupied Moscow, but it was to be a hollow victory, for a day later the city was burning.

Moscow was virtually destroyed. An appalled Napoleon watched the terrible conflagration from the top of the Ivan Bell Tower in the Kremlin and later wrote, "Such terrible tactics have no precedent in the history of civilization. . . . To burn one's own cities . . . a demon inspires these people! What a savage determination! What a people! What a people!"

Although Petersburg was unscathed, the whole city was caught up in the war effort. When Napoleon seized Moscow, apprehension grew in the capital and an evacuation of palaces and museums was hastily begun. The treasures of the Hermitage, of the Academies of Art and Science, and of many of the palaces were hurriedly packed. As the ruler of both Pavlovsk and Gatchina, Maria Feodorovna worried about the fate of the valuables of the two palaces in her charge, and she ordered cases made. As valuables were packed, they were sent far to the north to the cities of Sveaburg and Kargopol, with the Empress herself determining three categories of valuables: those most precious, those less so, and those there was a hope of hiding. Packing of valuables went on at night by candlelight, often with the Empress supervising. Lists of the time show that most essential to her were the pieces of furniture with embroidered upholstery done by herself and her daughters, and that these were the first to be carried away. She worried greatly about the bronzes and the paintings. There were several hundred paintings, among them a Rembrandt, a Reubens, and a Veronese, and thirty-one hundred engravings in the palace. All the paintings were packed and evacuated, accompanied by the painter Mettenleiter. Voronykhin, along with other academicians, was designated to lead further evacuations of valuables.

As it turned out, he did not have to, for after the burning of Moscow, as peasants burned their houses and fields, the French, cut off from their supplies and finding nothing but scorched earth, began to retreat. Then came the Russian winter. Miserable, dying by the thousands in the frost and blinding snow, the Grand Army struggled back toward Western Europe. As they fled, they were attacked by peasants with pikes, whose vengeful cries echoed in the forests. Fierce bands of Cossacks rode down on them and recovered most of the booty the French had stolen from the Uspensky Cathedral in Moscow. A Russian account says that 36,000 French dead were found in the Berezina River alone. In all, 125,000 men perished in battle, 132,000 succumbed to fatigue, hunger, and cold, and 193,000 were captured. Only 40,000 men returned alive from what was one of the greatest military catastrophes in history.*

When the news came to Pavlovsk that Napoleon's army had crossed the Berezina River in Byelorussia, it was judged that the danger to the palace had passed. Packed valuables were turned around en route. Orders were given to return all that had already been evacuated and to unpack and replace everything in the palace.

In December, as the French were in retreat, Maria Feodorovna wrote exultantly to her friend Nelidova: "A brilliant victory! . . . It seems to me that the charm is broken for Napoleon, and that he is no longer redoubtable as he was in the past; he is no longer an *idol,* he has descended into the class of men; and so he can be beaten by men."

In England, the same month that Napoleon had invaded Russia — hardly noticed during that tumultuous time — a brief obituary notice had appeared in *Gentleman's Magazine:* "At St. Petersburg, Charles Cameron Esq. formerly architect to the court of Russia." Cameron's actual date of death is unknown. It is said that he returned to Pavlovsk in 1811 to do the last work he would ever do in the first house that he had created, and that the Tsar was given the news of his death at Vilna in late April. He left no fortune. His wife made arrangements for the sale of his library and personal effects in November 1812, not the most propitious time for the sale of fine books, paintings, and furniture, and his collection was dispersed, leaving no trace. Emperor Alexander was generous with his widow, giving her an annual pension of fifteen hundred rubles, which was almost the entire sum her husband had received as Architect to the Admiralty. Four years later, in failing health, she was advised by her doctors to return to England and live with her family. The Tsar continued her pension until she died in 1817.

In the years he spent working at Pavlovsk, Voronykhin worked not only in the palace but in the park. In 1805 he built the Centaur Bridge near Cameron's neoclassical Cold Bath, and the Visconti Bridge, with its lacy grillwork that spanned the Slavyanka and floating fields of yellow water lilies.

His jewel was a little villa in the park with a round central hall and a small cupola, which he designed for Prince Bagration, whose family occupied it for a

* Legend has it that the average height of Frenchmen became inches shorter after the catastrophic battle with the Russians, as Napoleon's troops — the tallest Frenchmen of the time — were slain.

few years. Acquired by Maria Feodorovna in 1811, just before the war with Napoleon, she renamed it *Le Pavillon des Roses*. Like the Petit Trianon at Versailles, built for Marie Antoinette, the Rose Pavilion became Maria Feodorovna's favorite place and the center of her private life in the years after Paul.

Tended by veterans of the wars, whom Maria Feodorovna cared for and who called her *Matyushka* (Mother), the pavilion was an enchanting spot, entirely surrounded by rose bushes of hundreds of varieties, which grew, not in neat tended beds, but in a profusion of thick wild bushes whose scent perfumed the air.

When the Rose Pavilion was first acquired by the Empress, Russia was at war, therefore no special purchases were made for it, and it came to be furnished entirely by family and friends, who provided examples of work made by their own hands. Everything was decorated with a rose motif. Ladies and maids-of-honor contributed examples of their embroidery — rose-covered carpets, pillows, and even tables covered with embroidered cloths — executed in the long months of waiting for their men to come back from battle. Friends sent presents; in the summer of 1813 the Duchess of Württemberg and her daughter sent a vase made of yellow wood, and pillows embroidered with the double eagle and garlands of roses; Princess Shcherbatov gave a table embroidered with a rose cover. Later, the favorite china service was dark blue with many varieties of wild and cultivated roses on white medallions; each different, each copied from a book by Redouté, in the library of the palace. Porcelain plates mounted in gold frames with copies of paintings done by famous artists hung on the walls. A very poetic touch were the aeolian harps with long vertical strings, which, built into the frames of the windows, produced melodic chords when the rose-scented wind blew. On tables along the sides of the round study lay albums of drawings and colored engravings, and each day on a special table fresh newspapers and magazines were distributed for visitors. The albums, provided for the observations and suggestions of friends over the years, came to contain the comments, inscriptions, poems, and drawings of some of the greatest artists of the day, along with the more prosaic suggestions of friends, one of whom wrote one day: "Here in the Rose Pavilion there is everything one could ever want; it is a pity there is no forte piano." The same day, Maria Feodorovna ordered a piano placed there — one older than Pavlovsk itself, made in Germany in the eighteenth century.

After the war, on Sundays, there were often dancing parties. Famous authors visiting Pavlovsk regularly gathered there with the Empress and her friends to read their works. According to guests the magic and wonder of the Pavilion lay not only in its architectural beauty but in its perfect expression of femininity, its warm coziness and charm, peace and gentleness.

Voronykhin gave ten creative years to Pavlovsk, working there until the day of his death. On February 25, 1814, at age fifty-four, as he was working on Paul's mausoleum and a new Orangerie, he died. The circumstances of his death, as those of his birth, remain cloudy; some say he died of a stroke, others that he committed suicide. Sadly, this premature end to the life of one of Russia's most talented and romantic artists left many of his imaginative projects for the palace unfinished. A son of a serf mother brought up by a Russian nobleman had given to Pavlovsk its distinctive Russian character, and his art, combining as it did the best of Russia and Europe, became the synthesis of the great epoch of connection between the two.

Grand Duke Paul, late 1780s

Grand Duchess Maria Feodorovna,
by Alexandre Roslin, late 1780s

Pavlovsk Palace

The Private Garden, designed by
Charles Cameron, 1786

Volière, by Cameron, 1783

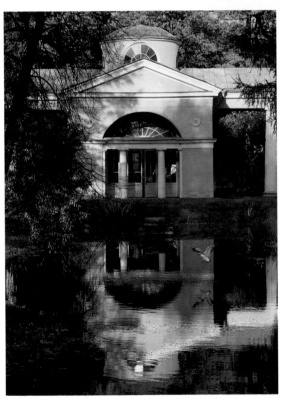

The Temple of Friendship, by
Cameron, 1780–1782

Opposite page: Library of Maria Feodorovna
Top left: Library of Paul I
Bottom left: The Little Lantern Room
Right: The Rossi Corner Salon

The Sèvres toilet set

Detail: cups with portraits of
Marie Antoinette and Louis XVI

Clocks from the palace collection

Top left: Lyre clock, Paris, 1780s

Center left: Clock with sculptural group illustrating scene from Mosigny opera *The Deserter* (France, 1770s) and box with musical mechanism (Russia, late eighteenth century)

Bottom left: Mother-of-pearl clock, Austria, early nineteenth century

Below: Vase clock, England, second half of the eighteenth century. The clock plays six pieces: a minuet, a gavotte, a march, and three songs.

Cylinder-top desk, made by serf
master Veretennikov, 1790s

Tula steel, gilded bronze, silver
encrustation dressing table and
chair — Tula master, Samarin,
1789

Detail of restored sculptural wall
decoration

Carved and gilded restored detail
of door

Above: Restored ceiling, Hall of War

Design for Throne Room
ceiling — Gonzaga, 1799

Dressing Room of the Empress:
trompe l'oeil fresco, Gonzaga

State Vestibule grisaille ceiling
decoration — Giovanni Scotti
1803; reproduced by Treskin,
1963

Designs of Andrei Voronykhin

Hall of Peace: Athénienne of crystal and colored glass, Imperial Glass Factory, 1808

Greek Hall: wooden carved gilt armchair, 1804

Pilaster Room: sofa and armchair, part of a set, early nineteenth century

Vase of Ural jasper, chased
ormolu — Ekaterinburg Stone
Works, 1802

Above: Pavilion of the Three
Graces (designed by Cameron,
1800): marble statue by Paulo
Triscorni, late eighteenth century

Right: Eighteenth-century copy
of antique statue in the palace
alcove

The Apollo Colonnade. Charles Cameron, 1782/83

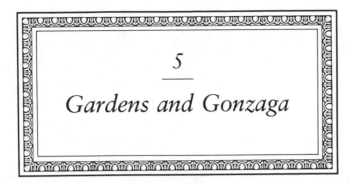

5

Gardens and Gonzaga

ON THE DAY OF HIS ACCESSION, Alexander raised the town of Pavlovsk to the rank of city. He also gave his mother Gatchina, but it was always Pavlovsk that remained the kingdom of her heart, her surest refuge from the sorrows of her existence. Paul was dead, but Pavlovsk was alive. Maria Feodorovna outlived him by more than twenty-eight years, and as her life took on the darker, richer hues of maturity, the palace took on wider national meaning. During the first quarter of the nineteenth century, Pavlovsk was gradually transformed from a royal residence, which magnificently expressed aristocratic taste, into a focus for the increasingly popular and flourishing new art and culture of Russia. It was to win a permanent place in Russian hearts as the place where a triumphant Tsar Alexander returned to celebrate one of the nation's greatest victories.

The park became ever larger and more important, a unique glory of the nation. Maria Feodorovna always loved the country and the life of the country. Her gardens and park were a consuming interest and she continued to embellish them until her death. Each architect who worked on the palace also worked on the park, and in the course of fifty years, as it was gradually shaped, left the special imprint of a unique artistic personality. The result of these decades of work done by great architects, painters, and sculptors as well as thousands of nameless workers, became a masterpiece of Russian landscape design.

The contribution of Maria Feodorovna, who all her life was a practical and dedicated gardener with a professional knowledge of botany, was immense. Over the years, under her careful eye were erected some thirty-seven pavilions, houses, monuments, obelisks, and "ruins" — of varying styles and moods, but always tasteful and elegant. Among them was a water mill known as the Pil Tower, the classical Cold Bath for summer bathing, a romantic play fortress named Bip, and two beautiful dachas: the Constantine, built for a much-hoped-for but never realized visit by her mother, and the Alexander, built for her son "on a hill where the thornless roses grow." * In 1786, the year that Thomas Jefferson, himself a dedicated gardener, set out for a tour of the gardens of Europe and began building at Monticello, Cameron at Pavlovsk laid out an intricate green maze, built a cozy theater seating 110 people, and designed the monument to Maria Feodorovna's parents.† Brenna in the 1790s created the New and the Old Sylvia. The Old Sylvia was a shady circular glade from which twelve *allées,* each adorned with a muse of the arts, radiated with a statue of Apollo in the center. The New Sylvia, connected to the Old by a small bridge, was a series of five corridors bordered with clipped acacia hedges in the forest which, running almost parallel to each other and punctuated with corners, grew wider until they formed a small circle with several clearings. Paul's mausoleum was placed in one of these.

The park owed much of its beauty to its hilly terrain and abundance of water. These water effects were heightened by creating pools and waterfalls. A large reservoir was dug alongside the Slavyanka, and a cascade made to pour down its bank, dashing over boulders strewn along the bottom of a shallow ravine in picturesque disorder. There were over thirty fountains and many graceful bridges designed to span ponds and river.‡ Gradually, forests were cleared, waters dammed, *allées* laid out. The park grew to eighteen hundred acres, crisscrossed

---

* This property was given by Catherine to her grandson when he was still a child. The young Grand Duke himself presided over the arrangement of park and pavilions. They took the form of an allegory connected with a moral tale in verse, which the Empress had written for the education of her grandson. In this tale a young prince named Chlore was led by the Princess Felitza through many difficulties toward the mountain on which bloomed "the thornless rose." Young Alexander imagined the idea of transforming the park of his villa into the form described by the tale of his grandmother. It contained many paths, complete with obstacles, a hermit's cave, a spring of life, and temples to Ceres, Flore, and Pomone, all of which traversed little bridges with allegorical significance. The paths finally led to a little hill on which there was a Temple of the Rose; inside was an altar in antique form on which shone a golden rose in a blue vase.

† Cameron designed the structure which is in the form of a small open temple. In or about 1807, a magnificent marble sculptured group done by Ivan Martos was placed in the temple.

‡ By Maria Feodorovna's orders in 1799, the Apollo Colonnade was moved from the original site where Cameron had placed it to the edge of the river, and a grand fountain was installed. Cameron had predicted that if moved to this location it would be flooded, and his prediction proved true. The colonnade was flooded and struck by lightning in 1817. It was never repaired, for the lightning damage gave it the romantic appearance of a real ruin.

with 250 kilometers of small roads and paths, the largest landscaped eighteenth-century park in the world.*

Even more than in the pavilions and interiors of the palace, Maria Feodorovna's hand was evident in the gardens, and she took a keen interest in the work of all the gardeners at both Gatchina and Pavlovsk. In the first years, her almost daily letters to Kuchelbecker are full of precise instructions for planting. She had dreamed of re-creating the charm of her childhood home, Étupes. To duplicate the buildings was one thing; the challenge of trying to duplicate the lush gardens of Württemberg in the cold north of Russia, with its yearly average of only ninety days of sun, was a far more difficult challenge.

Maria Feodorovna was familiar with all the theoretical works of the day on gardening and brought great ingenuity and persistence to overcoming the rigors of the northern Russian climate through the design of the gardens. She had fruit trees brought from Moscow, oaks brought from Finland, and personally attended to the planting and the protection of all the trees, supervising both Kuchelbecker and her head gardener at Pavlovsk, Visler.

She paid attention to the smallest details, as is evident from her letters to Kuchelbecker. On October 19, 1784, when she was twenty-five, she wrote:

> Ask Visler to calculate, my dear Kuchelbecker, how many linden trees we will need for the planting which is indicated, and mark on good quality paper the thickness, height, the kind and quantity you will need. You will remit this paper to me on Thursday. As the clumps of flowers here have spread extremely well I thought to please you by sending this drawing made to the exact measure of their size. This drawing can guide you for those you will make *chez moi* [Pavlovsk]. Remember that in the middle of these clumps of flowers are found lilacs and wild roses. I flatter myself to think that I will find a few beautiful groves of large trees planted on the main lawn.

On October 19, 1786, she wrote to Kuchelbecker.

> I am told that it is in Finland that one will most easily find a fine oak; that one could take it in the early spring, with all the roots and earth. We must at present dig the hole which will receive it and then cover it so that snow does not fall into it and when one plants the tree, which we will transport on a sledge, put a good layer of Holzerde [wood mold].

---

* Pavlovsk's park covers 1,800 acres. By comparison, Central Park comprises 840 acres, the park of Versailles 250 acres (1800 acres equal 728.45 hectares).

Linden trees for the splendid long *allée* leading from the palace were brought from Lubeck. Maria Feodorovna watched over their progress, writing:

> Mr. Swart advises me to remove the old braids with which the lindens are presently wrapped and at the first frost to put new and dry ones, so that old ones, being humid, do not freeze on the tree. One must also have put a pile of leaves at the foot of each tree.

On April 20, 1786:

> I have arrived from Gatchina at this moment and have examined with the most scrupulous attention the way of planting trees (especially the lindens and rose trees) of Sparrow and I confess that I was very surprised to see the difference between the care that he gives to it and the little that Visler brings to it. Sparrow, after having planted the lindens in black earth puts more on top of the roots and every two days has each linden watered and the roots covered with many pine branches. He does the same with rose trees and so all of these are green. . . . It is women who are used to water the trees. Try and find some for this work and starting tomorrow water my new planted lindens and roses. I conjure you to engage Visler to put more zeal, more care and more polish to his task. . . . Sparrow's methods seem very successful. I have therefore given orders to buy 500 wild rose trees. . . .

As a result of all this careful attention, from the cold earth of the north she and her gardeners coaxed luxuriant rose gardens where more than a thousand varieties bloomed. Her mother sent cuttings from Montbéliard, which she insisted on carefully tending herself.

Her passion for flowers never abated. Inside and out, she surrounded herself with them. She collected an important series of illustrated works on the most beautiful flowers of all climates. A description of Pavlovsk published in 1816 affirms that for the *parterres* of the Private Garden, which she could enter from her study by descending a few steps, each summer ten thousand pots of flowers were prepared.* From every window in the palace there were views of nature, joining interior and exterior, natural flowers echoed by embroidered flowers on upholstery, the soft greens of the birch on green silk walls.

Outside there were *parterres* of hyacinths in the red, white, and blue colors of the Russian flag. These bulbs she ordered herself from Holland, specifying varieties. In the archives one can find an order dated November 20, 1809, written

* Preserved in the library of Pavlovsk there is a project drawn to scale for constructing a temple entirely of flowerpots, which was happily abandoned.

in her graceful, feminine hand, finished by a regal signature, for: "double white hyacinths (Virgo and Heroine), red (Phoenix, Floras Rosenkranz), and double blue (Bouquet, Mon Amie and Duc de Luxembourg, Comte de Romanov and Comte de Buveen)" as well as for tulips, daffodils, and narcissus. From Holland also came hundreds of fragrant lilac bushes that bloomed in late May and June.

For her Orangerie, not far from the palace, and the many other hothouses she had built, she ordered seeds and cuttings from many countries. In these hothouses, hundreds of varieties of flowers and a wide range of fruit — apricots, cherries, peaches, grapes, and pineapples — were grown throughout the year. As early as 1784, only two years after the palace was begun, she wrote to Visler that the pineapples were not as good as the year before — but then congratulated him for the splendid carnations. In the summer, she had tubs of ripe grapes from the Orangerie placed along the walks of the Private Garden.

When she was in Petersburg, she would often have bouquets sent to her from Pavlovsk, saying they comforted and pleased her. When Catherine kept her children from her, she regularly sent bouquets to her sons, using flowers as her messengers of love.

Indeed, the all-consuming interest of the Empress in plants was so famous that they arrived at Pavlovsk from many parts of the world. Usually it was she who decided which plants were required and where to get them, but many others came as unsolicited gifts. A general officer in Georgia sent lilies from the Black Sea; the Russian Ambassador to Constantinople, specimens of Turkish roses. When a coral tree she expected from Amsterdam arrived in a special container, she left orders that it was to be put in her own apartment and not unpacked until she arrived to supervise it herself.

In 1793, having built a new hothouse, Maria Feodorovna wanted to acquire some of the new plant discoveries from the South Seas. She sent a request through the British Ambassador in St. Petersburg, and in 1795 this resulted in a rare horticultural gift — a collection of 126 plants from Kew Garden sent from London by George III. The King also graciously ordered that the plans, and elevations of a stove and Cape House at Kew be sent with them, as well as engravings and drawings so that Maria Feodorovna might know what to expect when the plants flowered. In addition, the King also dispatched one of his own top gardeners, Noe, to accompany them.

The collection, weighing over three tons including pots, was transported from England in the hold of the ship *Venus,* which was equipped with a special platform to accommodate them. Upon arrival, the plants were taken to the Imperial

Botanical Gardens in St. Petersburg and then in fifteen coaches, each with four horses, to Pavlovsk, where they arrived at midnight.

The next morning at 6, eager to see her new treasures, Maria Feodorovna arrived at the hothouse unexpectedly, disconcerting poor Noe, who requested a few hours in which to put the plants in order. She returned a few hours later, this time bringing Paul and seventy attendants, and ordered that the initials GR (George Rex) be inscribed on each pot. She then spent an hour in the hothouse each day, carefully learning the name of each plant and meticulously drawing each one as it came into flower. Among them was a rare plant known as "New Zealand flax," which, it was thought in England, might somewhere in the extensive domains of Russia find a hospitable climate and prove to be commercially valuable.

When Maria Feodorovna had to leave for Gatchina, she asked that Noe bring her each plant as it came into flower for her to inspect. She later offered him a position in Russia, which he declined, and when he went back to England, she presented him with a gold watch and three hundred rubles to buy views of the royal gardens and plants for her.

What Maria Feodorovna and her architects, Scottish, Italian, or Russian, strove for in the park was a perfect harmony of nature and art. The park was as meticulously planned as the interiors: each pavilion, bridge, statue, obelisk carefully conceived to fit into its setting and to serve as a key feature of a particular area.

Trees were chosen for their shape and color of foliage. The scenery of the Russian north was presented in an ever-changing diversity of lyrical moods; dark firs, white birches, maples and lindens, sturdy old oak trees, bright accents of red-fruited rowan berry trees, silvery willows reflected in the quiet waters of the Slavyanka.

Over the years, Pavlovsk became an encyclopedia of landscape architecture, reflecting all the main trends in European eighteenth- and nineteenth-century garden design, achieving a beauty that could satisfy all tastes and match any mood. The French regular and formal style, which echoed the richness of formal interiors, was used immediately around the palace; Brenna used the style of Italian villas with regular *parterres* adorned by classical statues in the Great Circles and beyond in the Amphitheater overlooking the lake, where one could watch pretty gilded sailboats as they glided over the mirrorlike surface of the lake. His long Italianate staircase guarded with bronze lions at the bottom and two fine white marble lions at the top swept dramatically up from the Slavyanka, giving the optical illusion of being wider at the top than bottom. Cameron used the cozy Dutch style for the intimate Private Garden he created for Maria Feodorovna immediately behind the palace, and the English landscape style in the Slavyanka Valley. In the great expanses of the outlying wooded areas the ideas of the *Encyclopedistes,* and especially Jean-Jacques Rousseau, the friend of Maria Feodorovna's family, paved the way for a different kind of park — one that would reflect the beauty of nature in its wild state and the idyllic life of the country.

There was one artist of very special gifts who came to devote many years to the park and Pavlovsk, and he, along with Cameron, is perhaps the most responsible for giving Pavlovsk its distinctive personality. This was Pietro di Gottardo Gonzaga, who worked under Brenna and continued to work closely with Voronykhin in the years after Paul, contributing his unique gift as a master of perspective to create illusions not only inside but outside the palace.

Gonzaga also knew Cameron, and although very different in character, one a reserved Scot and the other a hot-tempered and ebullient Italian, they became friends. This is not surprising, for both were highly original, stubborn, and completely independent artists. Both, unrecognized and unappreciated in their own lands, were to find in Russia their fullest artistic expression, great careers, and national fame.

Like so many of his compatriots who found their way to Russia in the eighteenth century, Gonzaga was a northern Italian. Born on March 25, 1751, in Longaron, in the northern Italian province of Belluno, he was the son of a provincial decorator and landscape artist. As a boy he dreamed of becoming an actor, and at fourteen, he began to work with Carlo Bibieni, member of a famous family of stage designers. At eighteen, after turning down an apprenticeship with the Bibienis, he went to study painting and drawing in Venice for three years. There he was introduced to Palladio, and fell in love with the landscapes of Caneletto. Yet he chafed at what he called "the precise and systematic discipline of painting" as it was taught to him, a discipline that he felt in essence consisted mainly of "study and memory." Nevertheless, swallowing his reservations, he decided that "the fault lay not in art, but with artists" and "the public could all the same distinguish and appreciate the most talented." And, still in love with the theater, in 1771 he went to study theatrical design for five years in Milan. His road was not easy. He was impatient with the conservatism imposed on his designs by both his teachers and the conventions of the theater. He wanted to stretch the boundaries, but his new and original approach to stage design was neither understood nor appreciated, and he had to wait several years before his work had its debut at La Scala in 1779. And even then, although he designed four productions each season for twelve years, he never won real fame or recognition. The problem, as he later wrote, was that "already what I was doing in the theater was not painting — it was another type of art, which needed a different name" and, as it turned out, a different country.

Quarenghi, his northern Italian compatriot from Bergamo, knew Gonzaga's work, and in 1789 invited him to come to work at the Hermitage Theater. This theater in rotunda, a jewel Quarenghi had designed for Catherine near her small, elegant Hermitage on the banks of the Neva, was equipped with a huge stage and the latest equipment capable of producing all the complicated special effects — including fireworks, fires, and floods — that were beloved in the eighteenth century.

But it was not until two years later that Gonzaga, at age forty, decided to try his luck in St. Petersburg, where Italian opera was very popular and well supported. Taking his wife and small son Paulo, he was to spend the rest of his life in Russia and there find at last the great career and fame that had eluded him in his native land.

From the moment he arrived, new creative possibilities were opened and his rise to professional success was swift. As Catherine's envoy to the Sardinian court of Amadeus III, Prince Nikolai Yusupov, an art critic and connoisseur of the theater, had seen Gonzaga's creations at La Scala. When Gonzaga arrived in St. Petersburg, Yusupov had become director of Catherine's music and pageants. He was also a close friend of Paul and Maria Feodorovna and a favorite actor in their amateur theatricals. He received Gonzaga as a house guest and introduced him to the Grand Duke and Duchess. In 1792, less than a year after he arrived, Gonzaga had already done a series of watercolors of the interiors of Pavlovsk. This proved to be the overture to a working association with Maria Feodorovna that was to last until her death thirty-six years later.

Quarenghi brought Gonzaga into the Hermitage Theater and there he staged his first famous work, doing the scenery for a production of *Amor and Psyche* in 1793. When he first arrived in Petersburg there were critics who looked with disdain at his "unfinished"-looking sketches, so different from the dry precise work of other Italian set designers in St. Petersburg. Yet when the finished production appeared they all fell silent — it was astonishing, incomparably new. A master of illusion, he produced works with extraordinary perspective, optical illusion, and fascinating shadow, which none of his contemporaries could imitate.

In March of 1798 he staged a *tour de force* for young Grand Duke Alexander and his friends — three hours of nothing but changing sets — no play or opera, no actors or music. In later years he was to create realistic sets of ephemeral and unusual materials. For a court masquerade at the Hermitage in 1807 he designed a "crystal tent" made entirely of pieces of glass, a set so beautiful and remarkable that it was carefully preserved and repaired for twenty years afterward.

In 1794, three years after he arrived, he was made a member of the Academy of Arts. By 1795, after designing eight spectacles, his name had become synonymous with stage decoration in Petersburg.

Like Cameron, Gonzaga was always sure of his approach. He was outspoken, critical, intransigent — tendencies that were only accentuated over the years and made him many enemies. They had reason to be jealous: Gonzaga was given marvelous working conditions and a private studio of his own in the Hermitage Theater. In 1796, the year of Catherine's death, he received a contract for the huge sum of 10,500 rubles a year (his nearest competitor made only 2,300) and his salary continued to grow with each subsequent contract. He designed scenery for stages not only in St. Petersburg, Pavlovsk, Gatchina, and Tsarskoe Selo but also in Moscow and Ostankino.

Gonzaga described his stage sets as "architectural mimicry" — and saw himself not only as an artist, but as an architect and theorist. All his life he dreamed of architecture, but his plans for theaters and palaces remained only on paper. He insisted that for him the borders of theatrical decoration, painting, and actual architecture did not exist. When people argued with him, in his characteristically stubborn way he never gave an inch, saying, "In spirit my profession is the same . . . in order to be an architect I need simply to exchange my materials and workers." And yet strangely, proud as he was of his art, he rarely signed his sketches or stage sets.

Gonzaga became the designer of not only the great theatrical entertainments, masquerades, and ballets of the emperors and empresses of Russia, but also the solemn spectacles of their life and death. It was to Gonzaga that Paul turned to design the dramatic funeral procession of Catherine and Peter III. By the orders of the monarch, the artist was then called on to design Paul's coronation in Moscow, for which he conceived ornate triumphal arches, and decorated both the Voskreseniye and Spassky Gates of the Kremlin. He was to design the coronations of three tsars — Paul, Alexander, and Nicholas — as well as both Paul's and Alexander's funeral processions.

But the energetic Gonzaga, always overflowing with ideas, grew bored with simply designing for the stage. He loved Pavlovsk, where he spent most of the summer and had a home. There he went to relax, once writing to an Italian friend: "If I did not spend the summer months in Pavlovsk, I would probably not be able to withstand the burden of work demanded in my theatrical decorating studio." Between 1798 and 1800 he drew up a set of plans for Pavlovsk, and beginning in 1798 at the time of Brenna, and later with Voronykhin, painted marvelous ceilings in the palace and many of the pavilions; ceilings that brought nature inside, as he had already done in his early work in Italy; ceilings that stretched space, "breaking" the walls, giving the illusion of soaring into the sky. He often made his painting grander and more monumental than the room itself — as if to stretch the limits of the architecture. He emphasized the main themes of the architecture of his friend Cameron, extending in his painted ceiling Cameron's architectural detail (for instance, painting cornices that imitated real ones). Always he precisely took into account the viewer's perspective of his work.

Although the exact date is not known, sometime in 1810 he painted a series of frescoes on the walls of an outdoor gallery, which was later named for him. These frescoes were one of his greatest achievements and one of the marvels of Pavlovsk.

The painted architecture and sculpture looked absolutely real. Approaching the palace from the Slavyanka, visitors could look past the colonnades of the gallery into the shadows of its canopied arcade. There in the passageways, arched corridors, decorated with winged goddesses, led into other galleries that seemed to exit into the depths of the palace. Tree and shrub prunings placed alongside the wall as ornamentation formed winged screens and served as an unobtrusive transition to the painted illusion of depth. It was all so realistic that a visiting Frenchman reported that "a poor little dog was fooled and smashed its nose until it was bloody trying to run into the nonexistent space." In 1814, when it was decided to rebuild the gallery, Gonzaga was called to measure and preserve the frescoes, and in 1822, when Carlo Rossi, the last architect to work at Pavlovsk, built the library over the gallery, Gonzaga's *trompe l'oeil* window and arch motifs served as the inspiration for the real windows of the library.

His talented hand was on most of the theatrical performances and celebrations at Pavlovsk. In 1798, for an elaborate outdoor celebration for the Knights of Malta, conducted according to ancient ritual, he constructed for Paul a fantastic black-and-red-striped canvas tent surrounded by bonfires decorated with tree branches and flowers. In 1811, for a performance given by children of the court for Maria Feodorovna, Gonzaga created an outdoor theater with walls, wings, and sets all constructed of greenery.

His most famous theatrical *tour de force* at Pavlovsk was the extraordinary celebration that Maria Feodorovna organized in 1814 for the triumphal homecoming of Alexander after the great victory over Napoleon. For this, Gonzaga created spectacular set designs that no one present ever forgot. The palace, its pavilions, and gardens shaped a spectacular celebration of a golden moment in Russian history, when Russians were hailed as the liberators of Europe, and because of this found a lasting place in Russian historical consciousness.

The celebration began when on June 9, Grand Duke Constantine, "The Messenger of Peace," arrived at Pavlovsk to announce the happy news of the signing of the Treaty of Paris on May 18, 1814. Cannons were fired, bells started tolling in all the churches, liturgies were held, and fireworks lit up the sky. At the palace a ballet and divertissement were staged, and at the Rose Pavilion, cupids and zephyrs scattered roses as they swung on rose garlands. But this was only the overture to the great event that followed when Alexander finally came home.

On July 12, Maria Feodorovna received the long-awaited news that the victorious Alexander had at last arrived at Tsarskoe Selo. His departure from Tsarskoe for Pavlovsk was announced by a mighty thunder of Cossack cannons. All the townspeople of Pavlovsk, joined by thousands more who had come from Petersburg, lined the roads, surrounded the palace, and thronged the entrance. Observers reported that Maria Feodorovna, who was waiting in the Private Garden, came out several times onto the Pavilion of the Three Graces to gaze down the road in anxious anticipation. Finally, her long wait was rewarded. The first horsemen appeared, followed by the steadily rising crescendo of cheers, which announced the appearance of the Emperor. Crowds in the courtyard of Pavlovsk witnessed the emotional reunion of the Imperial family. Maria Feodorovna, with Grand Dukes Nicholas and Michael, appeared from the lower chambers of the palace. Alexander leaped from his carriage and rushed to bow before his mother and kiss her hands, but she did not permit this gesture of formal courtesy. Instead, she embraced him as a mother, and burst into tears. At the sight of this intimate family scene, the crowd fell into respectful silence. Only when Alexander took his mother by the arm and began bowing to the crowd did they resume their thunderous hurrahs.

For weeks before, Maria Feodorovna had been meticulously planning the homecoming celebration, making suggestions, correcting songs and poems composed for the occasion, and personally overseeing the smallest details. Scheduled to take place on June 26, to her bitter disappointment it had to be put off until the twenty-seventh because of pouring rain, but on that day in the late afternoon the gala began. The Emperor was greeted by huge massed choirs in national costume singing a triumphal hymn composed by the court poet Nelidinsky-Meletsky. On their way to the Outdoor Theater, where an elaborate ballet had been choreographed for the occasion by Ivan Valberkh, the ballet master of the Imperial Theater, Maria Feodorovna led Alexander through a triumphal arch of greenery designed by Gonzaga. On it was a grandiloquent inscription which began:

> O you who return from war
> This arch is too small for you. . . .

Among the thousands of spectators were students from a new *lycée* created by Alexander at Tsarskoe Selo. Dressed in their special uniforms, blue serge jackets piped in red with high red colors and gilt buttons, white piqué vests, and rakishly plumed three-cornered hats, the boys watched the approach of the Tsar from a box hung with rose garlands. Instead of being awed by the Tsar's magnificence, one of the boys found it comical, and quickly made an impudent drawing that showed a corpulent Alexander, stuffed with too many state dinners, bearing down on the Triumphal Arch whose gate was too narrow to receive him as his panic-stricken generals rushed ahead to avoid disaster by enlarging the arch with their swords. The boy, then age fourteen, had only a few days before precociously burst into print with a poem in a St. Petersburg newspaper. Although no one could guess it that day, he was destined to become the most beloved writer and the quintessential romantic figure of his country and to bring Russia even greater glory than the Emperor who had conquered Napoleon. His name was Alexander Pushkin, and all his life he was to retain the free spirit that moved him to spoof a tsar.

The festivities then moved on to the Rose Pavilion. There, in just seventeen days, Gonzaga had built and attached to the pavilion a grand ballroom as large as the pavilion itself. It was covered with a paper ceiling (later replaced by an iron one) painted with garlands of roses surrounded by a semicircular balcony and open gallery. Gonzaga had outdone himself, making works of art of the props for this historic celebration. Inside, hanging from the ceiling, the decorated columns, and the wall sconces, were wreaths of both real and artificial garlands of roses, tulips, and narcissus made by students of the Smolny Institute. Maria Feodorovna herself ran up and down the stairs and attached small water tubes to each rose. Hundreds of candles, placed around the ceilings in front of the doors and in chandeliers of painted tin, gave off a sparkling light.

Lawns on all four façades of the pavilion had been cleared and converted into theater stages with wings made of green shrubbery and roses, and opposite the rear another large clearing was made. On the four sides Gonzaga painted special sets showing folk celebrations, using live trees and branches as wings and attaching the huge framed canvases to them. The first depicted children meeting the Emperor and his family with songs and dance; the second, youths prepared to give gifts to the victorious Tsar; the third showed soldiers meeting their wives; and the last portrayed the joy of old parents reunited with their soldier sons. The action occurring in these backgrounds was pure Gonzaga: detachments of guards marched by Russian cities, towns, villages, plowed fields and gardens. Even in daylight everything looked so real that people were fooled until they were almost on top of the canvases.

Before these remarkably lifelike sets a splendid pageant took place. Hymns and cantatas specially written by the Poet Laureate, Gavril Derzhavin, and Yuri Nelidinsky-Meletsky with music composed by Dmitry Bortniansky were sung by leading singers (including the extraordinary tenor of the day, Vasily Samoylev) and the mighty choirs of Russia. After each refrain, three times "hurrah" erupted thunderously from thousands of voices. Poets declaimed verses composed in honor of the victorious Tsar. Real detachments of soldiers marched before the villages designed by Gonzaga.

Afterward there was a ball opened by a Polonaise led by Alexander and his proud mother. The ball was interrupted by a splendid fireworks display, which ended with a fiery monogram of the Emperor emblazoned in a golden temple. The dancing continued until a late supper, held for the Imperial family and the highest members of the court in a specially constructed Pavilion of Peace, and for others under a large tent inscribed "For the Victors." During the supper a special work by Nelidinsky-Meletsky was sung, followed by Russian folk and soldier's songs as the Emperor and his mother, along with members of his family, made the rounds of each table accepting toasts to the victory. After the departure of the royal family the crowds strolled in the *allées* of the park, illuminated with Bengal lights, and the festivities continued until morning.

Gonzaga's native villages painted on gigantic canvases remained a subject of amazement among visitors to Pavlovsk for many years. They were left in place until they disintegrated entirely. More than a year after the celebration Mikhail Glinka, writing for the *Russian Messenger* in 1815, said:

> I walked by the Rose Pavilion and saw a beautiful village with a church, manor house and village inn. I saw tall peasant *izbas* with towers between them, hurdles, fences — and behind, green flower beds, piles of straw and stacks of hay. The only thing I did not see were people. Perhaps, I thought, they are working. I was certain of the existence of what I saw and I walked closer and closer. But suddenly my eyes began to make out some odd change . . . as if an unseen veil had been lowered over all the objects. The closer I came, the more the charm disappeared. The colors faded, the shadows thinned, the nuances were lost. A few more steps and I saw the taut canvas on which Gonzaga had painted the village. Ten times I took several steps back and forth and looked at it again. Finally I quarreled with my eyes, my head spun and I hurried to get away from this thing of wonder and marvel.

Two years later, for the wedding of Anna Pavlovna and William of Orange, Gonzaga designed other such outdoor sets, this time painting elaborate landscapes of foreign villages with the tents of soldiers returned from duty in the background, while real soldiers pitched their tents in front.

In the park, his artful painting transformed the Pil Tower into a romantic ruin; he painted charming *trompe l'oeil* ceilings in the New and the Old Chalets and the Elizabeth Pavilion. But of all his remarkable artistic illusions, the greatest were the ones he created in nature itself.

In 1808 Gonzaga wrote a monograph entitled, *The Music of the Eyes,* in which he set out the principles that governed his art. He loved the distinctive and emotional beauty of Russian nature and, like Pushkin, saw its poetic qualities. Now this subtle and very sophisticated artist boldly decided to apply his precepts in Pavlovsk and create in the park the subtle illusions he managed on canvas for the stage, carving them out of nature itself. If he could not be an architect of stone, he would be an architect of nature.

In a highly original work that took him many years, he sculpted new and vast areas of the park. Not relying on French and Italian formal patterns of royal gardens, which extended the life of the court into nature, instead he used trees as a painter uses colors and revealed the natural beauty of the park by creating images on a living canvas that echoed the landscape paintings of contemporary Russian artists.

The keys, he wrote, were "Variety and elegance, which prepare for us a strong operating philter against boredom and disgust. . . . For the music of the eyes, one needs a rhythm of space and modulations of colors."

Gonzaga believed that the human eye needed constantly changing vistas in order to stimulate the mind, and because of this,

> the art of the gardener consists . . . in knowing how to discern the character of visible objects which nature has scattered confusedly and to subject them to an order which increases their effect. The wise gardener in the distribution of his plan proposes a succession of different scenes artistically prepared according to the disposition of his terrain . . . and must pass judiciously from one to the other . . . here gaiety, there sadness, a little further tranquility . . . freshness, some places striking, romanesque, horrible — and here and there a touch of caprice, a little *bizarrerie* and even a few little extravagances, if the project is vast enough and needs a lot of variety.

For him, beauty was a synonym for order. He saw and loved the evocative elegance of trees, writing, "Even in nature, beauty includes periodic repetition and symmetry. Out of all that comprises nature — trees, flowers, grass — the most beautiful of all are Nature's most ordered part — leaves and branches — symmetrically dispersed and harmoniously colored." Interpreting as an artist the world that surrounded him he created a unique park, one that reflected the rhythm of Russian nature, which he loved.

To accomplish this required years of work in the damp swampy growth around the Slavyanka. With his helpers he tramped through the undergrowth carrying pots of white and black paint to mark the trees that would stay and those that were to be removed. He asked Maria Feodorovna not to deprive him of the opportunity of creating his landscapes with his own hands. Calling himself "a fumbling paper hanger," a "tree pruner," and "surgeon of nature," he insisted on cutting down and pruning the trees himself. Sometimes he would sketch his ideas on the ground. The Empress followed his work closely, studying each of his plans showing the space to be cleared, the old undergrowth to be cleaned out, the contours of the land to be accentuated or flattened; each bears in the corner the inscription "Approved. Maria" and the date. Even at seventy-five, Gonzaga would still go out early in the morning with his son, his assistants, and students to sketch and work in the park.

From impassable tangled forests and undergrowth, Gonzaga sculpted out of the vast park clusters of trees, paths, and roadways leading to this or that meadow, forest, and river, creating varied effects. In some places a group of slim birches gave the illusion of a group of village maidens dancing a traditional Russian round dance; in others, pines seemed to form a Gothic gallery; boughs of birches created fluid arches.

His genius lay in the rhythm of his plantings and the contrast between open and enclosed spaces. Without being aware of the subtle manipulation of a great artist, a stroller would suddenly, as if coming out of the wings of a theater, have an entirely new and evocative view opened out to him.

As in music, Gonzaga used rhythm and *leitmotifs;* as in painting, he strove for harmonious effects of color and composition. Since the court arrived in the spring and fall, he used colors of trees and foliage that were prominent then. "Form and color of trees create a very marked difference of feeling; there are some that are decidedly gay, gracious, others that are sad, proud, majestic." As a musician might, he used two primary themes — birches and pines — the distinctive mark of Russian nature, then he employed linden trees, maples, and oaks as sonorous or bright accompaniments. Light birches looked even more delicate next to the deep green needles of the pines; their slender white trunks seemed even more fragile placed alongside the strong red-brown evergreen trunks. In the fall, only the pines remained green while the rest of the park blazed with gold.

The result of Gonzaga's work is that depending on the season the park evoked many different media: graphics in the winter when the trees were bare, pastels, with the first trembling leaves of spring, watercolors in the summer, and oils in the brilliant autumn. The remarkable thing was that although all was carefully conceived and sculpted by Gonzaga, nothing looked as if it had been touched by human hands.

This highly original artist gave Pavlovsk thirty years of his life. In his native land, his name was never mentioned in encyclopedias of his own day and even in our time when it finally was, he was called a Russian artist. In 1827, at age seventy-six, by order of the State Senate he was finally given what he had so long desired, the rank of architect and the post of Architect of the Imperial Theaters. Four years later, in 1831, he died of cholera at age eighty in St. Petersburg in the country that had become his own. No portrait of him has ever been found, so we can only imagine what this great master of illusion, with his enthusiastic, flowery handwriting, looked like. Perhaps he would have liked it that way — he, that subtle sorcerer of the eye, who could make walls melt away into space, plaster ceilings rise into the sky, and who even managed to put Nature herself on stage.

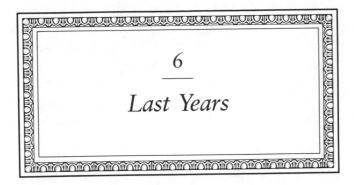

6

Last Years

To the end, Maria Feodorovna grieved for Paul. As long as she lived, liturgies were faithfully celebrated on his birthday and name day. At Pavlovsk, his study was preserved exactly as it had been. Instead of court livery, his former chamberlain continued to wear a Maltese uniform. Almost every day, leaving her maids-of-honor, Maria Feodorovna went alone to pray at his monument and those of her parents and daughters. But while in his lifetime her intense loyalty never permitted anything less than complete devotion to her husband, the years of her widowhood were a time when she could live more closely according to her own interests and permit herself a personal fulfillment impossible when Paul was alive.

In Paul's last years, intellectual life at Pavlovsk had become morose and as sternly regimented as his marches and drills. Now Maria Feodorovna made of the palace a Parnassus, surrounding herself with interesting and lively company, which included many of the notable literary, scientific, and artistic personalities of her day. Far more than merely an aristocratic salon, these gatherings provided a significant impetus for Russian culture. There were evenings of music, where virtuosos of the time performed, plays, poetry readings, and even an early aeronautical attempt, when in 1803 the Empress invited a French aeronaut, Garnier, to come to Pavlovsk and conduct a scientific experiment in which he attempted to fly a hot-air balloon carrying a cat over the park. A wick attached to a lead line was lit and the balloon rose into the air, but the firing mechanism functioned improperly, setting fire to the sling holding the cat. The experiment failed, but the cat survived, wafting safely back to earth in a specially designed parachute.

The Empress invited the greatest artists of the day to create works for important festivities at Pavlovsk. Gavril Derzhavin, innovator of the age of classicism in Russian poetry and Poet Laureate, wrote a play to be performed at Pavlovsk and also composed verses for Alexander's homecoming celebration. The poet Yuri Nelidinsky-Meletsky, for a time court secretary to Paul and then a friend of Maria Feodorovna, at the end of the eighteenth century wrote love songs that are still sung in Russia today. In 1805, this poet composed a long poem of a hundred verses called "Stanzas to Pavlovsk" and also contributed original work for many special Imperial occasions from birthdays to the celebration for Alexander.

Maria Feodorovna often wrote warm personal letters to writers and poets offering them the hospitality and peace of Pavlovsk for extended periods of time. She was especially pleased when the palace and park inspired artists to create, and often gave her own ideas for themes, particularly landscapes, and she preserved the works at the palace.

Pushkin's name is linked with Tsarskoe Selo, where he spent his schooldays and, later, summers, but that of the man he greatly admired and hailed as his teacher, Vasily Zhukovsky, is intimately connected with Pavlovsk.

A sensitive and kind man, Zhukovsky was the offspring of an exotic union between a Russian landowner and a Turkish captive. Invited to Pavlovsk in 1815 by Maria Feodorovna after she had read his patriotic ballads and poems written while he was serving in the Napoleonic war, he stayed at the palace for three days reading his work. He and Maria Feodorovna became friends, and for the rest of his life Zhukovsky remained closely linked with the court, living for long periods at Pavlovsk, sometimes in the guest quarters of the Bip play fortress. While at Pavlovsk, he fell in love with one of the great beauties of the day, Countess Samoilova, whose family owned a splendid dacha there. In 1825, he was named tutor of Maria Feodorovna's grandson Alexander, who was to become the "Tsar Liberator," and Zhukovsky is credited with giving the future Alexander II not only a fine education but many of his liberal concepts of government. Pushkin came to Pavlovsk to visit Zhukovsky, once as a madcap young man, arriving in the wee hours and waking him by imitating a monkey and then keeping him up until 2 A.M. carousing.

Zhukovsky's rich lyric verses introduced Romanticism to Russia, and over a period of ten years, a whole cycle of his work was inspired by Pavlovsk. Not only did he write many poems celebrating the palace and the park, but he also made a series of delicate pen-and-ink drawings. In the evening, with the rose-scented air wafting in the windows of the Rose Pavilion, he often read his romantic verses about moonlit nights on the Slavyanka, including his "Ode to the Moon" inspired by a luminous August night in 1822 when Maria Feodorovna went riding in the park with her entourage.

The jolly, fast-living Ivan Krylov, often called the "Aesop of Russia," was another regular member of Maria Feodorovna's literary circle. In his two hundred fables satirizing human weaknesses and social customs, some adapted from Aesop and La Fontaine, Krylov introduced the earthy spoken Russian idiom into literature. Catherine had frowned on the sharp commentaries of this merry man who loved to drink and gamble, and in 1794 forced him to leave Petersburg. But Alexander felt differently, and in 1806, when Krylov's first fables appeared in print, he was repeatedly invited to court to read his works, and from 1812 to 1841 he worked in St. Petersburg as an assistant librarian in the Imperial Public Library.

Maria Feodorovna loved to hear Krylov tell stories of his dissipation and gargantuan appetite, which, it was said in Petersburg, nearly equaled his talent, and he often came to visit at Pavlovsk. (Krylov's enormous appetite elicited many jokes and stories. Once a fellow guest chided him at a Pavlovsk dinner, "Come on, Ivan Andreevich, restrain yourself a little, give the Sovereign a chance to offer you something!" "But what if she doesn't?" replied Krylov jovially, as he helped himself to another generous serving.) When, in 1823, the Empress heard that he had suffered a stroke, she insisted that he come to convalesce at the palace, saying, "Under my supervision, he will recover sooner." He stayed for two months, and during this time wrote one of his most famous fables, "The Corn Flower," in which he compared the Empress to the sun and himself to a modest cornflower (a comical comparison as Krylov was a huge portly figure). He copied the work in his own hand into one of the albums of the Rose Pavilion. That same summer, he wrote his popular play, *Demyan's Fish Soup,* and volunteered to play a leading role himself.

The tall, elegant Nikolai Karamzin, Russia's first great historian, also became one of the Empress's circle of friends. Karamzin had been the editor of *Moscow Journal,* which, because it had shown sympathy for the ideals of the French Revolution, had been silenced and censored under Paul. After Paul's death, Karamzin resumed his writings and in 1803 began to work on his most famous and lasting achievement, *The History of the Russian State.* Alexander placed him on a salary of two thousand rubles a year to write his history, and gave him the official title of "historiographer." From 1819 until his death in 1826, he managed to complete twelve volumes.

Starting in 1814 Maria Feodorovna wrote to Karamzin, inviting him to Pavlovsk. In one of her letters, dated September 21, 1815, she urged:

> Summer has already passed, but the *Pavillon des Roses* is still known to you only by name and I am still talking to you only by letter . . . the more one expects something good, the more pleasant one feels when it comes, and believe me, the delay only enhances my anticipation to listen to your history. . . . I am greatly pleased with the success of your work, since it gives me the hope that you will come to our remarkable time, which surpasses the former one with wonderful events. . . . Come to us, the sooner the better, and meanwhile overcome your modesty and write, with no fear of being boring, something which, as far as I know, no one has ever found in either your work or your conversation.

The two met early in 1816. Karamzin wrote to a friend, "On the 4th of February I went to Empress Maria. . . . I was utterly surprised by her fresh and youthful look. She is a beautiful woman. . . . She speaks pleasantly, neatly, and with surprising ease. Our conversation lasted twenty minutes or even less, but one could touch on morality and the most abstract things, not forgetting naturally, history." In a subsequent letter he exclaimed, "A wonderful woman! Perhaps posterity will give her her due louder than we frivolous and thoughtless contemporaries." That year, Alexander offered Karamzin a house in Tsarskoe Selo, where he spent the next ten summers. He and his family were often invited to Pavlovsk, which he especially loved, and he formed a close friendship with both Zhukovsky and the Empress. On summer evenings after dinner, either at the palace or the Rose Pavilion, he read long extracts from his history aloud, while the ladies embroidered.

Karamzin was invited to every festive day at Pavlovsk, including the wedding of Anna Pavlovna to the Prince of Orange. At his suggestion, young Alexander Pushkin, then sixteen, was asked to contribute a poem for the occasion, which was set to music and sung at the wedding celebration. In thanks, Maria Feodorovna sent Pushkin a gold watch, but annoyed that the poem had not been performed the way he had written it, the young poet petulantly smashed the timepiece with his heel.

Karamzin noted that well into her fifties, Maria Feodorovna had preserved her beauty. She had delicate and fine features, a well-shaped nose, and the friendly smile that revealed her as the mother of Alexander. Her nearsightedness, noticed by Marie Antoinette at Versailles, was accentuated with age, but she seldom used a lorgnette. She grew a bit stout, but liked and was accustomed to tight lacing. Because of it, her way of walking was slightly restrained. Always elegant, she usually wore an ostrich feather toque, an ankle-length dress with a high waist and puffed sleeves, long kid gloves, and high heels. In memory of Paul, always pinned near her left shoulder was a small Maltese cross on a black ribbon. Her speech was quick and not always distinct, so people often had to pay close attention to understand her. Yet she was never impatient if a page or a servant did not understand her orders at once. In fact, the Empress never expressed anger. If she was displeased, she would simply not speak to the offender, which, it was said, was harder to bear than any outburst.

Her detractors were few, although there were some who called her haughty and criticized her for being too punctilious about the old rules of etiquette. It was true that at Pavlovsk, where every object and piece of furniture had some sentimental association for her, she surrounded herself with mementos of the past and preserved all the old courtly ways. She preferred to be served by young court pages in whom she took a maternal interest, even to supervising their studies. If she happened to see a page reading, she would often exclaim, "That is fine, very fine. Always study, read, but no foolishness — no novels!" When one was having trouble passing his exams in mathematics, she told him that when he came for his duties he should bring a slate and she would help him with his math. When pages graduated to the rank of officer, she gave them each a gold watch.

These young Pavlovsk pages accompanied her everywhere, even when she went to Petersburg or Moscow. At Pavlovsk every night at dinner, one would slide in her chair, then from the right side proffer a golden service plate on which she would deposit her gloves and her fan. Not turning her head, she would then reach backward over her shoulder with three crossed fingers into which a pin would silently be put, and with this pin she would tidily fasten her napkin over her bosom. After dinner the golden plate would be offered again for her to retrieve her long gloves, which a page would have carefully smoothed out and folded.

The old order at Pavlovsk gradually passed away. Quarenghi died in St. Petersburg in 1817 and Brenna in Dresden, in 1820. Carlo Rossi, Brenna's former pupil, was the last architect to work at Pavlovsk. Rossi, the son of an Italian ballerina and a Russian father (sometimes rumored to be Paul himself), became

Alexander's favorite architect. He designed several of the most beautiful and imposing buildings in Petersburg, including the General Staff Building on the Palace Square, the Synod, and the Senate buildings, and the beautiful Alexandrinsky Theater. He also put the finishing touches on Pavlovsk in 1815/16, and again in 1822 redesigned some rooms in his own neoclassical style, among them the Corner Salon. Rossi preferred native woods, Russian and Karelian birch, poplar, and walnut, and had all the furniture for the rooms designed to his specifications. To achieve a wide color range, he used a variety of woods and gilding. In the Lavender Drawing Room there are tall doors and furniture of warm honey-colored Karelian birch set within a color scheme characteristic of the day — violet and lilac walls of *faux marbre,* draperies of golden yellow silk with lilac edging, and white silk trimmed with yellow. In this room Maria Feodorovna received her guests at her desk in front of a window solidly banked with flowers. In 1824, above Gonzaga's marvelous *trompe l'oeil* frescoes, Rossi designed the library that bears his name, a library that held more than twenty thousand books along with rare collections of butterflies and coins.

As her family grew into a third generation, Maria Feodorovna, who had been deprived of some of her children as a young mother, happily made of Pavlovsk the center of Romanov family life. Throughout their childhood, twice a year, on her birthday and her name day, each of her children had presented her with samples of their drawings. Many of these, each signed by the young artist, were carefully framed in gold frames and hung in the family room and even spilled out onto the walls of the corridors. She kept others in her own room. All her children remained devoted to her; her sons, including the two who became tsars, sought her counsel. Alexander, when he was at Tsarskoe Selo, came to see her every day precisely at 3 o'clock.

The family was close and happy. At the time of Paul, the Romanov family had been rather small in comparison with other ruling houses. Paul had no brothers or sisters, and no cousins. The result was that the ten children of Maria Feodorovna and Paul were unusually close throughout their lives and retained very strong ties with each other. The murder of their father united the family still more. The three youngest — Nicholas, Anna, and Michael — formed a club, which they called the Triopathy, and had special rings made as a sign of their membership. (They made their mother an honorary member and had an additional ring made for her.) When apart, they wrote to each other constantly.

As the children married, new young brides and bridegrooms were welcomed at Pavlovsk; and then, to Maria Feodorovna's delight, she lived to know three granddaughters and two grandsons. In 1818 the birth of Alexander was a special joy for her. Her eldest grandson spent much time with his grandmother, and local people remembered the young boy who was to be their Tsar wearing the uniform of a Pavlovsk Hussar regiment, working in the garden, visiting with Pavlovsk's chief of engineering, practicing target shooting in the park, and studying sciences under the guidance of Zhukovsky.

The entire family gathered regularly at Pavlovsk. They were better educated than many members of royal ruling houses; all, including the girls, spoke several languages flawlessly, all knew how to draw and play instruments, and their family gatherings were animated with music and word games. When the weather was fine, traveling musicians sometimes entertained them at the Rose Pavilion in the evenings, with trained monkeys and dogs. On rainy nights, they gathered in the salon of the first floor and while the ladies busied themselves with their needlepoint, Zhukovsky read his verses. Grand Duke Nicholas, who would one day be known as the stern "Iron Tsar," was the most merry and animated. He organized and acted in family theatricals, made many drawings in the albums provided for this purpose by his mother, and often led the charades the whole family loved. (Once Nicholas acted out the word *corpulence* by stuffing himself with a pillow, holding his nose, and grabbing a lance that hung on the wall.)

With her family or alone, the days of the Empress were as regular and disciplined as they had been all her life. She was up by six, often earlier, and at work in her study reading reports, petitions for help, and the correspondence of students. At one, she went for a walk in the garden or a carriage promenade in the park. At two, there was dinner, and then she again busied herself with work or reading. At seven, guests of the court gathered for supper, conversation lasted until ten, and she was in bed by eleven.

Her regular reception day was Sunday at one o'clock after church. She greeted members of Polish noble families, because they especially revered Paul, other foreign guests, and members of the diplomatic corps. She had an easy way of talking to everyone, according to her own interests, and was so gracious and diplomatic that a contemporary, Count Musin-Pushkin, wrote: "When talking with her a clever man seemed to become cleverer and a limited one felt himself a clever man."

In 1809, one of the new ambassadors she received was John Quincy Adams, who described his first encounter with the Dowager Empress in his *Memoirs*. It was Adams's second stay in Petersburg. He had first come at age fourteen during the reign of Catherine the Great as private secretary to Francis Dana. He returned as the first accredited diplomatic envoy from the new young republic of the United States.

On August 5, 1809, Adams left his house on Nassau and Boylston streets in Boston and, with the bells of Charlestown and Boston ringing one o'clock, set sail on the simple merchant vessel *Horace*. With him were his wife, his sister-in-law, his youngest child, a chambermaid, and a black manservant named Nelson. After a tempestuous and hazardous voyage that lasted seventy-five days, during which Adams whiled away the time reading Plutarch and various sermons, the little group arrived in St. Petersburg.

The very next day, after the morning liturgy, Adams was received by Maria Feodorovna. He was taken to the Winter Palace, where, he writes:

> all the foreign ministers were assembled and I was soon called out to have a private audience of the Empress Mother; she is said to be very much attached to the punctilio of etiquette . . . but her Imperial Majesty is all condescension and affability; full of conversation and upon a variety of topics. She spoke about America, which, she said, was *"un pays bien sage."* I told Her Majesty that we were much obliged to her for the good opinion she had of us. She asked whether there were not great numbers of emigrants arriving from Europe. I told her not many of late years. "How so?" said she. I said that the ports of Holland and other countries from which they were wont to embark had been closed against our commerce and they could not find opportunities to go; that our commerce was shut out from almost all of Europe.
>
> "But," said she, "it is freely admitted here." I said yes, it was an advantage that we still enjoyed and very much cherished; that from the friendly dispositions which His Majesty the Emperor was pleased to manifest toward the United States I hope we would continue in the enjoyment of this advantage which was important to the interests of both countries.

Adams remained in Petersburg until 1814, when he returned home to become secretary of state, and in 1825, president of the United States.

During Maria Feodorovna's later years, in 1820 as secretary of state, Adams sent the former governor of South Carolina, Henry Middleton, to St. Petersburg as United States envoy. Middleton was from a distinguished family: he was the grandson of Henry Middleton, who was president of the Continental Congress, and son of Arthur Middleton, who had fought alongside George Washington and had been a signer of the Declaration of Independence. Middleton was to stay in Russia for ten years, longer than any American envoy before or since, representing the United States during the reigns of both Alexander I and Nicholas I.

Middleton arrived in St. Petersburg with his wife Mary, a beautiful red-headed English Regency belle, and several of his eleven children, including his son Williams, who served as his attaché and left impressions of his work and stay. Mary kept a lively journal of her time in St. Petersburg. She was delighted by "the magnificent buildings that one sees at each step" and pronounced the Nevsky Prospect "the handsomest street I ever saw; the houses are not homes, but palaces!" She commented on "how wonderful to see how clean the streets are kept," on the variety of frozen food in Russian markets, and on how well the Russians danced: "It is a pleasure to go to a ball here, for there is such a variety of dances. The *mazurka* is a beautiful dance and Russian officers in their long boots and spurs produce a great effect as one of the chief parts consists of making a noise with the spurs (to which in Poland they say, are affixed with bells). It is very difficult and I cannot yet dance it, but hope to learn it soon."

Middleton was a dedicated amateur botanist. He maintained close contacts with the famous French botanist André Michaux, who imported many exotic plants to America, including the camellia. Middleton Place, his seventy-thousand-acre rice plantation near Charleston, worked by a thousand slaves, was famous for its impressive library of over twelve thousand volumes and its splendid gardens, the first formal gardens in the United States and their *allées* of camellias, which a hundred slaves labored to plant over ten years, and thousands of azaleas. Like Maria Feodorovna, Middleton collected rare plants, and although it is not recorded, he and the Empress surely found a common topic of conversation in their mutual love of horticulture. Middleton and his wife both attended Alexander's funeral in 1825 and returned home with a rare book of watercolors showing the procession designed by Gonzaga, as well as large portraits of both Nicholas I and his wife, presented to them as a token of the Tsar's esteem, all of which remain at Middleton Place to this day, where Henry Middleton is remembered in the family as "Russia Henry."

In her mature years, basing them on models she had established years earlier at Pavlovsk, which were often far in advance of anything that had existed before in Russia and, in many cases, even abroad, Maria Feodorovna greatly extended public-spirited endeavors. Although many royal personages extended their patronage to charitable establishments, what was different about Maria Feodorovna was her active personal involvement in their creation and her continuing personal attention to the details of their management. All were marked with the stamp of her practical, thrifty, and compassionate character.

From the time she was a young Grand Duchess, Maria Feodorovna had closely preoccupied herself with the welfare of the people of Pavlovsk and Gatchina. Her correspondence shows her concern about the health of all the workers and artists at the palace. When the painter Giovanni Scotti and his son fell ill, she wrote Kuchelbecker every day to inquire about their health and progress. When a worker chanced to be injured breaking ice, she directed that he be compensated.

As Grand Duchess, she founded a public school in the town of Pavlovsk, and to encourage peasants to send their children to school, released those that did from their quitrent. The salary of the teachers was high for the time — six hundred gold rubles a year plus an apartment with all accommodations. Every month she was presented with the notebooks and drawings of students, and took a keen personal interest in the academic and family situation of each pupil. After final exams in December, she rewarded the best students with gold rings and pencils, silver pencil cases, and gifts of money.

In those early years, her measures for the health of the citizens of Pavlovsk were often undermined by the people's mistrust of medicine and doctors, which she tried with great energy to overcome. In 1789, when an epidemic of smallpox broke out, she went to Pavlovsk to set the example by having her own two children inoculated, and sent a doctor to inoculate the children of the town, writing to Kuchelbecker: "You must gather all the children who do not have smallpox so that Dr. Halladay may examine them and decide if they should be inoculated. . . . You will note for me tomorrow what Halladay has decided and send me a list of those he has chosen and their ages."

The effect of these vaccinations was noticeable — violent epidemics raged in surrounding areas but did not strike Pavlovsk. In April 1789, Maria Feodorovna wrote: "Thank all the peasants, especially the one who gave the example to all the other parents."

She also instructed doctors to take many other measures to protect the life and health of children, and paid close attention to the living and sanitary conditions of the town population, especially women. When she discovered that children of working mothers were often left in the care of brothers and sisters who were no older than six or seven, and that babies were subjected to traumas and sometimes left without milk, she ordered the town doctor to issue monthly grants of money to poor mothers so that they would not need to leave their babies every day for extended periods of time.

Always faithful to her adopted religion, Maria Feodorovna had the Church of Maria Magdalene built by Quarenghi in 1781, and turned the vessels and a large chandelier of ivory and amber herself. In addition she generously supported the Lutheran church of Saint Dorothy, which was also under her care.

In 1787, after she became Empress and had greater financial independence, she joined an almshouse, the Church Invalid, to the Church of Maria Magdalene; there, old men and women received pensions and lodging for themselves and their children. At the same time she also created the Marinsky Hospital. The people of Pavlovsk were extremely proud of this hospital, which was unusually well equipped for its time. Open to all, it provided free care to both men and women, free men and serfs, regardless of whether they were permanent or transient residents of Pavlovsk. A surgeon and two assistants were in charge. A doctor was responsible for free inoculations against cowpox. There was also a maternity home, and an out-patient clinic. A doctor made house calls to those who could not come in, providing all medicines and care without charge.

The Marinsky Hospital at Pavlovsk became the model for others she later created in Moscow and Petersburg. According to an article written in 1818, the Imperial Hospital for the poor in St. Petersburg, built by Quarenghi in 1803 at the suggestion of the Dowager Empress, had 242 beds in twenty-six rooms; a clean and extremely well-equipped institution, it had its own baths and chapel. Medicines were prepared in the hospital; women, supervised by ten nuns, cared for the sick. As at Pavlovsk, in this hospital in Petersburg and another she founded in Moscow medical care and medicine were dispensed free. In the years between 1803 and 1816, the Petersburg hospital treated 22,736 in-patients as well as 222,755 out-patients of all classes free of charge.

In Pavlovsk, Moscow, and Petersburg she founded convents, orphanages, and schools. She was always particularly interested in the education and status of women, and upon his accession Paul put her in charge of the Society of Education of the Daughters of the Nobility and the Institute at Smolny, which Catherine had created. Maria Feodorovna then created another school for young women, the Catherine Institute, and appointed Quarenghi to design it. She carried on a detailed correspondence with the architect about its construction, often making specific suggestions; among them were requests that the windows be made larger, to assure greater circulation of air, and that privacy be assured by partitions. Every week she visited the institutes and hospitals she directed, often making the long journey from Pavlovsk to the city by coach and back in a single day, returning late at night.*

As a widow, every day the Empress took long walks in Pavlovsk park, often meeting and chatting with strollers in the park along her way. One summer morning in 1806 she happened to meet the wife of General Acherdov, one of the tutors of Grand Dukes Nicholas and Michael, who was out walking with her young nephew. Conversing with her, the Empress learned that not only was this child deaf, but that he had two brothers and a sister who had also been born deaf. Deeply struck, she said, "Abroad, the fate of such children had long been paid attention to by governments. Special institutes have been established — but we have unfortunately done nothing in this respect." †

Writing later about his encounter with the Empress, the young boy Alexander Meller noted:

> The Empress having stroked my cheeks gave me sweets which she usually carried with her for the children she might meet while walking. She suggested that my parents send me to her brother, the Duke of Württemberg, who would see that I could enter an institute. But my parents did not want to part with me, and having expressed their gratitude did not accept the proposal of Her Majesty. The next day, when I was again strolling with my aunt in the garden I met the Empress once more. She said to my aunt, "Your nephew kept me from sleeping all night. I was thinking about his fate, and that of children like him until dawn. And today, as soon as I got dressed, I sent for Secretary Villamov and ordered that he should engage one of the most famous professors from abroad to establish a school for the deaf, where your children will be the first." My aunt, touched to tears, rushed to the Empress and kissed her hand. . . . Pastor Sikard-Sigismund came from Poland and organized the first college for the deaf in Pavlovsk, in the castle of Marienthal.

By October 14, 1806, the Empress's birthday, the plan for the experimental school for the deaf was executed with money allocated from Maria Feodorovna's own funds. All the children were to be taken from the Children's Home and to

---

* Petersburg was subject to frequent floods; the one of November 7, 1824, was particularly calamitous. Many perished, and thousands of families were left homeless. The Empress donated thousands of rubles for flood relief, placed widows and orphans in the institutions she had founded, and supplied hundreds of families with wood, food, and clothing.

† Even in Europe there were very few schools for the deaf at the time. Abbé Charles de l'Epée of France and Samuel Heinicke of Germany were the two most prominent early educators of the deaf. In 1755 Abbé de l'Epée founded in Paris the first free school for the deaf. In the United States the first school for the deaf was created in 1817, by a Hartford minister, Thomas Hopkins Galludet.

be educated, clothed, housed, and fed free. Children of noble families who wished to join them paid for themselves.

The school opened in 1807. As the Empress had promised, the first students were Alexander Meller and his brother, joined by two more boys and five girls. Pastor Sigismund was so skilled that within a very short time Alexander began to read, write, and even to pronounce some words. Maria Feodorovna was so delighted with his progress that she rewarded him with a gold watch. Meller remained in the school until 1812, and then was given a job in the Empress's administrative offices, where he worked for many years. The original school remained at Pavlovsk until 1810, when it was transferred to a larger building in Petersburg, and finally to its own building. A school for the deaf exists at Pavlovsk to this day.

That year, the Empress also founded a shelter in Pavlovsk for sick children from the St. Petersburg Foundling Home so that they could come and spend summers in the country. By her order, in 1811, the population was informed and invited to send their adult daughters to the new midwives institute she founded. Because of the low esteem in which the profession was held, responses were minimal at first, but within a few years, because of the active support of Maria Feodorovna, citizens of Pavlovsk from many different classes had enrolled.

Her school projects were varied and imaginative: she tried to open a school for practical agriculture by awarding it both arable and forest land, but was unsuccessful for lack of good teachers. She realized her idea of opening a school for cotton weaving for peasant children under the guidance of a German teacher, and in 1815 she began a school of botany and gardening, naming as its director the famous scientist and botanist Ivan Andreevich Vainman, who had become the Director of Gardens at Pavlovsk. A year later he submitted to the Empress a plan, which she immediately approved, for establishing in Pavlovsk a school with a four-year course for children from the Children's Home. Upon graduation students were given a prize of 150 to 300 rubles, which, according to the Empress's orders, was not given directly, but deposited in a bank in the student's name; according to their qualifications, they were also given work for six years in the Imperial Gardens.* Other students came to study hydraulics under the guidance of Pavlovsk's Chief Engineer.

All her life Maria Feodorovna paid special attention to the needs of invalid

---

* Eventually this school was transferred to Gatchina because of the greater variety of fruit trees. In 1827 it was moved to St. Petersburg to the Imperial Botanical Gardens on the Apothecaries Island. Only a small department was left in Pavlovsk.

soldiers and their widows, founding both homes and hospitals for them. The Military Hospital was the largest of these in Pavlovsk, and by the end of the eighteenth century sheltered 180 veterans. In 1812 during the Napoleonic invasion the hospital was enlarged, and after the war Maria Feodorovna created another hospital in Pavlovsk for junior officers and privates who had served and been wounded. Four more wings were added in 1817/18, called Montmartre in honor of the battle that had raged outside Paris in 1814. As usual, the Empress paid close attention to all details of construction, asking the committee in charge to report to her the slightest changes in layout, and giving specific instruction down to the size of the window frames.

At Montmartre, which became a landmark of Pavlovsk, married soldiers were given apartments and space for kitchen gardens. They were given undemanding salaried duties in the garden buildings of the palace, which were often quite profitable, as Maria Feodorovna loved to talk to these veterans while out walking, questioning them closely about their war experiences and the battles they had fought, and regularly giving them money from the purses she always carried for the purpose.

In all, the Empress founded (or took over the direction of those already existing) twenty-seven establishments, superintending their managements and receiving sealed reports direct from the administration. Under her guidance, as her children grew older, each was expected to devote a certain number of hours every day to work for the poor and for the charitable enterprises she had founded.

In 1827, an English doctor, Augustus Granville, who spent many months in Russia, said that in all her activities she was inspired by four main motives: a desire to promote and improve education among all classes of society; a wish to alleviate human sufferings; a disposition to support those without natural protectors; and a great zeal in encouraging national institutions.

Maria Feodorovna watched over every activity of the town of Pavlovsk, treating it as her extended family. From April to September during her residence in Pavlovsk she personally received all petitions. Solicitations were always answered, refusals were rare. In approving money grants, Maria Feodorovna often added a short personal note. Among these petitions were many humble requests: the town carpenter's cow died and his wife applied to the council for help. Maria Feodorovna gave her a cow from her own farm. In the majority of cases when people asked the City Council for a grant of money, she increased it from her own funds. By 1820 the petitions filled many volumes and had grown so numerous that she made a request of the council that those submitted immediately were to be in the following order: old men and women over sixty-five; cases of fire, death, or other disaster; peasants who lived under the jurisdiction of the City Council and were asking for reconstruction of their houses or funds to buy cattle.

The City Council had a discretionary fund for helping the needy of Pavlovsk, and in 1826, with the help of the Empress, a special capital of ten thousand rubles was created, the interest of which — five hundred rubles a year — was used to lend money for a term of two years to the people of Pavlovsk to buy horses, cows, and other domestic utilities. When the interest on the capital reached a thousand rubles, money was also lent without interest for the construction of houses. Each loan of more than a hundred rubles was approved by the Empress, and at the end of the year the directors submitted to her a full report on the state of the capital and the loans issued.

From 1812 on, all plans and façades for buildings to be constructed and built in Pavlovsk were submitted to her for approval. Considering these, she took into account the means of those who proposed them, and when necessary gave additional money. She knew that many people fixed up their houses hoping to attract people from Petersburg to rent them in the summer. Knowing that because transportation was poor it was difficult to attract such tenants, she stepped in and gave orders that an advertisement should be placed each year on behalf of the Pavlovsk City Administration in the newspapers of the city. Accordingly, in May of 1818, the following notice appeared in the *Academic News,* both in Russian and German: "In implementation of the will of Her Imperial Majesty Maria Feodorovna and the Pavlovsk City Council, respectable public is informed that those who wish to spend the summer in Pavlovsk can rent convenient houses, and walk, ride horseback and in carriages on paths and roads meant for these activities." Spurred by her, a post office was created, the town organized a volunteer fire brigade, fire tools were provided and kept in several houses of the town, and landlords were required to indicate on special metal plaques on their gates what fire-fighting equipment was available.

It was only after doctor's orders that the Empress, at fifty-nine, was persuaded to adjust her rigorous schedule slightly. This she did by rising at 8 instead of her usual 6 A.M. and by limiting her exercise to a gentle morning ride. In the morning a small horse, saddled in "gentleman's manner," was brought to her. Then, dressed in a gold knee-length embroidered velvet coat, white trousers, high boots embroidered with gold, and a small hat with a feather, she rode for an hour through the *allées* of the park, for that hour closed to the public to allow her privacy. She was always accompanied by a chamberlain; a court page rode ahead, carrying a wad of bank notes and two purses with gold and silver coins, plus a pack of pins in case something went wrong with a garment and repairs were necessary. If the Empress happened to run into a war veteran with a medal, she would stop to interrogate him closely, and after her departure one of her suite would discreetly deposit money for him behind his watch post. If she met peasants in the little village on the outskirts of the park, she would again stop her horse and distribute money.

The last years of her life brought her two more painful family losses. In January 1819, news came of the sudden death at thirty-one of her fourth daughter, Catherine, who had become Queen of Württemberg after the death of her first husband. Cruelly, a few days later, Maria Feodorovna received a letter from her daughter written shortly before her death, and for a time the grief-stricken mother tried to persuade herself that the first information was false and her daughter alive.

In 1825, she lost Alexander. On August 22, he came to visit his mother. His wife had been taken ill and it had been decided by the Tsar that to speed her recovery they were to go to the remote village of Tagonrog on the Sea of Azov where the climate was reputed to be like Italy. After dinner, mother and son strolled in the garden and went to the Rose Pavilion. There was a quiet melancholy in the air. In the cold north, autumn had already begun. The roses were gone and the leaves already turning to gold, but the pavilion looked beautiful, as all its garlands had been refurbished that summer. It was the last time that Maria Feodorovna was to see her son. A few months later in Tagonrog, after a sudden and unexplained illness, Alexander died.* On the morning of November

---

* The official report of Alexander's death states that he died in Tagonrog on November 30 of "natural causes," after falling into a state of weakness and delirium a week earlier. However, many believe (and in fact many members of the Imperial family were firmly convinced) that Alexander, deeply immersed in mysticism at the time, faked his death with the help of his confidant Prince Volkonsky, then retreated to Siberia, where he lived into the reign of Alexander III as a hermit-mystic under the name Feodor Kuz'mich. The heart of the mystery lies in the fact that Alexander had a closed coffin at a time when the ability to view the deceased was a vital part of the Imperial Russian funeral. Ambassador Middleton's wife comments in her journal how extremely unusual this was. Defenders of the official story of his death argue that the body was too badly decomposed to permit an open coffin; others argue that the body was really that of a Russian soldier, purposely allowed to decompose in order to provide this excuse. A great display of armed force was needed to prevent an excited populace from insisting that the coffin be opened. Maria Feodorovna was allowed to view the body, and commented: "Yes, it is my dear son, my dear Alexander. But oh, how terribly thin he has got." Perhaps, although not convinced it was he, the Empress preferred to think of him as dead, rather than as a demented mystic. When the Bolsheviks opened Alexander's sarcophagus, they found that the original coffin had been replaced by another under secret order of Alexander III, a seeming indication that the body was not that of the Emperor.

27, the church service devoted to the Emperor's health was interrupted by his brother, Grand Duke Nicholas. The priest raised a crucifix covered in black crepe to the lips of the Empress. She understood, and bursting into tears, fell to her knees before the altar.

After Alexander's death, there was a short period of confusion about the accession. Constantine, who wished to remain in Poland as Viceroy with his morganatic Polish wife, gave up his right to the throne in favor of his younger brother Nicholas. Taking advantage of the slight delay, on the day of Nicholas's accession in December, a group of aristocratic officers, demanding a constitution, organized a rebellion. Among them were the two sons of Pavlovsk's first director, Karl Kuchelbecker, both friends of Pushkin. The rebellion of this group, known as the Decembrists, was quickly and decisively quelled by Nicholas, who after this challenge went on to become a stern, conservative ruler, whose motto was "orthodoxy, autocracy and nationalism."

The death of her beloved first son was a blow from which Maria Feodorovna did not recover, and it seriously affected her health. Although she preserved her clear mind and mildness of temper, she, who had always been cheerful and full of energy, grew noticeably weaker. In Moscow, in 1826, for the coronation of Nicholas, her daily letters to her director were full of nostalgic thoughts of Pavlovsk: "How is my beloved Pavlovsk doing? Is the lilac in blossom? Does the small garden look beautiful? Are the nightingales singing already? . . . What trees have you planted? . . . This summer I shall not be able to come . . . because of this I ask you to write me more often and with more details about everything that is being done." In Moscow, she ordered two hundred roses for the gardens and as soon as she returned in September, although it was late in the season, she visited Pavlovsk.

The summer of 1828, the year of her death, Russia entered the Turkish war. In Pavlovsk, the Guards troops and Hussars were mobilized. The new Emperor and his brother Michael left with them, and along with the other wives and mothers of the town, Maria Feodorovna saw them off. Trying to comfort the other women, she repeated, "Don't cry my children, don't cry," as tears streamed down her face. She blessed the soldiers that were leaving for war and, with her usual efficient thoughtfulness, in advance ordered a table set for officers who had to stop in Gatchina.

That last summer, she lingered in Pavlovsk longer than ever. Even after leaving for Petersburg, she came back several times in the fall. She took special care of the buildings and the gardens. She made plans for 1829 for numerous improvements and even some new buildings. Her last orders were for some new hothouses and for refurbishments of Krak, one of the eighteenth-century hunting cottages where she had spent her first happy days as a young bride.

She saw her beloved Pavlovsk for the last time in late September 1828. Shortly after, she fell ill, and on October 24, fourteen days after her sixty-seventh birthday, she died in St. Petersburg. She was deeply mourned by her family and her people. The manifesto issued by her grieving son, the Tsar, ended, "let the Lord pacify her gentle soul, which was the receptacle of all tender feelings and values." Her friend the poet Zhukovsky composed a long poem, "At the Grave of Maria Feodorovna."

Careful and organized to the end, she left a long and detailed will, which contained forty-three statutes. Always very private about her personal feelings, she often asked that recipients of her letters destroy them. Now, in a great loss to history, although she had kept detailed journals all her life, she requested that her son the Emperor burn them, saying that as she had freely expressed her opinions about court figures, she feared that these might influence his attitude. Her dutiful son fulfilled the last wishes of his mother, but Grand Duke Michael, who implemented her will along with his brother, said sadly, "When I burned the papers, it seemed to me that I was burning my precious mother. . . ."

Realizing that she had at Pavlovsk created a rare ensemble, and knowing from experience that when the heir became Emperor this would necessitate changes for the palace, she left it instead to her youngest son, Michael, and his descendants, along with one million five hundred rubles for its upkeep. If Michael were to have no heirs, it was to pass to the second son of his brother Nicholas. She made provisions for her remaining two daughters, specifying that they were to be able to live at Pavlovsk whenever they wished, and for the care of all those who had served her, requesting that salaries be assured in their working years and their well-being in their old age. She left a special capital for the continued support of all the charitable institutions she had founded. She even remembered her plants, asking that Grand Duke Michael choose those he wished for the gardens and give the rest of her botanical collection to the Imperial Botanical Gardens. She further specified that as soon as her will was read a detailed inventory be done of both Gatchina and Pavlovsk, and that no piece of furniture or object should be dispersed or given away except those that she had specified. Her devoted children honored each of her requests to the letter, and every year on the anniversary of her death gathered to hear her will read to them again.

Michael had five daughters, none of whom survived, so upon his death in 1849, Pavlovsk passed to the second son of Nicholas I, Constantine Nicolaievich, who, on its hundredth anniversary in 1877, had compiled a detailed and extremely valuable historical volume on its history. Constantine left the palace to his widow, Alexandra, and later it went to their eldest son, Constantine Constantinovich. Neither Michael nor Constantine Nicolaievich ever lived in the palace, electing instead, when they were in residence, to live in one of the dachas in the park, and to keep the palace as a family museum.

Thanks to Maria Feodorovna's foresight, the palace largely escaped any changes in the later nineteenth century. Preserved almost exactly as she had created it, the serene beauty of Pavlovsk remained the finest monument to the Empress who was "only a woman, nothing more."

7

Musical Pavlovsk

WITH THE DEATH of Maria Feodorovna, the curtain fell on Pavlovsk's great aristocratic period. In Maria Feodorovna's last years, the gathering of poets and artists, the grand celebration for Alexander that had brought together Russia's greatest talents, had marked a transition for Pavlovsk from a royal residence to a focus for a new Russian culture and pride. Maria Feodorovna was gone, but through the halls at the striking of the hours a symphony of tinkling silver bells and chimes still played waltzes, gavottes, and airs from old operas — a graceful memory of days gone by that presaged the surprising new future. For as the country progressed, there was to be a delightful musical interlude in the history of the palace that would win for Pavlovsk a lasting place in the emerging popular culture of the nation and in thousands of Russian hearts.

In the eighteenth century, music was intrinsic to the life of the court, and from the beginning a rich musical tradition existed at Pavlovsk. In that time of the porcelain-figurine delicacy of powdered wigs and rustling silk, of the songs of princes and princesses playing in pastorales, it was the sound of the harpsichord and the harp that echoed in the palace. Music was considered an essential part of a proper education in that refined epoch, and all gently raised people were expected to learn to sing, to play one or more instruments, and even to compose. Princes and princesses, lords- and ladies-in-waiting, were often skilled amateur performers.

The country, it seems, was full of music, and not only in the court. Unanimously, foreign visitors commented not only on how much but how well Russians sang, and not only in their splendid church choirs, but everywhere else. Coachmen sang to their horses, boatmen sang while rowing their boats, soldiers as they marched, pedlars while selling their wares, peasants while working in the fields or resting. Every occasion, whether happy or sad, Russians marked with a song. This great native tradition provided a rich store of folk music, which, in the later nineteenth century, was mined by Tchaikovsky, Rimsky-Korsakov, and Mussorgsky for their new Russian operas and symphonies.

When Pavlovsk was built, Italian opera was in vogue all over Europe, and Italian composers were in demand at virtually every royal court to compose, perform their works, and teach young music students. Empress Anna Ivanovna brought the first Italian company to Russia in 1735, and Russian society soon became addicted to Italian opera. Extremely high salaries attracted the best Italian composers and performers, and Russians trained by these superlative teachers brought performances to a very high level.

Until the early years of the nineteenth century, great nobles in Russia kept their own serf orchestras and performers and spared no effort or expense to have serfs properly musically trained. Italian or French masters were imported to teach them singing, dancing, and how to play instruments. Noblemen sometimes even sent their serfs to Europe to improve their musical knowledge and ability; some became famous performers. This continuing lavish Imperial and aristocratic support provided a great impetus for the development and refinement of native Russian talent.

Although Catherine herself had a tin ear, writing to Grimm: "I die of desire to listen to and love music, however hard I try, it is noise and that is all . . . the only sounds I recognize are those of my nine dogs, who . . . in turn have the honor of entering my room; each one of whom, even from far off I can recognize by his voice," some of her lovers — notably Potemkin, Orlov, and Zubov — knew and appreciated music, and they guided the Empress. During her thirty-four-year reign, Catherine employed seven illustrious Italian *maestri di cappelli* who, while they were in Russia, composed thirty original operas, in addition to numerous ballets and religious and dramatic cantatas. Catherine also encouraged Russian opera, and personally wrote five Russian librettos herself. However, since her musical attention span was short, she decreed that operas last no longer than an hour and a half.

Giovanni Paisiello, born in Taranto and educated in Naples, was one of the most successful and influential opera composers of the eighteenth century. Ranked with Piccinni as one of the leading composers of comic opera, he was considered by Mozart to be the best Italian composer of his day. Not surprisingly, Paisiello's fame attracted the attention of Catherine, and in 1776 Ivan Yelagin, director of the Imperial Court Theaters, invited him to come to St. Petersburg as *maestro di cappella* for three years, at a handsome three thousand rubles a year. The Empress also agreed to pay all his traveling expenses, in addition to providing him with a comfortable apartment near the Imperial palace.

Such was the enthusiasm for music in Russia that arriving in St. Petersburg in 1776, Paisiello found himself in a more cosmopolitan artistic atmosphere than Naples; in St. Petersburg he lived and worked with artists, authors, and musicians from France and Germany, as well as Italians. His duties included composing all the operas, cantatas, and theatrical pieces required at court, as well as directing Catherine's theater and chamber orchestras. In 1777, Paisiello wrote three dramatic works in honor of Alexander's birth and, when Constantine was born, he wrote a new opera, *Demetrio,* to celebrate the occasion.

Catherine was enchanted with the handsome Paisiello, and after each new opera presented the composer and his wife with diamond-studded snuff boxes and other magnificent gifts. In 1778 his contract was extended and his salary raised to four thousand rubles. Not surprisingly, he decided to stay, and eventually spent eight years in Russia.

One stipulation of Paisiello's second contract was that for an extra nine hundred rubles a year, he was to teach the Grand Duchess. Maria Feodorovna, who eagerly studied painting and drawing, found to her sorrow that her nearsightedness sometimes hindered her and, forced to limit herself, she turned to musical studies. She worked with Paisiello for several years until his final departure from Russia. She was accomplished on the harpsichord and the pianoforte, and with her daughters regularly took harp lessons from Cardon, a French harpist who also played in Paul's mixed quartet.

Beginning in the 1780s, Pavlovsk's musical life became closely associated with Russia's great court composer and clavecist Dmitry Bortniansky. Like Voronykhin, Bortniansky, who became Russia's most famous musical personality of the eighteenth century, began life as a serf, born in Glukhov, a small town in the Ukraine, a region famous for its extremely musical people and fine voices. An Imperial Choir School was founded in Glukhov in the early eighteenth century, and children for this school were selected for voice training at eight or even younger. Bortniansky quickly attracted attention because of his beautiful voice and outstanding musical ability, and although a serf, like Voronykhin was singled out for a special education; at ten, he was sent to St. Petersburg to study at the

Military Academy for children of the nobility. By age eleven he had already performed alto roles in several Italian operas.

For the next six years in St. Petersburg young Bortniansky studied music with the famous Venetian composer Baldassare Galuppi, then *maestro di cappella* at Catherine's court; during that time he was freed. In 1769 Galuppi invited him to Italy, where he spent the next ten years. He studied in Venice and received a brilliant musical education at the Academy of Bologna, working with Padre Martini and the Bologna Philharmonic, writing his first compositions and two successful operas, which were produced in Venice and Modena. He traveled extensively and began what became an extremely valuable collection of paintings that included a good number of the greatest Italian masters.

In 1786, upon his return to Russia, Bortniansky was named Choir Master to the Imperial Court Chapel choir and came to Pavlovsk to teach music to Paul's sons, including Alexander. He also gave harpsichord and pianoforte lessons to all the other children, as well as to Maria Feodorovna.

For the palace's amateur theater, in 1786, 1787, and 1790 Bortniansky wrote three charming comic operas that were to greatly influence the development of Russian opera. The first, *Le Festivale du Seigneur* (*Comédie Mélee d'Arts et de Ballets*), was performed outdoors in the gardens of the palace, the second, *La Faucon*, had a libretto written by the Franco-German Franz LaFermier, a teacher of elocution and librarian to Paul. For this opera, a pastorale that took place in Spain, Bortniansky wrote the role of Ramiro especially for eleven-year-old Alexander.

All the performers were members of the court who loved art and music, and all had received musical training. Catherine Nelidova, who was blessed with a most pleasing voice, generally played the soubrettes, and lesser female roles were often filled by students of Smolny. These delicate and elegant chamber operas were performed in the Greek Hall or one of the pavilions of the park before small intimate audiences of courtiers and close friends. The costumes designed for the productions were magnificent; for *La Faucon*, Prince Dolgoruky, one of the participants, writes, "for the first act, we had costumes of cloth with gold lace, in the second, silk with diamonds." Paul and Maria Feodorovna lent their jewels. In the third opera, *The Rival Son*, a charming Mozartian work, Alexander, then fourteen, played the young romantic lead.

Musical life at Pavlovsk was colorful and varied. In the palace musical library voluminous reference books contained the overtures to most of the famous comic operas of the day. Not only Bortniansky's operas, but others, by Russian, Italian, and French composers, many of whom had lived in Russia, were performed. (One of Paul's favorites was *The Americans,* an opera written by the Russian composer Evstigney Fomin.) French troupes and German *Singspiel* orchestras came to perform. There was dancing in the pavilions of the park; in the Dairy, peasant girls sang folk songs. In the outdoor theater, children performed French comedy and ballets. In the evening, military brass bands would play on the parade grounds. For one festival, musicians in boats floated back and forth in front of the Temple of Friendship while cannons from Bip fired. Balls held in the Greek Hall opened with a polonaise of Kozlovsky, and then the company danced "The Matador," the gavotte, the *ecossaise,* the *Allemande* and the Russian *khorovod** — but not the waltz, which Paul prohibited because he felt it corrupted the temperaments of the dancers to dance with their arms around each other.

Upon his accession to the throne, Paul made Bortniansky both Director of the Imperial Chapel and a state councilor — a very high rank. His musical duties at Pavlovsk took on a new and more important character, and the Imperial choir became a fixed part of the life of the palace. He was also given a piece of land on the upper part of the Slavyanka across from the Bip fortress, which made his ties to Pavlovsk even closer.

Bortniansky, whose music perfectly embodied the Italo-Russian style born in Empress Elizabeth's reign, was primarily a composer of religious music, and he wrote some extraordinarily beautiful concerts and compositions for the Russian church.† Despite the fact that his training was completely Italian, he was the first Russian composer to return to the melodic foundation of Russian vocal music. For Pavlovsk he also composed a great deal of secular music: harpsichord sonatas for Maria Feodorovna, French romances, chamber music, and marches for brass instrumental music to accompany Paul's military parades. For Alexander's triumphal homecoming, he wrote a cantata to the verses of Nelidinsky-Meletsky, who wrote to a friend: "At first Bortniansky complained about how short the verses were and badgered me to add another four verses, but out of pride I refused. Finally he got down to work and changed the introduction where, according to him, the music required an exclamation . . . 'Russia take pride in her!' — this accompanied by the sound of trumpets — and it was all very expressive."

Bortniansky was a very delicate and affectionate man, always calm and agreeable, who avoided all political intrigues, concentrating on his art. Unfortunately,

---

* The *khorovod* is a traditional peasant woman's round dance.
† Tchaikovsky greatly admired Bortniansky's music, and in 1881 edited his complete sacred works.

he was never particularly concerned about the publication of his works, with the result that much that he wrote was never credited to him, and some pieces were even stolen. After a long and productive musical life that spanned three reigns, he died on September 28, 1825, just three years before Maria Feodorovna.

On the day of his death he summoned the court choir, saying that he wished to listen to his last concert. They sang his solemn and dramatic composition "Mournful Is My Soul," according to his wish, performing in an adjoining room. When the choir finished, they entered his room to find that the great composer had peacefully passed into the next world. He left his magnificent art collection to the Academy of Art where, because of his great knowledge of art, he had served as an Academician for many years.

In the early 1830s, after Maria Feodorovna's death, the prosperous little town of Pavlovsk, which lay just beyond the gates of the park, became, like nearby Tsarskoe Selo, a fashionable and elegant summer colony. Although the town was administered by a City Council, the owners of the palace continued to watch over it carefully. In a tradition begun by Maria Feodorovna, which endured until the Revolution, all plans for construction in the town, even to a humble hen coop, had to be approved by the current grand duke. Lists of those wishing to rent summer dachas in the town were submitted to Grand Duke Constantine Nicolaievich, Maria Feodorovna's grandson, who would veto those he did not like.

In the small town, life was cozy; people knew each other by face and name. Summer residents came to include a whole constellation of notable literary and artistic figures of the time, a lively and colorful group who visited back and forth and frequently strolled together in the parks.

In 1831 Pushkin rented a dacha in Tsarskoe, and there on May 20, he was introduced to Nikolai Gogol, then an awkward and shy young tutor spending the summer in Pavlovsk giving reading lessons to the retarded son of the Vasilichikov family. Gogol was thrilled to meet Pushkin and Zhukovsky, and whenever he had free time deliberately went for long strolls in the parks of Pavlovsk and Tsarskoe, hoping to run into the great poet — which he often did. Pushkin befriended him, and Zhukovsky sometimes joined them on their walks during which they talked about their work and plans for the future. That summer Gogol was writing what was to be his first literary success: *Evenings on a Farm near Dikanka,* a collection of comical tales of his native Ukraine. In the evenings he read selections aloud at the Vasilichikovs' and at the homes of other friends in Tsarskoe Selo. In August when he went to St. Petersburg to get the proofs, he found the typesetters laughing, the first harbinger of his popular success.

The famous Bruillov family of artists and architects also spent summers in Pavlovsk, living in a large wooden house with a tower that remains today in a fir glade called *Bruillovka*. Karl Bruillov, one of the most famous painters of his time, was an exact contemporary of Pushkin. He spent many years in Italy and there had achieved world renown because of a huge canvas he painted in Rome, *The Last Days of Pompeii*, which was hailed as a masterpiece. The most celebrated artists and foreign visitors flocked to his studio, including Sir Walter Scott, who, Bruillov wrote home with joy, sat in front of his painting for an entire morning and pronounced it an epic. Bruillov won many prizes in Europe, including the prestigious Grand Prix of the Paris Salon in 1834, and was made a member of the Academies of Bologna, Milan, Parma, and Florence; when he returned to St. Petersburg in 1836, he was received as a darling of society and made a professor at the Academy. He was the friend and portraitist of most of the literary and artistic celebrities of his day, painting Gogol, Lermontov, and Glinka as well as many of the notable aristocrats.

Other famous summer residents were the Klodt family who lived in Pavlovsk from 1839 to 1854. The father, Baron Pyotr Klodt, was the sculptor of the four monumental horses on the Anitchkov Bridge on the Nevsky Prospect, one of the landmarks of St. Petersburg. His son Mikhail was a painter of the "Wanderer" group. In his memoirs, Mikhail gives the flavor of their joyous summertime life:

> At Pavlovsk, life flowed freely and simply. On the day before father's name day on June 29, guests would begin arriving in the evening. The men would make themselves comfortable on piles of hay, in the towers, in the workshops, and around the stables, and would spend the night talking and joking. The women were all put up in the dacha. The next day there would be a big festive meal. . . . At Pavlovsk father acquired a horse, an entirely white pure-blooded English stallion that was an old veteran of the royal stables. The horse, named Sirko, was used by father as a model for the Anitchkov Bridge. Father often took us children for rides on Sirko along the paths of the garden. From the Emperor he later got another horse, named Almaddek, that also served as a model for the Anitchkov horses. Almaddek was a white Arabian with a faultless physique. Father trained her and at his command she would stand on her hind legs and assume all kinds of poses. . . . Our dacha was

the talk of Pavlovsk. Splendidly harnessed and decorated and pulling a char-abanc, the horse would rumble terrifyingly down the cobblestone road with our ingenious father looking like a Roman charioteer. Dogs would bark from the gateways and summer residents would stare and ask "Where is the fire? What is burning?" They would be calmed with assurances that this was only Baron Klodt amusing himself.

But the most significant event in the conversion of Pavlovsk into a great popular center was the coming of the first railroad in Russia, which made the town, palace, and park easily accessible to large numbers of people of all classes from the capital. In 1835, a German engineer, Anton Ritter von Gerstner, who with his father had built the first railroad in Austria in 1824, a year before the first one was to appear in England, sent a proposal to Nicholas I. Gerstner had dreams of gaining a monopoly over Russian railroad construction, and he proposed beginning with an extensive line that would reach from St. Petersburg to Moscow and then continue on to Nizhny-Novgorod, the site of Russia's greatest annual fair. A shrewd, aggressive man, Gerstner was the first railroad contractor to gain serious attention in high Russian government circles, but the Tsar was not prepared to commit the vast financial resources his project demanded. Instead, the Tsar and his ministers cautiously opted for a tiny experimental line, which would run from St. Petersburg to Tsarskoe Selo and then end at Pavlovsk. Financed by a stock company formed by Gerstner, two prominent Russian merchants and the wealthy manufacturer and sugar beet king, Count Bobrinsky, a champion of railroad building in Russia, construction began in 1836. Built by unskilled Russian laborers — twenty-five hundred serfs and fourteen hundred Russian soldiers who, steam shovels not being available, laboriously worked with picks and shovels — the line took a year longer to build than Gerstner had envisioned. Rails, locomotives, and drivers were imported from Britain, along with some engines from Belgium.

To bring the railroad to Pavlovsk, a way was cut straight through the park, passing through the green meadows and glades of Gonzaga's and Cameron's carefully sculptured vistas and cutting the park into two unequal halves. Tracks were laid in front of what had been the former Music or Circular Hall. Considering the care for preservation lavished on Pavlovsk by its owners, astonishingly no one seems to have worried about this — perhaps because railroads were the newest rage and considered the path to progress.

Despite many construction difficulties, the line was officially opened on October 30, 1837, with Gerstner proudly at the throttle of a locomotive pulling eight cars, which carried the Tsar and an entourage of foreign dignitaries over the twenty-six kilometers to Pavlovsk.

The travelers arrived at a large, elegant circular station building with a tower and an illuminated clock, designed by a British architect, which included game rooms, gardens, and a restaurant. Called the Vauxhall, in Russian, *Voksal,* it quickly became so popular with the public that the name passed into the language and remained the Russian word for all railroad stations. With the coming of the railroad, Pavlovsk, already a fashionable but exclusive retreat for elegant summer residents, quickly became a favorite country excursion spot for the Petersburg public of all classes.

Wanting to attract passengers for the railroad, the directors advertised in the newspapers of the capital, stressing the "pleasantness and ease of the means of transportation," and hit on the idea of inviting foreign conductors for the restaurant orchestra. The first such visiting conductor at the Voksal was Joseph Labitsky, "musical director from Carlsbad," a well-known Austrian waltz conductor who played with his small but choice orchestra of fourteen musicians on Sunday, Tuesday, and Thursday, and on "table days" before a gypsy ensemble performed. He was followed by the Moscow conductor Heinrich Herman, who from 1839 to 1844 played in a charming wooden pavilion constructed especially for him. Herman turned his attention to Russian music and began to play the new music of Mikhail Glinka, who often came to Tsarskoe to visit his sister, who had a dacha there.

Glinka, who is considered the father of Russian music, was five years younger than Pushkin, and his great admirer. The son of a wealthy landowner in Novspasskoe in Smolensk province, he had as a child developed a passionate love for music, learning piano from his governess and violin from a member of his uncle's serf orchestra. At school in Petersburg, Glinka continued his musical studies, and perhaps because a musical ear and a linguistic one go together, he mastered Latin, English, French, and German, and later both Italian and Spanish. He studied ballet for two years, and developed his good tenor voice with an Italian singing master. All his life Glinka was such a charmer of ladies that one of his contemporaries, somewhat awestruck at his prowess, wrote that "even when he was forty-five, the youngest and most beautiful girls would surrender themselves happily to him." In 1830 he went off to Europe to study music, but very much in the new spirit of his times, he dreamed of writing a truly national work in the Russian spirit. When he returned home four years later, Zhukovsky suggested to him that he write an opera based on the Russian story of Ivan Susanin and the first Romanov Tsar, Michael. It was the first opera with a purely Russian national theme, full of beautiful Russian melodies and suites of lively Polish and Russian dances. Nicholas I attended many rehearsals and it was he who named the new work *A Life for the Tsar.* The opera had its premiere in St. Petersburg on December 9, 1836, and both the Tsar and the public were delighted. Glinka was hailed as the greatest composer of the land; the Tsar presented him with a ring worth four thousand rubles and named him Director of the Imperial Court Chapel — a post he filled until he resigned in 1845 to start his European travels again.

In the summertime, whenever he was in Russia, Glinka came to Tsarskoe and Pavlovsk, where he visited Zhukovsky and spent jolly evenings with a group of close friends he called "The Brotherhood." In the Russian style, this merry group drank tea and talked all night. While at Pavlovsk in the summer of 1839, he was inspired to write his beautiful and haunting "Waltz Fantasie," dedicating it to his latest flame, Ekaterina Kern, the daughter of Anna Kern, to whom his friend Pushkin had dedicated one of his most famous poems. At the Voksal, Herman arranged Glinka's waltz for his orchestra and introduced it at his Pavlovsk concerts, where it soon became so popular that it was called "The Pavlovsk Waltz" — and sometimes, "The Melancholy Waltz" because of its haunting minor strains, which hint at tragedy and love unfulfilled. In 1846 and 1856, during his summertime visits, Glinka took the baton and conducted the Voksal orchestra himself.

This early musical activity was prelude to the arrival at Pavlovsk of the man who was to become its most popular and famous conductor — Johann Strauss the younger, "The Waltz King" himself.

It happened that in 1855 Strauss, recuperating from an illness at the Bad Gastein spa, chanced to meet the manager of the Tsarskoe Selo Railway Company. The manager could hardly believe his good luck at meeting the famous Viennese composer and thought that he was just the man to solve the railroad's problems. Although the railroad was enjoying a popular and profitable trade, the directors wanted to attract more of the "better people" of St. Petersburg, who, they felt, had not been sufficiently frequenting the Voksal. Strauss, reasoned the manager, was precisely the attraction needed.

Although Strauss was usually opposed to travel, he found it impossible to refuse the manager's munificent offer of twenty thousand rubles for the season of mid-May to mid-September — a sum that no one in Vienna could possibly match. Yet Strauss agreed to sign the contract only after he was assured that he would not be forced to live in a hotel and the railway company found him an elegant villa in Pavlovsk near the Voksal.

Before Strauss, no really serious thought had been given to the music at the Pavlovsk Voksal. The duties of the orchestra were limited to "pleasant songs" at mealtimes and dance music in the evening. In addition, in what became a lasting Pavlovsk tradition, there were always the fiery gypsy ensembles that Russians loved. To entice the public there were regular popular balls, where thousands of couples danced, and celebrations with fireworks ("with no special charge for admission," the railroad advertised). There were also elegant illuminations, announced in the newspapers of the city, when, according to one correspondent, "colored lanterns swirled around the gallery and the entire building was a triumph of light." Strauss was to change the emphasis and make Pavlovsk an important musical center where people came for the music first.

When the famous waltz composer arrived in 1856 he brought ten extra musicians with him, swelling the existing orchestra to thirty-five, a very large orchestra for the time. He was thirty-one, at the height of his talent, handsome, charming, romantically mustached. The newspapers extolled his "appealing and expressive appearance," his "modest and well-bred manner," and "refined taste." The eldest son of six children of the Viennese composer Johann Strauss the elder, he had written his first thirty-six bars of waltz music at the age of six, and with his great talent he went further than his famous father, developing a style of Viennese waltzes that combined rich melodies and gay wit, of which he became the undisputed master.

On May 6, 1856, the day of Strauss's first concert, the trains were overflowing. Benches were set up in the square in front of the station between the billiard hall and the restaurant to accommodate the overflow audience, and even then there was standing room only, a situation that was to continue for many seasons despite occasional chilly evenings.

From his very first notes, the Russian public was enchanted with the charm, elegance, vivacity, and sophistication of Strauss's melodies, which mirrored the glitter and *joie de vivre* of Imperial Vienna. He was forced by prolonged applause to repeat nearly every piece twice. The critics raved, one writing that "musical inspiration ran through the performance like an electrical current flowing from the Strauss baton out in the audience and then returning ever stronger back to the orchestra on stage." Strauss's unorthodox conducting style astonished his audiences: he would conduct with violin in hand and then suddenly, leaning his bow into the strings, explode with sound. Captivated by the effervescent lilt of his own music, he would sometimes dance about with his violin.

From 1856 to 1865 Strauss came back every year for ten superbly successful years. Even after his regular appearances ceased, he made return appearances in 1869 with his brothers Josef and Eduard, and again in 1872 and 1886. He introduced the Russian public to waltzes and polkas, and they went wild. One of his great admirers was Ivan Turgenev, who wrote, "Strauss — how much fascination there is in this name: royal palaces and barracks, cities and towns, silk slippers and wooden clogs, weightless fairies and stocky peasants all dance to the waltzes of Strauss. His melodies inspire the soul and speak to the feet." His orchestra grew to forty-two and his salary to the huge sum of forty thousand rubles a season.

Strauss became the idol of the Petersburg public — especially ladies. One cartoon of the day shows him being tossed in the air along with bouquets of flowers by a group of irate gentlemen; in another Strauss is shown playing his violin among crinolines surmounted with hearts while being drilled with evil glances by jealous husbands. The Tsarskoe Selo Railroad published a hundred thousand autographed pictures of him and did a brisk business selling them at ten kopecks apiece.

Strauss was deluged with flowers. Once, challenged to a duel by a Russian officer who complained that his wife sent Strauss roses every day, the composer led him to two unfurnished rooms in his villa entirely filled with flowers. "They have all come within the past two days," explained Strauss; "I will be glad to give you satisfaction but could you show me which ones came from your wife?" The officer withdrew his challenge and made his apologies. After several summers Strauss was so popular that the police were forced to clear the square in front of the St. Petersburg station so that he could make it to his carriage without being mobbed. And the manager was correct — he did attract the right people. He drew members of the court and the aristocracy, the rich bourgeoisie and, once, even the Tsar himself. The Tsar requested his favorite piece, "The Peasant Polka." *

Strauss's concerts were so popular that he would often be forced to play into the early-morning hours. The music would then come to a swift finish when the

---

* Strauss later wrote to his friend and publisher: "One day the Tsar came with the Grand Duke to the concert. He requested his favorite selection the 'Bauren Polka' which evoked a storm of applause such as no Beethoven symphony has ever received; even the orchestra members applauded wildly like the public and forgot that the composition is a miserable piece of trash."

station bell signaling the last train back to St. Petersburg rang, sometimes stopping him in the middle of a bar of music. One evening after Strauss had performed his new composition, "The Pavlovsk Forest Polka," the audience was so enthralled they refused to budge even after the last bell. Strauss agreed to continue the concert if each member of the audience would agree to donate two rubles to benefit wounded soldiers. They enthusiastically complied, and the music continued as the last train to St. Petersburg left the station. After the concert was over, the crowd, unperturbed, spent the rest of the night strolling in the park in the pleasant summer night until the first train rolled in in the morning.

While he was in Russia, Strauss composed a great deal and wrote a whole series of waltzes and polkas, including an autobiographical piece he titled "The Pavlovsk Polka." Some of these are difficult to trace today as many of the names were changed later — "Memories of Riga" was later changed to "Memories of Nice," the "Polka in the Woods of Pavlovsk" and the "Strelna Terrace Quadrille" to "Memories of St. Petersburg."

He also fell madly in love. It happened when Strauss was thirty-three, after a concert during the luminous white nights of June when he met twenty-year-old Olga Smirnitskaya, the lovely daughter of a Russian merchant prince. Olga's parents objected strenuously and refused to allow the match, preferring a man with a secure state position to any musician, no matter how famous. Because of their adamant opposition, meetings between Strauss and Olga were few and fleeting, although they did manage to carry on a voluminous correspondence by romantically leaving their letters ("bon-bons," the lovers called them) in a hollow tree in the park near Strauss's villa, where his secretary would retrieve them. Strauss was totally enamored. In one of his letters he wrote: "I am more and more convinced that you are destined for me by God, and there is no space within me which could harbor the thought of living without you." For her, he composed "The Olga Polka." Although their match was not to be, Olga's aura remained a part of him and her presence can be felt in his "Waltz das Reise-Abenteuer" and the polka-mazurka "l'Espiegle"; some even say that she may even have had a hand in their composition. Much later, his Russian experience lingered in the character of Prince Orlovsky in his famous operetta *Die Fledermaus*.

Strauss expanded greatly both the audience and the repertoire at Pavlovsk. He invited foreign musicians and choruses to perform with him and brought a wide Russian public into contact with contemporary Western composers. On Thursday and Sunday, the traditional musical evenings, Strauss began to play full evening concerts of serious music. He performed Bach's "Meditation" on many occasions, as well as the overtures to the Mozart operas, and parts of Beethoven's sonatas and symphonies. He was well acquainted with the work of Schubert and Mendelssohn and performed Mendelssohn's *Italian Symphony*. He devoted a great deal of attention to the music of Bellini and the new works of Verdi, playing portions of *La Traviata, Rigoletto,* and *Il Trovatore.**

With great determination, over the course of several seasons, Strauss performed the "difficult" works of Wagner, playing the overtures from the opera *Rienzi* and *Tannhauser,* choruses from *The Flying Dutchman* and fragments from *Lohengrin,* with the result that the public was well prepared to receive him when Wagner came to visit St. Petersburg in 1863.

Russia was developing a powerful school of national music, and Strauss played many of the new works of Russian composers. He devoted much attention to the work of Glinka, beginning in May 20, 1862, a series of all-Glinka evenings that became a tradition in his last years at Pavlovsk. Attending that first evening was young Nikolai Rimsky-Korsakov, then a naval cadet, who wrote to Balakirev: "The playing was a wonder, except for the *lezhinka.*" In a concert on August 30, 1865, Strauss played "Characteristic Dances," a piece composed by the young composer Peter Tchaikovsky, then a graduate student at the newly formed St. Petersburg Conservatory.

At the final concert of his last regular season, on September 19, 1865, Strauss played "The Grateful Polka," "Hommage au Publique Russe" and "Pavlovsk Is Finally Silent." Petersburg bid an emotional farewell to their beloved conductor. Before leaving that fall, Strauss wrote to the St. Petersburg newspaper, *Voice:*

> At the end of ten years of work in St. Petersburg I am filled with heartfelt gratitude. I must now leave this northern capital I consider my second home. I cannot find the words to express the fullness of the feelings with which I am imbued at this time and which I will experience when I say my final farewell. At the time of my arrival here I was greeted with utter cordiality, goodwill and unbiased appreciation for my work. I will never forget the happiest days of my life which I spent among you. They will remain an indelible memory in my heart. And as I bring you my most thankful salutations, allow me to cherish the hope that the people of St. Petersburg will remember me fondly.

Strauss crowned the first period of existence of the Voksal. The restaurant where people had come to both eat and listen to music was entirely converted to a concert hall where people went primarily to hear music. By the time he left,

---

* Verdi wrote *La Forza del Destino* on a generous commission of twenty-two thousand rubles from Russia and came to St. Petersburg himself to conduct the premiere in 1862.

two thousand people were able to sit and listen to concerts in a hall with perfect acoustics. He was responsible for establishing both a concert hall and concert conditions and transforming Pavlovsk into a significant and important center for Russian music.

By 1866 Pavlovsk had become a place of delight for thousands of people. The newspapers of Petersburg reported that up to a hundred thousand people would stream out during the summer to find enjoyment there. They came to hear music, to ride horseback, to promenade in carriages. Ladies strolled in the Pavlovsk park under ruffled parasols. On Tuesdays and Saturdays there were tennis competitions and equestrian shows. In a letter written in May 1866, Vladimir Bruillov, a son of the artistic family, gives an account of a public concert in which there were one thousand performers: "the violinists alone numbered about 200. The effect is beyond description." That day, the American Ambassador, Cassius Clay, a famous abolitionist from Kentucky, visited Pavlovsk for a local celebration arranged on his behalf. The warm relations between the United States and Russia were extolled.* "Speeches," continues Bruillov, "seemed to go on without end. The noise was so great that it was almost impossible to have a conversation. There were a great number of people — they say up to 12,000. Not bad!"

The popularization of Pavlovsk was so complete that there were even complaints. An article that appeared in the newspaper *Voice* on June 19 of the same year takes notes of the sharp increase of visitors to Pavlovsk — six thousand on one Sunday alone. The writer disapprovingly speaks of the "democratization" of the square in front of the Voksal, which in his opinion made the square unrecognizable, especially since "the public was far from a choice crowd."

By the end of the century Pavlovsk was such a famous retreat for citizens of St. Petersburg that it passed into literature when Dostoevsky placed much of the important action in his novel *The Idiot* there. His heroine, Nastasiya, attends concerts at the Voksal, and in the climax of the novel, the aborted wedding of Prince Myshkin and Nastasiya and her abduction at a Pavlovsk church, Ragozhin wraps her in a mantle hastily bought from a woman on the platform and spirits her away on the train.

The departure of Strauss and his brothers after so many years of complete

---

*In 1863, Alexander II had sent a Russian fleet to support Lincoln during the Civil War. Lincoln hailed the timely arrival of the Russian fleet in his Thanksgiving Proclamation of that year as "One of God's bounties which cannot fail to penetrate the heart." Alexander II freed the serfs in 1861, two years before Lincoln's Emancipation Proclamation, and was hailed as a hero in the United States.

dominance of the Pavlovsk stage marked the end of the epoch of "garden music," but the importance of Pavlovsk as a beloved musical center continued to grow. Although the conductors who followed Strauss also had to conduct music at public balls and perform a potpourri of traditional "summer music," they considered the performance of serious music their real vocation. In 1872, an additional large wooden theater, constructed in picturesque wooden gingerbread dacha style by Nikolai Benois of the artistic family, was built. There, operas, operettas, and ballets were performed by members of the Imperial Theaters, as well as plays presented by Russia's finest actors. Until the First World War, every great Russian singer and musician performed in either this new theater or the Voksal. Continuing what was a Pavlovsk tradition, famous gypsy orchestras, notably that of Ilya Sokolov, played for many seasons. At the end of the century there were also the new Great Russian orchestras of balalaikas and singers, including the famous orchestra and chorus of Vasily Andreev.*

During these years of music at the Voksal, the descendants of Maria Feodorovna continued to spend their summers living quietly at the palace, sharing their park with thousands of visitors. Grand Duke Constantine Nicolaievich and his wife usually preferred to live in one of the dachas rather than the palace itself. They often attended concerts, sitting inconspicuously in a small box at stage right instead of the grander Imperial box in the center of the theater. Constantine Nicolaievich died in 1898, and after his wife's death Pavlovsk passed to their eldest son, Constantine Constantinovich. The last Grand Duke† to live at the palace, the tall, handsome, bearded Constantine detested politics and preferred the company of artists and academics. He was an accomplished pianist and published poet (he signed his verses KR — Konstantin Romanov). In a silver-embossed notebook preserved at the palace are a series of touching love poems he dedicated to one of the reigning beauties of the day, Princess Zenaida Yusupova.‡ Many of the Grand Duke's verses were set to music and are sung in Russia still; his translation of *Hamlet* into Russian was considered the finest until Pasternak's. From 1889 Constantine served as president of the Academy of Science, and is credited with being an original sponsor of Pavlov and his famous research. He was also a military commander and a progressive Inspector General of Military Schools.

---

* During this Slavophile period, Alexander III not only put the Russian army back in Russian dress but issued an ukase ordering all soldiers in the army to learn to play the balalaika.

† The title Grand Duke can be used only by the son or grandson of a Tsar.

‡ Princess Zenaida, from the powerful Yusupov family, was the mother of Prince Felix, who in 1916 was a member of the group that assassinated the mystic Gregory Rasputin.

Constantine, his wife (the German Princess Elizabeth of Saxe-Oltenburg), and their large family of nine children spent their summers living in a wing of the palace. His last child, a daughter, Vera, who lives today in the United States, was born in Pavlovsk in her mother's bedroom on the ground floor. Their cousin, Nicholas II, and his family lived in a wing of the Alexander Palace in neighboring Tsarskoe Selo, and there Alexis, the heir to the throne, played happily with his sisters, sliding down a special mahogany slide in the ballroom on a silk pillow, or in his playroom filled with marvelous toys, which included an elaborate train and a real Indian tepee.

Accompanied by his nursemaid, Alexis would often ride over in his little horse-drawn carriage to meet his younger cousin Vera as she rode about the Pavlovsk park in hers. Vera remembers that once when the two carriages met, Alexis invited her to get in his and, leaving the two nursemaids behind, took her off. When they came to a large puddle, he mischievously suggested, "Jump in." Vera, who greatly admired her older cousin, obeyed, and was found by her horrified nursemaid a short while later with her immaculate white dress, hat, and muff covered with mud.

The household in those days at Pavlovsk numbered eleven servants, including a butler. The head of the stables, Vera's riding master, was a sergeant in the Cavalry School and an Old Believer.* Her godmother was Empress Alexandra, who, along with the Emperor, would often come to take tea and to eat the delicious strawberries that grew in Pavlovsk in the spring. One day, Vera recalls, a member in the Emperor's Company who had recently been raised to sergeant was serving them. The Emperor exclaimed, "How grand you have become! And I have remained a simple colonel!"

At the Voksal that summer season of 1912, when Vera played with Alexis, Chaliapin and Sobinov sang, and a series of concerts by new young composers were featured. The concertgoers who flocked to Pavlovsk heard the first works of Igor Stravinsky, *Fireworks* and *Firebird,* and the first concert of young Serge Prokoviev, who performed his First Piano Concerto. In June, a gala concert celebrated the seventy-fifth concert season with works of Strauss, Glinka, and Tchaikovsky.

By this time, several generations of the people of Petersburg had learned to

---

* Old Believers are an Orthodox sect that split from the established church during the reign of Ivan the Terrible. The main issues in the schism, or *raskol,* were the form of worship, including the proper way to make the sign of the cross, and whether the Orthodox Church was to remain congregationally led or become a hierarchy controlled from Moscow.

know and love Pavlovsk. In Pavlovsk's park they had fallen in love, courted, rested under the birches, and watched their children frolic. It evoked the warm lazy days of summer and the luminous white nights, a place of peace in busy lives, the familiar background of thousands of family photographs.

In June of 1915, at the palace, Grand Duke Constantine was struck by a heart attack and died. His was to be the last Imperial funeral; he was the last Romanov to be placed in the family vault at the Peter and Paul Cathedral. His death presaged not only the end of the monarchy, but also the ending of eighty years of music at the Pavlovsk Voksal. For after the war, the storm clouds burst, and the lilting strains of Strauss's "Olga Polka" and Glinka's "Pavlovsk Waltz" were heard no more at the Voksal, replaced by the more militant sound of revolutionary songs.

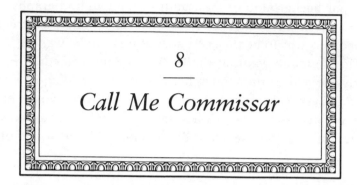

8

Call Me Commissar

FOR A HUNDRED AND TWENTY-FIVE YEARS, history had been kind to Pavlovsk. There had been points of danger: the disastrous fire of 1803, the threat of Napoleon's invasion, the death of Maria Feodorovna, when the beautiful ensemble she had created might have been dispersed or irrevocably changed. In each case, the palace had been spared. Now the tumultuous twentieth century was to bring danger on a far different and infinitely more perilous scale.

In 1914, Russia was leading the world in the arts. Diaghlev's Ballet Russes, which demonstrated Russia's extraordinary talents in dance, art, and music, had taken Paris by storm. In 1913 Igor Stravinsky had ushered in the twentieth century with his titanic composition *The Rite of Spring*. Avant-garde painters in Russia had gone into pure abstraction and imagined the modern world. Russian artists were the symbol of everything that was bold and daring and free. Although Russia was increasingly restive against an antiquated, autocratic regime, economically she was the bread basket of Europe, and industrialization was proceeding so rapidly that in 1913 its rate of economic growth surpassed that of the United States. Then came the First World War and in its vortex the Revolution.

In 1914, Nicholas II, in a burst of wartime patriotism, decided to change the name of the city from the Germanic-sounding St. Petersburg to the more Russian Petrograd. Early in March 1917, in the city short of food and tired of war, unruly crowds took to the streets, breaking the windows of bakeries to get bread. In the following days, strikes and demonstrations erupted. Soldiers sent to disperse the disorders joined them instead. On March 15, in a railroad car that was bringing him back to the capital from military headquarters, the last Tsar, Nicholas II, pressed by the leaders of the Duma,* abdicated for himself and his son, ending a dynasty that had endured since the seventeenth century. Russia was left in the hands of the Provisional Government headed by the prime minister, Prince George Lvov. The Tsar, his wife, and five children were confined to the Alexander Palace in Tsarskoe Selo. The swift downfall of the dynasty was startling. On January 22, 1917, only a few weeks before the abdication, Lenin, then in exile in Zurich, pessimistically had told a group of Swiss workers, "We older men may not live to see the decisive battles of the approaching Revolution."

From the beginning the Provisional Government was beset by dissension and indecision. On July 20, Lvov resigned and the Minister of Justice, the fiery Socialist lawyer Alexander Kerensky, replaced him. In August, fearing for the safety of the Imperial family in the face of rising revolutionary bitterness in the capital, Kerensky sent them into exile in Tobolsk, a remote provincial town in the Urals, in action that was inadvertently to seal their doom.

After only eight months, overwhelmed by events it could no longer control, the Provisional Government fell. The second revolution came in early November,† and with it the radical Bolshevik regime led by Vladimir Ilyich Lenin, who rode to power promising "Bread and Peace" to a population exhausted by war.

In the space of a few months, as ministers, leaders, and governments changed in a frenzied relay, the old world vanished and the country spiraled downward into revolution and civil war. During these months of upheaval the most basic assumption of society — that law and order is being kept by someone, whether friend or enemy — collapsed. Undisciplined soldiers felt free to roam the streets, break into houses, get drunk, and pillage. In a time of rapidly shifting authority, people claimed the right to carry out real, misrepresented, or even nonexistent orders. Citizens lived in fear of arrest and death, never knowing what the next day would bring.

What in such a time was to be the fate of works of art? Fragile and irreplaceable as hothouse flowers, silent witnesses to the sense of beauty of another age

---

* The Duma, a broad-based elected legislative assembly, was established by Tsar Nicholas II after the 1905 Revolution. Although it was given limited legislative and budgetary power, real power remained in the hands of the Tsar. The first three Dumas, too liberal for Nicholas's taste, were dissolved; the fourth, based on a much more conservative electoral process, survived until March 1917.

† In February 1918, the new Soviet government officially adopted the Western (Gregorian or New Style) Calendar, which is thirteen days ahead of the Julian (Old Style) Calendar that had previously been used in Russia. The Bolshevik Revolution, which actually occurred on October 25, 1917, according to the old calendar, is therefore celebrated on the new date of November 7.

and a culture now despised, scores were wantonly destroyed and stolen. Yet in that time of the whirlwind, as the old order crumbled and the new ruthlessly struggled to assert itself, miraculously Pavlovsk found a defender who stepped forward and, with singular dedication and courage, managed to save it.

In 1917 Alexander Polovtsov was a distinguished member of what soon was to be called "the hated bourgeois class." Himself an official of the Foreign Ministry, his father had been an important Tsarist official; Secretary of the State Council, his brother was a general. A gentleman of taste and sophistication, Polovtsov was a great connoisseur of art and director of the Art Institute and Museum of the Applied Arts founded by his grandfather, the immensely wealthy banker, Baron Steiglitz.* He lived not far from St. Isaac's Cathedral, on what is today Herzen Street, in a grand house containing rare tapestries, magnificent chandeliers, and famous Bronze and Gold Salons. Although he modestly referred to himself as a "dilettante," Polovtsov was in fact a preeminent expert in the applied arts. He spoke and wrote French with graceful perfection and his book *Les Trésors de la Russie sous le Régime Bolshevik,* written with detachment and flashes of ironic humor, provides a unique personal glimpse of the turbulent months immediately following the abdication of the Tsar.

At the time of the March Revolution, concerned about the fate of the Imperial palaces and the unique art treasures they contained, Polovtsov left the Foreign Ministry to join a group of friends who were determined to protect this national heritage. Although at the time they decided to form their group there had as yet been no serious incidents of pillaging, mobs had sporadically mutilated buildings by tearing down Imperial Eagles, and Polovtsov and his friends anticipated that much worse was to come. "We thought," wrote Polovtsov, "that it would be useful to form a nucleus of people dedicated to the conservation of the artistic riches of two centuries which had accumulated in the capital and its immediate environs . . . ready to defend and save that which represented in our eyes the most precious product of civilization in our country. We resolved to do our work no matter what the politics of the moment might be . . . no matter who the men in power were, by right or by fact. We understood that the worse the situation was, the more necessary would be our activity."

The original group was comprised of Polovtsov, Count Valentin Zubov (founder and director of the Russia Institute of the History of Art), and Peter von

---

* According to an intriguing rumor, Baron Steiglitz had an adopted daughter who was actually the natural daughter of Grand Duke Michael, Maria Feodorovna's youngest son and owner of Pavlovsk. If so, then Polovtsov was in fact Maria Feodorovna's great-grandson.

Weiner, who had since 1907 published the most prestigious art journal in the city, *Stariye Godi*. Like the Dutch boy in the tale who steadfastly kept his finger in the leaking dike, during the next fifteen months, as their nation, their city, their culture, and their personal lives were being destroyed, this small group and those who later joined them heroically attempted to stem the tide of destruction and save what they could of the beauty of the past.

Animated by a selfless love for art, they intervened and protested expropriation of historic houses and tried to protect the contents of the former Imperial palaces by making inventories of the art treasures they contained. In a scientific and orderly fashion they worked to turn the palaces into protected museums and thus preserve their treasures for their nation and future generations. This they did at great personal sacrifice, often risking their lives, staving off the ignorant and often incompetent bureaucrats of the new regime, hostile soldiers, and their own imminent arrest. This dedicated group, yet to be mentioned in any Soviet account of the history of the palaces, deserves immense credit for their selfless work to save the art of Petersburg from the chaos and vandalism that characterized the first months that followed the Bolshevik Revolution.

In June 1917, with the approval of the Provisional Government of Prince Lvov, Polovtsov, Zubov, and Weiner, along with a dozen students chosen from the city's art institutes, began to work in palaces that had belonged to the Emperor and were now, because of his abdication, without a master. They started with the huge job of doing a systematic inventory of the accumulated treasures of the immense palace of Gatchina, where the paintings alone numbered four thousand.

As the summer progressed, the political situation deteriorated, and by September Polovtsov began to worry about Pavlovsk, which, having passed to a younger branch of the Romanov family, was not counted directly as an Imperial residence but as a private estate and thus stood in danger of being summarily expropriated. The question of its status was being hotly discussed by a special commission that had decided to admit the principal of private property, but the government had been impressed by a strident revolutionary argument that since this palace had been built at the time of Paul I, when public and private monies were not clearly defined, the domain should be nationalized. Although the verdict was not yet in, Polovtsov felt that, whatever the outcome, it was vital to begin an immediate systematic inventory of the palace's contents; "For we knew," he said, "it contained marvels." The matter was urgent, for in the weeks after Kerensky assumed power, revolutionary sentiment was growing stronger among the population.

More and more people were asking why anyone should obey anyone else, and anarchy was increasing each day. Despite the fact that they were working with the authority of the Provisional Government, the local soviet* had begun to interfere in their activities and had sent sullen armed soldiers to watch them as they worked. The situation at Gatchina, Polovtsov said, "was charged with electricity."

Just at this time, the manager of the affairs of Prince Jean, the eldest son of the late Grand Duke Constantine, approached Polovtsov, asking him to recommend someone for the job of doing an inventory of Pavlovsk. "I offered myself," says Polovtsov," and Prince Jean greeted my suggestion with enthusiasm. He said that he himself did not know what his palace contained and that he had on several occasions suspected servants of the disappearance of furniture and objects."

At the time of the Revolution, the late Grand Duke Constantine's eldest son, Prince Jean, his wife, Helen, the daughter of the King of Serbia, and their two children were living in apartments in the right wing of the palace along with Constantine's sister, Queen Olga of Greece,† who was nursing wounded soldiers in hospitals she had created in the area. There were also the apartments of Jean's mother, Grand Duchess Elizabeth, and her two minor children, the youngest, little Princess Vera, who was then eight. Although the Grand Duchess and her children had left to live in Petrograd in 1915/16, they came to spend what were to be their last summer weeks at Pavlovsk in 1917.

Polovtsov was lodged in guest rooms in the center of the palace, just below the central dome, where there were no other inhabitants. With one collaborator he started to work in an empty apartment far away from the daily life of the palace.

Relations between the town and the palace were extremely tense. The local Cossack regiment had disappeared to join General Kornilov, commander in chief of the army, who that summer had mounted an abortive counterrevolutionary campaign against Kerensky. Left to protect the palace were only a few members of a battery of mounted soldiers. These, fearing trouble from radical elements in the town, kept a constant guard around the palace by order of their own revolutionary committee.

---

* Local soviets (elected councils) were set up in every province, district, city, town and village. They were responsible for managing local affairs and for electing the soviet of the next higher level of government. Often weak and disorganized because of short sessions, large memberships and crowded agendas, the local soviets were nevertheless a radical element in the countryside.

† Queen Olga was the wife of George I of Greece.

On September 3, the city of Riga in Estonia had fallen to the German army. In Petrograd, so widespread was the fear of an imminent German invasion that two trainloads of treasures from the Hermitage had been hurriedly packed and evacuated to Moscow. Crates from the Steiglitz Museum had also been prepared, and Polovtsov, as director, was to accompany them to Moscow. But arriving at Pavlovsk the Sunday before he was to leave, he found that since the night before even the few soldiers who had been guarding the palace had mysteriously vanished. Upon investigation he learned that emissaries from the revolutionary committees of the town had been sent to taunt them, making accusations that under pretext of guarding the palace they were actually forming a rampart behind which members of the Romanov family were living in peace. Stung, the soldiers had deserted their posts.

Deeply concerned about the vulnerability of the palace and its inhabitants, Polovtsov advised Prince Jean to leave immediately for Petrograd, where he would be less in evidence and better protected. But the prince, says Polovtsov, "a profoundly pious man, assured me he feared nothing, and accused me of putting him out of his palace." Polovtsov firmly stood his ground, telling the Prince that he thought his course of action folly and that he had no intention of being massacred. Adamantly Polovtsov insisted that if the Prince was determined to stay, he would leave; but if the Prince left, he would stay and continue his work. Prince Jean went to consult his wife and the next morning, with their children, they all left for Petrograd. The Queen of Greece, who came to the palace only at night, as she spent all her days caring for the wounded, stayed alone with the remaining servants.

Leaving Pavlovsk in charge of his colleague, Polovtsov left for Moscow on November 6. On his way to the station, he stopped at the office of the Fine Arts Commission in the Winter Palace, where he found the atmosphere extremely tense. Although the commission did not yet know it, Kerensky, facing growing disorder in the capital, had left the palace late the night before, escorted by a Pierce Arrow from the United States Embassy flying the American flag, to seek the support of a commander of Cossack troops stationed at some distance from the capital. A few hours later, without disturbing the night life of the city, a handful of Bolsheviks captured the railroad stations and key government buildings.* While the ministers of the Provisional Government were still conferring,

---

* An artist living today, who was a student at the Academy of Art, remembers that the students, locked in for their protection by their professors, partied all night; when they emerged the next morning, the Revolution was over.

the Winter Palace was defended for a few hours by a battalion of women and a few officer cadets. The battleship *Aurora*, manned by revolutionary sailors, fired a single blank shell. The women's battalion surrendered. It was in fact such a small skirmish that on November 8, the greatest problem for the Bolsheviks who took it over was to find the correct staircase (there were 117) and room in the immense palace to which they were at length led by a dignified palace flunky with powdered hair. In the former private dining room of Nicholas II the waiting ministers surrendered peacefully.*

In Moscow, Polovtsov and his wife chanced to stay in a house sandwiched between a Bolshevik headquarters and a factory, directly across the river from the Kremlin. The Kremlin was being defended by a group of young boys from the Military School, who shot wildly in their direction — occasionally shells fell in their garden. Horrified, Polovtsov witnessed Bolshevik shelling of the historic buildings of the Kremlin; the Cathedral of the Assumption was partially destroyed, along with the Tower of Ivan the Terrible, the Bell Tower of Ivan III, and the Treasury of the Patriarchs.

Deeply worried about the fate of the palaces, he rushed back to Petrograd and from a newspaper bought on his way to the station learned that "one of the new masters of my unhappy homeland, a man named Lunacharsky, had proffered anathemas against the destructors of the Kremlin and even announced that he would refuse to take part in the government if immediate measures were not taken to safeguard works of art. In the inexpressible desolation which I was feeling, this was a ray of hope." The two men — the revolutionary and the gentleman of the *ancien regime* — were soon to be joined in the common cause of saving Pavlovsk.

Anatoly Lunacharsky, a man of ideals and artistic knowledge, was one of the most interesting figures of the Revolution. A friend of Gorky, and a talented playwright as committed to the theater, literary criticism, and fine arts as he was to Marxist philosophy, he described himself as "an intellectual among Bolsheviks . . . Bolshevik among intellectuals." In the first days after the Revolution, Lunacharsky was named Commissar of Enlightenment — the equivalent of minister of education for the new Soviet government agency known by its acronym,

---

* The Revolution was hardly a popular choice. As Adam Ulam says in his book *The Bolsheviks,* "After their October coup the Bolsheviks — who remembers it now? — proclaimed their regime but a 'provisional Workers' and Peasants' government until the meeting of the Constituent Assembly.' "

*Narkompros.** This agency, which implemented the experiments in mass education that were a special interest of Lenin's wife, Krupskaya, also became responsible for the former Imperial palaces, and by the close of 1918 included a department of museums and preservation of historical and artistic monuments.

From the beginning, Lunacharsky recognized the need to act quickly to preserve the palaces from looting. Describing them as "these pearls of art, this splendid history lesson, this beautiful scene for strolling and public holidays," he firmly believed that the "consummate artistry" and "dazzling scale and artistic sweep of these masterpieces of the past" should continue to entertain and inform the masses of the new proletarian Russia. He expected that the palaces would become inspirations for great public buildings to be created in the new socialist epoch. Yet although he was respected both at home and abroad, Lunacharsky was never really trusted nor admitted into the confidence of inner party circles. His perceptions were deemed "too liberal" and not doctrinaire enough to suit party firebrands, and he remained always in the fringe role of specialist, never of leader. He was to play an important role in saving and preserving the art of the Tsarist era, but overworked, idealistic, and not always practical, he was to find that his influence was often deflected or overridden by more rabid revolutionaries.

Both before and after the October Revolution, perhaps in part because of Lunacharsky's influence, Lenin wrote and spoke theoretically of the importance of preserving the monuments of the past for the education of the future; his remarks are still admiringly quoted today in the Soviet Union, yet Lunacharsky's efforts were often the target of Lenin's biting criticism. Telegrams reflect Lenin's rising impatience with what he saw as Lunacharsky's "softness" regarding the remnants of the old cultural establishment. In September 1918, he reprimanded Lunacharsky for his delay in putting up monuments to Karl Marx and other revolutionary figures. In January 1922, in a note to Molotov, calling Lunacharsky "the accused," Lenin demanded that he be summoned for carrying a proposal through the Politburo assuring the preservation of the Bolshoi Opera and Ballet.

Nevertheless, Lenin respected Lunacharsky, and the two were joined in their criticism and opposition to the ultraradical *Proletkult* group as well as the extreme left "destructionists" within Bolshevism, led by Bukharin, who demanded the immediate creation of a socialist culture and the destruction of all cultural manifestations of the past.

Once he arrived in Petrograd, Polovtsov rushed immediately to the Winter

* *Narodnyi Kommisariat Prosveshchenie:* People's Commissariat of Enlightenment.

Palace only to find that in the few days he had been away the atmosphere had drastically changed. The palace was now surrounded by armed soldiers. Admittance required a complicated procedure of special permissions and passes. Finally penetrating the chambers formerly known as "the third reserve apartment," he found

> a heteroclite group of well-known artists plus unknown people, all very dirty and hirsute, who seemed absorbed in debating grave questions. A magnificent regulator which had once belonged to Potemkin marked the hours; on the table a bronze Minerva which decorated an Empire clock contemplated the crowd with a skeptical air. On the walls some awful portraits of distant relatives of the Imperial family, Prussians, or perhaps Hessians, ornamented with multicolored orders, seemed firmly decided to ignore the revolutionary hurly burly. I asked a disheveled secretary to whom I should address myself: "To Lunacharsky," she answered, "That's him sitting in the corner."

Waiting until the crowd that surrounded Lunacharsky had dispersed, he quickly seized his chance. Boldly he went over and declared, "Pavlovsk must be saved!" Lunacharsky, says Polovtsov, "Put his head in his hands and looked at me through his bifocals with small troubled eyes. 'Pavlovsk?' he exclaimed, 'Yes, I think it should be saved. What needs to be done? Say it and I shall do it.' Quickly I answered, 'Name me commissar of the palace.' 'All right, but who are you? Write your name. It will be done.' " A few days later he received an official document naming him "Commissar Curator of the Palace of Pavlovsk."

After his brief conversation with Lunacharsky, Polovtsov stayed and took part in a "crowded and disorganized meeting. All present, each in their turn, proclaimed the necessity of saving the artistic past of Russia, without however having any practical program to propose to achieve this result." It was eventually decided to send commissars to Gatchina, and the next day an unlikely threesome — made up of the elegant Polovtsov, a newly arrived and very stubborn revolutionary émigré, and a former officer who was arrested a few days later for allegedly robbing the Winter Palace — went off to inspect the damages at Gatchina, which had been stormed by a mob when Kerensky had briefly taken refuge there.

Zubov had valiantly tried to save the most precious things from the apartments that had been invaded, but when Polovtsov arrived he found a dismal sight:

> The portrait of Empress Elizabeth bayoneted, the bronze ornaments of the mahogany furniture pried off, small paintings stolen. All the personal effects

left in my room had disappeared and part of our inventory was gone, rolled and burned for cigarette paper. Zubov and his helpers were in the middle of a terrible mess of paintings, porcelain, small pieces of furniture, vases and clocks, which were lying on all the chairs and windowsills and even piled in the bathtubs.

Many rooms were filled with sailors, lying indifferent or half asleep, who refused to move when commissioners tried ineffectively to persuade them to leave.

After having seen the disorder and damage at Gatchina, Polovtsov was enormously relieved when he arrived in Pavlovsk the next day and found that, thanks to his able adjutant, everything was in order. Sailors had brusquely arrived at night to make a search and look for arms, but the quick-thinking adjutant had asked them, given their large number, to choose delegates with whom he would make a tour of the palace. When the sailors wanted to break open furniture, he cooperatively opened the cupboards instead, and only a few contemporary sabers had been taken.

Notified of the invasion by her servants, the Queen of Greece had courageously come to meet the hostile intruders. She spoke to them warmly, telling them that she had always had a particular affection for Russian sailors and had many friends among them who used to come to Piraeus. She wanted to see, she said, if among these nocturnal visitors she would find any old acquaintances. Subdued by her gracious words, the sailors left peacefully without any acts of violence.

Alarmed by this unwarranted intrusion, Polovtsov energetically confronted the situation by seeking the president of the local Pavlovsk Soviet and asking when he could come to a meeting in the new "house of the people." Pavlovsk had no factories, which Polovtsov notes "was a fortunate circumstance for the safeguarding of the palace," for there was no rabidly revolutionary working-class population in the town. When he arrived at the meeting, he found a large group composed of soldiers and others who represented the "proletarian" element of Pavlovsk. These turned out to be mainly porters and gardeners of the summerhouses, along with a few doctors and railroad employees. He explained that the council of commissars of the people had confided in him the safety of the palace. But, that as all power had passed to the soviets, he could not work peacefully in the palace unless he had their confidence. As the palace had now become the property of the people, it was his duty to transform it into a museum, and he emphasized how important this would be for the people and guaranteed that his work would make it more attractive. He then offered to answer questions. The soviet, as it turned out had only a few: Could townspeople use the park to make vegetable gardens and could they take the dishes of the palace? Was it really for the people that he was working and not in the hope of handing over the palace intact to the Imperial family one day? Polovtsov deftly managed to deflect all suspicions and then asked for a vote of confidence, which was granted.

Yet knowing that this might be withdrawn at any moment, he then immediately asked for an audience with Queen Olga. "I had to confess to Her Majesty that I had only assumed the painful role of commissar in the hope of saving the palace and that my work would be easier if, in the eyes of the people, there were no more links with the Imperial family." The Queen, he says, "deigned to agree" and a few days later, on November 15, 1917, left to live in Petrograd, severing the last link with Maria Feodorovna and the past.

Now alone, Polovtsov set to work in earnest. The din of the revolution outside faded in the silent palace halls, and he lost himself in the world of Maria Feodorovna. The serene beauty of the palace was a revelation, and like others before and after him, he fell under the spell of its charm and refined intimacy.

Marveling at the beauty of the State Apartments, he wrote:

> I know no other dwelling of this period where the moldings, paintings of the ceilings, and sculptured panels attain such a harmonious perfection. Each room had different dimensions, but the more one lingered in each of them, the more one felt that the proportions were correct . . . exactly what they should have been. By some extraordinary good fortune the succeeding generations had barely touched the original work, Michael (died 1848), grandson Constantine (died 1898) and great grandson Constantine (died 1915), although they lived in an epoch which had little respect for the past and none had had a formal artistic education, each in their turn bent their efforts to conserve the original appearance of Pavlovsk and it is thanks to them that the middle of the nineteenth century, so distant from our ideas of the history of art, only brushed Pavlovsk without harming it.

He found that in the beginning of the twentieth century, Grand Duke Constantine, an accomplished poet and pianist who had served as president of the Academy of Science, had taken it upon himself to research the inventories of the past and to return objects to the places for which they had been created:

> Although a single inventory was used, that of the twentieth century, and despite the insufficiency of the results, the true principle of reconstitution was acknowledged, and when it was given to me to find in a forgotten corner the inventories of 1802, 1811, 1828 and 1849 I was able, little by little to follow the history of each object and trace its peregrinations from salon to salon.

The only fault he found was the parquets, which, burned in 1803 and never redone, had been replaced with what he called "squares without grace or character."

As for Maria Feodorovna, "her taste for certain combinations of colors proved with what research and perfection the artistic effects at Pavlovsk were created. Everything bears the imprint of a person very sure of her taste, disposing of the means to express it and surrounding herself with artists not only of talent but sometimes of genius."

Working among objects, reading through old diaries, he immersed himself in the eighteenth century. He found the many souvenirs of Maria Feodorovna's trip to Europe where she had traveled as a radiant young bride. All of these had been preserved at Pavlovsk, and he was able to trace every step, for "methodical and orderly, she classified and kept in her library all the papers that she had gathered on her trip in special briefcases . . . and one could still read on scattered pages the way she had spent her days." He was to find that her taste was so personal and corresponded so logically to her way of life that by studying her papers he was able to reconstitute the rooms exactly as they had been. By her orders, the disposition of the paintings had been reproduced on a sheet of paper with the number of each painting, the name of the painter, and a description of the frames, so that he was able to rehang them in the identical spot where they had been over a hundred years before.

In the freezing days of the end of November, he managed to heat one floor of the left wing of the palace with wood stoves, then worked as he could in the rest of the palace, which in January fell to minus twelve or thirteen degrees Centigrade. Trying first to protect objects that could be easily stolen or broken, he and his colleagues inventoried clocks and vases, porcelain, and crystal in two small heated rooms behind an iron door to which only he kept the keys. To help him, he engaged four young people, and later, when the weather was warmer, an archivist, who inventoried manuscripts, as well as a specialist in antique sculpture. To inventory the five hundred paintings and three thousand gravures of the palace, he found a young specialist from the Hermitage who volunteered to do the work without pay.

He took precautions to protect the palace and the grounds, ordering that all the gouaches and furniture from Krik and Krak and the Rose Pavilion be brought to the main palace — a prudent measure that saved them, for in the winter vandals broke into the pavilions and were forced to leave empty-handed. As thieves had tried to break into the first floor with axes, he had all the windows of the first floor boarded up — then engaged former soldiers to stand guard, accepting only those who had had long service records and who could present serious recommendations.

The entire fall, despite his meeting with the local soviet, he was constantly bothered by regular delegations of new "comrades" from the town who wanted something from the palace. "It seemed to them that they had had nothing and that there was a palace full of marvels, which was now theirs for the taking." First they demanded dishes for the community kitchen. Polovtsov sent them modern copies with the initial *M* in blue and gold and was disgusted to learn that once given, instead of going to the "House of the People," the dishes had found their way to the families of the members of the council and from there were sold to antique dealers. Next, was "the siege of the tables." The council wanted sofas to sleep on and tables for their offices. "They screamed that I was refusing to give them because emperors had sat on them and they were just as good. One of the worst moments came when a delegation came to take the library that the people, they said, deprived of education, wanted to read."

The original core of this rare and historic collection had been made up of Catherine's "traveling library" — which Maria Feodorovna, with her lively spirit so eager for knowledge, had completed and made into the ideal library of a literate person of her century.

> It contained the whole eighteenth century in first-class editions, beautifully bound by the best bookbinders in Europe. The botanical section was extremely important; there were unedited manuscripts — including those of Lavater, with whom Maria Feodorovna corresponded and from whom she bought original drawings which illustrated his theories. Besides this, there were a great number of bulletins sent from Paris before and during the Revolution so that they could be well informed of the news of the day. A number of volumes were annotated in the margins by the Empress herself. It was a collection which was all the more valuable because it had not changed for a hundred years. The idea of seeing these treasures ripped from the shelves and thrown to the fantasy of the mob awakened my fighter's instinct.*

* Maria Feodorovna's library included twenty-two different sections — approximately twenty-two thousand volumes and manuscripts. The entire eighteenth century was represented, including all the best editions of the *Encyclopedistes,* Voltaire, and Corneille, and rare Russian editions. Many French editions included fine engravings, and a number of Italian books were in Venetian bindings of embroidered silk.

Polovtsov had the rare talent of always finding the correct tone and words for each person he confronted, of knowing when to be firm and when to bend, and was always ready to try every strategy in order to gain his objective. In this case he amiably took his keys, opened the shelves and showed the members of the delegation everything, seriously discussing with them how to pack the books and how many trucks would be needed to carry them away. Gradually, disarmed by his kindness, the delegation began to ask him about the choice of volumes. Quickly he handed them the heaviest encyclopedias, and they were forced to admit that it would cost a great deal to transport these without their furnishing much of interest to the reading room. They parted, says Polovtsov, "the best of friends," and the unique library was saved.

Every day brought new challenges. Clearly incompetent people would arrive at the palace proposing themselves as potential collaborators, sometimes even presenting official credentials signed by Lunacharsky himself. When he complained, he found that sometimes Lunacharsky absentmindedly signed orders without reading them. As rules and authority changed almost daily, soon even signatures became less and less effective. It became more dangerous even to protest decisions, as people were summarily arrested and sent to languish in prisons and sometimes even shot simply for having "bothered people." When Polovtsov was briefly arrested for the first time, he went to complain to the Bolshevik Commissioner of the Arts at the Winter Palace after his release. The man simply shrugged and said, "Why get upset about it? It happens to everybody. I was arrested recently. If it happens that you get dragged off to prison, you will always find a way to let us know and we'll see that you get out. Don't worry about it." In a world where rationality had disappeared, there was no longer any guarantee of anything. "As in the primeval forest a man was responsible for his own survival, and that of his treasure," said Polovtsov. "Having chosen Pavlovsk as mine, I defended it as well as I could. . . . This required *sang froid,* a great element of chance and considering all that was happening, an impassively philosophical attitude."

Despite all interruptions, alarms, and threats, he patiently continued his work. He went through the magnificent collection of porcelain, which numbered in the thousands of pieces, and traced the history of the family, the palace, and the pavilions: the beautiful service of the Rose Pavilion with its dark blue background of many varieties of domestic and wild roses painted on white center medallions, the Wedgwood service of the Farm on which, by order of the Empress, everyone who came was served a small meal. To his astonishment he found that everything he touched was original, and when occasionally he came upon objects that he thought were copies, further research would confirm that he was mistaken.

So personal was the palace that everywhere he felt the invisible presence of Maria Feodorovna. Walking through her Private Garden at sunset, it seemed to him that "I would surprise the literary circle that surrounded the Empress — certainly here is where Zhukovsky read his 'Ode to the Moon,' and Krylov imagined 'The Corn Flower.' " The many unusual plants, including mahonia bushes, unknown in the north, which she had imported and managed to keep alive were still flourishing. In the Family Room, he inventoried all the drawings done by her children. These, still in their original golden frames, stretched along a long corridor, each bearing the name of the young artist and the date of the anniversary. He found drawings done by Paul himself, and even a unique historical example — a painting of a vase of flowers done by Catherine. (Catherine, he noted, was infinitely superior as a stateswoman than as an artist.) After having found the documents and seeing which rooms had been changed, he had partitions in the dining room removed to restore them to their original aspect. When he found original pieces of furniture that had been disfigured by chintz and had had their gold frames crudely painted over in white, and others that had found their way to servants' rooms, he carefully grouped them together by ensemble in order to make it possible to restore them.

So he worked, but sometimes as he walked alone in the still serene park, "full of the shadows of yesteryear; timid and charming shadows so eloquent when a pious hand retains them . . . but vanished forever once vandalism is perpetrated against them," a rare outburst of passion expressed the tension, the incongruity of what he was doing. Outside, brutal anarchy raged more fiercely each day; within his palace, he was as fiercely devoted to "gentle phantoms of the past, to saving in its entirety this atmosphere of an eloquent epoch so full of allegories and allusions." A year before he had been a member of the elite Imperial Chevaliers Gardes, now, to pursue his task he had become a commissar of a regime he despised. "I was ready to don any disguise," he wrote, "to suffer any insult, to let myself be called by any alias, that of commissar as well as any other. Am I to be 'Comrade Polovtsov'? If that may please you, but you must allow under this mask full liberty to the one who will be in fact only the posthumous secretary to the orders of Her Imperial Majesty Empress Maria Feodorovna."

9

To the Last Chandelier

TWICE A WEEK Polovtsov went to the Winter Palace to discuss with other curators the common measures they could take and the results they hoped to attain. "It was a time," he says, "of interminable and incessant meetings presided over by Lunacharsky or his colleagues where the most grandiose plans were discussed for the conservation of all things and the elaborate measures to be taken to encourage the arts. Simultaneously the habit of destruction became more and more fierce around us; the arts were in a quagmire and the population was beginning to feel the first pangs of famine. The new Bolshevik commissioners," he continues, "would talk about preserving things and then a few weeks later appropriated the Alexander Palace and the Kremlin for their offices."

The damage that could be caused to art by using historic buildings for other purposes was woefully evident in the Winter Palace itself. Kerensky had quartered sailors in the former salons of the Empress Alexandra. Soldiers sleeping on the floor on mattresses had amused themselves by ripping out the cherries and apricots of the mosaics with their bayonets. Albums of watercolors, decorated with medallions in enamel and bronze, given by Bulgaria to Alexander II, had been forced open and the watercolors reduced to shreds; icons had been stolen; miniatures had been ripped from their frames; and the splendid portrait of Nicholas II by Serov destroyed. Clothes taken from the cupboards then fought over were left in rags on the floors. In the Rotunda, all the eyes and faces of the portraits of the sovereigns were pierced with bayonets. In the apartment that Kerensky had occupied, the invading mob had broken everything. Outside the city, estates and historic houses were pillaged. Five hundred kilometers from the capital, Polovtsov owned a castle full of eighteenth-century furniture, porcelains, and rare objects. Polovtsov learned in December that everything had been destroyed, but of his personal loss he stoically wrote only: "One reason more to try to save the things which one could defend by one's presence."

Like a fireman fighting brush fires, he raced around the city trying to save as much as he could. Grand Duke Nicholas had an extraordinary Russian porcelain collection with unique pieces from the eighteenth century. Sometime before the Bolshevik coup, Polovtsov had written the Grand Duke, who was fighting in the Crimea, and secured his permission to have his collection moved to the Steiglitz Museum. It was still waiting to be packed when a group of soldiers came and affixed a seal of appropriation to the entire collection. Polovtsov rushed to Lunacharsky and managed to obtain a document authorizing him to transport the collection to the museum. After confronting the surly commander with his paper, and after much argument, he was given only three days to pack and crate the three thousand pieces. By working day and night, curators and watchmen of the museum succeeded in transporting all of it to the museum with every fragile piece intact. Polovtsov retrieved twenty-five crates containing a rare collection of enamel miniatures and silver that had been stopped at the border, had them brought to Smolny, and after much struggle obtained permission from the authorities to have all preserved in the Steiglitz Museum. A few days later he faced down a roomful of armed and hostile soldiers, none over twenty years old, who were determined to seize the museum itself. Somehow, Polovtsov managed to convince them that an institution where more than a thousand students received an artistic education was worth saving.

Arbitrarily, incomprehensibly, everything in society was being overturned. Each day life became more difficult and perilous. Letting off servants became a dangerous proposition; a denunciation from a disgruntled lackey could bring imprisonment or death. Banks and everything in them were expropriated, money became worthless; people sold what they could ("A few optimists," says Polovtsov with a flash of irony, "tempted by the low prices, bought"). Foreign antique dealers came like jackals and found ways to export their purchases by greasing the proper palms. When commissars coveted something, they simply had it expropriated.

Armed bands of soldiers broke into houses on the pretext of looking for arms or abolishing wine cellars. Shortly after the November 7 Revolution, coveting the rich wine cellars of the Winter Palace, larger and larger crowds threatened to overcome the soldiers posted to guard it. Machine guns were brought with orders to shoot into the crowd. Yet one night the crowd broke through. Polovtsov wrote that it was

> an indescribable bacchanal . . . the whole quarter was full of drunken soldiers, swilling out of the same bottles, stealing bottles from one another, screaming, gesticulating, shooting off their guns. Unfortunate inhabitants barricaded behind their windows saw and heard columns of drunken armed men, fearing that any minute they might break into their houses. The pillage did not stop until the cellars were flooded by firemen; some were drowned. Afterwards, the snow around the palace was mottled with large stains of wine, the streets full of empty bottles, and the walls around the Hermitage nauseating with the smell of alcohol.

Systematic armed raids of private cellars followed throughout the city. For Polovtsov, the first such raid came in late November as he was sitting down to dinner after returning from Pavlovsk. A band of soldiers shot at his windows until he and his wife were forced to flee. The next day not a bottle was left in his cellars, and his servants were all drunk.

During the next ten months he was subjected to five more such raids. In February 1918, he was awakened at 2 A.M. to find himself surrounded by armed soldiers calling themselves "The Extraordinary Committee to Battle Counter-Revolution." Electricity was now turned off at midnight, so by the eerie light of flickering candles they searched his drawers, stole his wife's diamond necklace, and arrested his nephew. They left, threatening to come back the next day to take all his clothes. The following day when Polovtsov went to complain to Lunacharsky about these violations and the committee's threat, all Lunacharsky could find to suggest was, "Why don't you try to take as much as you can to Pavlovsk."

Bands of criminals infested all quarters of the city, freely roaming the streets at night. The Fontanka Quay was so dangerous that carriages refused to traverse it; thieves would come out of boats moored along the dark canal to rob pedestrians and kill those that resisted them. At night, when Polovtsov returned from Pavlovsk, there were no longer any taxis and the trolleys overflowed with soldiers who traveled free, hanging like human grape clusters along their sides. So at night, Polovtsov walked home through dimly lighted streets where the few pedestrians walked in the middle of the sidewalk, apprehensively trying to avoid each other. One of his friends, seeing a lone woman in a dark side street one night, gallantly went over to offer to escort her. As he approached, she fainted dead away in fright.

As the months wore on, getting to Pavlovsk became ever more difficult. Trains no longer ran on time and were often abruptly stopped by wildcat strikes. In January the temperature in the unheated cars fell to thirty below zero. So icy was the floor that even hardened soldiers with heavy boots would climb up on the train benches. "Even when one managed to squeeze into one of the packed cars, one often stood for an hour or two in this arctic atmosphere before the train departed. If one came on time and found a way to sit down, one traveled under two or three layers of humanity. If late, often one could no longer get in the door, so passengers perched on the roof, between the cars, or even hung onto the exterior sills. During snowstorms people died and the Bolsheviks prohibited this way of traveling — to no avail." Later additional empty freight cars were added where people stood packed in like cattle. Early in the morning at Pavlovsk, which was at the end of the line, trains would arrive full of desperate people who had gotten on at earlier stations simply to get a seat to ride back.

Overnight, a poisonous bureaucracy flowered, which nourished itself by requiring ever-changing new documents. There was no way these could be avoided, for without having the proper document of the moment, citizens could be prohibited from entering or leaving a railway station or would simply be arrested. Since these changed almost daily, it became necessary to stand in line for hours and always at a different office. "One could," said Polovtsov, "get everything and anything by paying, until the day when a denunciation sent both payer and payee to prison or into the other world."

Lengthy and boring meetings in which less and less was decided were now required for everything — "always the same, always repeating the extraordinary benefits of the Revolution." Polovtsov developed the habit of never asking anyone for anything unless he needed a signature or an official measure. "I understood that in order to obtain rapidly what was needed one had to exploit the very human taste for contrast and be very brief; one had to demand, never explain." Once a month he addressed himself to Lunacharsky directly. After March 1918, when the new Soviet government moved the capital of Russia back to Moscow, catching the elusive minister was no easy matter. He received people at unpredictable hours, sometimes in the Winter Palace, at other times in the Ministry of Public Education. A large enthusiastic untidy man, full of his latest plan, he usually arrived late, waving his arms in animated conversation surrounded by a group of acolytes. "When I was very pressed for time," wrote Polovtsov,

> I installed myself behind his desk despite all the "entrance prohibited" signs on all the doors and I would explain myself to him between deputations. Another system was to go down to the kitchens of the palace where those who worked in the building had set up a makeshift lunchroom. Lunacharsky came down to lunch around three and I could talk to him while he was eating.
>
> His life was full of the unexpected. He had the Bolshevik manner of improvising everything without putting any order in plans, giving promises to speak in public in such and such a place, making constant trips to Moscow now that his chiefs had settled there, and always the problem of deflecting intrigues which, it was said, were regularly mounted against him. All this made the possibility of a reasonable and sustained decision very ephemeral.
>
> One day I told him that he would be doing me a favor if he would come one day to Pavlovsk to speak to the soviet on preserving the integrity of the park as some of the inhabitants wanted to increase their vegetable gardens at the expense of the landscapes of Gonzaga.

Lunacharsky kept promising but never came, and Polovtsov had almost gave up hope when he heard by chance in Petrograd that Lunacharsky was coming to Pavlovsk the next day. Still not believing, he nevertheless took the train and saw Lunacharsky, wearing, as he always did in winter, a huge fur coat, the kind that merchants wore under the old regime, a gift to him from the Red Army. Surrounded by his usual group of acolytes he was on his way to Tsarskoe with the idea of coming to Pavlovsk.

Polovtsov had grown accustomed to a constant stream of visits from ignorant functionaries curious to see the palace and expected that this would be yet another such tedious official visit. To his surprise, as soon as he began showing the palace, Lunacharsky went straight for the finest objects and talked knowledgeably about each one. Seeing this, Polovtsov confessed, in what for him was the highest possible compliment, that he thought at the time that "if such a man had presented himself as a collaborator, I would have taken him immediately. . . . I have often wondered since how he had been able to form his taste, living as he had the communal existence of socialist refugee."

Lunacharsky lingered so long that dusk was falling when he reached the Rossi library. He could not tear himself away. He asked Polovtsov to open one of the cabinets, and at random began taking out works of Russian poets of the eighteenth century, despised by the public of the time. "I'll wager," he said, "that you have never read Hemnitzer; neither have I. Let's see how he wrote." "He then," continued Polovtsov, "began to read aloud the solemn hexameters which were the delight of the century of Catherine the Great, revealing their antiquated beauties. . . . Finally he said, 'Chase me away, or I will never leave.' I let him go off in a sleigh without accompanying him but my goal was realized, and since then I always found in him a champion ready to defend the beauties of Pavlovsk against all those who wanted to despoil it."

How well Polovtsov had succeeded was evident when, a few years later, in a series of essays called "Why We Save the Palaces of the Romanovs" written in reply to criticism from Sir Martin Conway, a British Member of Parliament who accused the Soviet government of destroying incomparable works of art, Lunacharsky gave the highest praise to Pavlovsk. Extolling the beauties of the park and the palace he called them "the highest level of exquisite taste," and described Maria Feodorovna as "a child of her century who brought her love of elegance to Russia where she gathered the most talented artists in all of Europe . . . giving them unlimited freedom."

Others were not as successful as Polovtsov. His friend, the gallant Count Zubov, fighting the increasingly tyrannical local soviet in Gatchina, was submerged. Despite the order of the Bolsheviks that the palaces were national property and had to be administered by a representative of the Commission of the Arts, local demagogues were able to appropriate Gatchina, where Zubov had done so much work, along with all its contents. Zubov, protesting their action, passionately exclaimed that he would rather see the treasures abroad and safe than destroyed in Russia. He was arrested on the spot and saved only by Lunacharsky, who sent him to Moscow. Crowds then broke in and looted, destroyed windows, and tore down and stole the draperies.

Everywhere but at Pavlovsk, thefts continued unabated. At Tsarskoe, soldiers broke into the first floor of the Alexander Palace. The eighteenth-century statues and forged iron benches of the park were stolen, taken apart piece by piece, and sold for a few cents at the iron market. At Peterhof, soldiers broke into the halls after climbing up the old linden trees and forcing the windows of the first floor. They wanted the curtains to make dresses for their girlfriends. Curators succeeded in packing up the main treasures of Mon Plaisir, Peter the Great's charming pavilion by the sea, and although much of historic importance remained, it was used for balls for soldiers and cooks. At Orienbaum, Peter III's house was pillaged and his unique and historic collection of toy soldiers stolen, along with quantities of rare porcelain and silver.

Polovtsov was thoroughly disgusted when in what seemed to be a desecration of all the principles he enunciated, Lunacharsky appropriated the Alexander Palace for himself and settled himself in rooms of the suite adjoining the former apartments of the Tsar's children. The palace was to be turned into an educational establishment where Lunacharsky would set about forging the new education. Said Polovtsov:

> In order to raise the children in the socialist spirit, and most especially to prevent them from receiving a religious education they were to be taken away from their families who would no longer know them and be concentrated in special schools. As Tsarskoe Selo was located on a height renowned for its fresh air and water, it was decided to create a group of boarding schools there. The town was rebaptized Detskoe Selo [Children's Village]. The first model establishment was to be created in the Alexander Palace not because it was the most easily adaptable but because it was a palace — and what is more the most intimate of the dynasty. The first step of the propagators was to install themselves there, along with a few of their friends. As for the apartments of the former Tsar's children, Lunacharsky proposed to distribute to schools and hospitals all the toys and books that were there.

The curator of the Catherine Palace, the eminent art specialist and historian George Lukomsky, hotly protested in writing and in person, trying unsuccessfully to explain what a crime against the science of history it would be to destroy such an ensemble. By pointing out that the books of the Tsarevich marked with his personal *ex libris* and distributed among schoolchildren would no doubt end up sold to booksellers, Lukomsky managed to save them, but the toys were all dispersed. "Yet," continued Polovtsov:

> the apartments remained unoccupied — due to the difficulties of heating and the fact that families did not willingly wish to give up their children and opted instead to flee to the country. Several houses in Tsarskoe were taken as nurseries and from the street as I passed, I saw the apathetic little pale faces of children clustered around the windows. In September 1918, when the first frosts arrived, there was not enough wood to heat the babes. Lunacharsky called me with a desperate appeal: the children installed at Tsarskoe were perishing of cold. As I had received my provision of wood for Pavlovsk I sent a few of my loads there.

The unsuccessful educational experiment was quickly abandoned.

At Pavlovsk, Polovtsov managed to surmount every new challenge with toughness or cunning. In order to save objects of art, he began to use his own authority to "confiscate" valuables from private houses in Pavlovsk, which the local soviets now claimed the right to expropriate and pillage at will. He demanded that Lunacharsky allow him to make an official list of buildings and pavilions that could not be touched. To protect the palace, he often had to act in a way that contradicted his own deepest sympathies. In the autumn of 1917, a Bolshevik decree had appeared prohibiting the celebration of religious services in chapels belonging to the state. Before the Revolution there was not a hospital, ministry, or administrative building that did not have its own chapel — many of which were marvels of architecture, with precious vestments and chalices. As the parish churches were overflowing and many people worshipped in these chapels, this was a devastating blow, which caused great consternation. The little group of curators protested, then insisted on making photographs and lists, but despite their efforts the cathedral of Peterhof was transformed into a movie house, the Izmailovsky Regiment Church auctioned off. Wanting to give no pretext for the expropriation or despoiling of Pavlovsk until he could open it as a museum, Polovtsov closed the chapel of the palace and remained unshakable at the insistent demands of the population — even the shrewish female chief of the local soviet — to celebrate Easter service there.

In May, he began talks with V. Taleporovsky, an architect who settled in Pavlovsk with his wife and son, and like so many others soon became devoted to the palace. Together they began repairs. Despite all of Polovtsov's efforts, several of the pavilions in the park had been damaged or vandalized during the winter. The picturesque *Vieux Chalet,* Maria Feodorovna's beloved retreat where her children had planted gardens, had been broken into and its entire contents destroyed. The windows of the Elizabeth Pavilion and the Temple of Friendship had all been smashed with rocks, and water had seeped onto the floors. The monument to Paul by the sculptor Martos, lovingly erected by Maria Feodorovna with an inscription "to the spouse benefactor," had been crudely vandalized. Intruders penetrating from underneath the gates had broken the fingers of the statue and taken the marble urn which weighed over 100 kilos. Although Polovtsov repaired the chains and locks, it was repeatedly vandalized until he was finally able to obtain a heavy marine chain from a warship.

With the first rains of March, Polovtsov noticed that the roof of the palace was leaking, threatening the beautiful painted ceilings. He began preparing estimates for the commission, but with inflation rampant and prices rising every day, he decided not to wait for the interminably long decision. Advancing the money from his own pocket, he purchased all the necessary materials. These were extremely difficult to obtain, and finding a way to transport them was even more so, but Taleporovsky managed to commandeer some military cars. Workers agreed to do the work for one price, only to immediately change it the next day, but with Taleporovsky's help, they managed to finish everything during the summer — even to having their estimates accepted — so that in the end Polovtsov was largely reimbursed.

Having looked all winter for someone who could do a proper inventory of Pavlovsk's paintings, Polovtsov determined to ask Lunacharsky for Zubov, who had been dispatched to Moscow after the Gatchina debacle. Once again he prevailed. Zubov returned and settled himself in Pavlovsk with a secretary and finished the inventory by September. Many of the paintings were in poor condition and needed restoration. There were no materials, but they managed to obtain a little alcohol and did some basic restoration themselves.

While Polovtsov continued to keep at bay ever more strident demands from the female chief of the local soviet to turn the palace into a working community for proletarians, a hospital for scrofulous children, or a workroom for the unemployed ("Mostly," he said acidly, "wanting to provide her family with well-paid administrative posts"), he and Taleporovsky planned exhibition halls, rehung paintings in their original places, and prepared an exhibition of porcelain in the Throne Room.

To help him complete the inventory, he recruited a whole group of talented experts. A woman who specialized in the work of Russian women of the beginning of the nineteenth century took over the responsibility of making a catalogue of all the drawings signed by the young Grand Duchesses and the students of Maria Feodorovna's school for young ladies. Another woman, a permanent member of the direction of the Hermitage, took over the inventory of drawings, gouaches, and albums, leaving a complete and definitive work. A professor of French literature, an authority on books, undertook the work of cataloguing the library. A specialist in embroideries began the study of the immense reserve of fabrics and embroidery that filled several large armoires, not only describing them in detail but also personally restoring many pieces. A former naval officer who had become an archivist began to systematically catalogue the enormous archives of Pavlovsk which had been collected and stored in the play fortress Bip. Polovtsov had been unable to prevent the municipal council from expropriating

Bip, but he had seen to it that by the time they took over the premises all the archives had been removed.

In the course of his own work Polovtsov discovered an invaluable historic collection of architectural designs. All construction, including the hen coops and ice houses at Pavlovsk at both the palace and in the town, had to be approved by the sovereign of the palace, a custom begun by Maria Feodorovna that lasted until the Revolution. Each project bore the signature of the successive owner of Pavlovsk, for no matter where they were — in Warsaw, Moscow, or the Crimea — decisions concerning Pavlovsk were too important to entrust to anyone else but the owners. He also found all the original plans and sketches for both the park and the palace, which had been assembled for Grand Duke Constantine, and grouped them according to author.

He established fundamental principles of work and held a meeting each week where all gathered to discuss problems and how to restore them. Everyone, said Polovtsov, agreed on one thing: that their work in the middle of the beauties of Pavlovsk helped them to endure and even sometimes to forget the catastrophes that were accumulating around them.

The more they advanced in their work at the palace the worse the conditions of their daily life grew. Famine was increasing and food was ever more difficult to obtain. In Petrograd, Polovtsov's wife had a trusted person who did nothing but search for food at any price for them and their servants. In exchange for carrots and potatoes, they sold their possessions and clothes. Polovtsov's hunting boots brought a good price, their curtains were snapped up to be transformed into dresses, even — to Polovtsov's amazement, as he could not imagine why anyone would want it — the chauffeur's livery. Nevertheless, they were always hungry; Polovtsov comments in passing that "I lost 20 kilos under the Bolshevik regime."

The entire economic system of the country was paralyzed. As the weeks passed, the only way of obtaining food was through soldiers who raided trains and filled their bags with whatever they could lay their hands on, which they then sold at exorbitant prices, or from peasants who occasionally brought milk and vegetables to the city. Railroad stations were full of starving people with empty bags, bottles, baskets, feverishly waiting for the arrival of village women. Whenever Polovtsov got off the train, desperate crowds surrounded him to ask where he had come from and whether they were bringing anything from the suburbs. Sporadically Red Guards would seize everything from housewives and then, said Polovtsov, "it was cries, floods of milk on the sidewalk, potatoes trampled under foot and general desolation." Peasants were less and less willing to exchange their products for depreciated bank notes, all the more so as there was nothing to buy. As the summer advanced, they refused to come at all, afraid that since the Bolsheviks had nationalized everything, they would be despoiled.

Clothes and shoes vanished. Queues began to form in front of shoe stores at ten o'clock at night. People slept on the sidewalk in order to be the first when the stores opened in the morning. Bringing supper and breakfast, they stayed, sleeping on the sidewalk even in the rain and wind. "I never understood as clearly as I did when seeing these lines of people, in no way embittered, perfectly resigned, with a joke on their lips, how easy it is to govern the Russian people."

In desperation people went themselves to remote villages to exchange their clothes and shoes for food. Polovtsov saw elegant women arriving at Peterhof with bags in hand, crossing the entire huge park in order to get potatoes, which they were forced to dig up themselves. The watchman of the Chinese Theater at Tsarskoe and his wife took turns sleeping in their vegetable garden, as every night people came to raid it. Polovtsov brought food to his colleagues at the palace when he could and then formed a cooperative vegetable garden, until without any warning the entire local soviet at Pavlovsk was arrested by Red Guards, who then imposed a rule that no food could be taken out of the town and proceeded to search every package at the station.

All meat except horsemeat disappeared, along with butter and all starches. Not only were people constantly suffering from hunger, said Polovtsov, "but one had to add to that the boredom of listening to everyone talk about nothing but food. Great expeditions were mounted to the center and east of Russia — expeditions full of danger, which necessitated intermediaries, special passes, quantities of money," only, on the way back, to have half the merchandise stolen or confiscated. All small restaurants, cafés, and pastry shops, which formerly had grown like mushrooms on every corner of Petersburg, disappeared during the winter. Then Red Guards began raiding larger restaurants, arresting all who had the bad fortune to be found eating there. By October all restaurants were closed as well as all the hotels. People lined up at soup kitchens, there to be insulted if they did not look sufficiently "democratic."

By the early summer of 1918, Bolshevik decrees authorized not only the occupation of houses by the proletariat, but pillage as well. In desperation, crowds of people, all trying to save objects of art, brought what they could carry directly to the Winter Palace. Fine bronzes, sculptures, paintings accumulated, piled helter-skelter along the walls, and the little group of curators was overwhelmed.

To help deal with the flood of requests, Polovtsov and the others recruited friends, until there were seventy-six people who divided the city by quarters. Racing from one end of the city to the other, on foot or on the overcrowded trolleys, hoping to arrive in time, they tried to influence their local soviet and retrieve from houses either before or after pillage everything that they could declare national property. By dint of great and courageous efforts they were able to convince the authorities to declare a few of the great houses museums. Later, Polovtsov was to write: "Days were too short to do the indispensable. Every hour there were new despoiling decrees. . . . I grieve to think of all that we could not do, of everything that perished because we were too few, because certain among us were not lucky or clever enough to avoid prison." Yet any effort was worthwhile if only "one day they will have the joy of seeing the objects of art for which they so valiantly fought definitively saved from destruction."

Every day new rumors, many of them unhappily true, swept the city: Bolsheviks were determined to destroy all the statues of former sovereigns in the city. The Arts Committee protested and demanded that a commission be formed. Next, they wanted to seize the portraits of sovereigns, including a famous portrait of Catherine II by the eighteenth-century Russian painter Levitsky, and use the canvas for revolutionary works. Again the commission raised a storm of objections and prevented this wholesale destruction.

On May 1, 1918, Polovtsov with undisguised horror witnessed the first "Parade of the Proletariat." "The Bolsheviks decided to cover the façades of certain houses with colossal constructive and patriotic painted banners." Walking to the station that morning, he saw one of these hanging on the Palace Square:

> A worker four stories high threatening an invisible adversary with his hammer with all around him a legend destined to terrify the "enemies of the people." Everything was loud, vulgar, badly drawn and of doubtful taste. It seemed to be flapping in the wind of a desert, for the inhabitants seemed to have passed the word to avoid these gatherings; only in the afternoon was there a procession of Red Guards and workers who filed by this ugliness — and the workers had stipulated that for doing this they would receive an extra ration of bread. Later they dragged a chariot with an enormous doll that represented the overthrown ruler.

Polovtsov did not hide his disdain for the clumsy attempts of the new regime to bring "art" to the masses — an art so opposite to his refined ideas of beauty. Lunacharsky installed a movie theater in the enormous Nicholas Hall of the

Winter Palace where the Tsar had once received foreign ambassadors. Every day there were long lines of people waiting to see free spectacles. To Polovtsov's disgust, artists were lodged in a studio in the Winter Palace and there turned out what looked to him like "charades of multicolored spots." In the meantime, he said triumphantly, the only real step toward popularizing genuine works of art was made by the Commission of the Arts. "In June, 1918, we opened the palaces of Tsarskoe Selo, Pavlovsk, Gatchina and Peterhof to the public two or three times a week."

After all his patient and dedicated work, he had won. Pavlovsk was now confiscated, but with all its treasures intact, and it became a national museum officially protected by the government. As soon as the palaces were opened as museums, huge, eager crowds appeared to see the magnificent palaces for themselves. At the Catherine Palace at Tsarskoe alone, more than a thousand people came on the first Sunday. Every week the crowds grew larger. So many came, in fact, that to preserve the magnificent inlaid parquet floors, Lukomsky created the *tapachki,* rough slippers made out of pieces of old rugs, which could be attached to any shoes.* They were afraid at first that soldiers would not accept these, but to their surprise they were mistaken. So respectful were the crowds that when once a man refused to don his slippers, the crowd surrounded him and adamantly refused to enter until he put them on.

At Pavlovsk it was the same story. So many people came that Polovtsov was forced to designate helpers to guide them through; but as they, too, were often overwhelmed he frequently stepped in to guide tours himself, reminding the public that it was forbidden to touch objects and furniture. Everyone always peacefully observed the rule, and never was anything disturbed or stolen. He was struck by the number of intelligent questions that were addressed to him and the eagerness of people to learn. Organizations of all kinds came to visit, and Polovtsov was touched by the many letters he received asking him about points he had raised during their tours.

Yet even as the eager crowds were filing in to see the beauty Polovtsov had saved, the descent to naked terror had already begun. On July 16, 1918, in a cellar in their last place of exile, ostensibly by orders of the extremely radical local soviet, but actually of Lenin, the Tsar and all his family, their doctor, cook, and parlormaid were brutally assassinated. The maid, who survived the first volley of

---

* *Tapachki* are still used in all the palaces today.

shots, was pursued and stabbed more than thirty times. As he lay moaning in his death throes in the arms of his dead father, the Tsarevich, Alexis, fourteen years old and a hemophiliac, was brutally kicked in the head with a heavy boot. Two more shots were then fired into his ear. After this hideous regicide, every member of the Romanov family that could be found by the Bolsheviks was murdered. The day after the assassination of the Tsar, in the town of Alapayevsk in the Urals, the pious Prince Jean — who, only nine months before, had told Polovtsov that he feared nothing — his two brothers Constantine and Igor, and the saintly Grand Duchess Elizabeth, a nun, sister of the Tsarina, who had resisted all offers of security and escape, were taken in peasant carts to the mouth of an abandoned mine shaft. They were thrown alive into the pit, with heavy timbers and hand grenades thrown after them. Not all died immediately. A peasant who timorously approached the pit after the murderers had left heard hymns being sung at the bottom of the shaft. When, a few days later the White Armies found the bodies, young Igor, the great-great-grandson of Maria Feodorovna, had his mouth full of dirt — whether fighting pain or hunger could not be known. His wounded head was bound with the Grand Duchess's nun's veil.*

In Petrograd, no one knew of the grisly murder of the Tsar. There, both before and after the Peace of Brest-Litovsk,† people expected invading German armies to arrive any minute. Other rumors had it that it would be the Czechs and then, the Allied armies. What no one believed was that the Bolsheviks would last — even the Bolsheviks themselves were terrified, sometimes whispering to Polovtsov when he came to the commission at the Winter Palace that they were convinced that the moment to flee had arrived. Some were making plans to get away to America. In August 1918, Polovtsov chanced to meet the editor of *Pravda* on a streetcar and asked him how things were going. "To the devil," he answered, "from bad to worse." "How much time do we have?" Polovtsov asked. "At most three or four more weeks." "And then?" The man drew an imaginary knife across his throat — "Yes, yes," he said, "I am resigned to it." Then adding, "And don't think you will escape either" as he jumped from the trolley.

---

* A few months later, Princess Vera, the youngest child of the last Grand Duke of Pavlovsk, along with her brother, her mother, and the widow and children of her murdered brother Prince Jean, escaped on one of the final boats to leave for Sweden.

† There was dispute within the Party over the signing of a separate peace treaty with Germany and withdrawal from the war. The German proposal at Brest-Litovsk demanded very harsh territorial concessions from Russia. Because of Lenin's insistence that peace was necessary, the Treaty of Brest-Litovsk was signed on March 3, 1918. Russia paid a heavy price, losing 34 percent of her population, 54 percent of her industrial plant, and 89 percent of her coal mines.

The death of the Tsar was a stain of blood that spread until it engulfed the whole land. At the end of August Socialists began assassination attempts against Bolshevik leaders. In Petrograd, two local chiefs, Volodarsky and Uritsky,* were killed, Lenin and Zinoviev were wounded. These attacks provoked massacres in September for, said Polovtsov, "the public was complaining louder and louder against the regime . . . and these assassinations were used as a pretext to institute a terror, the real reason being to try to subdue all opposition."

By some ill fortune Uritsky's fleeing attacker had managed to slip into a back door of the Club Anglais and then escaped; when the Red Guards arrived, they arrested everyone who happened to be in the club at the time, including those peacefully playing billiards. During the following days, a massive wave of arrests and summary shootings spread throughout the city. In a single day the official Bolshevik journal announced that five hundred victims had been killed in Petrograd and Kronstadt. Prisons were overflowing, and wives were prohibited from bringing food to their imprisoned husbands. "In the street," said Polovtsov, "one saw long processions of prisoners, many of them women and old men. Often families learned of the arrest of their near and dear only from having seen them in these doleful processions. In September," he continued, "almost all our friends were in prison."

To assist in their executions, the Bolsheviks, said Polovtsov, used brigades of Chinese. Originally brought to Russia as laborers on the Murman railroad line when successive mobilizations had taken all the Russian workers, they had stayed on after railroad work ceased and spread through the city working as janitors and at other menial jobs. They were a very rough group; for some time before the Bolshevik coup, Chinese names had figured prominently in the newspaper crime lists. Now the Bolsheviks formed them into revolutionary brigades and billeted them in a camp not far from Tsarskoe Selo, which made Polovtsov fear greatly for Pavlovsk. In the trolleys of the city they insulted terrified passengers. "The cruelty they exhibited during the massacres corresponded to what one might expect," wrote Polovtsov. "The Bolsheviks had found the perfect instrument for their methods and procedures."

The Bolsheviks now feared everyone. All "counterrevolutionary" gatherings were prohibited. Spies were posted everywhere; houses and all who went in and out of them were closely watched. Polovtsov's situation became more and more thorny. At Pavlovsk an informer had been sent to replace the former head of the

---

* Uritsky was the hated president of the Extraordinary Committee to Battle Counter-Revolution, Speculation and Sabotage.

servants committee, and he noted that a spy was now permanently attached to him. An ominous new decree demanded that all members of the arts commission declare themselves Bolshevik. "It was only a matter of chance when everything else in my existence that did not have to do with the arts would serve as a pretext to arrest me: it could be for having been against the nationalization of the Ural mines, for being a member of the New Club, for continuing to visit a Grand Duke, for being a friend or related to someone already in prison." He knew that if he were arrested Pavlovsk would certainly be ransacked to find proof of his "counterrevolutionary tendencies." His colleagues would be molested, and even perhaps his friends working in other palaces. All his work to save the palace could be destroyed.

He decided to make one last appeal to Lunacharsky, asking him for his help in getting rid of the spy who constantly followed him. Lunacharsky promised to try, but nothing happened. "My last weeks in Petrograd and at Pavlovsk made me understand that if I stubbornly stayed, I could easily put in jeopardy the work to which I had devoted myself for more than a year. I had sacrificed everything for it up to then, not sending even the debris of my fortune out of the country for had I done so at the beginning, I would have been forced to leave immediately, and I wanted to do nothing that would keep me from staying."

Now, however, he began to think about leaving:

> No material consideration influenced my resolution. The human animal is so adaptable that each progressive turn of the screw finds him ready to adapt himself to the new vise . . . the lack of security, the absence of all comfort, the lack of objects necessary to existence, were no longer felt as acute suffering. Perhaps we were weakened by privations, and less capable of reacting; but on the other hand, there was indubitably a certain element of sport, I would say almost amusement, in doing without those things which we had formerly thought indispensable. Along with this was joined the satisfaction which all thoughtful human beings experience when sharing the fate of their country, compared to the horror of exile, and this passive patriotism helped to make one forget the dangers and disappointments of the Bolshevik regime.
>
> Nevertheless, after much vacillation my wife and I decided to leave, and at the end of October 1918, we arranged to do so. Without a passport or any papers, with few suitcases, deceiving our servants — in a word, almost as if we were criminals, we crossed the frontier to Finland.

Even his colleagues at the palace did not at first suspect that he had left permanently; for as a final act to try to protect Pavlovsk, before he left his beloved country, Polovtsov wrote one last letter to Lunacharsky, with instructions that it be delivered after he left. In it he said only that he was going into hiding until the informer assigned to the palace had been removed. Later, in exile, he learned that this had been done. The capable and devoted Taleporovsky took over and became an outstanding director of the new palace-museum.

The little band of friends who had been ready "to fight down to the last chandelier" had lost many battles, but they had won the most important one. When in exile in 1919, Polovtsov wrote the account of his harrowing days in Petrograd; he glimpsed their true victory:

> The mentality we had been able to inspire hypnotized the crowd so that they considered palaces to be untouchable; this mentality prevailed. I know that neither Pavlovsk nor the other palaces, once transformed into museums, suffered any damages.

The man who had accepted the designation of commissar in order to save beauty had succeeded. By saving Pavlovsk from the bureaucrats and ideological dogmatists he helped to preserve the history and art, indeed the soul, of a nation. The transformation of the palace was complete. It now belonged to the public. Like a beacon it would allow the generation that came after him to follow the traditions that the Revolution sought to destroy. The eager crowds continued to grow — to be touched by the palace and to ponder. For although the form of society had changed, the values of beauty that the palace represented remained alive, and once it was given to the Russian people, they would protect it as fiercely as Polovtsov through the even darker days to come.

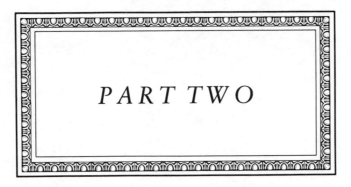

PART TWO

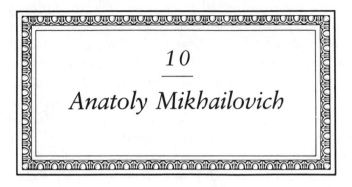

10

Anatoly Mikhailovich

The past is not a bad witness.

— Russian proverb

POLOVTSOV ALMOST SINGLEHANDED had saved Pavlovsk from the chaos of the early revolutionary period. But worse was to come. Two tyrants now arose, Hitler in Germany and Stalin in the Soviet Union, who were to pursue their ideological goals with unprecedented cruelty and ferocity. Both made the destruction of culture and memory a keystone of their strategies, and both turned on the culture of old Russia. How could the fragile beauty of Pavlovsk hold out against these onslaughts, which made the trials of the early Revolution and all other disasters that had fallen on Russia — including the Mongol invasion — look like child's play?

Even as Polovtsov left, the conflict was growing more deadly. In the bitter Civil War, the newly formed Red Army, the Whites, the Greens (Ukrainian Partisans), the Blacks (Anarchists), and other assorted parties grappled for victory. In Petrograd in 1921, the sailors of the Kronstadt Naval Base rebelled against Bolshevik rule and were overcome. The final action came in February 1921, when the Red Army invaded and occupied Georgia.

Shortly after the Red military victory, between March 1922 and March 1923, Lenin suffered three strokes, and finally died on January 21, 1924. Joseph Stalin was General Secretary of the Communist Party. Originally a relatively unimportant position within Party ranks, it was used by Stalin to gain extraordinary influence within the government, and by late 1930 he had expelled or exiled all of his critics and assumed the dictatorship of the Party and the nation. Under his direction the Party began the forced and bloody collectivization of the peasants, which was fiercely opposed. Two-thirds of the horses in Russia were killed by farmers, who refused to have their beasts fall into the hands of the Bolsheviks. In 1929, Russia suffered a poor harvest, the first of an endemic problem in the USSR ever since, which made food rationing necessary. Nevertheless, the government continued to export grain, creating the first man-made famine in history. In 1932/33, millions of peasants starved to death in the traditional breadbaskets of Russia.* In 1932, internal passports were made mandatory and have remained in force to this day.

Within the Party, there were fierce internal struggles. On December 1, 1934, Sergei Kirov, a popular independent leader of the Leningrad Party organization, was murdered in what was supposedly the act of a disaffected Party member named Nikolaev — in reality, by order of Stalin. Kirov had received more votes in a Politburo election than Stalin — a vote that became, in effect, his death warrant. Hundreds were shot outright. Within a month of Kirov's death, thirty to forty thousand people in Leningrad were imprisoned. By 1941, more than fifteen million people were in forced labor camps.

From the time Stalin seized control, the new rulers set out to obliterate all achievements of the past and the memory of all that had gone before them, including the revolution that had brought them to power. With growing ferocity, the Soviet regime waged a relentless war against art, culture, and religion. History was swallowed into the black hole of the Big Lie. Books were locked up in libraries and access to them banned; facts of history were changed; encyclopedias rewritten not once, but many times, according to changing Party lines. The tsars disappeared, their names and achievements striken from the historical record, their statues and portraits removed, and along with them the respected old flags, standards, and orders of Russia. Familiar names of beloved villages, streets, and buildings were changed to bear the names of the new leaders and their police chiefs; treasured national holidays, including Easter and Christmas, were prohibited and replaced with others glorifying the new regime.

---

* The death toll of farmers and peasants from both collectivization and famine in the 1930s is staggering. The exact numbers are still being studied and debated by both Western and Soviet scholars. Current estimates have now risen as high as 17 million dead or disappeared.

An all-out war was declared on religion. Ancient churches, which contained treasures of the people, were blown up or turned into warehouses, movie theaters, and swimming pools; church bells melted down; and thousands of priests massacred. By 1929 there were only four bishops left, and by 1939 only a hundred functioning churches in a country that had had fifty thousand.

All art and free expression were stifled as the new regime attempted to commit a lobotomy on the nation, to erase its cultural memory, and to impose a new socialist order. Works of Tolstoy and Dostoevsky were expurgated and banned entirely. Eighteenth-century and avant-garde paintings alike were locked away in dark cellars and never exhibited. Writers, artists, musicians, and poets were shackled and silenced. By 1925, all the avant-garde artists, most of whom had sympathized with and championed the Revolution, had fled into exile, been imprisoned, or were dead. Then, as Socialist Realism imposed the tyranny of banal "optimism" and "glorification of the proletariat," those who remained and refused to bend to the regime's will either perished or were forced into lives of grinding poverty, obscurity, and surreptitious creation "for the drawer."

Countless art treasures of the nation were callously sold. In the 1930s, the wife of the American Ambassador was taken down to the storerooms of the Kremlin by Mrs. Molotov to choose items she fancied; the value of silver and gold chalices of the time of Peter the Great were determined by their weight. Foreign agents came to purchase objects of art, including religious vestments and icons roughly ripped out of churches, which then found their way into American and European collections.

But as much as the new leaders labored, culture proved impossible to destroy. Preserved in the unconscious of the nation, it continued to live silently in the minds and hearts of the people, passed down in the stories of grandmothers to grandchildren, in poetry committed to memory and recited in whispers, in treasured family objects and photographs hidden and shown to only the most trusted friends. So strong was the Russians' love for their past that it could not be ripped out of them; its spirit endured, even as they were being cut to pieces.

One of the great qualities of the Russian people is that they are deeply spiritual, sensitive to beauty and mystery. Their greatest weapons are patience and a calm stoicism in the face of disaster. Enduring all, they outwait, outlast, and finally swallow every conqueror. Their culture had survived two hundred and fifty years of Mongol rule and one hundred years of westernization imposed from above, and it was to survive communism. For just as a sapling mysteriously grows in the trunk of a felled tree, nourished by the dying trunk and its roots, even as everything was being destroyed, in unexpected places, those who were to protect and nourish the culture of the Russian past were beginning their lives.

How the ordeal was survived is an astonishing record of the resilience of the human spirit. Some clues as to how it happened are to be found in the story of Anatoly Mikhailovich Kuchumov, who was to play a leading role in the saving of Pavlovsk during our time. He and all his contemporaries grew up, reached adulthood, and began their work of preserving the beauty of the past against this background of war, revolution, and terror.

Anatoly Mikhailovich was born on June 9, 1912, in the heart of old northern Russia, Yaroslavsky Oblast, or as he still calls it in the old way, *Gubernaya,* in the small city of Mologa, which then numbered about four thousand inhabitants. Mologa, situated five hundred miles southeast of St. Petersburg on the left bank of the Volga in one of the most densely forested regions of all Russia, was a colorful, ancient, bustling merchant town recorded in sources of the thirteenth century. For centuries Mologa was known as the ship and barge building capital of Russia, and the Mologians as a hardy, resourceful breed, renowned for their trustworthiness in service; they were energetic and enterprising folk, geared for survival. The peasants managed to extract twice as much from their poor land as their neighbors. The people of the region were famous for their skill in woodworking and for their fine flax — in the sixteenth and seventeenth centuries the tsars bought their linen there.

Anatoly Mikhailovich spent his childhood in Latskoe, a tiny village 26 kilometers away from Mologa, which then numbered some four hundred souls. There, until he left to seek his fortune in faraway Leningrad, he lived in a large log *izba,* built by his grandfather.

The year he was born, it would have been impossible to believe that a humble peasant boy, born in a small town on the Volga and Mologa rivers in a remote part of northern Russia, would become the caretaker, protector, and savior of the palaces of the tsars. The world was a stable place. Grand Duke Constantine Constantinovich lived at Pavlovsk and music played at the Voksal. The Romanov dynasty, which would celebrate its three hundredth anniversary the following year in great national pomp and rejoicing, was securely in place. Yet in a few short years this ordered world was utterly swept away in the whirlwind. Even the town where Anatoly Mikhailovich was born was to disappear, flooded into oblivion by a hydroelectric station.*

His great-great-grandmother had been a serf of the local Prince Cherkassy, sold at the age of fourteen. His father was a peasant, a self-taught carpenter educated in the village schools. His mother worked as a carrier, using their horse and cart to haul kegs of water to the station. When Anatoly was a small child, his father went to work in Petrograd restoring and repairing old furniture for the brand-new Hotel Astoria, built in 1911, and the elegant, older Europe Hotel. His mother followed, working until the Revolution at the famous firm of Fabergé, glueing boxes. Little Anatoly was left at home to be cared for by his *babushka* (grandmother) — who is the key figure in the life of every Russian child, and for centuries, from generation to generation, passed on the lore, the tales, and the wisdom of the nation; without her, the soul of the nation would perish.

Life still moves at a slower pace in Russia today than it does in the frenetic West. The hours seem longer. There is more time for talking, and remembering the past. Stories in Russia unfold slowly, and when Anatoly Mikhailovich talks about his early life in his small village, where the perils and trials of his country were a faraway echo, it is in the unhurried calm accents of a Russian fairytale. "When I was a child, we most often stayed at home, my grandmother and me, in our big *izba*. That's how life unfolded. My grandmother worked no more no less than forty years as a maid in the hotels of St. Petersburg near the Hay Market, and she told me many stories of the life of that turbulent neighborhood. If you look at her photograph, you would say she was a *grande dame* and yet she signed her name with difficulty and could not read Russian, only Slavonic — the Gospel, the Bible, and religious literature.

"I never saw electricity — of cinema I had no knowledge, yet from my earliest years I had some idea of beautiful things living within me, drawing me towards them. I was given toys — bears, dolls and wooden cabins — but I was never very interested in them. Other beautiful, artistically made things interested me more. When I was about four years old, we had a lot of porcelain in the house from the Kuznetsov factory, which was widely distributed then, things which I found lovely — pink-gold glasses with crystal edges, really magnificent things. When mother wasn't home, Grandmother would let me play with the service. I would

---

* The Rybinskoy hydroelectric station was built in the early 1940s; people living in the areas flooded to form the reservoir, including the town of Mologa, were resettled.

spread them out. I fitted wooden shelves into the walls of our log house with wooden chips. Then she would put the cups in my hands and I would spread them out, according to my taste, and would admire my 'museum' exhibition. But once, when I set up things in the kitchen on a shelf, under the weight of the service the shelf fell. Cups, glasses flew off and were broken. Babushka just said, '*Nichevo!* We'll buy more.' But mother when she came home was angry and groaned, 'How can you give God knows what to the child — everything he asks to play with?' But Grandmother never refused anything.

"Grandmother's brother worked in a print shop in St. Petersburg and brought home a whole set of reproductions from the Tretyakov Gallery. We had Repin's 'Ivan the Terrible,' and paintings by Vershchagin. Although father was born a peasant, and became a self-taught carpenter, he knew an extraordinary amount about history and art. He loved books about artists and knew the significant works of both foreign and Russian masters. In his trade he exhibited much creativity and loved to do artistic carving. Our *izba* was decorated with shelves and furniture made by his own hand. He made frames for the reproductions of the Tretyakov Gallery and we had a whole picture gallery, about fifteen, hanging on our walls.

"On the eve of the Revolution, my parents left to work in Petrograd. I remember the day of the February Revolution, the overthrow of the monarchy. I was five years old. I had over my bed a great many portraits of tsars, because of my uncle's work in the publishing house. He would bring home great packages of pictures and portraits. The walls of our *izba* were plastered with them. I loved it when Grandmother would tell me 'And this is the Sovereign Emperor, and this is the Empress and this . . .' I knew all of them. And so when once I woke up and saw that not a portrait was left, I burst into tears and cried even harder when I saw that the portraits were on the floor all torn up. Grandmother said, 'Be quiet.' I saw a soldier sitting there. The soldier came from the front. He explained that there was no Tsar, there is a revolution. Grandmother of course quickly destroyed these portraits. I began to yell. She promised to buy new ones. She went to the store but there were no more tsars, only 'boyarinas' working on sewing machines.

"Grandmother was very much a peasant. We had a lot of flax. We worked it and sold it. Latskoe had sixteen fairs a year and on one of these market days after a successful sale, we would go drink tea in a tearoom. Grandmother would order a large kettle of tea and about two kilograms of biscuits. We would sit there, drink tea, order seconds and thirds. After this we would go to a store and Grandmother would buy me cloth for my shirts, any kind I liked. I remember pink flowers on cotton. Then we would buy pillowcases, linens. Every year, after the sale of the flax, we always bought manufactured goods and somehow improved the household.

"At the village cemetery there stood a seventeenth-century church with a wonderful carved iconostasis. Inside the cupola was the Savior, painted on wood, split in two. Grandmother told me that lightning had struck this icon and set it on fire and knocked off the arms and head of the silver-plated angels that stood on the iconostasis. I wondered why the injuries were left as they were, why no one fixed them. There was a very old icon, more than three hundred years old. How I remember that huge blackened board, how the eyes of the Mother of God projected forward from her countenance! On the church balcony hung a picture — a green snake, horribly portrayed. When I went into the church I would try to squeeze sideways, so as never to stand beneath this terrible icon. As a child I was afraid to go into this church because in the narthex there was what seemed to me to be an enormous 'Last Judgment.' On it were portrayed all the passions to which sinners were doomed in the other world. Grandmother would lead me to it and say, 'You see, he who lies is hanged by his tongue, and he who steals is fried on a skillet.'

"The memory of these depicted passions never left me. Many years later I became interested in the fate of the 'Last Judgment' of my youth. It never reached a museum because the directors of the *kolkhoz* [collective farm] that was formed there decided to make a shed out of the church in 1936. They vandalized it, and threw all the icons out. Some of the local inhabitants gathered them, including my grandmother. She covered pails of water with them, saying, 'The board is good.' She considered herself a Believer, but apparently her faith turned into some kind of convention. Then people from the Yaroslav Museum came to collect all the surviving artistic valuables from each house, but the most important icon was destroyed. Eventually someone was punished for this free-spirited destruction of old churches, but then, that time had its price.

"There was on the premises of the local seminary a village school, but somehow I couldn't get in there, so when I was nine years old I was designated for the school of the second level in Mologa, the capital city of Yaroslavskaya Gubernaya, twenty-six kilometers away from our village. Grandmother hitched up a horse. A suitcase with a rim of iron etched with a frost pattern design was bought for my things. When you turned the key you would hear music. Because in those first years we walked in *lapti** made of birchwood — which I actually liked a great deal for they were very easy to walk in — there were in the suitcase foot wraps, as well as a pair of shirts, and my books. What I liked most of all is that whenever I needed a book I had to spring the lock and music would play. Besides that, Grandmother loaded onto the wagon a bag of potatoes and a pot with linseed oil and so took me 'into society.' "

While the Civil War raged in Russia, little Anatoly began his studies. Occasionally the far-away tempest that was shaking Russia had its echo even in his remote village. "I first became acquainted with real art, and its sad situation, when I was eleven years old. I was sent to a Pioneer Camp about ten kilometers from our village where the estate of the Master of the Stables of His Highness, Shebeko, once had been. The estate was called Murzino. The nobleman's house had been burned by peasants at the time of the Revolution. There was a hatred for the rich in those days, and it was expressed in such fires. Only the external constructions remained, white columns, wings, very beautiful among the foliage, which already had grown over the ashes. But close by, about two kilometers away, the Andreyevskoe estate, which had once belonged to Prince Kurakin, had survived — at least some stone and some wooden buildings. Kurakin had been the representative of the local nobility of the *uyezd*.† He had built a splendid school on the estate, which was considered the best in the area. An excursion for us Pioneers was organized and we saw this school. It awed us — large bright classrooms, wonderful staircases, laboratories for physics and chemistry, which were, for those times, excellently equipped. We couldn't help but compare them with our poor school, which had nothing. As I remember now, after school we asked them to show us the residence of the old nobility. It stood all boarded up. Someone said we must look for a key. Someone else said, 'We don't need a key, we need an ax.' A man came, tore the boards off, and we went into the house, all drooping and neglected. Yet, in some places stood cabinets of mahogany and large paintings, but mostly frames without pictures. There were still mirrors on the walls, and marble fireplaces. I even remember that the fireplace was made of Dutch tiles. In some rooms there was decoration in false marble with decorated ceilings and walls. This nobleman's house, even half destroyed, with its uncommon artistic decoration, gave me, a village lad, the impression of a fairytale. A

---

* *Lapti* are sandals made from bark. Their name derives from the Russian word *lapa*, meaning paw.
† The *uyezd* was the lowest geographic administrative division, equivalent to what is today called the *rayon*.

The future Alexander I, 1777. Overjoyed at his birth, his grandmother, Catherine the Great, gave his parents the original parcel of land for Pavlovsk.

Krik: Maria Feodorovna and Paul spent happy days as newlyweds living in one of the two small hunting lodges on the thickly forested land given by Catherine.

The Temple of Friendship, the
first Doric building in Russia,
and the first building designed
for Pavlovsk by Charles Cameron. Gottleib Schwenke

Charles Cameron, 1740–1812.
Much remains mysterious about
this Scottish architect, including
this disputed self-portrait.

Giacomo Quarenghi, 1744–1817

Vincenzo Brenna, 1745–1820

Carlo Rossi, 1775–1849

Paul, Maria Feodorovna, and
nine of their ten children; a bust
of their daughter Olga, who died
at the age of three, is on a pedestal. Carl-Ferdinand Kügelgen,
1800.

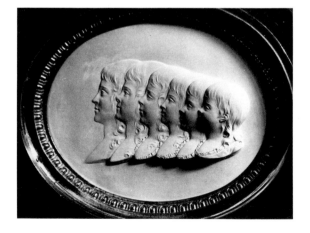

Plaster medallion with copper on
glass profiles of her six eldest
children made from the drawings
of Maria Feodorovna, 1791

Pavlovsk Palace in 1800. Carl-Ferdinand Kügelgen

Paul I in 1800, one year before his death. Semyon Shchukin, 1800

Maria Feodorovna as a widow wearing a medallion of Paul. She outlived him by twenty-eight years. J. Voile

Andrei Voronykhin (1760–
1814), self-portrait, 1812

Count Alexander Stroganov.
Jean Laurent Monnico

Alexander I. George Dawe,
1812.

Sketch of the Rose Pavilion
ballroom constructed for the
homecoming celebration of
Alexander I

New Chalet

The Dairy

Old Chalet

Bip Fortess

Illuminations at the Pavlovsk
Voksal in the 1870s

1856 cartoon showing Strauss
being tossed in the air by his
enthusiastic public

1856 г.
Публика въ неистовомъ восторгѣ отъ своего любимца.

Concert Hall of the Voksal, 1914

Grand Duke Constantine holding
his son Prince George, 1904

Princess Vera with her dolls in
her room at Pavlovsk

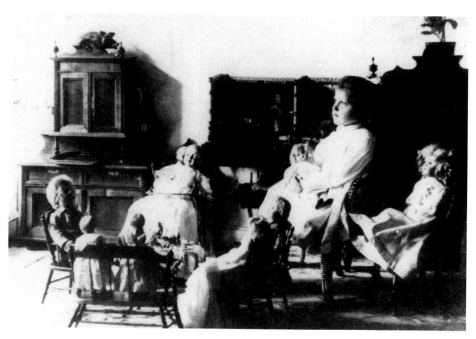

Grand Duke Constantine with
seven of his children

ЕЯ ВЕЛИЧЕСТВО КОРОЛЕВА ЭЛЛИНОВЪ
ОЛЬГА КОНСТАНТИНОВНА.

Queen Olga of Greece, sister of
Grand Duke Constantine

Anatoly Mikhailovich Kuchumov
in 1941

Kuchumov reading in the Mauve
Boudoir of Empress Alexandra,
Alexander Palace, 1940

Anna Ivanova Zelenova in 1941

Blockade days in the cellars of St. Isaac's 1941/42. Anna Zelenova with muff is on the right.

Nazi registration of local inhabitants for slave labor, 1941

Pavlovsk burning

Pavlovsk Palace,
1944

Ruins of palace
interior: The Throne
Room stoves are
visible.

Pavlovsk Park: Area of the Great Star, 1944

Ruins of Rose Pavilion, 1944

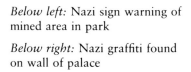

Below left: Nazi sign warning of mined area in park

Below right: Nazi graffiti found on wall of palace

Anna Zelenova and Natalia
Gromova at work

Women's brigade unearthing
buried antique statues in
Pavlovsk cellars, 1944

Women workers unearthing buried statue of a muse in Old Sylvia, 1945

Women workers digging out stumps in park, 1945

Sapgir's soldier brigade working
in ruins of Greek Hall, 1944

Women volunteers replanting
trees in white birch area, 1946

Feodor Feodorovich Oleinik,
first architect of Pavlovsk
reconstruction, 1950

Palace enveloped in scaffolding,
1954

Sophia Popova-Gunich working on palace restoration

Restoring palace façade, early 1950s

Chief staff members of Pavlovsk Palace: (first row left to right) S. Popova-Gunich, architect; A. Zelenova, director; O. Gendleman, engineer-contractor; A. Kuchumov in second row. Late 1960s

Workers who restored the Temple of Friendship

Restoring the Greek Hall, 1967

N. Belinskaya and E. Anokhina
restoring plaster molding in
Greek Hall, 1967

N. Mal'tseva restoring molding
of Hall of Peace, 1967

N. Varlamov restoring gilding of
the State Bedroom, 1965

A. Ivanov and V. Karnaushenko
reassembling chandelier of State
Bedroom, 1967

P. Nikanorov restoring fireplaces
of the Greek Hall, 1967

Above left: V. Kornaushenko, restoring furniture, 1966

Above right: V. Fedotov recreating parquet floors of State Bedroom

Left: Finished parquet floor of State Bedroom

Anatoly Treskin, self-portrait

Treskin restoring ceiling
of Pilaster Room, 1958

Treskin restoring the ceiling
of the Rossi Library, 1963

Anatoly Kuchumov and Anna Zelenova holding tray with traditional bread and salt at ceremony marking the official opening of first Pavlovsk rooms, 1957

life or existence in the midst of such an enchanted world seemed to me an impossible dream.

"We were led around and told, 'You see how the reptiles lived!' And we answered, 'How good it was that they were chased out.' But at the same time we had seditious thoughts of how good it would be to set up a museum of art on this estate — to preserve what was left and show it to people. I noticed that of the furniture only those things remained that could not be used in peasant life. Later I found in many houses tall mirrors, propped up on their sides because they were too tall to stand up in *izbi*. Sometimes gilded or mahogany objects also turned up in the *izbi*. The house was taken apart, moved to the Volga station, and reconstructed for worker housing. The artistically carved doors were used in a milk processing plant and the pictures all scattered; one sees some of them today in the Yaroslav Museum. There was a Murillo painting, *The Resurrection of the Madonna*, a copy of the Raphael Madonna. I did not know, of course, what they were then, but later, when I did know, I remembered. Once, I recognized the furniture. I had seen it in the old pre-Revolutionary journal *Capital and Countries*, which showed Andreyevskoe and the furniture with the embroidered upholstery given to the Princess on her birthday. Because of all this, my interest in the art of the past grew more and more — but all detached information, unorganized knowledge.

"In 1925 when I was thirteen, by some fortunate circumstance I was settled with Aunt Masha, the old guardian lady of the local Mologa Museum. Most of the time when I was not in school, I spent in the museum. The only director was an artist who had finished the Academy of Art with a silver medal — Vassily Vassilyevich Tsitsin. He became my first teacher. As the whole staff of the museum was comprised of this director and Aunt Masha, my assistance was extremely useful.

"From Vasily Vasilyevich I received a systematic education, pulling together the scattered bits and pieces I had gathered. He knew art splendidly, especially Russian art, and since during his period in the Academy he had traveled to many different cities and villages to do work from nature, he was especially interested in the architecture of old Russian cities. He had been in the militia, spending his time of service in the 421st Tsarkosel'sky Infantry Division, and he would often tell me of the storybook beauty of the parks and palaces of Tsarskoe Selo. Starting in the fifth and sixth grades, I began to go to museums. Tsitsin noticed my interest and picked me out from the rest of the children. He would tell me of many things, taught me what to respect, and would say, 'Here, read this book, and then that one.' I would sneak into the library and take things that interested me. By the eighth grade I already knew more than any of the teachers. Later we traveled together through the old estates near Mologa. We bought Saxon porcelain, paintings from former merchant houses. In the Mologa Museum there was a room done in the old Russian style. There we exhibited all that we were able to collect from old estates, merchants' homes, and half-destroyed churches. I hung and arranged things myself and was very proud. Although I was a schoolboy, I tried my best and what I did was almost always approved of by Vasily Vasilyevich.

"According to rural standards the museum was quite large, perhaps twelve rooms. Although there was a department of nature, I was more concerned with old paintings, sculpture, frescoed ceilings. And so even in this provincial town, while still at school, more and more I entered the world of the art of the past, which later became for me the beloved and only essential work.

"From Mologa every weekend, I would walk the twenty-six kilometers home, there to warm up, have a filling meal, help with the household chores. During one vacation, with a friend, we began to organize a museum. I used some curtains as a panel to hang over the door. We made a roof over the shed and began to collect exhibits. Someone found a carved chest, another some fabric, a carved grouse, a horse. But our museum endeavor ended badly. We were laughed at. Then one fellow locked us in this 'museum' and poured two buckets of water on the roof, drowning all of our exhibits. But my attraction to this occupation did not drown.

"And then, when I was nineteen, and my ten-year term at the school was behind me, I left my home town, the village on the river Latskaya, and Mologa as well. I wanted to go to Leningrad."

The year was 1931. In seventeen years, reflecting the changing political currents, the city had changed its name twice. By the time Anatoly Mikhailovich arrived, it was no longer the proud capital of Russia. Lenin in 1918 had "temporarily" moved the capital back to Moscow. In 1924, at the time of Lenin's death, the name of the city was once again changed — from Petrograd to Leningrad — the explanation of one official being that "We wanted to give him the best we had." Not only the city's name was changed, but the familiar old names of streets and squares, sweeping away history and memory.

Anatoly Mikhailovich arrived during the period of the brutal collectivization of the peasantry. In Leningrad, food supplies were short; there was rationing. "I could not allow myself to sit as a freeloader on the backs of my father and mother who lived there. I urgently had to find myself a job. At that time, it was not easy. There could be no thought or discussion of art. I went to the Labor Registry Office and there I was offered either the cooking school or the electrochemical FZU [*Fabrichno Zavodnoye Uchilishche*]. I finished FZU Factory Plant School and was appointed to the Okhtinsky Chemical Plant, where I worked as an electrochemical worker for exactly three months. Doctors freed me from this occupation because of my worsening vision. I had to put on glasses. But even at FZU, the dream of a museum did not leave me."

From the first moment he arrived, Anatoly Mikhailovich had been stunned by the beauty and majesty of the glorious city on the Neva, with its golden spires and sparkling blue river, its wide boulevards, green parks, and splendid buildings. "I loved Leningrad; I actively learned about its sights. And when I saw the Hermitage and the Russian Museum, I was infected with art, incurably and for all time. I made an important decisive step. While still at FZU, I applied and was accepted at the so-called Worker's Group of the Hermitage. For this opportunity, I am without question indebted to the Soviet government. These were night classes at the Hermitage, and every Sunday tours or lectures for young workers interested in art. Important and famous historians gave courses, Levinson-Lessing, Dzhevilegov, Tartakovskaya — many old experienced colleagues of the Hermitage. I did not limit myself to the meetings and seminars. I was interested in history and art history memoirs. And what is wonderful is that the library of the Hermitage organized an office and evening hours for us after work. One could sit there and calmly read and study until ten o'clock. I took full advantage of this — I studied a great deal by myself, but you know we learned more from all these old learned people than from books. For instance one of the old curators of the museum, Professor Vel'fold, was a great expert on furniture. I remember how as we walked through the Hermitage he would say, 'Well here, this thing is German and why? — because a German would do it this way and a Russian that way, although the journals say otherwise.' That is because in the journals of the old days many things were simply determined by the eye."

Anatoly Mikhailovich's fate was determined by an accident. Often on weekends he went out to the palaces in the country. One day he went to Tsarskoe Selo* and was taken through the museum by an old doorman of Tsarist days — this was in 1932. "There were many of them still there, for at the time of the

---

* In 1917 the name was changed to Detskoe Selo; in 1937 it was changed again to Pushkin because the great poet had attended the *lycée* adjoining the palace. A recent poll taken in Leningrad revealed that the majority of those questioned wished to have the name changed back to Tsarskoe Selo.

Revolution they were not chased out, but continued to work at the palace as servants. I went for a walk in the garden. It was spring, water was running in the ditches. I decided to go look at the personal garden of Nicholas II. I stepped on the ice, it cracked, and I fell into a ditch. My shoes were full of water. What to do? So I went to the Catherine Palace, knowing that in the entrance of the waiting room there was a fire where I could dry my feet. I asked for permission from an old lady, removed my shoes, and began drying my socks. And we struck up a conversation. I told her who I was, and said how much I envied those who worked in the palace. She, it turned out, was the former parlormaid of the Duchess Mecklenburg-Strel'nicheskaya and later her husband worked at the Chinese Theater of the palace. She told me how they were under arrest together with the family of Nicholas II. Since they were not permitted out of the park, they simply lived there. She said, 'This is how they hire us. Try.' But I was afraid. I was sent to the commandant of the palace. He was an imposing man with long whiskers, a handsome dark-eyed sailor, who had formerly been on the Tsar's yacht *Standart* — one Mikhail Martinovich Kalita. He took me through the halls to the director of the research department. I boldly told him, 'You need workers. Let me work here.' They needed knowledgeable people, he said, and asked me what I knew, interrogating me about the furniture and porcelain — who were its makers. I answered him, this is such and such a style, this is Louis. He set up a whole examination for me. He asked me to write a statement requesting employment as an inventory taker. I answered that I was afraid of working in the Catherine Palace, that I wanted to work in Pavlovsk. When he asked why, I answered that my aunt lived there, although I had none. I was just frightened of working with such authorities and then I had first seen Pavlovsk in 1930 and had fallen in love with it.

"I will never forget the date, April 5, 1932, when I was twenty years old, that was the day I became an inventory taker at Pavlovsk. From that day my whole life became tied to the palaces of Pushkin and Pavlovsk — which at this time was one museum union. I did a description of all the interiors, and all the furnishings. When I first began I was not allowed to touch anything for two weeks. I had two supervisors, women, one German and the other Russian, both artists. They taught me an approach to artistic things. They would make me lie on the floor to look at objects and furniture. They showed me how to move a sofa. Once, when I was working alone in the Tapestry Study, on a fireplace stood two pink Sèvres vases. I decided to adjust one of them but it fell off. Somehow I caught it, held it close to me, and slowly straightened up. It was such a lesson! If I had broken this vase I would have instantly been relieved of my duties.

"I think they say in such cases that I sort of recommended myself. For after four months I was listed on the staff as a scientific technical worker of the Pavlovsk palace museum. The director said, 'Anatoly Mikhailovich, you have a phenomenal memory. You remember what hung or stood there, what was in every hall of the palaces. Isn't that so?' It was true, for of course, if I saw something once I remembered it for the rest of my life. We even had a sort of game before the war: I would walk through a hall and look at the exhibits, then walk out the door. Someone would move something from its place. I would have to guess what was moved. Each thing in the museum had its place. I can say exactly how many things stood in any palace room. I know because in my youth I studied this — I really looked. With my eyes closed, I can tell the distance between things. But memory is memory; it helps me, but it is also important that all or almost all of the objects of art in the palaces of Pavlovsk and Pushkin passed through my hands. I held them, looked them over, registered them, described them."

In the early 1930s, Anatoly Mikhailovich also witnessed the doleful time, when despite all of Polovtsov's efforts and their own former decrees establishing the palace as a museum, the Soviet government threatened to close Pavlovsk. "There were many ideas at the time," he says. "They wanted to close the palace and make it into a rest home for architects and such things. In 1926 they closed the historic rooms in the Winter Palace, as well as the Yusupov, Sheremetyev, and Shuvalov palaces — all were museums. They gave away furniture to different organizations, paintings to the Hermitage. Much went to Moscow."* As the authorities began to sell many treasures, fearful museum workers tried to hide as many objects as they could. The precious Sèvres toilet set and the gilded Jacob bed of the State Bedchamber narrowly escaped being taken, but there were other terrible losses. Anatoly Mikhailovich remembers bursting into tears one morning when he arrived at the palace to find only bare walls where the Gobelins tapestries given to Paul and Maria Feodorovna by Louis XVI had once hung. They had been taken and sold. (Shortly after, when a visitor to the palace dared to

---

* In 1926 as there was already a People's House of Recreation in one wing of the palace and a technical school in the other, the question of closing the entire palace museum and turning it into a house of recreation arose again. A great battle in the press ensued. Reading the journals of the time, one can find a number of articles pro and con. However, the Architectural Society protested so vehemently that they were somehow able to overcome all opposition and prevent the threatened closing of the palace.

ask aloud what had happened to them, he was arrested and disappeared into the camps.)

The talents and industrious nature of Anatoly Mikhailovich were so remarkable that four months after he had begun working at Pavlovsk he was transferred to the Catherine Palace museum as an assistant to the head curator. At twenty, barely two years after he had left his little village, the keys to the palace storerooms and closets were given to him. "As curator I made the last rounds, checking that the exits were locked and everything was in place, sealing it with a thread and a wax seal and marking it with my own signet."

In 1934, age twenty-two, he was assigned as a curator to one of the departments, and within two years was named Head Curator of the Catherine Palace. In 1937, at twenty-five, he was named Director and Chief Curator of the Alexander Palace.

He met his wife at the Catherine Palace. Anna Mikhailovna was a student at the Art Institute, and in 1932 was sent to the palace to lead tours. Anna Mikhailovna was immediately attracted to the sturdy young man with light brown hair, strong practical hands, and bright blue eyes, which had such an inquiring intelligent glance. When he smiled, a dimple creased his cheek, and although his dark-rimmed glasses gave him a serious look, she found that he had a mischievous sense of fun. When he laughed, which was often, his mirth consumed him entirely. He was so energetic, so organized, and hardworking — and so knowledgeable. "It was very interesting to be with him," she says, "for he knew a great deal compared to me, although I had finished the Institute. And what was so remarkable, was that he could identify absolutely accurately by a single detail — the look of an elbow rest or a foot — the exact period, artist, and even what museums the object came from. When I finished the Institute a year later, they wanted to send me to the Russian Museum, but I asked to be sent to the Catherine Palace, and there I saw Anatoly Mikhailovich again." As for Anatoly, he found the petite blue-eyed blonde who shared his interest in art quite irresistible. They were married in 1935, although he remembers, "We were not wealthy enough to have a wedding."

Although his friends teased him, calling him "The last guardian of the last palace of the last Tsar," Anatoly Mikhailovich loved the Alexander Palace. For, he says, "It was the last residence of the Tsar and tied with the family's life under arrest. It was the first place where one could sense the aroma of the epoch, the character of the people. Imagine, you opened a table in the study of Alexander II and the documents and papers were inside. In the dressing table of Alexandra

Feodorovna there were even little boxes of medicine. In the bedroom of Nicholas II and Alexandra Feodorovna, there were various relics, icons, a *lampadka** with icon oil — rose oil. The scent of rose oil remained until the war. One had the impression that the people who had lived there had just gone into another room a minute ago. In the bedroom, for instance, one even felt uncomfortable to be alone. If my assistant left, I went into the next room — because there was a sense of the unseen presence of a person and this was disturbing.

"We would keep the palace open until midnight, all lit up with electricity. In one of the salons we would wind up the old gramophone with the records of Chaliapin and Vyal'tseva. The light would be warm, streaming from under the art deco glass lamps. You would sit on a soft couch and listen to Chaliapin. He performed more than once in the palace. He finished the Cadet Corps and was in the first performances before the Empress Alexandra in the Alexander Palace in the Corner Salon. We heard many stories about Chaliapin. Once the palace servants had to register, receiving small photographs for identification, which were certified by the palace commandant with a stamp. One had to show the card to be permitted in, and several actors of the Imperial Theater had to submit to the same thing. Chaliapin refused. 'I won't sing,' he said. Once he sang in the small salon in which we sat, and after the applause of the audience he bent down from his great height and whispered something in the Tsar's ear and clapped him on the shoulder. This was shocking, because one mustn't whisper in the presence of others, especially to the Emperor. It turned out that what Chaliapin said was, 'We, the *Kostromichi*, won't let anybody down.' That is, he was referring to the Romanovs' ancestry as coming, like himself, from Kostroma.

"Not long before the war, our palace was often open at night. In 1940 we organized an exhibit of costumes for the seventh of November. On our day off, we gathered all the mannequins from the shops in the city of Pushkin and made some ourselves, and took the ones from the palace and put costumes on them. We put them in the front hall, all in dress trains. Under the light of the chandeliers, these court costumes sewn with gold and silver were magnificent. It was like a fairytale. In the semicircular hall, we staged a formal palace reception — but as we were lacking enough mannequins, we took church candle stands, made abdomens out of pillows, and put on the costumes. This lasted for only two days, because after the holiday we had to return all the mannequins.

"We put a great effort into our restoration of the palace. I checked whether

---

* The *lampadka* was the traditional small oil lamp placed in front of icons to illuminate them.

everything stood in its place, I read old lists — where everything should be moved. We brought the palace to order. We had original extra material and re-upholstered furniture.

"The Soviet authorities, having overthrown the Tsar, did not chase everyone out who worked in the palaces. Those with titles left, but the little people, those who worked, they continued to work — and there were many such people. There were old butlers and lackeys who helped us a great deal. They were living annals. So not only the things themselves spoke, but people spoke of the past too. At Pavlovsk there were old women who had lived there in the time of Constantine Constantinovich. Kalita, at the Catherine Palace, had not only been on the *Standart** but until the First World War had been commandant of the doormen of the Catherine Palace. Until the Revolution he had been a commander of the children's half of the quarters of the daughters of Nicholas II and had worked as a butler in the Tsarevich's quarters.

The old lackey Dektayerev, who had a long beard, worked until 1940. We would laugh when he would say, 'I held the Princess in my arms when she would jump out of her carriage. She would have fallen, but I would catch her and put her on the ground.' I was led through the palace in 1936 by someone who had been a butler in Alexander II's time. He was eighty-seven years old and had entered into service at the palace at the age of fourteen. We walked through the halls with him and he would say, 'This chair should be placed like this' or moved there. And, 'I was sitting near this stove stoking the fire for Tsarina Maria Alexandrovna [wife of Alexander II]. We had to patch up the stove opening with clay, so that the coals would not fall out.' And of the dressing room of Alexander II when we asked what pictures hung there? he answered, 'There were these frivolous pictures — all sorts of nude women — the Tsar liked them a great deal.'

"Another caretaker of the rooms of Alexander II had been the maid of a certain countess. You see the way these rooms were used was very relevant and important for us. Here in the living room the sofa must stand so that a person might walk up to it without touching it and sit down. It must, therefore, be three-quarters of a length away from the table. She explained all this to us. 'I would have many things to do of course,' she would say. 'The duchess would come, sit down. I would bring the footrest, place a pillow behind her. Then she would sign something and I would have to wipe the quill pen. I had many duties.' It was from these people that we learned how things were used. There were many

---

* The *Standart* was the Russian Imperial yacht, built for Nicholas II. It was used both for official visits and for the relaxation of the Imperial family.

everyday things in the palace. They would actually rinse their teeth at the table. A special cup made of colored glass with water was brought. You would rinse your mouth, spit into a dish which would be left right there. The English, French, American way of life are completely different. We were able to learn about the style of life in Russia from these old people." *

These were the happiest years of his life. While he worked at the Alexander Palace, carefully studying and assembling his archives, Anna Mikhailovna worked at the adjoining Catherine Palace. A son, Felix, was born, and the young couple lived in a little house on the grounds of the Alexander Palace where the sailor Derevenko, protector of the hemophiliac Tsarevich Alexis, had once lived. His copper name plate was still on the door. On June 9, 1941, Anatoly Mikhailovich celebrated his twenty-ninth birthday. He had achieved his dream and was looking forward to continuing his work.

For those who live in the northern latitudes, Midsummer's Eve, June 22, is the most beautiful day of the year — a day for worshipping the sky and the light after a long dark winter. These are the white nights in Leningrad, when there is no darkness and the sky retains a glowing mother-of-pearl luminosity the whole night long, a time when no one sleeps — not even the birds.

Hesitantly, Leningrad had begun to breathe a little after the Stalin purges, which had begun in 1934 with the assassination of the independent Party chief, Sergei Kirov, and then spilled over the land during the 1930s. Stalin always mistrusted the glamorous former capital of Imperial Russia, Peter's Window on Europe, that so fruitfully mingled two cultures. It was after all, the cradle of the Revolution, and he was determined that no one was ever again going to rock the cradle. In 1926 and in 1930 there was a threat that the palaces of Leningrad would be closed permanently, to be put to use as rest homes and children's schools. In 1926 Pavlovsk was closed for a time, and during the following five years many of its treasures were sold by the Soviet government to collectors abroad, including those in the United States. But because of the determined opposition of the city, the palaces were not closed for good, and in 1941 the majority were preserved as museums. Despite the Revolution and Stalin, the beautiful parks and interiors had survived, and now, every inkwell in place, all were looked after with diligence and love. The people of St. Petersburg—

* In his memoirs Trotsky mentions the old Imperial lackeys who continued working in the Kremlin after the Revolution. In one anecdote, he relates the story of the flunkey Stupishin, who, while serving dinner to Lenin and Trotsky, went around the whole table carefully adjusting the plates so that the Imperial double-headed eagle would appear right-side-up to face each guest.

Petrograd–Leningrad, whatever the twists of their fate, tenaciously maintained their independence of spirit and their pride in their magnificent city where, a poet wrote, "Even in anguish one can live."

And on that June day in 1941 how beautiful it was! The Neva sparkled in the sun. Sea gulls cut white crescents against the blue sky. Overflowing riverboats took people to the beach at Peterhof. There they picnicked, rode in painted boats, and strolled among the sparkling fountains cascading to the sea. The smell of lilacs from the thick bushes on the Mars Field wafted through the city. Touched by the glow of the midnight sun, the golden spires of the Admiralty and the Peter and Paul Church gleamed. Summer at last after the long dark winter! Schools were closing, and during the long twilight of the white nights, to the accompaniment of accordion and guitar, students sang along the embankments of the river, and at 2 A.M. stood to watch the great nightly spectacle of the bridges of the city slowly opening to permit the stately procession of ships to sail out into the sea. At Pavlovsk the thousands of white birches, which the Russians love and believe are inhabited by the souls of their ancestors, had only a few weeks before burst into leaf. Summer! A time for rest and relaxation, a time for love, all the more precious because in the north this time of light is so brief.

In his journal Anatoly Mikhailovich in nearby Pushkin described this idyllic day:

Sunday, June 22, 1941. Summer was just coming into its own. The fresh green foliage of the old parks, gardens, and squares, which encircled the town and its remarkable palaces, perfumed the air. From early morning orchestras were playing — bold and happy songs — full of energy and joy. Through the streets streamed a variegated crowd. There was the old silver-haired professor who was a constant museum visitor, workers in bright kerchiefs, and so many students, newly released from classes and come from all parts of the country. In one flow, the holiday crowd moved toward the palaces. There, old men rested on the lawns, young people danced to the music of the *bayan.** Others played volleyball, and in a constant stream, crowds flocked into the museums to see the work of those artists of genius — Rastrelli, Cameron, Quarenghi. One group after another, flowing as if on a conveyor belt through Rastrelli's gilded *enfilades*. It would go on like this until evening.

In the afternoon they headed for the Alexander Palace where we, as usual, were waiting for them. Morning at the Alexander Palace was always quiet. For us, the big crush came in the afternoon. The guides waiting for groups

---

* A *bayan* is a traditional Russian folk instrument akin to the concertina.

were sitting with the museum staff and carrying on their usual endless shop talk. Each museum worker had put their own rooms in especially fine order. As it was a holiday weekend, many of them had removed the covers from their furniture to better show off the palatial rooms in all their splendor. From the square, we could hear the sounds of the band music. It was nearly noon. The first groups had just arrived to be greeted one by one by their assigned guides.

Everything was just as it always had been when suddenly Klava, the supervisor, rushed into my study with the breathless news that Molotov was to go on the air with an emergency announcement. I ran through the room to the palace colonnade where there was a loudspeaker. A large crowd was already gathered listening to Molotov's voice, gruff and full of emotion uttering simple, terrible words: "Today at four o'clock in the morning, without presenting any claims to the Soviet government and without any declaration of war, German troops attacked our country, attacked our borders at many points and bombed our cities. . . ." His message finished with the words, "Our duty is right. The enemy will be vanquished. Victory will be ours."

Everyone stood motionless. Smiles disappeared. War. New trials. New disasters. The whole happy new life of summer vanished and in its place there was only trouble and the premonition of terrible grief. In a half hour everything changed. The crowd of people at the gates burst into tears. The sounds of music disappeared. The park emptied. I passed through the halls of the palace. Several groups were still there, but I could see by their worried faces that they had lost all interest, that their thoughts were working in another direction, and that they were looking only from a sense of obligation.

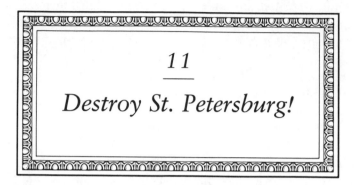

11

Destroy St. Petersburg!

ON THAT JUNE DAY, the dimensions of the disaster to come were still unknown to them. Massed on the northern borders in East Prussia preparing to drive for Leningrad were half a million Nazi troops. There had been no warning, no suggestion that the country was on the brink of war. The Soviet government had repeatedly assured Leningrad and the rest of the Soviet Union that the Nazi-Soviet Pact signed on the eve of the war in 1939 would guarantee the country against attack. Over and over at Party meetings, Party propagandists had stressed that under the treaty each nation was solemnly pledged not to carry out aggression against the other.

Yet as the news of war in Europe grew grimmer, and, closer, people in Leningrad worried. Rumors proliferated, but to suggest anything other than the official view was considered close to treason. After all, it was pointed out, Andrei Zhdanov, chief of the Leningrad City and Regional Party, had left as usual for his summer vacation on the Black Sea; surely this was a reassuring sign.

In fact, Hitler had decided on the date of his attack on Russia more than two months earlier. Operation Barbarossa, which consisted of three army groups, was commanded by Colonel General Franz Halder. Aimed like a dagger at the heart of Leningrad was Army Group Nord commanded by sixty-five-year-old Field Marshal Wilhelm Ritter von Leeb — Bavarian aristocrat, professional soldier, seasoned veteran of many campaigns. Under him were two armies: the Sixteenth, commanded by General Ernst Bush, and the Eighteenth, commanded by General Georg von Küchler. These included the Fourth Armored Group, the First Air

Fleet, and the Fourth Panzer Group. They were to be followed by the Totenkopf S.S. Death's Head Division, formed predominantly of former concentration camp guards, with the sinister skull and crossbones emblazoned on their black uniforms and all their equipment, including motorcycle sidecars. It was a formidable military force, which included twenty-nine divisions, three armored and three motorized, equipped with twelve thousand heavy weapons, fifteen hundred tanks, and over one thousand planes.*

Hitler had given one implacable order: "Destroy St. Petersburg!" He hated the city, which he saw as the despised cradle of Bolshevism. He considered the Baltic a Teutonic lake and himself the leader of a great crusade, which would recapture that sea once controlled in medieval times by the Teutonic Knights from their fortress strongholds along the Baltic and in Malbork in East Prussia. Because of Hitler's obsession, Operation Barbarossa specifically provided that Moscow be attacked only after Leningrad was annihilated. According to Nazi plan, von Leeb was to capture the city within four weeks — by July 21.

Such was the unexpected lightning force of the attack that within the first twenty-four hours, 85 percent of Soviet planes were destroyed on the ground. This meant that Soviet troops, who were badly armed and positioned, fought without air cover. They had old model tanks, three-quarters of which needed repair. Fortifications had not been prepared. Stalin's relentless purges of 1937/38 had decimated and dangerously weakened the Soviet army. Every commander of an army corps had been shot, along with every division commander. One-third to one-half of all Soviet military officers, some seventy-five thousand, had been arrested; in the high ranks the percentage was even greater. In the army that was left, only 7 percent of the officers had had advanced military education — 37 percent had never had a course in a military institution. The army was completely demoralized, and discipline had not been restored.

With a rapidity that astonished even their commanding officers, the Nazi forces moved across the land smashing, destroying, certain that Russia would fall apart in three weeks.

At the palaces no one could guess how much time they might have to save the treasures. Stalin had ignored all early intelligence of the forthcoming Nazi attack. No advance precautions had been taken. Speed was essential but the task was

---

* There are discrepancies among German, Soviet, and other sources regarding the exact size and composition of the Nazi forces that attacked on June 22, 1941. As Harrison Salisbury notes in *The 900 Days*, some Soviet sources estimate that forty-two or forty-three divisions with some 725,000 men, 500 tanks, 12,000 weapons, and 1200 planes comprised the initial attacking force. Other Soviet sources vary — some say twenty-nine divisions, including three tank and three motorized divisions. German sources cite twenty-eight divisions.

staggering. In Pavlovsk alone, there were 22,500 objects of value, not counting the Rossi Library of more than twenty thousand books and rare collections; in the Catherine and Alexander Palaces some sixty to seventy thousand; at Peterhof, Orienbaum, Gatchina thousands upon thousands more — in the Hermitage more than two and a half million. In all the threatened museums and palaces of Russia curators and employees rushed to save everything they could.

At the Alexander Palace, with the museum still open and the last tours finishing, Anatoly Mikhailovich and his colleagues started working immediately. Closing the door of the Corner Salon, where only a short time ago they had happily listened to Chaliapin, they began to pack crates under the famous portrait of Empress Alexandra by Paulbach.

The next morning, a meeting was held on the square in front of the Catherine Palace. In quiet even tones, Vladimir Ladukhin, the director of both palaces, informed the assembled group of museum curators and workers that they were to execute a previously conceived "Mobilization Plan." Artworks and treasures of the palaces and museums of Leningrad were to be evacuated into the interior of the country to a secret destination. Kuchumov was appointed to direct and carry out the first echelon of the evacuation of the palaces of Pushkin and Pavlovsk. This first echelon was to be followed by others as quickly as they could be readied. Afterward, Ladukhin took Kuchumov to his office, opened a safe, and handed him notes on the museum objects judged to be of greatest value and to be evacuated first in case of war — instructions that had been drawn up in 1936 by a special commission, which included two of the most prominent art experts of the Hermitage Museum.

On the first floor of the Catherine Palace seals were removed from an emergency reserve room in which were stored a quantity of boxes and packing cases. Exhibits were removed from the halls and carried in relays down to this room.

Packed was the collection in the fabled Amber Room of the Catherine Palace, where caskets, boxes, chessmen, chairs, and tables were all made of amber.* Fragile amber caskets and chests were disassembled for easier transport, but over two centuries the famous eighteenth-century panels of amber that overlaid the walls had become brittle; the sheets began to crumble and proved impossible to

---

* Even the walls of this magnificent room were completely overlaid with panels of honey-colored light amber. Peter the Great first saw these panels in the palace of Mon Bijou in Berlin when he passed through in 1717 on his way to Paris. The story is that he persuaded Frederick William of Prussia to part with them in exchange for a number of recruits, all over six feet tall, for Frederick's Corps of Grenadiers. The panels lay unused until 1750, when Rastrelli found them. An Italian master amber specialist labored with Russian assistants for five years to repair the panels, and Rastrelli had them fitted into the Amber Room.

remove, so they finally had to be left in place. At Pavlovsk, the priceless Sèvres toilet service given to Maria Feodorovna and Paul during their trip to Paris in 1780 was judged to be the single most valuable exhibit in the palace. At the Alexander Palace, it was the Gobelins tapestry portrait of Marie Antoinette, given as a present by the President of France to Empress Alexandra. "It hung above her writing table," says Kuchumov — "it was the first thing we packed and it took up half the crate."

For some inexplicable reason the original list contained only some two hundred items; in the palaces there were thousands. "The most valuable things we were able to pack away very quickly," says Kuchumov. "Only after putting away these things could we see if anything else would fit." When he saw that indeed they would, Kuchumov called the director to ask permission to pack more. "The director simply said, 'Anything you consider valuable, put away.' " For Kuchumov, of course, that meant everything. "In that first group of crates we were able to pack eight hundred articles instead of the proposed eight."

Fearing air raids, within ninety-six hours after the announcement of war, Kuchumov took the first group of crates by horse-drawn cart away from the palaces. So as not to draw attention to the contents, the crates were simply marked *"Pushkin Museum: This Side Up"* and covered with tarpaulins. He pretended to head for the station, but in reality turned back into the park and made his way to the Arsenal Museum of Weapons of Nicholas I, where, under the stern watchful glance of a member of the NKVD* who stood at the doorway, the crates were stored and sealed in the deep dark cellars of the building to wait for the moment when freight cars could be found. All those in the operation were sworn to secrecy.

"We had not nearly enough packing material," remembers Anatoly Mikhailovich, "so we mowed grass and packed the things in fresh hay — but hay is always susceptible to rot, and mold threatens objects made of wood. Therefore we would first check the composition of objects and use wood shavings when we could, or paper scraps. I ran through the rooms, removing things from cabinets and shelves and putting them on the floor. I asked the assistants and tour guides to take everything I designated and pack it away. Soon there were no

---

* The NKVD (*Narodnyi Kommisariat Vnutrennikh Del* or People's Commissariat of Internal Affairs) was the precursor to the modern day KGB (*Komitet Gosudarstvennoi Bezopasnosti* or Committee for State Security.) At the time the war broke out, members of the NKVD served as secret police, border guards, foreign agents, and concentration-camp guards. In 1943 the NKVD was divided into two directorates — NKGB, which assumed the secret police functions, and NKVD, which retained all others. In 1946 these departments were again renamed — MVD and MGB, the Ministries of Internal Affairs and State Security, respectively.

more crates. In the storerooms we found the Tsar's trunks with clothing and uniforms — among them two trunks taken to Tobolsk* by Empress Alexandra and then returned to the palace. We used these trunks for the porcelain and crystal. But when all the available packing materials had been used up we still needed to pack away the crystal lanterns, which now hang in the Egyptian vestibule at Pavlovsk. We decided to pack them in the clothing of the Empress Alexandra Feodorovna. We would put a dress on a large sheet of paper, roll it up, and use these packets to put around the lanterns. Thanks to this the dresses of the Empress were saved — otherwise they surely would have been lost." For other items they used dress uniforms of Nicholas II. However, when the time came to transport the trunks it was noticed that the Tsar's double-eagle crest and the Imperial Crown were emblazoned on all the trunks and canvas covers, clearly identifying that inside were tsarist treasures. Attempts were made to cover the crests with black paint — to no avail; the crests continued to shine out. Finally the palace carpenter brought oilcloth and quickly glued canvas over the crests on which was simply written *"Pushkin Museum."*

During one of those frantic days and nights of evacuation in the palace there was a strange apparition. As Anatoly Mikhailovich relates it: "During the packing there was always a night watch. Inside one had to make the rounds without light, although during those late June days the nights are light, which provided some illumination. One could tell where one room began and another ended by counting the steps. I could easily get around that way. The halls were dark, only here and there we had small lamps burning. I went through the first hall, then the second. Suddenly I saw coming toward me silhouetted against the light background of a doorway the dark figure of a woman, tall, dressed all in black. As I would have been caught in the doorway with her I stepped aside, off the carpet and onto the parquet to let her pass. I said, 'How are things?' But the figure was silent. As I stepped aside, the figure disappeared. I couldn't go farther. I turned back. When I was asked why I didn't finish the rounds I said, 'Let's wait a little.' Then I asked a comrade to accompany me." To this day, he believes that the apparition he saw was the ghost of the last Empress.

On June 30, eight days after the declaration of war, freight cars were finally secured. The crates were brought out of the cellars of the Arsenal and transferred

---

*These trunks had originally been packed by the Empress while the royal family was being held at Tsarskoe Selo in August 1917. Told that they were being moved for their own safety, they were instructed to pack as many warm clothes as possible, then were secretly transported to Tobolsk in Siberia. Somehow some of the trunks found their way back to Leningrad after the family was murdered in July 1918.

by a convoy of drivers and loaders to the freight station. Anatoly Mikhailovich bade farewell to the director and his co-workers, leaving behind all kinds of instructions for packing everything that was left.

At midnight Anatoly Mikhailovich went through the palace that had become his home for the last time. His footsteps echoed in the empty halls. Covers removed from objects that had been sent off still lay on the floor. On the marble walls, bereft of paintings and portraits, empty frames hung forlorn. On the floor, vases and candelabras, bronze clocks, and furniture had been massed together for protection and future packing. Over all this upheaval, the luminous white nights shed an unreal, eerie light. In the libraries, in mahogany cabinets of Pushkin's time, were nearly eighteen thousand books, albums, and collections. As he took this last look, he managed to pick out unique works such as an original fifteenth-century edition of Olearius's *Travels through Muscovy,* as well as a collection of engravings that had belonged to Prince Potemkin. At the last moment he remembered a valuable collection of drawings of all the Russian cities from Petersburg to Astrakhan and all kinds of Volga boats and barges, 150 sheets in all, kept in a massive album bound in silver. He thought a moment, removed the sheets from the ornate album, which he knew would attract attention, and hid them in a simple, shabby box that lay open on the floor, hoping that in this way they would survive.

Anatoly Mikhailovich walked out into the courtyard and for one last time gazed on the beautifully proportioned eighteenth-century colonnades of Quarenghi, trying to implant them forever in his memory. In the courtyard, his father was waiting to say goodbye. As there was a curfew in Pushkin, and it was necessary to have a special pass to move about in the town, his father was not permitted to leave the park. At the gates of the palace, father and son parted, not knowing if they would ever meet again.

Anatoly Mikhailovich walked alone along totally deserted streets toward the railroad station where the freight cars stood waiting. "It was five A.M. The morning was marvelous, the air so fresh. Birds sang. The rays of the sun gilded the cupolas of the Feodorovsky Church. I did not know if I would ever return or if I did, what I would see there. With me I took only my briefcase and my shaving kit."

In Pavlovsk's history women have always played a key role. Inspired and created under the direction of a woman, in the desperate days of the twentieth century another woman was to save it. For both, Pavlovsk was the work of their lives.

The paths of Anna Ivanovna Zelenova and Anatoly Mikhailovich Kuchumov ran close in their early lives, sometimes nearly touching, but never intertwining until the war. Like Anatoly Mikhailovich, Anna seems to have been called to her vocation, destined to accomplish the work that she was to do so faithfully and brilliantly. She was born a little less than a year after Anatoly Mikhailovich, on February 29. All her life she delighted in that leap year date, which made it possible for her to skip birthdays, a very feminine weakness. She grew up in an apartment across the street from the Europe Hotel, where Anatoly Mikhailovich's father worked repairing furniture, next door to St. Petersburg's famous Philharmonic Hall, and only a few steps away from the Mikhailovsky Square. This green and shady square with its statue of Pushkin directly in front of the grand yellow and white former palace of Grand Duke Michael,* brother of Alexander I and youngest son of Maria Feodorovna, is one of the most enchanting squares of Petersburg. Anna loved this place, absorbing its beauty from her earliest childhood. Close by was the bustling life of the Nevsky Prospect — the Fifth Avenue of St. Petersburg — but in the square there was always something mysterious and silent. "It reminded me of a theater, before the beginning of a performance," remembers Anna Ivanovna. "The low houses around the square seemed empty, as if a curtain had just gone up and a play were about to begin. The cozy, shady square was the foreground — behind it the great white columns of the yellow Michael Palace." At first she saw it sitting on her father's shoulders, then holding his hand, then as she ran alone along the paths.

Both her mother and father were orphans of humble background who had met when Anna's mother worked as an assistant in a Petersburg corset shop. There she had once made a corset for the famous ballerina Kschessinskaya, briefly the mistress of the future Nicholas II. Her father was a sailor at the Kronstadt naval base. Anna was their cherished only child, but perhaps in memory of their own lonely childhoods, all their lives her parents welcomed orphan children into their household. Anna shared with Maria Feodorovna an abiding love for children, although, unlike the Empress, she never married or had any of her own. To her death she was to have only one abiding love — Pavlovsk — to which she gave forty-nine years of her life.

She was born in the most turbulent years of her city and lived through her city's most harrowing ordeal and brilliant triumph. A few years before her birth, Bloody Sunday had taken place in the Palace Square not far from her home. As

---

* The former palace of Grand Duke Michael is now the Russian Museum.

she grew up, revolutionary ideas filled the air. The year of her birth was a year of splendid ceremonies and parades commemorating the three hundredth year of the Romanov dynasty, celebrated with all the pomp and ceremony of Europe's most magnificent court. When she was one, Russia entered the First World War, which was to topple the ancient monarchy and change the course of history for her country. That year Nicholas II changed the name of St. Petersburg to Petrograd and by the time she was eleven, it had become Leningrad. Yet despite all the changes of the city's name she, as most of its inhabitants, with the fidelity to the past that is one of their most endearing characteristics, continued to call it affectionately "Piter" — as indeed they still do.

After he had finished his naval service, her father became a metalworker and locksmith. It was said of him that he had "golden hands" that could open anything. When the Revolution came he was called on by the bank next door to crack safes to get at the deposits of those who had fled or were now deemed enemies of the people. Anna's father was also considered a great furnace specialist. In those days, as each building in the city was still heated separately,* her father was often called to the Philharmonic Hall, to the Maly Theater, to the Russian Museum, all on her beloved square, which despite all the turmoil had retained its distinctive serenity and beauty. With him, Anna would enter the elegant theater entrances. Then he would go down to the boiler room and she would go upstairs to hide behind the cool marble columns to watch and listen. Sometimes it was a marvelous actress, sometimes a ballet, sometimes a violin quartet, or the symphony. All this, she later said, "educated her soul." She grew up in an atmosphere of beauty and learned to cherish it. Anna always believed that her childhood passed in Mikhailovsky Square and her later connection with Pavlovsk were inseparable.

When it was time to go to school, her father sent her around the corner, down the Nevsky toward the Admiralty, to the closest school to their apartment. At this school, called Peter Schule, founded at the time of Peter the Great and one of the oldest in Petersburg, all classes were taught in German.

The Russians say, "When you know a language, you can get into the soul of a people." Anna's Germanic schooling was to prove invaluable for her and her country. By the time she was through her classes, Anna could compose verses in both German and Russian and spoke German fluently. The school inspired in her a lifelong love of study — not only what was required, but also an enduring

---

* All of Leningrad's heating is now centrally controlled. In the early years after the Revolution, however, buildings produced and controlled their own heat by means of individual furnaces.

taste for independent investigation, which for her was always essential. Efficient Germanic habits of method and organization were instilled in her, which were to prove to be of the greatest advantage for the work she was called upon to do. At the end of the seventh grade, another school was added to Peter Schule; her father sent her to a drafting school, saying in the manner of those whose life has not been easy: "It's time for you to learn a trade. There are too many of you educated ones in the work force."

She might have become a good engineer, but like Maria Feodorovna before her she had weak eyes, which meant that she always had to wear heavy glasses. Nevertheless, she easily finished three years of a machine-building institute, where she received a prize as the best draftsman of the construction department. But while she was still in her teens, she had an accident. "It happened after a fall from a scaffolding," she said. "I was then working as a building measurements technician. Afterward I walked with a cane. I suffered for many years from tuberculosis of the bones." Still, the thought of becoming a museum worker never crossed her mind until one day, when the young students were called on to make a model of a six-sided pinion, she had a revelation. "Although I was able to do it easily, it suddenly struck me — this doesn't interest me at all!" She decided to enroll as an auditor in a special course for the Excursion Translation Department, which prepared those with a knowledge of foreign languages to be guides for the Society of Proletarian Tourism.* She began to lead tours — to the Hermitage, to the Russian Museum. She developed thematic tours — "The Antique," "Holland," "France" — but, she remembers, "When I saw Pavlovsk . . . it immediately showed me how little I knew." She fell in love with the palace, which was to become the passion of her life. For her it was a temple of art, the most beautiful place in the world. She was, in the best sense of the word, obsessed by it. When pressed to explain her love, she would answer, "Pavlovsk speaks to all moods of all people of all ages. It was a remarkable time. Derzhavin was still alive, Pushkin had already arrived. And in the Little Lantern Room of Maria Feodorovna there reigned such an airiness, such a remarkable lightness. Everything sang, chimed. It is true that architecture is crystallized music." Two years after she had enrolled in the evening courses, she was able to enter the university. She then studied for another year in the literary department of the Herzen Ped-

---

* The Society of Proletarian Tourism was founded in 1929, the same year as Intourist. The society promoted and organized tourism within the USSR for Soviet citizens, whereas Intourist handled tourism for foreigners within the Soviet Union, as well as travel abroad by Russians. In 1936, the society was replaced by the Tourist Excursion Administration.

agogical Institute, which is still a prestigious school for advancement in the Soviet Union today.

In 1930, when Anatoly Mikhailovich had just come to seek his fortune in Leningrad, Anna Ivanovna was a technical draftsman at the Special Institute for Metalworkers. When at twenty, he began to work as an inventory taker at Pavlovsk, nineteen-year-old Anna led her first tours to Pavlovsk and there they met for the first time. When he went to the Catherine Palace in 1931, she became an official Pavlovsk guide, and from 1936 to 1940 she worked there exclusively, first as a guide, then as a Research Fellow and Deputy Director of the Scientific Section. She learned to know Pavlovsk in winter and summer, spring and fall. She was happy in that enchanted park where Pushkin had strolled, Glinka had listened to the murmur of the oaks, and Dostoevsky had sought seclusion and peace.

The photographs of her youth show a slender, thoughtful, serious young woman, with a romantic old-fashioned air. Behind her bookish dark-rimmed glasses there is a dreaming glance. But this is deceptive, for Anna was a decisive person with a quick mind and tongue. As many people were to discover, it was hard to best her in any argument. She chain-smoked and loved to dance the Charleston.

She wrote profusely. All her life she kept detailed journals, wrote poetry and plays, and was an inexhaustible correspondent; when parted from close friends, she sometimes wrote three times a day. She especially loved corresponding with children, with whom she kept contact their whole lives.

But like the leafy garden that was the foreground of the square and the stage set of her imagination, her early life was only the prologue to the true drama of her life, which began on June 22, 1941, when she was twenty-eight years old.

In 1940, Anna had been called to work as the administrative secretary of the Museum of the City of Leningrad. It was there that she heard the fateful noon announcement. In those first days of the war, the city was plunged into turmoil and confusion. Men rushed to mobilize; women and young people began building barricades and digging trenches. On July 6, a few days after the first convoy of palace valuables had left, Anna received a call from the Directorate of Evacuation asking her to go immediately to help supervise the continuing evacuation of Pavlovsk. She left the museum, and without stopping off at home, went straight to the Vitebsk Station to take the train to Pavlovsk, assuming that she would be returning that evening. She did not return for more than two months.

The first list of valuables in the evacuation list — thirty-four crates — had already gone with Kuchumov. As at the Catherine and the Alexander Palaces, there had been in this list unique works of art, but a relatively small number.

The responsibility for the evacuation had fallen on the shoulders of the director, Ivan Mikryukov. He had conscientiously prepared tarred crates, boxes, and the packing material necessary to send delicate museum valuables on their long journey to the interior. He had successfully made arrangements for vehicles to carry the heavy crates to the Pushkin railroad stations. But he desperately needed the help and knowledge of museum objects that Anna could provide.

As soon as she arrived, she saw that there would be no going back, that she would have to work without stopping. Most of the men had been called to the front immediately, leaving the packing to women and a few older men. When Anna appeared, looking for museum workers, she found them in the library with their heads and shoulders peeping up among huge wooden crates that were meant to hold books. Anna discovered that these books were not from the library at all — those were stacked about in various corners of the first floor. Instead, what was being packed were court journals accumulated over many years by the proprietors of the palace, which simply recorded an endless stream of names of visitors and did not constitute a bibliographic rarity.

All her life Anna was an extraordinarily well-organized person who planned each day and kept meticulous lists. Now she immediately took charge. "I gave instructions to unload the journals from the crates and place them in smaller boxes. I called a meeting of all museum workers to determine what had already been prepared for evacuation, make lists of what had not yet been entered on the original evacuation list. Before my arrival, all objects from the main halls had been gathered on the ground floors, which seemed safer from air raids.

"It seemed such a short time ago that our relationship with Pavlovsk was so carefree, so idyllic," she writes, "and now we were deciding what to save. It was impossible to carry away everything." Yet she was determined to try, and imposed a systematic organization. "We made preparations to protect the palace from air raids, trying to preserve the palace walls, the sculptures in the park, from bomb shrapnel and shock waves. On all the windows we attached thick shields made of boards, this work done by the remaining old carpenters who hung huge hammocks in front of the palace and thus nailed in the wooden shields." Sand was spread on the floors to protect against shrapnel and to absorb the shock of bombing attacks.

By mid-July, the Nazis were threatening Leningrad. They had taken Pskov, 276 kilometers away, Novgorod, 204 kilometers, Luga, 139 kilometers, and

Kingisepp, 137 kilometers distant. "As the days passed and the Nazis moved closer and closer to Leningrad, it was necessary to expand and expedite the task of evacuation. Every object in Pavlovsk was unique. The extreme haste meant that we had to work both night and day. We were desperate to send as many things as possible away from the bombardments and shooting."

Anna Ivanovna supervised all this frantic activity from a work table set up in the mirrored Egyptian vestibule, with the twelve-foot-high black Egyptian statues representing the twelve months of the year looking on like frozen guardians. She made her lists, checking each crate that was prepared for evacuation. "They were brought in through every door," she writes, "and the statues, reflected in the mirrors, seemed either to advance on me or retreat, to the point where I became dizzy. The bombardments and shooting were almost constant. Once, two pieces of shrapnel fell right onto my desk. I saved them." On another occasion during an air assault, Anna threw herself bodily on a crate of porcelain to protect it.

"These were days and nights of unbelievable haste. Air assaults became more frequent. The windows of the palace were boarded shut. There was no electricity. Work was done by candlelight, then we burned rope and twisted paper." Although the pressure of the time was intense, nevertheless great caution had to be exercised in packing all these delicate objects. Two palace curators, Weiss and Bazhenova, took time to draw diagrams of how the bronze rims and crystal garlands on the chandeliers were positioned before they were carefully taken apart and packed; the crystal in cotton, the bronze in hay. Porcelain vases had to be dismounted from their bases, along with the interior metal bolts connecting the main portion of the vases with neck and base. Eighteenth-century furniture had to be artfully dismantled, table tops removed from consoles. Pavlovsk contained one of the finest collections of eighteenth- and nineteenth-century clocks in the world. During the evacuation each had to be taken apart, diagrams made, and mechanisms packed separately from the body.

When crates were used up, they took apart fences; when packing material was exhausted, they went into the fields and cut hay. The entire work force consisted of some thirty people — several women curators, and a small brigade of women whom the City Council of Pavlovsk had sent to help. "Women lifted the heavy crates, loaded them onto trucks. The most valuable collections of the palace — paintings, chandeliers, crystal, porcelain, vases of jasper and rhodonite, rare furniture, works in ivory and amber — were prepared and sent off into the interior of the country."

From each set of furniture several examples were taken. The rest had to be left behind. "But the palace sculpture," she continues, "the extraordinary collection of original Roman and Greek antiquities, second only to that of the Hermitage — this was an especially difficult problem. Heavy, frail, priceless, these statues stood in the emptied halls, so beautiful it was frightening to touch them. We decided that it would not be safe to send them on the long journey. But we could not leave them in the halls. We thought of the heavy vaulted palace cellars."

Women removed the statues from their pedestals and dragged them on carpets, then down wooden planking laid on the stairs, deep into one of the secluded corners of the cellars. There they were placed together as tightly as possible. To the statues of the palace gallery were added all the muses from the Rossi Library. The compartment was sealed off with brick. But the wall still looked treacherously fresh. Cunningly, they washed it over with water and then bombarded it with sand and dirt. The compartment became unnoticeable.

By the third week of August, in less than sixty days, thirty people had succeeded in packing off and evacuating thirteen thousand objects plus all the documentation of the palace, which proved invaluable after the war. As the weeks sped by the second echelon of forty-two crates had gone off to Gorky, the third, of sixty-three crates, to Sarapul. The last echelon ("Crates loaded illegally three crates high," wrote Zelenova), containing 3,168 objects, left on August 20, 1941 — this time toward Leningrad, as it was no longer possible to leave for the interior. Among these last evacuated objects were the unique chandelier from the Italian Hall, a table of Paul I's with ivory legs, and the Strizhkov vases of jasper from the Greek Hall. Anna had already signed the accompanying documents when she decided to take one more look in the Rossi Library. She quickly ran by show cases and glassed tables; throwing open the doors of bookshelves in the last cabinet, she noticed folders. She opened one and found some original drawings by Rossi for his work at the palace. Opening the next and the next, she found other original architectural drawings of Cameron, Quarenghi, and Voronykhin. Although most had been evacuated earlier, somehow these precious drawings had been left behind. In her reminiscences she wrote, "For such folders a standard crate would not do. The carpenters fortunately had not left. I gave them the measurements. There were no more boards." She ordered them to break a chest where all the sofa cushions had been packed. "While they were making the crate I committed what was for me a blasphemy." She had constantly worried over the unique Voronykhin furniture made especially for the palace in the first years of the nineteenth century, which had coverings of the finest French tapestry.

According to Anna's account, "They had not been removed and now it was apparent that it was impossible to take away the furniture. But the coverings! Every piece was attached to the seat with hundreds of small gilt rosette upholstery nails." She boldly grabbed a knife and began to cut the tapestry coverings away, trying to keep the slashes close to the nails. They packed the folders in the new crate, laying the valuable Gobelins between them. She did not know it then, but this was to be the last convoy. The next evening, August 21, Anna received a phone call from Leningrad. "I could hear only very poorly but I understood that the call was from the Directorate of Palaces and Parks of Leningrad. I was told that as the director of Pavlovsk would soon be leaving for the front, I was appointed director and had to take all measures to hasten the evacuation. Then the connection was broken. I could not protest. There was no one to protest to. The thought did not occur, why had this choice fallen on me? In those days we did not judge or deliberate. I suddenly felt older. Such an immeasurable responsibility." A few days later, on August 30, the Mga station, the last rail link from Leningrad to Moscow, was broken. Leningrad was cut off, and German long-range artillery was already battering the city.

From mid-August on, a stream of refugees had been pouring into Pushkin and Pavlovsk — refugees from Pskov, from the Baltic, from Velikiye Lugi, and Gatchina only about twenty kilometers away. More than two thousand people, sick and invalid, elderly, women and children, huddled in the cellars of the palace.

In his memoirs, *From the Neva to the Elbe,* Lieutenant General Semyon Nikolaievich Borshchev, then a major just out of the Frunze Military Academy, writes of those days of fierce fighting at the end of August 1941. During the fall of 1941 Borshchev served on the Leningrad front as the operations officer for the 168th Rifle Division, which fought in Pushkin and Pavlovsk. On August 27, the staff officers made a reconnaissance tour of the Leningrad-Moscow highway. They found the road from Pushkin and Pavlovsk engorged with refugees fleeing the advancing Nazi armies. He writes, "Old men, women, mothers and children, dragging small carts with their household belongings shuffled along, despairingly staring at the ground." Nazi planes periodically strafed and bombed the fleeing refugees; the road was littered with the corpses of women and children. Citizens of Leningrad, women and students, were digging trenches. One of the women explained to Borshchev that they were doing the same work around Kingisepp, Luga, and Gatchina. Shaking her fist at the sky the woman exclaimed, "Those vermin are bombing us from morning until night!"

By August, the Nazi advance had been slowed by fierce Russian resistance. At first the invaders progressed at a rate of five kilometers a day. This had been slowed to only 2.2 kilometers. "But," wrote Borshchev, "none of us was calmed by the fact that in August the Nazis were moving slower than in July. Now enemy clouds were billowing over Leningrad." On August 28, the Germans were shelling the southern and southeastern suburbs of Leningrad from Tosno, less than thirty kilometers away. By August 29, in a pincer movement, the Germans were attacking Pavlovsk on two sides, along the road to Pavlovsk and Pushkin and the road to Krasny Bor, Yam-Izhora, and Kolpino. Germans taken prisoner would give no information, disdainfully repeating only *"Russe kaput."* *

Pavlovsk was now the front line, and fierce battles were raging only a few kilometers away, yet Mikryukov, Zelenova, and their few co-workers continued their packing. From August 31, for eleven days, Soviet Division Headquarters was installed in one of the wings of the palace; in another, the headquarters of local defense. On August 31, when Borshchev arrived at the new Division Headquarters, he noticed the pile of crates at the entrance to the palace and the feverish packing activity that was going on:

> All this work was being directed by a young woman around thirty. She introduced herself to me, crisply saying:
> "Zelenova, Chief of the PVO Objective."
> "What objective?" I asked.
> The woman threw me a piercing glance and answered, "This objective, the Pavlovsk Palace Anti-Air Defense Unit." It was painful for me to realize that the palaces of Leningrad, the creation of great artists, had now become "objectives."
> "Who is the director?"
> "I am the director of both. Tell me, are the Germans far away? We need time to get these treasures away."
> "You will succeed." I reassured her, and saw how her face brightened.

Pavlovsk was now a main target for attack. The destruction of a staff headquarters, which it had become, is a classic martial tactic for demolishing the opposition. The park also offered the tactical advantage of elevation over the adjacent countryside as well as offering prime fields of fire and observation. Now fighting raged around the palace itself. By September 8, according to Borshchev, "Airplanes came in wave after wave, methodically dropping bombs." Although Germans were suffering major losses, they seemed to disregard them, continuing

* "Russia is finished."

to bring in fresh forces, while the Russians were experiencing an extreme short-age of men, equipment, and ammunition. On September 9, says Borshchev, "The enemy, determined to seize Pavlovsk park, was throwing machine gunners into the battle, putting them in new tanks for protection." Russian artillery was able to delay the advance of the Nazis for several hours, allowing reinforcements to arrive, but by the twelfth, German units had penetrated into the eastern edge of the park area and Nazi Junker pilots began massive shelling. The Russian 260th Regiment pulled farther back into the park, until their command post was less than 800 meters from the Division Headquarters in the palace. An artillery bat-tery took up a defensive position on the northern edge of the park and repulsed the enemy three times. The forward edge of battle was now no more than a ten- or fifteen-minute walk from the palace.

During the weeks of evacuation Anna directed the burying of the remaining park statues.* She wrote, "In the park, bombardment and shrapnel had already damaged many trees. The same threatened the park statues. They were priceless, but it was impossible to evacuate such a great number. It was decided to bury them right in the park."

Under waves of Nazi bombardment, women dug pits. Based on her knowledge of the German language, and her study at Peter Schule, Anna made a cunning gamble. "The Germans are highly precise and accurate people. They will expect that statues will be buried at one meter eighty. We shall bury them deeper, they will not dig further." And so they did — going sometimes as deep as three meters. Earlier, in the serene Old Sylvia, where Maria Feodorovna had loved to stroll, the beautiful bronze eighteenth-century copies of Roman and Greek antique sculpture had been wrapped in canvas and placed deep in the Russian earth: first Apollo, then the nine Muses, Flora and Venus Kallipiga, then the children of Niobe and their weeping mother. Even in those desperate moments, Zelenova found time to notice that "The park was so beautiful. The only joyful thing in those terrible times. The noise of the battle from faraway streets did not penetrate into the quiet forests of the New Sylvia. Then reality burst in with the screech of Messerschmidts and the cacophony of bombardment that followed."

In the Brenna Circles, the marble sculptures had been placed in wooden crates lined with tar paper. On the crate in which was placed the famous marble statue of Peace, an early-eighteenth-century work by the Italian sculptor Pietro Baratta, bought by Peter the Great, a worker found time to scrawl, "We will come back

---

* The first burial of statues occurred on June 26, while Anna was still working in Leningrad.

and find you." Burial places were covered with grass, then scattered over with early fall leaves, which camouflaged the hiding places even more securely. Although the famous "Three Graces," a statue of three maidens carved from a single block of marble by Paulo Triscorni in the eighteenth century and presented by Alexander I to his mother in 1801, measured fourteen feet high and weighed almost a ton, it was somehow dragged and buried over three meters deep immediately at the foot of the stairs of the pavilion in Maria Feodorovna's Private Garden in which it stood.

During one of the desperate days of early September an incident occurred that neither Borshchev nor Zelenova ever forgot. As Anna described it, "One day returning to the palace I saw heavy, dusty military motorcycles with the gas tanks still hot, right at the entrance to Maria Feodorovna's Private Garden, resting against invaluable lilac bushes planted at Pavlovsk by Dutch gardeners. It was clear. They were ours, but whose?" Irate, she stormed up to the headquarters of the division on the second floor of the palace. "There, sitting at a table angrily cranking the handle of a field telephone, sat a major with an expression of anguish that shocked me. Something grunted on the phone. In an exhausted voice — it was apparently not the first time that day — the major was trying to convince someone that it was not he who had hung up the phone — that the line was being constantly disconnected and that he had already told them he had no more men. The phone continued to grunt angrily. The major slowly lowered the receiver back to its hook." In decisive terms Anna announced, "Tell your soldiers to remove their motorcycles from the Private Garden immediately!" "Whose private garden?" the weary major asked. Anna proceeded to treat him to the history of the artistry of Cameron, who had created this part of the park. The major, vanquished by Anna's vehemence, ordered the messengers to remove their motorcycles. "Just show them where," he said wearily. "I'll show them!" exclaimed Zelenova happily as she ran off without even asking his name. The major was so astonished by this irate young woman worried about Pavlovsk's Dutch lilacs in the middle of battle that twenty-five years later, having fought all the way to Berlin and survived the war, he came back to look for her at Pavlovsk.

It was on September 15 that the head of the kitchens of the regional defense suddenly appeared. Upset and out of breath he exclaimed, "No one was here to accept my shipment! I know you are waiting for vehicles. I have a few pounds of rice, macaroni, cocoa. I can't wait! I have a family — children! I must get back to Leningrad!" Zelenova signed for the shipment and had it distributed to the people in the cellars. "We must leave," urged Nikolai Weiss, the faithful co-worker who had remained with her. Still Zelenova hesitated. She could not bring herself to leave all the crates readied for shipment and everything that still had to be packed. Despite all their efforts almost eight thousand objects still remained. "Let's go on working," she said, "they know in Leningrad we are waiting for vehicles. Surely they'll send them." They continued their packing.

The next day, September 16, the division commander decided to move division headquarters to another location. Only Borshchev and the command posts of the 402nd and 412th regiments remained behind at Pavlovsk. Zelenova and Weiss decided to send what they could to Leningrad by horse-drawn cart.

In an account she later wrote Anna described the events that followed. As they were escorting the driver to his wagon, a green jeep screeched to a halt in front of the palace and a lieutenant jumped out, shouting authoritatively: "Why are all of you here! And who are you?"

Anna explained that she was the director and that these were workers.

The lieutenant exploded: "Everyone is evacuated from the town!"

"I am also evacuating and I am waiting for vehicles," she answered.

"There won't be any more vehicles. Lucky for you I happened to stop by to check whether everyone from the division had left. Get in! Now!"

"I can't leave," answered Zelenova, "even with your orders, because I am the head of the unit by orders of the highest authorities."

The lieutenant barked, "Understand that Pavlovsk is no longer a front, and not even a battle zone but already German territory. Get in — I am telling you for the last time!"

But Zelenova still refused.

"Devil knows what kind of broad you are!" he cried, angrily slamming the door of the jeep behind him as he drove off.

Zelenova and Weiss went down to the cellars. Stepping over samovars, sewing machines, and household paraphernalia, she made her way to the place in the cellar where inhabitants of the town were still hiding. "I must tell you," she said, "they are no longer defending the town. The children, the old, and the sick can be put on wagons. The rest must go on foot. It is not a short walk, but at least it will be thirty kilometers farther from the Germans."

But the frightened people cried, "Where will we go? Where will we be taken? We won't even reach Pushkin, both the horses and we will be killed." Mothers refused to take their children out while they heard bombing and shelling outside.

Moments later, one of the foresters rode up on his bicycle. Screeching to a halt in a cloud of dust in front of the palace, he cried, "Leave! Leave, for God's sake! German motorcycles are already in the park! I just saw them myself at the loop road at the White Birches!"

Anna ran to the Egyptian Vestibule to find Weiss, exclaiming, "Nikolai Viktorovich, we must leave immediately!" Looking down the beautiful linden *allée* that led to the palace, she could see that the horizon was glowing pink with fire.

Quickly she filled an old briefcase with all the evacuation documents and the plans that showed the hiding places of the statues buried in the park. Clutching it under her arm, she rushed from the palace. "It was the 16th of September," she wrote, "the blackest day of my life."

Deciding it was too dangerous to go through the park toward the train station, they decided to skirt around the northeast end of the town through the Five Corners. It was already dusk. At the first turn they were caught in gunfire and jumped into a ravine. When everything quieted for a moment, they continued. Shooting and bombs had torn deep craters in the roads of Pavlovsk and Pushkin. Felled telegraph poles, torn and hanging wire, obstructed the road. Hampered by her nearsightedness, Anna stumbled often and tangled herself in the wires. Afraid that she would break her glasses, she walked sideways. Nikolai Weiss led her off to the side of the road. They lost their way and came out in Pushkin. They saw Catherine's beautiful Chinese Theater burning. From the Pulkovo heights artillery boomed. Afraid of running into Germans, they made their way cautiously along the fields. Stones kept getting into her shoes and Weiss waited patiently for her to shake them out.

"We had already gone a long way, but there was not a single living soul anywhere. The closer we got to Kolpino, the lighter it seemed to get. Then we saw — the Izhorsky metal factory was burning. Quickly we passed the edge of the burning town and once again we were in darkness. The road here was in better condition and nearing a fork we heard the sound of engines. For some reason, past Kolpino we were convinced that they were ours. We decided to risk it. Three trucks were going toward Leningrad. The last one stopped for us." The driver opened the door. "Take us to Leningrad," she pleaded. "We are museum workers, from Pavlovsk, we were waiting for vehicles. We were evacuating the valuables."

The driver frowned, then said, "We'll take only the girl. Get in." Weiss firmly took her elbow to help her in. Zelenova writes:

Then I imagined myself speeding toward Leningrad, and Weiss remaining all alone. At home his wife and children were waiting. I got out and slammed the door. "Stupid woman," said someone next to the driver, and the vehicle took off. Without the sound of the motor, the explosions sounded even more frightening. I burst into tears. I explained to Weiss what he should tell my mother if I were to be hit by a bomb. Promising to remember everything he took me by the elbow and led me along the side of the road, reassuring me all the while that the shooting would soon stop, that we had chosen the right road, that we would be picked up.

Ten minutes passed and the attack did stop. Everything was quiet. About two hours later some trucks overtook us. Weiss, standing in the middle of the road, stopped one. I don't know what he said to the driver but in a moment he ran up and said, "Get in." I pulled myself onto the side of the truck and saw that it was full of severely wounded men. For the first time I feared for Leningrad. Passing Shushari, the driver stopped the truck, "Get out, we have to turn here." The remaining way seemed very short. We passed Srednaya Rogatka.* Trolleys were no longer running.

They had managed to cover the thirty kilometers in five hours. "At 10 o'clock I entered Saint Isaac's Cathedral where my nine hundred days of the Blockade began." On September 16, the Nazis occupied Pavlovsk.

* Shushari is twelve kilometers from Leningrad, Srednaya Rogatka within the city limits.

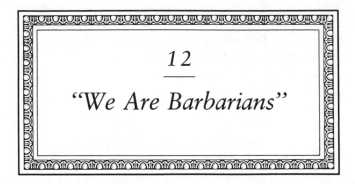

12

"We Are Barbarians"

Hague Convention Regulation 1907
"Seizure, destruction, willful damage
to historic monuments etc. are subject to
legal proceedings." (Article 47)

"Pillage is forbidden." (Article 56)

THE GERMANS ENTERED PUSHKIN on September 17 at 5 A.M. It was still dark. The assistant to the commandant of the Alexander Palace was lame, so she could not leave. She lived in the building of the old lyceum, and her windows faced the road. She looked from behind her curtains, trembling, because she had the keys to the Alexander Palace. Now the Germans would demand the keys. What would she say? From her window she could see Nazi trucks. The tarpaulins were thrown back; they were loading furniture from Nicholas II's bedroom. The hours went by. At nine o'clock they still had not requested the keys. They never did. They simply broke down the doors and immediately began equipping the headquarters of their generals with looted furniture. Later in the day, she was summoned to the palace to show them where to turn on the lights. She saw vandalized cupboards, broken tables, books tossed everywhere. On the floor, torn dresses of the Empress Alexandra, and her hats, trampled on the floor. Distressed, she picked up a veil that had belonged to the Empress along with a small vase from the Mauve Boudoir. A German officer allowed her to keep them.

At Pavlovsk, old women museum guardians were keeping watch on the first floor, shaking with fear. They heard a noise of motorcycles and the loud barking of police dogs. Officers jumped off the motorcycles and entered the palace. There was the sound of boots on the parquet floors. The Nazis demanded to be shown the palace, and immediately went upstairs. The upper halls were empty. Roughly, they began to question the women about where the valuables were. The old women answered that something had been taken away, but they didn't know what. All the remaining furniture and valuables were there on the first floor. In the Corner Salon there was a crate, nailed shut, which had not made the last evacuation. They broke it open. In the crate was Maria Feodorovna's collection of cameos — twelve thousand fine glass copies of those in the Hermitage, a present from Catherine the Great. German officers began shoving them into their pockets. In the same crate was a collection of sacred spoons, which Constantine Constantinovich had brought from Jerusalem. They took those as well. Then they chased out all the women, and the palace was theirs.

These are the first impressions of those who were there that day — the beginning of the greatest orgy of organized looting and premeditated destruction of artworks in the history of the world. What the Nazis attempted in the East was to art what the concentration camps were to people — a Final Solution that would totally obliterate the spirit and the historical memory of a nation. Contemplating the terrifying statistics of Nazi destruction in the East, one cannot refrain from once again asking helplessly, were these the Germans who prided themselves on their civilization and culture, the lovers of Bach and Beethoven, Schiller and Goethe? How, if they are still alive, can they live with the memory of their behavior? Men in war have always destroyed and looted, but none with the premeditated, organized, demonic thoroughness and efficiency of the Nazi armies on the eastern front. In the Soviet Union, since the war, it has been rumored that the German embassies and consulates have had a special problem of personnel suicide. Certainly there is cause for overwhelming remorse, and anyone contemplating the acts of the Nazi armies can only feel the most profound compassion for their guilt-ridden compatriots, driven to suicide because of the impossibility of coming to terms with the awful truth. Yet the terrible question remains: How did it happen?

Adolf Hitler had a dream. The Führer, a one-time house painter, had fantasies of being an architect. When he came to power, one of his most cherished personal goals was to make the small provincial city of Linz in central Austria, where he had lived as a child, a great monument to his glory. Linz was to be entirely rebuilt on a grandiose scale, to outshine Vienna and Budapest. There was to be a library of a quarter of a million volumes, plus a large collection of Austrian medieval manuscripts. Hitler's mausoleum, designed by himself, was to be in the center, and, as the crown jewel, there was to be the world's greatest art museum, dedicated, with the sentimentality that was a mark of this evil genius, to his mother. The firm plan was conceived sometime in 1938, after a visit by Hitler to Italy; the official title of the project, which was to remain top secret, was *Sonderauftrag Linz* (Special Operation Linz). The authority for making high-level appointments for this operation was given to art expert Hans Posse, who had been director of the Dresden Art Gallery, and on June 26, 1939, he was formally commissioned to create the Linz museum. The collection headquarters were to be in Munich, not far from Hitler's mountaintop retreat, Berchtesgaden.

The art to fill this fabulous museum was of course to be seized — or, as the Nazis preferred to say, "safeguarded" — from all over Europe. As Hitler's power and conquests increased, his dream for Linz became ever more obsessive; the model of his proposed dream city grew to be the size of a room. All during the war Hitler spent many hours fondly gazing at the huge model. He talked of how he would retire there, accompanied only by Eva Braun and his beloved dog Blondi. Many of Hitler's top henchmen also had art-collecting aspirations — Himmler, Bormann, von Ribbentrop, and, leading the list, *Reischmarschall* Hermann Göring, who was obsessed with collecting and determined to amass the largest private collection in the world. As early as 1933, Göring received approval from Hitler to form his own art gallery, and his collection subsequently was to rival Hitler's own. Each had his special preferences: Hitler, whose taste was provincial, loved genre pictures and heroic sculptures; Ribbentrop fancied the Italian Renaissance; Göring's taste ran to nudes — he had a splendid painting of a nude Europa hanging over his bed in his majestic estate of Karinhall, where fine paintings, many by Old Masters, covered the walls. Each of Hitler's henchmen had his favorite art experts and dealers; they all became involved in what was a gigantic art looting operation in which they managed, while giving the Führer his due, to collect a mountain of booty for themselves.

In 1940 Alfred Rosenberg, a cold-eyed, rat-faced man, was formally put in charge of the Nazi confiscation enterprises throughout the occupied territories. Rosenberg was born in 1893 in Revel, Estonia, in what was then the Imperial Russian Empire. He studied architecture in 1910 at the Institute of Technology in Riga, which, as the German-Russian front line approached, was moved to Moscow; there, in 1918, he received his diploma as an engineer and architect. During his trial at Nuremberg, this man who had committed such horrors in the countries of his birth and education testified that his principle interests were architecture and painting. He declared that at the university he read Goethe and Herder, that he was influenced by "the social ideas of Charles Dickens, Carlyle, and Emerson," and had studied Schopenhauer, Kant, and the philosophy of India. In 1919 Rosenberg left his native Estonia and went to Munich, where he met Adolf Hitler, and in 1920 he joined the Nazi party. Why he was chosen for his high post is a mystery. He was never popular in upper Nazi circles. He owed his fame in Germany to a single book, *The Myth of the Twentieth Century,* which even Hitler called boring, and Goebbels expressively described as "an ideological belch." But the book had enjoyed a wild success in Germany, selling over a million copies, and Rosenberg was hailed as the "philosopher" of nazism.

Rosenberg's organization was known as the E.R.R. (*der Einsatzstab Reichleiter Rosenberg für die besetzten Gebiete* — the Reich Leader Rosenberg Task Force for Occupied Countries). Its headquarters were in Paris in the Hotel Commodore, and the main storage facility was the Jeu de Paume Museum in the Tuileries gardens. Its first task was an ideological mission — to loot all Jewish and Masonic archives, libraries, and places of worship for a future academy in which young Nazis were to be educated to understand properly these evils. Then, in September 1940, thinking of Linz, Hitler abruptly directed them to enlarge their activities to include "stateless" Jewish art collections, starting with the immensely valuable Rothschild collections, which were to be transported to Germany; other categories of acquisitions were "safeguarding" and confiscation from enemies of the state; art was also to be purchased (either legally or forced) with *Reichskassenscheine,* invasion marks worth one-fourth of their face value.

The E.R.R. quickly grew into a complex, highly specialized bureau, which included art experts, packers, appraisers, and cataloguers. As the E.R.R. enlarged its art seizing activities, the top Nazis began to struggle for its control. Himmler, von Ribbentrop, Frank, and Bormann all vied to achieve domination of Rosenberg's task force, but Göring eventually won out, since he had control of major transport facilities. (Göring made twenty visits to Paris within two years to check on things.) A vast army of art dealers from Germany and the occupied countries eagerly collaborated in the slimy business of making fortunes from the Nazi art-collecting mania.

The E.R.R. was an extremely efficient organization. The orderly Germans kept precise records, cataloguing and photographing everything. Photographs were placed in handsome brown leather-bound albums, which Bormann from time to time would present to Hitler, who loved to peruse them as if he were going through a mail-order catalogue. He chose what he liked for Linz and then dispensed the other items to his favorite museums in Breslau and Königsberg. On one of his visits to Paris, Göring decided that the collection being gathered by Rosenberg's E.R.R. should be divided into four categories, in descending order: for Hitler, for Göring's personal collection, for centers of higher education, and finally for art museums and galleries.

All of Western Europe, including Hitler's Italian and Austrian allies, was subject to forced purchases and "safeguarding," but there was an important and sinister difference between Nazi policy toward art in Western countries and in the East.

In the West, the Nazis were anxious to preserve a veneer, however thin, of legality. Artworks, if not "purchased," were to be "safeguarded," or "confiscated from internal enemies of the state" (mainly French, Belgian, and Dutch Jews whose property automatically fell forfeit to the state). Museums were generally spared. The major treasures of the Louvre had been stored in one of the châteaux of the Loire in Vichy France. Hitler showed great respect for Napoleon's tomb, considered the Louvre sacred, and forbade confiscation from French state art galleries until final peace treaties, in which France would be forced to cede treasures as reparations. Because of the Linz museum plan, all stolen artworks from the West were strictly protected with the famous German thoroughness and efficiency. The first large shipment from France was sent off in thirty carefully heated baggage cars. Treasures and Old Masters were stored in special hiding places, safe and far from the war. One main repository was the fairytale castle of mad King Ludwig, patron of the arts and friend of Wagner, perched on a mountaintop in Neuschwanstein in the Bavarian Alps, where twenty-one thousand art treasures, including six thousand paintings, were carefully stored. Another was the castle of Nuremberg, which had a series of chambers sixty feet underground hewn out of solid rock. The most extraordinary was the Alt Ausee salt mine in the mountains near Salzburg, which served as a cache for ten thousand paintings, sixty-eight pieces of sculpture, and thousands of other objects.*

---

* After the war, astonished experts attached to the Allied Monuments, Fine Arts, and Archives Section were led to the treasures, through gleaming white passageways, by dwarfs whose families had lived and worked in the mine for generations. They spoke an archaic language similar to the German of the Middle Ages.

Eventually there would be some two hundred such storage places in southern Germany alone. Hitler made it clear through the chain of command that he was to have first claim on any great art from Western European countries, and when he learned of mass looting and pillage in the West by soldiers, he issued a stern order that all works of art in occupied countries must be handed over to the proper German authorities appointed for that purpose — an order that was not lightly ignored.

This was not so in the East. Cynical and terrible as it was, the plundering in Europe seems child's play, a mere prologue, to what happened in the East. Hitler's hatred for the Slavs was as intense as his loathing for the Jews. In his diseased mind, he lumped them together. He considered it his historic crusade to eliminate the Bolshevik *Untermenschen;* "subhuman" Slavs had to be exterminated like vermin. "This enemy," he once said, "consists not of soldiers but to a large extent only of beasts." He would not even consider any "subhuman art" from the East for his collection in Linz — refusing even to look at photographs, which his art director Posse, who knew much better, endeavored to show him.

The E.R.R. approach to collecting reflected the Nazi philosophy — the farther East, the less valuable the art. There was no pretense of any kind, no more talk of "safeguarding" — automatic confiscation without the slightest justification was the rule. And, although Hitler personally affected to disdain it, he generously had no objections if other Nazis felt differently and wished to collect "subhuman" art themselves; his henchmen vied and often collided with each other in their rapacious desire for Eastern treasure. "We are barbarians," said Hitler, "and wish to be barbarians. It is a noble calling." The noble Nazi barbarians outdid all previous invaders — the Romans, Visigoths, Vandals, Huns, the Mongols under Ghengis Khan and his grandson Batu, who devastated Russia in three invasions during the thirteenth century, even Napoleon, holder of the previous record for mass looting. The guiding rule was expressed by Göring in a speech to the Reich Commissioners for Occupied Territories in 1942: "Whenever you come across anything that may be needed by the German people, you must be after it like bloodhounds. It must be taken and brought back to Germany."

The Linz dream helped to spare Western Europe from indiscriminate pillage and destruction. With looting there is at least the hope of eventual restitution. In France a heroic French patriot, Rose Valland, an experienced art historian, managed to infiltrate herself into the heart of the E.R.R. operations and kept track of where stolen artworks were being taken. But in the East, even more than plunder, total destruction was the premeditated aim in a bestial, brutal, bloody war of ideologies that permitted no compromise.

"We do not have to kill the people," said a Nazi commander, "we only have to destroy their memory." Nothing that happened in the West can be compared with the naked barbarism in the East, in Poland, and especially Russia, where, in a systematic effort to obliterate the cultural memory of a nation, uncounted thousands of great masterpieces of art were annihilated in a holocaust of art destruction that was to hurl Europe several steps backwards toward the Dark Ages.

At the outset Rosenberg and his E.R.R. were given primary authority for art operations on the eastern front. He was given a new title: Minister of Occupied Countries. To Rosenberg's responsibility for art looting was added another responsibility: the looting of people for slave labor in Germany.

Two months before the June invasion, all his plans were made, and Rosenberg's chief of staff, Gerhard Utikal, was placed in command. Once again, as they had in France in 1940, the E.R.R. brown-shirted special units, along with civilian art experts, moved in like jackals on the heels of the invading army. The headquarters of this organized, uniformed band of thieves was in the ancient Byelorussian city of Smolensk. They were given the authority to work with the army quartermaster, who was to supply them with all the needed manpower from military units as well as the transport for their operations. Cutting their teeth, the Rosenberg Nazi army units made short work of Smolensk, destroying all four museums in the city after stealing all the icons, bronzes, porcelains, metal castings, and textiles. They then desecrated and burned down all the ancient monuments and set fire to all the libraries of the city and twenty-two schools — 646,000 volumes were destroyed. The historic old city was left in ruins.

In his disdain for *Untermenschen* art, Hitler seems to have been quite alone, for the riches of Russia were so tempting and so vast that very soon Rosenberg found he had many extra helpers, often colliding in their rapacious greed and complaining to each other and to the Führer about overlapping authority. Göring immediately sent in his specialists. Despite Hitler's objections, Posse dispatched his deputy, von Holst. Himmler also instructed his Gestapo to take a hand. In August 1941, three months after the invasion, Hitler commanded Joachim von Ribbentrop, the foreign minister, to add his special expertise to the systematic looting of Russian towns and cities, giving him direct orders to "seize and secure immediately after the fall of great cities and towns their cultural centers and all objects of great historical value; to select valuable books and films and finally dispatch all seizures to Germany." *

In order to carry out the Führer's orders efficiently, von Ribbentrop organized a special art-looting battalion, made up of four companies, each of two hundred men, which were to be under his personal direction with headquarters at 104 Hermann Göring Strasse in Berlin. As commanding officer he appointed his previous emissary to France, Baron von Künsberg, a major in the Waffen S.S.† One company was assigned to work with Rommel in Africa, the other three were sent to Russia, one for each Operation Barbarossa Army group, where they worked in close cooperation with military command.

So that looting could be conducted on a strictly "scientific" basis, civilian art experts and connoisseurs were specially drafted into this "art battalion." Among these were experts on paintings, engravings, and sculpture; men who knew their field, knew what they were doing, and knew precisely the value of what they were stealing. Such a man was *Obersturmführer* Dr. Norman Paul Föster, who testified at Nuremberg that

> In August 1941, while in Berlin, I with the assistance of my old acquaintance from the University of Berlin, Dr. Focke, then employed in the press section, Foreign Ministry, was transferred from the 87th Tank Destroyer Division to the Special Purpose Battalion attached to the Foreign Office. . . . Prior to our departure for Russia, Major von Künsberg transmitted to us Ribbentrop's orders: thoroughly to comb out all scientific establishments, institutions, and libraries and all the palaces, to search all the archives and to lay our hand on anything of definite value.

In the sinisterly elegant black uniforms of the elite S.S., von Ribbentrop's men followed in the immediate wake of assault troops. Their sector of the front was museums. Sometimes they would first carefully study the institutions that were to be stripped, politely speaking with the directors. Then they would scrutinize

---

* Joachim von Ribbentrop was appointed Hitler's foreign minister when the Nazis seized power in January 1933. His biggest coup was the German-Soviet Treaty of Nonaggression, signed on August 23, 1939, which cleared the way for Hitler's attack on Poland in September 1941. Found guilty on four counts by the Military Tribunal at Nuremberg, he was hanged on October 16, 1946. At his trial he stated: ". . . during the war neither I myself nor the Foreign Office confiscated or claimed any art treasures whatsoever . . . it is possible that these art treasures were temporarily removed for safekeeping."

† Waffen S.S., or Armed S.S., were special military S.S. units trained and equipped along the lines of the regular army. The Waffen S.S. was divided into three subgroups: Hitler's personal bodyguard; thirty-nine divisions that served as elite combat troops; and the infamous Totenkopf (Death's-Head) battalions that administered the concentration camps.

catalogues and classify. The best pieces went to Berlin, second-class goods to agents in neutral countries; "degenerate" art was mutilated. Rosenberg's Brownshirts began the job, but it was Ribbentrop's Blackshirts of the 2nd Company who descended on the region of Novgorod and the palaces of Leningrad. With the help of the German army and the men of the Spanish Blue Division and the Dutch Waffen S.S. Division, they methodically raped and destroyed all the palaces, museums, and monuments, stripping them of everything that was left in them.

They could not have done so well without the enthusiastic help of the German troops and commanders. Dehumanization is the core of barbarism, and German commanders encouraged such dehumanization among their troops in a series of merciless orders. General Hodt of the Seventeenth Army demanded that his subordinates make certain that "the sound feeling of vengeance and repulsion toward everything Russian should not be suppressed among the men, but on the contrary encouraged in every way."

One such notorious order was "On the Conduct of Troops in the Eastern Territories" (described by the Führer as "excellent") of Field Marshal Walther von Reichenau, commander of the Sixth Army, dated October 10, 1941. Von Reichenau, the son of a diplomat and a veteran of World War I, was one of the most fanatic Nazi generals. The very picture of a Nazi movie villain, von Reichenau had a tight, cruel mouth, a merciless face, piercing eyes, and wore a monocle. He led the Sixth Army in the invasions of France and the USSR and later commanded Army Group Sud. In his famous directive, issued two days after his fifty-seventh birthday, the general wrote, "The most essential aim of war against the Jewish-Bolshevik system is a complete destruction of their means of power and the elimination of Asiatic influence from the European culture . . . the disappearance of symbols of former Bolshevistic rule, even in the form of buildings, is part of the struggle of destruction. Neither historic nor artistic considerations are of any importance in the Eastern Territories." In the same month he issued another directive ordering the extermination of Soviet prisoners of war and civilians.

At the beginning, the special units and battalions provided some faint discipline, but as the war grew more bitter and German casualties mounted, even they were swept aside. In retreat, as blind hatred overcame greed, German officers made no attempt to restrain their troops from desecrating everything that was sacred in Russian eyes. German soldiers lent themselves to an unrestrained rampage in which all human creation was to be destroyed in a *Götterdämmerung* of annihilation. What is perhaps most appalling is that in all the testimony, official depositions, and accounts there is not a single recorded sign of opposition to this deluge of villainy. While this might be expected from the Nazis, there were millions of German fighting men on the Russian front, and there is no evidence recorded of a single redeeming act from either ordinary soldiers or even those who called themselves Prussian aristocrats. There were some officers who objected to Hitler's military orders and criticized his strategic plans, but not the seizing and destruction of art, nor, with few exceptions, his occupation policies. One such exception was General Erich von Manstein. This brilliant, aristocratic general, who commanded the Fourth Panzer Group in Army Group Nord and has been rated by many military historians as the finest strategist in the German army during World War II, refused compliance with Hitler's decree that all commissars were to be shot on capture. Von Manstein also frequently criticized Hitler's military decisions in the Russian campaign, and in 1944, after a final disagreement with the Führer, resigned. Nevertheless, as a senior commander, he was held responsible for the actions of his German troops, and because of the Nazi scorched-earth policy in the Crimea, he was judged by a British tribunal and sentenced to twelve years imprisonment in West Germany.

Eyewitnesses in Pushkin during those early days of the occupation testify that from the first hours of the invasion the Germans began their systematic looting. "From the time they first arrived," said a citizen of the town, "along the lake we could see a long line of wagons and cars full of palace furniture. All of this went through Pavlovsk to Gatchina, then to Germany." Another reported: "They immediately made the palace and surrounding houses their headquarters. From the first day they began hauling paintings, rugs, and porcelain out of the palace. What they could not for some reason take away, they destroyed. Along the streets one could see soldiers, carrying furniture, draperies, mirrors." A German prisoner of war from the Second Company said, "We ripped the gold decorations from the walls. Our commander, Major Fink, did not tell us not to do it. We burned the middle of the palace. We destroyed and looted the home of Pushkin." Another captured German prisoner testified: "In 1940/41 the commission loaded all valuable property of Pushkin palaces on trains and carried it away to Germany. I do not know what quantity of valuable property was taken, but in any case, everything was taken."

They labored so effectively that only five months after the invasion, Reich Commissioner Rube reported that goods sent from Byelorussia ran into millions of rubles. Freight cars packed with Russian loot reached Germany at the rate of forty to fifty a day, most of it being roughly sorted in East Prussia before it was moved on to Berlin and other German cities.

In the Alexander Palace all rooms were used as barracks. German squads and members of the Spanish Blue Division billeted there ransacked all the furniture, wantonly broke all the doors, carried away all metal decorations down to the doorknobs and locks, smashed the marble finish in the front halls, and carried away all the remaining furniture and the large library containing seven thousand volumes in French and five thousand in Russian.

At the Catherine Palace the Nazis succeeded in doing what Kuchumov and the Russian museum workers had been unable to do. They had the time, labor, and transport to dismantle and pack the heavy fragile amber panels of the Amber Room, fifty-five square yards of exquisitely carved panels backed with silver foil (conservatively valued at some sixty million dollars), in twenty-four massive boxes. Because of its German origin, this fabulous treasure was first on the Nazi list to be officially "confiscated" under the direct orders of Hitler himself. It was destined for the Prussian Fine Art Museum in Königsberg, which boasted one of the world's most famous amber collections. It is suspected that the bloody "Brown Tsar of the East," Erich Koch, gauleiter of East Prussia, was the person who coordinated this operation.*

All the ceilings of the antechambers of the palace were covered with fine canvases of the artists of the middle of the eighteenth century. Unable to remove these, the Germans simply cut the huge canvases to pieces. The eighteenth-century painted Chinese silk that covered the walls of the Chinese Drawing Room, and the bedroom of Alexander I, along with the Russian eighteenth-century yellow silk with woven swans and pheasants, was cut or simply ripped off. The priceless inlaid floors of the Lyons Salon and all others were pried up and removed. The Rastrelli enfilade of rooms, more than three hundred feet long and one of his architectural masterpieces, was burned. The blue and gold palace chapel, among Rastrelli's finest interiors, was entirely laid waste — the iconostasis smashed, the icons carried away, ceilings pried off, floors torn out, gilded molding chiseled off — and then used as a motorcycle garage.

---

*Erich Koch was named Reich Commissioner for the Ukraine after the German invasion, having previously served as the chief Nazi civil officer in eastern Poland. Headquartered for most of the war in Königsberg, he directed the looting of art treasures as well as deportations to death camps. He personally developed trucks in which people were gassed to death. Koch escaped advancing Soviet forces at the end of the war, but was arrested in the British Occupation Zone in 1949. In Warsaw he was tried and convicted for war crimes and was sentenced to life in prison. He died in November 1986 at the age of 90, reportedly still an unrepentant Nazi.

The fact that Catherine the Great had been one of their countrywomen did not spare her. Her private rooms decorated with fine glass, bronze, and porcelain mirrors were utterly destroyed. Senselessly smashed into smithereens were all the plates of fine opal, violet, and blue glass that covered the walls of the famed *Tabatière* and the Empress's bedroom, one of the finest of Cameron's works.

There was in Tsarskoe Selo a collection of antique boats and sailing vessels both Russian and foreign, some dating from the time of Peter the Great, as well as a great rarity, the amazing Hottorp Globe, made in the seventeenth century and presented to Peter. This enormous globe, with an inner surface that bore a map of the heavens, rotated in conformity with the rotation of the earth and was fitted inside with a table and bench for ten persons. The globe vanished, never to be found again. The boats were used by German soldiers for pleasure boating on the ponds and, when they tired of them, were sunk. The Turkish bath with its finishing of gilded marble was blown up; Catherine's Chinese Theater with its irreplaceable rare lacquer walls was burned.

Finally, in retreat, determined to destroy whatever was still standing, the German armies placed eleven huge delayed-action bombs weighing one to three tons each under the Cameron Gallery.

Inhabitants of Pushkin hiding in the cellars of the palaces were hauled out and sorted in the corridors. Some were sent to the study of Alexander II, where the chief of the Gestapo sat. Others were sent farther along the arcade of rooms to the stairs and the basements, where there was a prison from which there was no return.

During the two-and-a-half-year occupation of Pavlovsk, the Gestapo was housed in the main building of the palace. German photographs show the commandant of the palace standing outside of the stairs of the palace supervising the registering of a long line of inhabitants; some were taken for slave labor, some were sent to concentration camps. In the Egyptian Hall, where Anna Zelenova had conducted her packing operation, the marble floor was found useful for tortures and beatings.

Officers were quartered in the salons of the first floor. In these rooms stoves were installed by breaking all the mirrors and shoving stovepipes through crudely made holes. In the lower rooms of the first floor of the North Wing a stable was set up; barracks were located in the upper North Wing, and hospitals in the South Wing. The ballroom was transformed into a garage for motorcycles and cars. The wall between two windows was torn out, a ramp was made from tree logs chopped down in the park, and vehicles driven into the hall.

German troops were quartered in the park. The little houses of the Marien-talsky Pond housed members of the Dutch or Fleming Division, and in Paul's mausoleum were quartered members of the Spanish Division. These two special divisions fought with the German army in Novgorod and on the Leningrad Front. As non-Germanic volunteers, they did not rate elite S.S. uniforms, but standard German issue, the Spaniards distinguished only by their shoulder shields in Span-ish red and gold national colors with the word *España*.

The Spanish Blue Division, recruited on June 27, 1941, was a 17,736-man expeditionary force of Spanish volunteers sent by Franco; as Catholics, they con-sidered the war in the East a crusade against atheism. At the outset, the Blue Division was commanded by Augustin Muñoz Grandes, a short, chain-smoking, swarthy man from a working-class background in Toledo, well known by both the British and the Germans as one of Spain's finest warriors. He was replaced as commander in 1942 by Emilio Infantes Esteban, who was also at Pavlovsk.

The Germans, while respecting their bravery, considered the Spanish lacka-daisical and sloppy, mentioning in reports that they constantly composed songs and poems, chafed at eating German food, and eventually insisted on having garbanzos, Spanish wine, and tobacco shipped from home.* But, however lack-adaisical and full of Iberian charm they were, in 1942, while they were quartered at Pavlovsk, these troops enthusiastically participated in the ransacking and de-facing of the palace, and besides amusing themselves by painting graffiti all over the walls, left indisputable traces of their presence by hacking out on one of the marble porticos in Maria Feodorovna's Oval Boudoir the inscription *"Viva l'España"* — an inscription that remains to this day.†

Ribbentrop's Second Company and squads from Rosenberg's headquarters also kept themselves busy. Despite all efforts of Russian evacuation, some valu-ables remained in the palace, and the invaders carried away to Germany precious eighteenth-century inlaid furniture in addition to that designed by Voronykhin, as well as drawings by outstanding eighteenth-century artists. Sculptures and marble vases were barbarously mutilated. All ornamentation was ripped off the walls, including the bronze decorations of the doors. Then the doors of rare wood were removed, used for bunks, or chopped up for firewood. Only the statue of Paul I was spared; the Emperor's statue was used as a telephone pole with wires

---

* Goebbels once remarked, "The Spanish are extraordinarily valiant, but have military peculiarities that we can't comprehend. They don't assure, for example, that the horses have care and food. Nevertheless, they launch themselves against the enemy like Blücher."

† Kuchumov states that he was ordered to remove the sign, but refused to do so, agreeing with the local Party head that it should remain as proof of what the Spanish had done.

strung about the neck to connect dugouts and positions in the park. Yet despite their meticulous sacking, neither Rosenberg's nor von Ribbentrop's men ever discovered the antique statues that Zelenova and her women helpers had so cunningly concealed behind a false wall in the cellar; the Gestapo unknowingly sat above them during the entire occupation.

Near Pavlovsk there was an active partisan group operating behind the lines. One of the older women workers at Pavlovsk, who had served at the palace before the Revolution as a parlormaid for Grand Duke Constantine, tried to protest the brutal treatment of Jews by the Gestapo in the palace. When threatened with hanging for her protest, she managed to run off and join the local partisans for whom she became a cook.

Fighting behind enemy lines, these Russian partisans were very active and effective. At the end of 1942, there were about three thousand in the Leningrad region, and these increased to about thirty-five thousand by January 1944. During thirty-two months they killed about 114,000 enemy officers and men, blew up and burned a large amount of military equipment, destroyed bridges and communication lines and enemy storage dumps. When they were caught, the Germans executed them immediately, usually, as an example to the population, by hanging them from the porches of dachas, lampposts, and trees, and decorating them with signs: "I am a partisan, fighting against the enemy." In Pavlovsk, the favored spot was the clearing of the Old Sylvia, where all trees were cut down except for the sturdy oaks. There, stiffening bodies of partisans dangled above the secret burial places of the statues of Apollo and the Muses.

Like locusts, the German armies descended on the palaces that surrounded Leningrad and stripped them of everything. At Gatchina, Rinaldi's Florentine palace of the north, everything that was left in all five hundred rooms and the storerooms was taken. On September 23, 1941, after breaking into Peterhof, the Nazis embarked on a wholesale plundering of the entire area and were occupied for several months carrying everything away.

Peterhof, Peter the Great's "Versailles on the Sea," designed by the French architect Le Blond, whom Peter called his "treasure," and later enlarged by Rastrelli, was an enchanted spot, with vast parks full of beautiful pavilions and dachas built over two centuries by a whole line of tsars. The first day of the spring, when the cascades of fountains that flowed down into the sea were turned on, was a traditional holiday for all the population of Leningrad. Crowds streamed out to Peterhof on riverboats and waited expectantly as the bands began playing, a prelude to the marvelous moment when the fountains bubbled forth, first slowly and then growing higher and higher, sparkling in the sun and splashing over the golden statues of Samson and Neptune. Perhaps knowing the importance of these fountains to the population, within the beginning weeks of the occupation, one of the first acts of the Nazi armies was to remove the magnificent gilded bronze statue of Samson wrenching open the jaws of a lion — a masterpiece of the eighteenth-century Russian sculptor Kozlovsky — as well as those of Neptune and the figures representing the Neva and the Volkhov rivers. The town population who lined the streets wept as they saw their beloved statues trucked off to Germany to be melted down, along with all the fine wrought-iron railings that lined the promenade overlooking the park and the fountains. For good measure the Nazis blew up the intricate system feeding the fountains, devised by a group of French *fontaniers*, which brought water from thirteen miles away.

Despite the evacuation, there remained in the Grand Palace and all the other buildings and pavilions 34,214 museum exhibits, paintings, art objects, and sculptures as well as 11,700 valuable books. All these were carried away or destroyed. In addition, from the main palace, as well as the pavilions of Marly, Mon Plaisir, the Cottage Dacha, and others, 14,950 pieces of unique furniture of English, French, Italian, and Russian design made during the reigns of Peter, Elizabeth, Catherine, and Nicholas I were also plundered; as in Pushkin, all the silk and Gobelins tapestry coverings were torn off the walls.

At Peter's charming tiny retreat of Mon Plaisir, where the Tsar loved to look out at the sea and often perched in a tree peering through his telescope, floors were torn out, beams sawed through, doors and window frames, windows, and wainscotting destroyed, as were the interiors of the study and bedroom and the fine Russian-made lacquer walls of the Chinese Room. The central and most historically important part of the early-eighteenth-century pavilion was converted into a pillbox, and the Western Pavilion into a stable and latrine.

The Hermitage Pavilion, built in the time of Catherine the Great, was ransacked and turned into an artillery emplacement. The remarkable eighteenth-century elevating mechanism, similar to one that still exists at Versailles, which raised and lowered a large table into the upper dining room, was destroyed; then German troops used the charming ballroom as a shooting gallery, with the eighteenth-century portraits and busts as targets.

In the northern part of the park — the Alexandria, a place of romantic trails, wildflowers, and splendid trees — they blew up the favorite country retreat of

Nicholas II and his family, as well as destroying the Alexandria Gate, the pavilions of the Adam Fountain, the pylon of the main gate of the Upper Park, and the Rose Pavilion. After their capture of Peterhof, the troops of the 291st German Infantry Division amused themselves by lobbing nine thousand heavy artillery shells into the famous English Palace built by Quarenghi for Catherine the Great, which took care not only of the palace but of the entire picturesque English park and all the park pavilions. In the town of Peterhof they took time to destroy all the churches and the Serafim monastery. In retreat as grief-stricken townspeople watched, prevented from trying to extinguish the flames, they burned the Grand Palace, leaving it a blackened shell, and had the satisfaction of knowing after they left that Marly was blown up by specially placed delayed-action mines.

A scale model left behind in one of the few remaining buildings that had been used by the Nazis as their headquarters testified to the fact that the Germans deliberately included the historic palaces and parks as important parts of their defense system, so as to place them in the path of Russian shelling. This may in part explain the extraordinary ignorance of General von Manstein, who in 1942 in the Caucasus, far from the events in the north, wrote, "I was sad to learn that several of the Imperial residences I knew from 1931 — the lovely Catherine Palace in Tsarskoe Selo, the smaller palace where the last Tsar lived and the delightful Peterhof on the Gulf of Finland had fallen victims to the war. They had been set on fire by Soviet shelling."

What von Manstein said in ignorance has been repeated since by apologists seeking to minimize the crimes of the Nazi armies. Even some Russian citizens, led by their hatred and suspicion of Stalin, have echoed this argument. One woman in Leningrad said that as a little girl, after the war, her father took her to Pavlovsk and showed her the damage, saying, "They [meaning the Soviets] did it. I want you to remember this all your life."

It is evident that Soviet shells must have fallen on the palaces, even though Soviet officers insist that their possibilities of attack on the palace defensive outposts were hampered by orders to use only limited air and artillery support so as not to bomb or shell monuments. The palaces of Pushkin and Pavlovsk, they say, were specifically excluded from aerial fire.

But the major damage of Pavlovsk and other palaces came not from shelling or bombing, but from organized destruction, plundering, mining, and finally torching. For this, only deliberate Nazi policy can be held responsible. Occasionally, German apologists give yet another argument to minimize responsibility.

They point the finger at the Spanish. Indeed, the Blue Division did ransack and deface the palaces in which they were quartered, but they were under direct German orders and were only a very small part of the German army.

Everywhere the Germans passed, the horrors were repeated. Everything sacred to the Russians was marked for desecration and annihilation. Storming through large cities and tiny villages, they left everything in ruins. They paid special attention to national sanctuaries such as the Pushkin Reservation, where in 1941, striving to protect this precious national memorial, Red Army units evacuated the district without fighting and retreated toward Nozorzhev. Despite this, the Germans bombed the historic Svyatiye Gory Monastery, along whose wall Russia's greatest national poet, Alexander Pushkin, was buried. Then, in 1943, as the front line approached, they blew up the main monastery church, a sixteenth-century building, and before their retreat completed the job by destroying the two ancient churches in the monastery and leaving nothing but heaps of bricks, iron, and smashed boards. Icons, including the Icon of the Apostle Peter, were found riddled with bullets, the floor littered with pages torn out of prayerbooks and the ancient documents of the monastery. Pushkin's grave was covered with rubbish, his old house and the cottage of his beloved nurse destroyed, the museum sacked, his manuscripts sullied and destroyed, and his portrait riddled with bullets. Knowing that arriving Russian troops would go first to the grave of the nation's greatest literary figure, the Nazis prepared a complicated network of high explosives destined to blow up Pushkin's grave — a plan thwarted only by the timely arrival of Russian sappers who uncovered three thousand additional mines in the surrounding territory.

In Tikhvin, the home of Rimsky-Korsakov was reduced to rubble; in Istra, the home of Chekhov was looted and burned, with nothing left standing but a chimney. Tchaikovsky's large, beautiful wooden house in Klin was turned into a motorcycle garage, where the troops kept warm by burning the great musician's scores in their stoves. In Kaluga, in the house of aeronautical Russian pioneer Tsiolkovsky, his portrait was used for target practice, his valuable models of dirigibles, along with plans and instruments trampled underfoot, the furniture burned, and one of the rooms turned into a hen coop.

The Nazis spent six weeks at Tolstoy's historic home at Yasnaya Polyana. There they turned the room where *War and Peace* was written into a hayloft, destroyed the house, deliberately made a cemetery for Nazi soldiers in the Tolstoy family cemetery, and covered Tolstoy's grave with garbage. When a museum worker went so far as to ask a German officer named Schwartz to cease heating the stove with the great writer's furniture and books, the answer was, "We don't want firewood. We shall burn everything connected with the name of your Tolstoy."

Churches, too, got special attention. Troops organized bloody orgies in holy buildings, stabled their dogs and horses in churches, made bunks out of large icons, and dressed up in rich ecclesiastical vestments to amuse each other. Then as a rule, before retreating, they would drive the population of villages into churches, lock them up, and set fire to them.

At Istra, they made an ammunition dump of the famous New Jerusalem Monastery, with its unique decoration of seventeenth-century tiles, and when leaving reduced it to rubble. At the holy Pecherskaya Monastery in Kiev, the oldest monastery in Russia, the relics of the monks were plundered and the abbey blown up by order of the High Command.* "It was," said a witness, "as if a terrible hurricane had passed over the abbey, overthrowing everything, scattering and destroying the mighty buildings." Blown up also was the Uspensky Cathedral, an eleventh-century treasure founded by Prince Vladimir.

At the beginning of their crusade for power in Germany, Nazis had burned piles of books, but in Russia their pyromania reached its apogee. Everywhere on occupied Soviet territory they devastated and burned libraries, from small club and school libraries to the most valuable collections of rare manuscripts and books.

In Kiev, they blew up one of the most important centers of Ukrainian culture — the T. G. Shevchenko State University, founded in 1834. In the fire perished all the treasures that for centuries had represented the scientific and educational basis on which the university was founded. Over 1,300,000 books were destroyed, along with two million zoological exhibits. Plundered from other libraries were four million books. In the Museum of Ukrainian Art, of the original forty-one thousand exhibits, only fourteen hundred were left. All the paintings were taken. Of one hundred fifty schools in Kiev, the Germans destroyed all but ten. Ribbentrop's Fourth Company, in the Kiev Laboratory of Medical and Scientific Research, confiscated the entire laboratory as well as all the scientific materials, documents, and books. At Nuremberg the Soviet prosecutor, Rudenko, stated that "there was nothing of value left in the entire city of Kiev."

In Kharkov, after plundering the Korolenko Library of several thousand valuable books in rare editions, the remaining books were destroyed or used as paving

---

* The Nazis also removed holy relics, including the uncorrupted bodies of saints, from Novgorod, and put them on trains headed west. Their reasons for doing so will probably never be known.

stones in the muddy streets in order to facilitate passage of German motor vehicles. In the hospital, twenty thousand volumes perished.

In Minsk, every cultural and educational institution was destroyed and the contents of all the libraries were carried away. In a letter dated October 3, 1941, addressed to Kube, the Commissioner General for Byelorussia, Rosenberg said, "Minsk possessed a large, and in part very valuable collection of art treasures and paintings which have now been removed almost in their entirety from the city and sent to the Reich. They are worth several millions. Should have gone to Linz and Königsberg."

The Reich Commissioner of the Ukraine reported that sixty-five cases of objects of art evacuated from Kharkov and Kiev had been taken to Germany for "safekeeping" in noble estates in East Prussia. "Among the pictures," he said, "are a great number of very ancient icons, works by famous masters of the German, Italian, and Dutch schools of the sixteenth, seventeenth, and eighteenth centuries. On the whole, this property consists of extremely valuable works of art which have been removed from the public Ukrainian museums and whose value, even at a rough estimate, amounts to the sum of many millions."

Öbersturmführer Föster, a member of Ribbentrop's special Fourth Company, testified at Nuremberg, "We reaped a very rich harvest in the library of the Ukrainian Academy of Science, treasuring the rarest manuscripts of Persian, Abyssinian and Chinese literature, Russian and Ukrainian chronicles and first-edition books by the first Russian printer, Ivan Feodorov."

No region was spared. Novgorod, one of Russia's most beautiful and historic cities, where in the eleventh century the prosperous merchant citizens developed principles of self-rule long before the Magna Carta, was pitilessly demolished. A whole series of ancient churches, among them the eleventh-century Church of St. Sophia, with its rare twelfth-century frescoes, were blown up. A German prisoner testified, "On May 13, 1943, when passing through the Novgorod Kremlin, I saw German soldiers removing the gilded sheets from the church domes. Sheets no less than a meter in size were lying about on the ground. Major General Wilke himself stood at the foot of the cathedral and watched this scene. His chauffeur told me that Wilke had ordered the battalion paymaster Stinzkof to have dishes, goblets, and a tea set made for him out of these sheets." The rich museums of archeology and art were also ransacked. Of the three thousand icons of the Novgorod school, one of the three great schools of painting in Europe of the fifteenth century, only three hundred are left in the city today. Ribbentrop's battalions also pillaged the scientific library and collections of the photographs and bibliographical index of the Institute of History. Much of the population was abducted to slave labor in Germany. When Novgorod was liberated, of 2,436 residential buildings only forty remained, and only thirty residents in a town that before the war had numbered forty thousand; in the entire Novgorod district, of eighty thousand inhabitants only nine hundred were left.

While already in retreat in 1944, the orderly German employees of the E.R.R. in Paris carefully recorded the exact figures of their French art campaign: 29 shipments, 138 freight-car loads of 4,174 cases of art containing 21,903 objects confiscated from 203 Jewish-owned collections.

In Russia no such records were kept, but the staggering scope of the disaster can be glimpsed. In 1944 Rosenberg reported with great satisfaction that from the work of his special units alone, 1,418,000 freightloads of valuables had been removed from Russia, plus 427,000 tons shipped by water. And this of course was far from all, since indiscriminate looting and destruction were the rule, and only a small portion was taken out in an organized way. In Europe, with the exception of those destroyed by air raids, very few museums were razed to the ground. By contrast, of the 992 museums existing in the USSR, 427 were destroyed, and these were in the most important historical and cultural centers of the land. In addition, 1,670 Orthodox churches, 237 Catholic churches, 69 chapels, 532 synagogues, and 238 other church buildings vanished forever. The German armies were so thorough in their extermination of the Slav "vermin" that thousands of Russian villages were erased from the face of the earth, burned to the ground along with their inhabitants, who were herded into their barns and churches and then burned alive. By the time the Nazis were hurled back, more than twenty million people in the Soviet Union were dead — an inordinate number of these civilians — leaving a wound on the nation that has never completely healed.*

At his trial at Nuremberg in 1945, an alternately whining and unrepentant Alfred Rosenberg was to boast, "Between 1940 and 1944 our organization carried out the greatest art operation in history." For his crimes against civilization and humanity, he was hanged in October 1946.

Relatively few others have ever been judged for their crimes in Russia. The top military commanders — von Leeb, Manstein, and others — were judged at Nu-

---

* The terrible impact of all of Russia's combined calamities, the Revolution, Civil War, Stalin's Terror, plus World War II, can be glimpsed in one dramatic demographic fact. In 1950, eighty-five million Russians who should normally have been alive were not. Of these, forty-five million men — one in two — were, in the parlance of demographers, simply "not there."

remberg, a few others in the Soviet Union, but most of those who participated in these horrors and survived the war got off scot-free, and some must be alive today.

We in the West have known little about this holocaust in the Soviet Union — there have been few witnesses to step forward and give testimony in orderly fashion. The Russians estimated their total war losses at 629 billion rubles, and at the Yalta conference asked for ten billion dollars — or half the entire Allied reparations payments proposed.*

In reading the long trial testimony at Nuremberg, the feeling grows that Russian artistic losses were given somewhat less attention than those of the West. There are some possible explanations for this. In his obsessive paranoia, Stalin had cut off his people and his nation from the world for so long that few in the West knew the country or the culture that had been so devastated. The Cold War had already begun; suspicion of the Soviets and of Stalin certainly played a role. Traditional Western condescension toward Russian art may also have played a part; somehow the better-known works of artists of Western Europe seemed more important. There was general ignorance of Russian treasures and what they meant.

As the war in the East went on, Hitler, who despised Russians, began to revise his opinion about the detested *"Üntermenschen."* To Speer, his Minister of Armaments and War Production, Hitler expressed this contradiction to his long-held belief, saying, "Today the Siberians, White Russians and people of the steppes live extremely healthy lives. For this reason they are better equipped for development and in the long run biologically superior to the Germans." "At the beginning," writes Speer, "Hitler, captive to his theory that the Slavs were subhuman, called the war against them child's play. But the longer the war lasted, the more the Russians gained his respect. He was impressed by the stoicism with which they had accepted early defeats. He spoke admiringly of Stalin, particularly stressing the parallels to his own endurance."

In April 1945, just before the end, Hitler was still obsessively working until the early hours of the morning on his plans for his dream museum in Linz. After his suicide, the plans were found floating in the muck of his bunker by an American correspondent. Somewhere in the dark recesses of his soul Hitler knew what

---

* The issue of reparations is complex. The Western Allies declined to fix an exact monetary limit, preferring instead that each victorious country take what it wished from its zone of occupation. The total value of goods extracted by Russia from East Germany, including entire factories that were shipped east, cannot be calculated.

he had done, for when he confessed to Speer his irrevocable decision to commit suicide, he also admitted that he had come to his decision because, if caught, he might only be wounded, and he feared his body might be mutilated. But his greatest fear, confessed Hitler, was that he might fall into the hands of the Russians.

13

Siberia

AS THEY LEFT that early June morning of the white nights in 1941, Kuchumov and his colleagues could have no idea of the horrors of destruction that only a few weeks later would be perpetrated on their country and their beloved palaces, nor how precious the cargo of original treasures they had managed to spirit out ahead of the invading armies would become. For three years, enduring great hardships and traveling more than three thousand miles, they were to protect and care for the works of art that had been entrusted to them.

In the early-morning dawn, guarded by sentinels with machine guns, the long train slowly lumbered out of the Pushkin station. There was no friendly departing whistle — that once cheerful sound was now used only as an air-raid warning. Seventeen freight cars carrying 402 crates of palace treasures — thirty of them from Pavlovsk — accompanied by sixteen museum workers and their children, some still babies, began their journey toward the interior. Only Anatoly Mikhailovich knew their destination. After the first meeting on June 23, Ladukhin had taken Kuchumov aside and confided, "The museum treasures are to be stored in the city of Gorky. They have prepared special storehouses. This is a major state secret and must remain strictly between us."

This was all he knew. What awaited them, who would meet them when they arrived, and where the valuables were to be stored were still in question. Every time he had pressed Ladukhin for more information, he had been told, "Don't worry. They will meet you and then you will find out everything." Anatoly Mikhailovich was totally in charge of the convoy and responsible for its preservation.

From that moment, he never left the treasures for a single day during the entire three years they were away.

Their destination, the city of Gorky, 920 kilometers southeast of Leningrad, was situated at the juncture of two great rivers, the Volga and the Oka. Called Nizhny-Novgorod before the Revolution, a city lined with warehouses and market facilities, it had been famous since the fourteenth century as one of the greatest trading centers of Russia. Before the Revolution, every summer the city had been the site of the largest and most spectacularly colorful fair in Europe. In 1914 the last fair, in two summer months, had attracted four hundred thousand visitors; goods equivalent to two million dollars of those times from all over the Imperial Russian Empire were sold or exchanged.

Despite the assurances of the palace director, when Kuchumov arrived in Gorky he found that the city's storage facilities were already overwhelmed. Every day from Peterhof, the Russian Museum, the Ethnographic Museum, and others, treasures poured into the city. At first the city authorities proposed that they lay out their crates on a wharf along the river, and then store them in a house that had once belonged to a rich steamboat merchant and was now a local museum. This they did, only to discover that the available storage space was already exhausted. Eventually Kuchumov's convoy of palace treasures was put in the Stroganov Church, one of the finest monuments of Russian architecture of the late seventeenth century. In this sanctuary the 402 crates were placed beside those of Peterhof, which had arrived only two days before, and those of the Ethnographic Museum.

The church boasted a splendid carved iconostasis of wooden gilt work. The altar doors were carefully removed from their hinges so that even this area could be used, and the heavy crates were carefully eased behind the altar without harming the delicate wooden lace. The church was finally so crammed that only a narrow passageway was left in the center. The little group was sent to live across the river on the opposite side of the Volga in the town of Bor, and there they were safe for a few months.

"We kept things in Gorky until early November," says Anatoly Mikhailovich. "According to instructions I had no right to open a single crate — only those in special storage and only in the presence of authorities. But one day, when I was making the rounds, I saw a wood louse crawling out of a Pavlovsk Palace crate that stank of rot. The hay inside was still damp — it had not had time to dry out completely after we gathered it. Inside was a blue dressing table, and a Roentgen table. We managed to find wood shavings and then we repacked hundreds of boxes. For instance, we had packed a sofa and two tables in crates so big they wouldn't fit in the door, so we removed the articles, brought them in, took apart the crates, and put them back together again."

But by the end of October and the early days of November, as the battle grew closer to Moscow, the Nazis began bombing other important industrial cities, including Gorky, which was only 400 kilometers away from the capital. One day Kuchumov's wife, Anna Mikhailovna, was out walking with their little son, Felix, when she came upon a silent, motionless crowd all staring fearfully at the sky and a strange plane. "Not one of ours," she heard someone say, and then the word *Junker*. It was the first Nazi reconnaissance plane.

That night, the air assaults began. Multicolored anti-aircraft rockets streaked the sky, and the city glowed with fire. The treasures were no longer safe. Everything from the combined evacuated museums then in Gorky would have to be moved again. But where? One possibility was the city of Sarapul, 600 kilometers east, where all the evacuated treasures of Gatchina and three other echelons from Pavlovsk, Pushkin, and Peterhof had already been sent directly from Leningrad. But Kuchumov, afraid that Sarapul, too, might become vulnerable to the enemy, argued for sending their crates as far away as possible — deep into Siberia. Also, he had discovered that conditions in Sarapul were bad. The local museum, which was the proposed storehouse, had no central heating and had to be warmed by large wood furnaces, which consumed a huge amount of wood; the ceilings did not have proper supports, and the roof leaked. Besides these evident disadvantages, storing such a large amount of treasures in one place was, he felt, too risky. Instead, Kuchumov insisted on going to Tomsk, which was more than 2,400 kilometers farther east.

On November 7, the little group began the weary business of loading again. Local military sections, provided for protection, along with recruits helped with the loading. But the railroad workers, who had set aside a group of freight cars, had neglected one important thing. Sitting on open platforms next to the crates of museum treasures from Leningrad, Gorky, and Smolensk was a new shipment of tanks, which provided an inviting target for Nazi aircraft. Indeed, the attacks started as they were loading. While museum workers scurried for shelter and huddled under an overhang watching the battle, Russian anti-aircraft batteries managed to deflect the attack and the loading continued into the night. Just as the train prepared to leave, and museum workers from Leningrad and artists and workers from the Gorky Department of Art had scrambled aboard, it was suddenly discovered that a part of the museum group was missing. They were on the other side of the Volga and trying to rejoin their colleagues, a tortuous trip that took twelve hours riding on horses pulling carts carrying the children. There was only one bridge that led from Gorky to the opposite bank of the Oka and from there into the heart of the country. At 1 A.M., another Nazi assault began, with the bridge as its main target. The railroad workers insisted that they could wait no longer, for if the bridge were destroyed there would be no way to evacuate the treasures. At that crucial last moment, the missing few arrived. The train was forced to cross the bridge during the battle, in the midst of falling bombs and anti-aircraft fire, but miraculously it managed to make its way over the bridge to the heavily wooded opposite bank, and momentary safety.

In those wartime days, the railroad routes were overloaded with military echelons and the machinery and workers of the evacuated factories. The twenty museum cars, and a whole string of cars of other organizations, reached a local station, where they had to wait for many hours until railroad workers, acting on their own initiative, decided to try to hide the long convoy by shunting it off to a side branch, which led deep into the dense forests to a lumber mill. There, concealed between huge piles of birch logs, the museum convoy waited until it was judged safe to send it farther. Anatoly Mikhailovich recalls, "We hid there for two weeks. The closest settlements were eight to ten kilometers away and there were almost no inhabitants. When someone did ask, 'Did you come to us for lumber?' we did not reveal that this convoy contained great treasures, but instead, said that we had come to prepare birchwood logs. And indeed — with the help of soldiers — we used the chance to fill all the platforms of the cargo wagon with logs. In this way we gathered enough wood to last the whole way, to fuel the stoves in our own cars and the storage cars as well."

Running out of rations, they had to go foraging in a remote village in the forest for potatoes and milk for the children. This lost and isolated place was still populated with many Old Believers. Some met them abusively, others gave away their last food. One old man, crumbling a large dry potato, said, "My children are fighting and perhaps someone is offering them something. Take this, good children."

It was mid-November. "After these long freezing hikes," says Anatoly Mikhailovich, "sometimes we were even able to have a bath. We concocted a makeshift bath house by hooking up our old steam engine (called affectionately 'the Cuckoo' at the lumber works), which burned wood, puffed, huffed, and emitted clouds of sparks to a cold interior and then directed the steam inside."

After two weeks they were given the signal that they could leave, and the train started rolling again. This time the friendly "Cuckoo" nearly caused a tragedy. In the cars people slept on two levels of plank beds — women and children on top, men underneath. One night Kuchumov had the watch. Everyone was asleep, and as the train clattered along he sat half dressed and in galoshes reading by the light of the stove that heated their car. Suddenly those on the top bunks awoke, loudly complaining about smoke and burning eyes and asking him to put out the stove, while at the same time those on the bottom complained about the cold. A few moments later there was panic. The women on the top bunks saw that the ceiling was burning, ignited by sparks from the engine falling onto the wooden eaves beneath the metal roof. "Tongues of flame were running along the roof and the ceiling of the train," Anatoly Mikhailovich remembered. "We yelled at the engine car, signaling with a bucket, but they did not hear us. We were in the forest, so no one saw us. The engine ran on wood and there were many sparks, so they didn't stop. Women were preparing to throw themselves along with their children out of the moving train into the snow. One worker and I tried to douse the fire with boiling water from the bucket we used as a teakettle — but as I tried to jump toward the ceiling I only succeeded in scalding myself. Finally a courageous fellow from the Museum of Ethnography climbed up the braces and supports and out onto the roof of the moving train where he was able to put out the fire with snow. The first car was the military guard, the second was ours, but after us our seventeen carloads of cargo followed, and if the fire had spread back there it would have been horrible. Everything would have been destroyed."

When they arrived back at the station of Sukhobezvodnaya, where they had originally been shunted off into the forest, railway workers repaired the car and set up a new stove, yet even then the women refused to get back in the car, insisting they still smelled smoke. Anatoly Mikhailovich finally lost his temper, but the stubborn women would not budge. And they turned out to be right. Further investigation behind a closed door of a cargo car revealed that, behind the veneer, cracks jammed with wood shavings and string insulation were, indeed, still smoldering.

A straight way to Siberia now lay before them. For a long time all was darkness; train stations were lit only by dim blue lights. Everyone had to grope in the gloom. But once past the Urals, and the mountaintop summit with the signpost that marked the demarcation between Europe and Asia, stations were suddenly brightly lit again. As they traveled through the vast wild land, it seemed as if they had suddenly been transported to another planet, as if the war were nothing but a bad dream.

After nearly a month of travel, late one freezing night at the beginning of December with the temperature reading minus 55 degrees Centigrade, they arrived in Tomsk. Under the misty haze of bitter frost the illuminated snow-covered city, with its nineteenth-century wooden buildings and their elaborately carved gingerbread-lace window frames, looked like a storybook town. At the station they were met by representatives of the Moscow Committee for Artistic Affairs, who had been previously evacuated there.

For members of the committee, the unexpected appearance of such a large number of art treasures was a shock for which they were totally unprepared. Despite the late hour, accompanied by Kuchumov, they went off on wide horse-drawn sleds to inspect the few available storage places. The rare stone buildings of the city were mainly dilapidated churches with broken windows, frozen and encrusted with ice. One was proposed, but Kuchumov adamantly refused it. While the convoy waited, hasty telephone negotiations were begun with Novosibirsk, 225 kilometers southwest, where the Tretyakov Gallery had been evacuated since the summer. To add to the trouble, at that moment the railroad workers turned surly and insisted that they be paid ten thousand extra rubles — an enormous sum, which of course the museum workers did not have — to transport the cargo farther. Thanks to the firm intervention of the Tretyakov administration, the problem was resolved, and the train set off again. At long last, on December 22, 1941, almost two months after leaving Gorky, the Pavlovsk group finally reached Novosibirsk.

The train lumbered to a stop at a virgin clearing in the forest near a small railway junction on the Ob River. "Where shall we unload?" asked Kuchumov. Onto the snow, they were told. Snowdrifts were over three feet deep and the temperature subzero; not a warehouse or even a dry station house was anywhere near. Again Kuchumov refused and protested vigorously, first to the head of the railroad and then up the entire bureaucratic chain of command to the General Party Committee. "I was taken to the procurator. All the authorities used stern words with me but still I insisted. I told them that it was essential first to cover the crates — for things don't fear cold, but do fear snow." Once again the Tretyakov Gallery museum curators and administrators jumped in to support their Leningrad colleagues, insisting that if the snow, which would get into the crates, melted during transport, everything inside would rot. Under pressure of the military attorney, to whom Kuchumov had also appealed (as well as to the entire military leadership), the 402 crates were unloaded in a long pile that stretched the length of the train. The Party General Committee collected all the rugs, tarpaulins, and canvas stage decorations from the local theater to cover them. Guards were placed at both ends, and at long last, after their two-month journey, the workers were transferred from temporary shelters in the station to the cellar of the Novosibirsk Theater, where they were destined to live.

Although not quite finished, this huge circular theater was one of the finest in Siberia. Copies of antique statues stood between the columns of its enormous colonnaded amphitheater, which could accommodate several thousand people. In a large basement room with a concrete floor Kuchumov's group, along with their children, set up housekeeping. Everyone contributed whatever he or she had. Anatoly Mikhailovich unrolled a large carpet of Alexander III's time, which he had taken from the Alexander Palace to keep warm, and there, on the Tsar's rug, the museum workers took turns sleeping. This cellar room in the Novosibirsk Theater was to be their home for over two years.

The distance from the unloading site to the theater was only about one and a half kilometers, but the transfer of the valuables took almost three weeks. There was minimal manpower and very few means of transport, so most of the hauling had to be done with horses and sleighs. A crate would be placed on a sleigh and someone would have to lead the horse. "Seventeen cars," said Anatoly Mikhailovich. "Imagine that pile of crates! Anna Mikhailovna and four women escorted the sleighs, trooping through the snow in the summer shoes in which they had left Leningrad. While things were being loaded they would run into the driver's cab to warm up. The Tretyakov Gallery workers joined in to help us."

It would have been dangerous to bring the frozen crates directly into a warm place, so they first had to cool down the theater vestibule — yet not so much as to freeze the heating system of the theater, which would have left them all without heat in the Siberian winter. Crates were stacked, doors and windows opened, the temperature was dropped to 2 degrees Centigrade, and then gradually warmed so that no condensed moisture would collect on the precious cargo.

Maria Feodorovna's prized gift from Marie Antoinette had made the long journey to Siberia. Anatoly Mikhailovich had warned everyone about crate number one, which contained the priceless Sèvres toilet set. "I emphasized it should be moved with the greatest of care, and above all, not be dropped! When everything had been moved, I went down to check everything and found that this crate stood upside down! I did not sleep all night! In the morning we called the head of the Tretyakov Gallery Commission. Together we carefully turned over the crate, opened it, and found that the bronze Imperial crown and double eagle at the top of the mirror was jammed into the top of the crate. Behind the mirror was a metal shaft which supported the crown — and this heavy bronze crest had stood firm. Nothing was broken. It was a miracle."

Astonishingly, despite all the hardships of the long hazardous trip almost nothing was damaged. There was one accident, when a sculpture was unloaded at night by lamplight. Students were working, a heavy crate overturned, and the Dancing Satyr from the Italian Hall at Pavlovsk spilled out. The braces were torn off and the heavy base damaged, but it was restored. In another crate from Pavlovsk there were four vases: two monumental Sèvres vases, presents from Napoleon, and two smaller ones of Russian porcelain. The heavier ones had crushed the other two. "In time we inspected everything, obtained wood shavings, and repacked everything so that nothing would be damaged on the way back. Everything was checked, and more detailed documents were inserted in each crate." Empress Alexandra's dresses were carefully replaced in their original trunks.

During the two years, working with the Tretyakov Gallery and using crates as shelves, the museum workers organized exhibitions. One was "Treasures Saved from the Germans": Voronykhin furniture and paintings from Peterhof and Gatchina. These lifted the spirits and the morale of the townspeople as they heard the grim news from the front. "It was a cold and hungry time," said Anatoly Mikhailovich. "We drank coffee made of grain, we carried a couple of handfuls in our pockets. When we walked we were dizzy — there was very little bread. Later they gave us American supplies called 'melange' (egg yolks in a can), and then powdered eggs, which helped, and things got better."

They were far away, totally isolated. News trickled in rarely, and when it did, it was bad. As the terrible news of the Blockade reached them, Anatoly Mikhailovich remembers sadly, "We sat in Siberia, packed and repacked, and wondered: What would the future hold? Where would our treasures end up?" They were able to deflect a threat that for them was nothing less than blasphemy. "We were very upset when some bureaucratic bosses started suggesting that as the palaces were no doubt destroyed, and there was nowhere to take the things, and that in Leningrad we had the Hermitage and Moscow was so much poorer, then all these valuables evacuated from our museums should be transferred to Moscow. Such a resolution was even taken, but we raised a big outcry with the Leningrad bosses. They had even already transferred some of our convoy, including mine, to the Committee for Artistic Affairs, of which the Tretyakov was a part, to make it easier to take them away. But after our protests, they changed their decision and all stayed with us Leningraders, because when we had written the complete details, of course Leningrad could not agree to such a thing, that all the treasures which had been saved from our palaces should be given to Moscow — this was simply not possible!"

It was a blessing that they did not know how bad things actually were in Leningrad or they might have lost heart completely, for their city was in agony and dying.

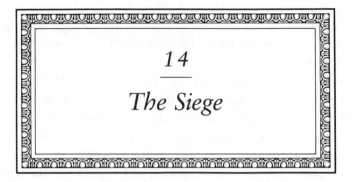

14

The Siege

"Looking at these stones, remember: no one has been forgotten, nothing is forgotten."

— Memorial Wall
Piskarevskoe Cemetery

LENINGRAD IS MORE THAN A CITY — it is a symbol of hope, a state of mind. Poised on the edge of Russia facing the sea, it stands looking toward the West, which is only a few miles away. Situated at the end of the Gulf of Finland, on the latitude of Hudson Bay in the northwest corner of a nation that stretches halfway around the globe to the Pacific, it is the largest northernmost city in the world. Its architecture is grand, startling, beautiful, a city of dreams made eternal in stone. A single man, the greatest Russian Tsar, Peter the Great, willed its creation, but his vision became reality because of the hard work and sacrifice of many thousands of Russian people. Western architects helped to create it, but it remains a monument to the imagination, ruthlessness, boldness, and sense of beauty of the Russian sovereigns who ordered it and to the artists and workers who built it. It owes its continued existence today to that indomitable Russian spirit, which has often astonished the world — a spirit that understands how to survive even the most impossible ordeal.

It is a Western cliché to speak of Petersburg as "not Russian." Certainly it is not the Russia of *izbi* and babushkas, of earthy proverbs spoken by peasants in bast shoes. Petersburg is Russia's graceful offspring of the eighteenth century —

a thrust to the stars, a leap of centuries, a challenge to Europe, neither entirely Western nor entirely Russian, but something entirely its own.

Younger than New York, it is a city built almost at a stroke. On May 6, 1703, Peter scratched a cross on the marshy land of the Finnish gulf where the Neva River flows into the sea. He chose the site solely because of its proximity to the sea and to Europe. If he considered the difficulties of construction at all, it was only to dismiss them.

And the difficulties were extraordinary. The islands of the Neva channels are flat, the low-lying marshes exposed to floods. The northerly location and the evaporation from the swamps make the climate damp and severe. Winter lasts from November to April. The Neva is frozen solid for six months. One hundred, perhaps two hundred, thousand people lost their lives in the course of trying to build a granite and stone city on wooden piles sunk in the shifting watery ground — so many that it was said the city was built on bones. Peter wanted his city immediately and, indeed, only twenty years after he scratched the cross in the marshes there was a city. Peter wanted it to rival the most beautiful cities in the West, and he imported the finest architects he could find. Under dire threats, he ordered his nobles to leave Moscow and build houses of stone in St. Petersburg.

From the first it was to be a city of ideas. There Peter created the first learned academies in Russia, the first libraries, and intended that Petersburg's contact with all that was good in the West be close and fruitful. From the moment of its founding the city became the focus of the struggle between the conservative heritage of Russia and the liberal ideas fostered by the Enlightenment in Europe.

After Peter's death, construction continued unceasingly on both sides of the Neva River as succeeding emperors and empresses erected splendid baroque and neoclassical palaces, libraries, theaters, and museums. Catherine the Great ordered the famous granite embankments of gray and pink Finnish marble along the Neva, which gave to the city a strong, regular appearance reminiscent of ancient Palmyra. As it grew, the city's wide avenues crossed by canals and rivers combined severe and stately buildings and planned squares with green parks adorned with marble statues and sparkling fountains. Over the years, the city spread to cover nineteen islands, which were all then connected by stone and wooden floating bridges. (Today there are 480.)

But St. Petersburg–Petrograd–Leningrad has always been more than a collection of buildings and monuments. There is about it an atmosphere that excites and continually creates new dreams. Water and sky reflect each other, and a human being feels forever suspended between them. In summer, the city is mellow and warm, full of lupin and poppies, wild roses and lilacs, whose scent, blown by the fresh wind of the Neva, fills the streets and perfumes the white nights of perpetual dawn.

Illuminated by iridescent light in summer and sunk in mysterious darkness in winter, human relationships there attain a strange intensity. Every monument, every street speaks of a great past, of poetry, music, adventure.

The inhabitants of such a city cannot be easily separated from it. They are what they are, think what they think because these sights are not only in their eyes, but in their souls. For two hundred years St. Petersburg was the capital of Russia and the center of all that was best culturally, artistically, and scientifically, inspiring myths and art as few other cities in the world have done. It was a city born of the collision of two cultures, and the tension arising from this collision became a persistent theme of many of Russia's greatest artists. Dostoevsky called it "the most abstract and artificial city on earth," and used its misty canals and mysterious streets as the setting for his celebrated novels. In 1842, when the visiting French poet Théophile Gautier first viewed the long horizon of the city broken by its golden spires, he was moved to write: "Nothing is more beautiful than this city of gold on a horizon of silver where the sky retains the paleness of dawn."

But if it was showered with gifts at birth, also from the beginning it has had a heavy share of tragedy. Nature has attacked it. It is prey, still today, to recurring floods, which in earlier times periodically swept away whole neighborhoods. Flood marks are regularly painted on the sides of buildings. It has also been almost overwhelmed by the floods of a tumultuous history. The Revolution was born in Petersburg — because nowhere else did ideas flourish as they did there — and its atmosphere began to take on a different and darker cast when in 1918 the capital was "temporarily" moved back to Moscow. For if from the moment of its founding it was to be a special city with special people, it was also to become for Moscow an enduring symbol of all that was new, stylish, and dangerous. To this day, Moscow has never learned completely to trust the glamorous northern city that supplanted it for so long. Today the rivalry is suppressed; when Stalin was in power, it was deadly.

After the capital was transferred to Moscow, whole libraries went too. During the 1930s, cultural establishments were gradually transferred. Petersburg, the traditional home of the Russian ballet, had to accept that from now on the Bolshoi was to supplant the proud, historic Imperial Ballet. When Moscow became the place where appropriations were decided, money for Leningrad became less available, and then not available at all, thus choking off cultural and artistic establishments. Stoically, the Empress of the Baltic accepted being humbled to the rank of a provincial city, always maintaining her independence and pride. Cultural downgrading was only the prelude to political suppression. The terrible purges of the 1930s began there and then spread over Russia like a deadly plague.

These attacks pale before the greatest disaster of its history, the Nazi siege of 1941–1944. Yet from this nightmare there emerged a shared glory, which turned disaster into triumph.

The siege of Leningrad is one of the great epics of heroism and endurance in war. In September 1941, when the last link with the interior of Russia was severed, the population of the city was 2,544,000 including some 400,000 children. Some 343,000 more people lived in suburban areas within the siege lines. For nine hundred grim and heroic days the city lay isolated and dying. Miraculously, it survived. In all history, no other such large city was ever called on to endure such a prolonged siege. No other famous siege of modern times — notably that of Paris, which lasted from September 19, 1870 to mid-January 1871, and in the United States that of Vicksburg, from May 18 to July 4, 1863 — was so long or involved such a large population; nor did other cities suffer such added trials as the fierce Russian winter, unceasing modern air and artillery attack, and a total paralysis of transport and communication facilities in a city spread over sixty-five thousand acres.

On July 10, 1941, as the frantic evacuation efforts were going on at Pavlovsk, Nazi armored units broke through the Soviet defenses south of Pskov and rolled in a wide stream toward Luga. Leningrad was only some two hundred kilometers away. At the speed at which they were advancing, the Nazi armies needed only nine or ten days to reach the city. On July 21, Hitler visited the headquarters of his commander, Field Marshal von Leeb, in Latvia and demanded a swift finish to the campaign for Leningrad. The outcome was a foregone conclusion. The Nazis had five or six times as much matériel as the poorly equipped and unprepared Soviet forces. Considering themselves unconquerable Goliaths, the Nazis were overflowing with confidence and certain of victory — so certain in fact that on August 8, Hitler's press secretary issued this statement about the fate that awaited Leningrad: "It is the first time in world history that a city of two million will literally be leveled to the ground."

This was indeed Hitler's intention: to reduce the fabled and beautiful Venice of the North to rubble, leaving it, like the ancient cities of Carthage and Troy, to survive only in legend. The seal was opened. The four horsemen of the Apocalypse thundered toward the city. Leading them, says the Book of Revelations, was the mighty conqueror with bow drawn; the symbol of false religion, crowned with enormous power. Close behind him was the red horse of war and destruction.

By August 30, with the severing of the last railroad link to the interior at Mga, Leningrad was caught in a steel vise — Nazi forces had completely encircled the city from the south and southwest. On September 4, the Germans began artillery shelling from Tosno, fifty kilometers southeast of Leningrad. From six entrenched positions along the heights overlooking Leningrad using the largest siege guns in Europe — 400- and 420-millimeter monsters capable of lobbing a projectile the size of a small Volkswagen, weighing over a ton, more than twenty-seven kilometers — they began battering the city.

On September 6, threatening leaflets fluttered down over the city taunting, "We shall do the bombing on the 6th. You will do the burying on the 7th." (A defiant Leningrad slogan responded, "Leningrad is not afraid of Death. Death is afraid of Leningrad.") That day, enemy aircraft, which controlled the air over the city, broke through Leningrad's anti-aircraft defenses and bombed the city for the first time. On September 8, with the fall of the small fort of Schüsselburg, near the mouth of the Neva, forty kilometers east of Leningrad, the city was completely cut off by land. The siege had begun.

That evening, first appearing over the city at dusk, Nazi planes rained 6,237 napalm bombs on the city and later the same night heavy bombers dropped 48 high explosive bombs. On September 9, von Leeb began preparing his final assault. By mid-September the Nazis were at the gates of Leningrad. The Palace Square was only fourteen kilometers away, the Kirov Steel Works six kilometers, and the front, in some places only three kilometers away. Jubilantly the Nazis planned their victory celebration at the Hotel Astoria; the invitations were already printed. They were soon to learn the truth of an old saying: "Russia is always stronger than her enemies believe." For there, at the gates to the city, they were stopped. One hundred and fifty thousand badly armed Russians held von Leeb's mighty army of three hundred thousand at bay, and the Nazis never advanced a single step farther.

Frustrated in their initial plan to take the city by storm, the Germans decided to change tactics. Now they determined to dig in, then bomb and shell the city into submission. On September 21 a special memorandum was presented to Hitler on the question of Leningrad:

> As a beginning we will hermetically blockade Leningrad and destroy the city if possible by artillery and air power.
>
> When hunger and terror have done their work in the city we can open the single gate and permit unarmed people to exit.
>
> The rest of the "fortress garrison" can remain there through the winter. In spring we will enter the city (not objecting if the Finns do this before us) sending all those who remain alive into the depths of Russia, or take them as prisoners, raze Leningrad to the ground and turn the region north of the Neva over to the Finns.

A few days later, on October 29, a secret directive was addressed to staff officers by the Chief of Staff of the Navy:

> The Führer has decided to erase St. Petersburg from the face of the earth. The existence of this large city will have no further interest after Soviet Russia is destroyed. Finland has also said that the existence of this city on her new border is not desirable from her point of view. . . .
>
> It is proposed to approach near to the city and to destroy it with the aid of artillery barrage from weapons of different calibers and with long air attacks.
>
> The problem of the life of the population and the provisioning of them is a problem which cannot and must not be decided by us.
>
> In this war we are not interested in preserving even a part of the population of this large city.*

Yet the closer the Nazis came, the more determined the resistance they met. Encirclement was not victory. By September 25, the Germans had already suffered 190,000 casualties.

The fanatic defense of their city by the people of Leningrad astonished the Nazis and the world. For nearly three years, until January 27, 1944, the besieged city lay starving, dying — but it did not yield. Instead, after twenty-eight months of vicious modern warfare, having suffered extraordinary losses, it was the mighty, once arrogant German army that retreated, broken and vanquished. Leningrad became the grave of the Nazis, but also of more than a million and a half Russians, both civilian and military — more than half of the population of the city. Almost fifty years later, there is still no adequate explanation of how a

* Staff directive number 1-a 1601/41 of September 29, 1941.

population could have withstood such sustained and prolonged hardship. Perhaps only a city with a touch of divine fanaticism could have done what Leningrad did — for in the beginning victory did not seem likely.

The boom of the cannon shot from the Peter and Paul Fortress to mark the noon hour each day is a beloved Petersburg custom.* On June 22, 1941, the familiar report of the cannon unexpectedly brought with it the radio broadcast and Molotov's voice announcing the Nazi attack and the beginning of war. Leningrad was unprepared and virtually unarmed when the catastrophe struck. After the broadcast, the city was in confusion. People rushed to the stores, buying everything they could. There was a run on the banks, which soon ran out of money. The halls of the Hermitage, which had opened its doors as usual that morning, were swiftly deserted and museum workers told that evacuation of the two and a half million treasures of one of the world's richest museums would begin immediately. Storehouses of packing materials were thrown open and massive crates of pine boards were hastily put together. Workers were given six days and six nights to pack up the first shipment of half a million exhibits. Twenty-two freight cars, with gems placed in special armored cars, protected by soldiers and anti-aircraft guns mounted on two open platforms on either end, left on July 1, destined for Sverdlovsk, there to be hidden in a Catholic church in the industrial town in the Urals where the last Tsar, Nicholas II, and his family had been assassinated. The second evacuation train of twenty-three cars left on July 20, with 700,000 objects in 422 crates. Packing went on until August 30, when the line at Mga was taken. By this time, the Hermitage workers had used up fifty tons of shavings, three tons of cotton wool, and sixteen tons of oilcloth. All stores were exhausted and no carpenters were left to make crates. Despite their superhuman efforts they had managed to evacuate only one and a quarter million objects — the 351 crates prepared for the third evacuation never left. Over one million art treasures remained, all of which had to be carried down to the ground-floor rooms and the cellars of the gigantic palace museum, where they remained throughout the Blockade.

Hastily, human and material resources were mobilized. Brigades of marines were formed from the personnel of ships, naval units, and academies. The people of the city hurried to form nine divisions of "People's Militia," simply throwing on their overcoats and rushing off to fight — youths with rifles in their hands for the first time, middle-aged men, in some cases armed only with hunting knives,

* The cannon at the Peter and Paul Fortress was set off by electric current from a control switch at the Pulkovo Meteorological Laboratory, on the Pulkova Heights nineteen kilometers south of Leningrad center.

who had fought in the Civil War. Quickly they were given elementary military training and sent off to face the armored might of the Nazi army. Three of these divisions, fighting as early as July, were cut down mercilessly because of their lack of preparation and their rudimentary weapons.

Everyone able to lift a shovel, some half a million people, the majority of them women and students without any previous experience, along with collective farmers from surrounding districts, went out to build defensive positions around the Leningrad zone. Factories worked around the clock turning out prefabricated reinforced-concrete gun and machine-gun pillboxes, armored artillery emplacements, and reinforced concrete pyramid-shaped obstacles, which were then installed in one of the fortified areas in a defense network. In the inner defense belt and the approaches to the city, antitank ditches were dug, as well as fire and communication trenches. Fortified areas were armed with artillery. Everywhere hundreds of thousands of people worked to transform Leningrad into a fortress. In a remarkably short time these untrained brigades of women and young people completed a girdle of anti-tank ditches 626 kilometers long, managed to dig or emplace thirty-five kilometers of open trenches, and built fifteen thousand reinforced concrete firing points, thirty-five kilometers of barricades, and forty-six hundred bomb shelters.

Yet in July and August, even as the enemy moved inexorably closer, still no one really believed that they would actually threaten Leningrad itself. There seemed to be no accurate perception of the extreme danger. The population was told that there were food supplies for many months (in fact there was only enough for one month) and reassured that the Soviet anti-aircraft system was invincible. Although food rationing was introduced in Leningrad and all over Russia on July 18, supplemental rations and supplies were still being distributed liberally in Leningrad. Bureaucracy continued to function in full flower — essential supplies were controlled by a hundred different bureaus. No plans for an extensive evacuation were made. Indeed, at the end of June and in early July children were sent off to the usual summer camp locations into the teeth of the advancing German armies. Only a few weeks later frantic mothers were trying to retrieve them; many fell into enemy hands. To compound the city's problems, refugees from the Baltic republics crowded into Leningrad, living in freight cars shunted onto railroad sidings and straining the city's fast-dwindling resources. Party officials announced, "Our population is ready to work in the front lines and it will not leave Leningrad." Civilians eager to leave were made to feel officially that wanting to leave the city was somehow not quite patriotic, with the result that in July and August only four hundred thousand people — many of them refugees and not inhabitants of Leningrad — were evacuated from the city before the escape routes were closed. Only a few weeks before the merciless Nazi shelling began, the population was being assured that Leningrad would never be shelled. In fact, there would only be short periods during the entire siege when they were not shelled. During the course of the Blockade, over a hundred thousand shells rained down on the city, not to speak of showers of heavy bombs and incendiary bombs; the Kirov factory alone took 770 bombs and 4,419 shells, and somehow managed to rebuild and continue turning out tanks.

Even by September 16, when Anna Zelenova, exhausted from her precipitous flight from Pavlovsk and the advancing Nazi armies, arrived at St. Isaac's Cathedral, neither she nor anyone imagined the terrible trials that lay ahead for them and their city. Her first reaction was one of relief; her first thought, "All the Pavlovsk things lay safe in the cellars of St. Isaac's and my heart was a little lighter."

The Soviet government placed its hope on unity — on the legendary patience and endurance of the Russian people and their long tradition of working together in times of crisis. This hope was not mistaken. After the initial period of confusion, united in the crucible of war, the population rallied and continued to rally with extraordinary heroism.

From the first, men had rushed to enlist, people's militias had been formed, and hundreds of thousands had turned out to dig trenches; now, sixty thousand people, including children, took turns standing air-raid watch on the rooftops of their city. Thousands of others worked to camouflage the celebrated landmark Petersburg buildings. The Bronze Horseman statue of Peter the Great and other famous city statues were sandbagged. The dome of St. Isaac's was painted gray, and the Admiralty spire splattered with paint. The baroque Smolny Cathedral, masterpiece of the eighteenth-century architect Rastrelli, was so cleverly masked that it could not be clearly discerned at even low altitudes.* Famous artists of the city turned out to help. Dmitry Shostakovich worked as a fire warden, Anna Akhmatova stood air-raid watches, the famous ballerina Galina Ulanova sewed camouflage nets. People were taught shooting and hand-to-hand fighting. Three hundred thousand Leningraders of all ages participated in civil defense. Young girls learned how to defuse delayed-action bombs. Women took over for men in factories, youngsters worked in auxiliary labor battalions, carried shells, and

---

* The gilt spire of the Peter and Paul Fortress also had to be camouflaged. The volunteers chosen to accomplish this task were given extra food for three or four days so they would have the energy to climb the spire.

acted as messengers. Mobile partisan units mined roads and bridges. Citizens and regional defense committees readied the city for house-to-house fighting and last-ditch defense of every block. All bridges, factories, and institutions were mined. Regional troikas were given explosives to blow up every important object in their districts if the Germans reached the city. Charges were placed on ships, under bridges, in factories, under cranes and presses, and within fuel reservoirs in evacuated factories.

In October, enemy aircraft dropped more than twelve thousand incendiary bombs — twice as many as in September. The outnumbered Soviet air force defended itself valiantly — when they ran out of ammunition, Soviet airmen took to ramming German planes to destroy them. Thousands volunteered to help extinguish the fires. The enemy bombarded at various times of the day, but concentrated their heaviest fire when the workday was beginning or ending and the streets were full of people, so as to hit as many as possible.* In her diary, Anna Zelenova wrote: "Those days were like a terrible dream. Bombs. Fires. I was amazed that people, above all else, tried to save not themselves, but all that was most worthy — our history, our memory: books, paintings, museums. I felt first and foremost a terrible terror for our Pavlovsk."

The palaces and churches of the tsars, built for the ages of marble and granite, with their deep cellars, offered the best protection from the unceasing bombardment. Thousands of people took refuge in these Imperial buildings and lived in them for months and even years. The twelve vast cellars under the former Winter Palace, which housed the Hermitage Museum, with its eleven hundred rooms and halls stretching for kilometers, could hold thousands of great works of art. In one such cellar, hundreds of pieces of delicate eighteenth- and nineteenth-century porcelain were half buried in masses of sand to protect them from the shocks. More than two thousand people lived, worked, and died in these Hermitage cellars during many months of the Blockade.

The last thirty-two crates of evacuated treasures of Pavlovsk were stored in the cellars of St. Isaac's Cathedral. There Anna watched over them during the entire nine hundred days of the Blockade. This huge cathedral, the largest in Petersburg, begun in the time of Alexander I in 1819 and not finally completed until forty-four years later in the reign of his grandnephew Alexander II, was lavishly constructed at a cost of twenty-three million gold rubles. The cathedral was surmounted by an impressive gilded dome, larger and higher than St. Paul's

---

* The German heavy gun emplacements were fixed; because of the trajectories taken by the shells, bombardment was heavier on one side of the street than on the other.

in London, rising to a height of 101 meters, dominating the city's skyline, visible at a distance of 60 kilometers. Built in the shape of a cross, the cathedral is 110 meters long and 95 meters wide, approached by wide granite steps from porticos on each side, the two largest adorned with sixteen monolith columns of polished Finnish red granite 16 meters high and 2 meters thick. Four colossal bronze doors richly decorated with sculptures lead inside. The walls are lined with polished marble of various colors and two hundred paintings by Russian artists. On the 68-meter-long iconostasis, flanked by semicircular columns faced with lapis lazuli and malachite, are thirty-five large mosaics of saints. Huge chandeliers of bronze and fifteen enormous chandeliers of pure silver hang from the ceiling.

During the entire siege, this monumental palace of God built by the tsars sheltered several thousand people in its deep cellars. Every nook and corner was occupied. Curators and museum workers from Pavlovsk, Pushkin, and Peterhof along with their children lived in these subterranean rooms. From the first day they arrived they were ordered into a barracks regimen by the Directorate of Leningrad Palaces and Parks. Evgenia Turova, an art historian from Pushkin, spent all of the first weeks of the war building defensive constructions around the city, leaving in St. Isaac's, under the care of others, her five-year-old son, who played with the two small children of Nikolai Weiss, the brave and stalwart curator who had stayed with Anna until the last, and sustained her as they escaped. He did curatorial work in the cathedral cellar, while his wife worked in the hospital, returning only late at night, exhausted from nighttime shifts.

Most had no homes in Leningrad and even those who did went home rarely. In the chancery of St. Isaac's they slept in their clothes on hastily set up planks. The huge unheated stone cathedral was dark, damp, and cold. Footsteps on the marble flagstones echoed hollowly off the vaulted ceilings. There, for many months alongside their crates of treasures they lived, worked, starved, and, in many cases, died. In the cavernous spaces, Anna wrote, "The office and academic section were set up in the side entrances to the altar. There too was set up a small *burzhuika* stove.* We heated water and dried our Blockade bread on it. We had to determine our responsibilities and all urgent matters for ourselves. The two most important assignments were the recording and protection of the museum valuables in our care."

During the first months of bombardment and shelling they carefully unpacked and inventoried everything that had been evacuated. Unemotionally Anna noted

---

*The *burzhuika* stove derives from the word *bourgeois* because it resembled the fat belly of a bourgeois capitalist as depicted in Soviet propaganda.

that "current events" often distracted them from their scholarly work — meaning that, among other problems, after the daily air raids they would have to sweep the huge interior clear of shattered marble slabs, crumbled plaster, and peeling vault painting. Much more difficult, she says, was the second part of their assignment — protection. "The marbles, works in stone, glass and porcelain seemed the safest. They only had to be immediately removed from the damp hay, which, in the haste of evacuation, had been used, and then everything had to be safeguarded from accidental shoves. Works in metal and bronze presented a great difficulty — in the dampness, corrosion could appear. The furniture was the worst — from the dampness and cold glue became soaked, veneer would fall off, expensive and rare Gobelins and silk tapestry were threatened by mold."

September and October were the trial of fire. The early days of that fall were unusually warm and beautiful, the leaves bright with color, but every night the sky turned blood red with the glow of fires. The city was being bombed and pounded to death, the air grew thick with plaster dust, it was hard to breath. Yet far worse was to come. Behind the red horse of war came the black horse of famine, and, by his side, the pale horse of death.

In the winter months of the north, darkness comes early. For six full months the pale northern sun barely appears. In November by three or four in the afternoon it is pitch dark in Leningrad. Winter came early that year — the coldest winter in a hundred years. The first snowflakes began falling in mid-October; by November heavy snowfalls engulfed the city. It is often said that it was the Russian winter that finished off the Nazis — what is sometimes forgotten is that it very nearly destroyed the Russians, too.

The period from November 1941 to the end of January 1942 was the worst of the entire Blockade. The whole city was covered with a thick layer of white. Large drifts accumulated along the streets and boulevards accompanied by a bitter icy wind that drove the snow through the broken windows of hospitals, stores, and apartments. With each passing day the city's transportation system progressively deteriorated until it came to a complete halt. Trams stood frozen on their tracks. Workers and employees living in distant parts of the city had to walk several kilometers to work, struggling from one end of the city to another in deep snow. Hoarfrost covered houses both inside and out.

Fuel supplies ran out. The last kerosene ration was given out in September, and there was no more until February 1942. Soap vanished. There was no heat, no light. In her diary, Anna wrote: "In that first winter of the Blockade, darkness oppressed everything. There was darkness in the streets, darkness at home —

and the white nights were so far away!" The streets were so black that people groped their way along with their hands outstretched, trying to avoid bumping into people or obstacles. In freezing apartments behind broken boarded-up windows people sat in darkness.

Electricity was shut off. Leningrad now lived by the light of small homemade wick lamps that sputtered and smoked. The Hermitage was lucky enough to find a cache of church candles in their cellars, and when these ran out, Tsar Alexander III's former yacht, the *Polar Star,* now an auxiliary vessel for the submarine squadron of the Baltic Fleet, provided them with electricity for a time when they laid a cable from the ship across to the museum. In St. Isaac's, Anna and her colleagues found altar lamps and burned seal fat that they had obtained from the zoo. In January 1942, the water mains burst from lack of heat. Fires from bombing attacks now had to be put out with snow, and weakened people had to haul water drawn from ice holes in the Neva, the Fontanka, the Moika, and the Karpovka rivers in heavy buckets over long distances.

Normally one hundred and twenty trainloads of wood were required each day to warm the city — now there were only three or four. Brigades were organized to take apart all wooden houses for fuel — nine thousand were demolished. People burned fences, furniture, books — all of which were consumed and extinguished with the heartbreaking swiftness of fireworks. Still the temperature continued to fall. That winter it hit record lows of minus 20 degrees and then minus 40 degrees Centigrade. It was so cold that sometimes Nazi planes could not fly because the fuel froze in their tanks. Sparrows froze in midflight and fell stiffly to the ground. Inside the marble and granite St. Isaac's it was so cold that, Anna wrote, "In those severe winters the frost was easier to bear on the street than in the dank cold of St. Isaac's. We would go out and warm ourselves on the portico."

It was Hitler's plan to use hunger as a weapon to conquer the city.* On September 8, during the first bombing attacks of the city, a terrible disaster occurred. The Badaev warehouses, where most of the city's stores were kept, were hit and totally burned. Meat, lard, three thousand tons of flour, and two and a half thousand tons of sugar went up in smoke, leaving a slimy crust on the earth. Two months later people were paying two hundred rubles on the black market

---

*Following a "plan of organized hunger," the German army and occupation authorities sent thousands of trains to Germany loaded with pillaged foodstuffs from every spot their troops overran. From Poland alone during the first two years of the war, the Nazis confiscated and exported more than 950,000 tons of grain, 800,000 pigs, and 100 million eggs.

for a jar of the sugar-soaked earth. Food supplies diminished every day. Office employees and workers harvested the last potato crop at night, creeping over fields on their hands and knees, exposed to artillery fire, hiding in shell holes, and lying prone to dig up potatoes and pile them in heaps. As the noose tightened during September and October, the bread ration was steadily reduced. In November it was cut three times, until the ration for dependents and children was a quarter pound of bread a day — four little cubes that were lost in the palm of a hand. Other than that, there was nothing.*

Fifty-three days into the Blockade the search for food became an obsession. Scientists at institutes worked on converting wood into edible cellulose, which began to arrive at bread factories at the end of November. Cellulose made the bread white, but the taste was bitter and grassy. Layers of flour dust that had been accumulating for years on the walls and floors of flour mills were gathered, processed, and used for making bread. Every sack that had ever contained flour was shaken and beaten. Finally, by November 1941, the composition of bread deteriorated to small amounts of corn and rye flour supplemented by a foul mixture of cellulose, cottonseed-oil cake, chaff, flour sweepings, and dust from flour sacks. Ghastly black macaroni was made of rye flour with 5 percent flax seed cake. In the harbor, two thousand tons of sheep gut was found; all was used for food. As people made sheep gut into jelly, ate boiled calfskins found in the tannery warehouses, seaweed, carpenter's and fish glue, and plaster from the walls, all sensation of taste was lost. Medicine cabinets were raided, and castor oil, vaseline, and glycerine consumed. Virtually every dog and cat was killed and eaten. Guinea pigs and mice vanished from laboratories. Birds disappeared, gulls and pigeons were gone. The rats abandoned the city and turned up in the soldier's front-line trenches where there was more food.

The siege brought out extraordinary heroism in people but also the most vicious side of humanity. There were exploiters who used their high positions to get food when others were starving, egotists who would snatch bread from their neighbors and even their own children, managers of bread stores who sold customers bread at false weight (those found doing so were shot). There were swindlers who tried to obtain more ration cards, who forged them and stole them, and apartment building managers who conspired with janitors to obtain cards

---

* In Leningrad during the Blockade, monthly books of ration cards were issued with daily coupons for each group of foodstuff: bread, sugar, meat, fish, fats, cereals and macaroni. Rations were divided into four categories, in descending quantity: workers, office workers, dependents, and children under twelve.

from dead, evacuated, or imaginary tenants. When ration cards were registered, the loss or theft of a card was an almost certain sentence of death. The black market flourished. On New Year's Day in 1942, a kilo of bread cost six hundred rubles. By the end of the Blockade a rare kitten cost five hundred rubles, vodka three hundred fifty rubles, and felt boots thirty-five hundred rubles. There were dark tales of cannibalism — people were afraid to let their children out in the streets for fear they would disappear. Human heads were sometimes found in snowdrifts.

Yet the spirit of heroism prevailed. No bakeries were ever looted. There were instances where bread trucks were overturned and not a piece stolen, and there were people who gave up their own rations to save others.

As nourishment deteriorated and the bitter cold made new demands on people's health, jokes and laughter ceased entirely. People forgot how to smile.* Blood no longer clotted. Men and women faded before each other's eyes. Old men went first because, according to a Leningrad doctor, men had less fat than women, and thus less to sustain them. People progressively moved more slowly, talked slower, then the emaciated body slipped quietly into another world.

Death overtook people anywhere. It claimed men as they worked at their machines. People would be walking on the street, fall, and never get up — go to bed, and never wake up. As there was no public transportation, the dead, without coffins, sometimes wrapped in makeshift shrouds, were carried on children's sleds, which became a macabre symbol of the Blockade. Two or three relatives would pull the sled through the dark, snowy streets, often losing strength and abandoning the sleds halfway to the cemetery. Corpses piled up along the streets; frozen bodies, half drifted over with snow, lined the cemeteries and their approaches. Hospitals were so piled with the dead that sometimes it was difficult to make a path through their halls. Trucks went through the streets gathering up bodies. A strong disinfectant of pine oil was thrown on them. This deathly smell stayed suspended in the frosty air, permeating the nostrils. Every week the toll rose, until thousands were dying every day. In November the death toll was 11,085, in December 52,881, and in January and February 1942, 199,187.

The only possible salvation lay forty-five kilometers north of Leningrad across

---

* Olga Bergholz, a Leningrad poet who read her works over the radio during the Blockade, said that Leningraders were so sapped of energy that "People, even children, did not laugh and did not cry." Another woman, recalling her first smile after all her suffering, noted how surprised she was "by those unaccustomed movements of the face muscles."

Lake Ladoga, the largest lake in Europe. Two hundred kilometers long and one hundred twenty kilometers across at its widest point, with depths ranging from twenty to two hundred ten meters, it is in reality an inland sea. A stretch of sixty-five kilometers along the lake separated the Germans at Schüsselburg from their allies, the Finns, on the Karelian Isthmus. This small breach in the Nazi armor became the place where the Russians, at great risk and with enormous effort, established their base for the supply arteries of water and ice that were to save Leningrad.

In the months of September through November, a long roundabout lake route for ships and barges, maintained with difficulty under Nazi bombing attacks, kept a minimum of supplies for Leningrad coming across the water. Anticipating the coming winter, the Russians began planning for an ice road as early as mid-October 1941. The route was to begin at Osnivets, a small fishing village fifty-three kilometers from Leningrad to the hamlets of Lednovo and Kabona — a distance of forty-five kilometers across the ice, and from there overland to railroad junctions. The territory directly bordering on the lake on the south was a front-line sector occupied by the Germans, and the route was under enemy observation all the way. In some places it would have to pass within range of German artillery. But there was no other hope for the city.

Officially called "The Leningrad Military Automobile Highway No. 101," the winter ice road quickly became known as "The Road of Life" — the tenuous, but sole, lifeline that prevented the Germans from achieving their goal of starving the city to death in that terrible first winter of 1941/42.

It was an enormously risky undertaking. No one had ever tried such a thing before, and no one could predict whether an ice road could be built at all. No one knew how thick the ice really was, and since the lake level rose and fell from one and a half feet to four feet even in winter, the ice shifted and moved. Scientific calculations determined that a minimum of eight inches was required to support trucks carrying supplies. During the month of November, as the city was starving to death, perversely, the temperature on the lake fluctuated capriciously. Finally the decision was made that they could afford to wait no longer. On November 20, twenty-eight to thirty-two meters apart, stretching in a column of over eight kilometers, three hundred fifty horses and sleighs started over the ice, and on the twenty-second, the ice was judged just thick enough for trucks to inch their way gingerly across. Within the first week, forty trucks broke through the shifting ice and sank to the bottom. Once on the other side, in order to reach the first Russian railway depot, trucks had to cross a tortuous land route of 350 kilometers hurriedly hacked out along ancient forest routes through swamps, bogs, and dense wilderness — often impassable because of snow.

On December 9, 1941, there remained in the city only enough grain for nine or ten more days; all other reserves had been consumed. On that desperate day, in a bitter battle, Soviet forces retook Tikhvin, a small city one hundred forty-five kilometers east of Leningrad, a vital link that had been in enemy hands for a month. This victory, and the recapture of the northern railroad as far as Mga, made it possible to establish a reliable link with the interior. This was a vital turning point in the defense of the city, no less crucial to the fate of Leningrad than the final breaking of the Blockade itself, and it saved thousands of people from death.

At first there was just a trickle. Leningrad required a minimum of a thousand tons of supplies, food, fuel, and munitions each day, and the ice road averaged 361 tons. But even this meant that on December 25, the bread ration was slightly increased. In the streets of Leningrad, people hugged each other and wept for joy. One woman wrote, "It was like the glorious day of Easter Sunday! It was such happiness!" The improvement was minuscule, but the effect on morale was tremendous.

Gradually, over the winter months there were sixty routes over the ice, and as the ice gradually grew thick enough to accommodate larger trucks, more supplies came in, among them some sent by the United States. Both the construction and maintenance of the ice roads were fiendishly difficult. First-aid stations, traffic control, repair points, snow-clearing, and bridge-laying detachments were all built on the ice. By midwinter, some nineteen thousand people were involved in the effort to keep ice roads functioning. Bitter icy winds blew over the lake. Temperatures ranged from minus 30 to minus 40 degrees Centigrade. Anti-aircraft defenses and traffic guards, themselves weak and undernourished, stood guard twenty-four hours a day under these extreme conditions. The Nazis pounded the convoys with artillery and bombed them — largely unsuccessfully, for as bombs fell through the ice and exploded underneath, the Russians quickly marked the craters with long poles topped by fir branches, and the drivers detoured around them. On the south shore of the lake, Russian machine gunners with chemical heaters in their pockets lay on straw mats on the ice guarding the road behind barricades of snow.

Earlier, people had tried to cross the treacherous ice on their own and many

had frozen to death. Such crossings now became against the law. Andrei Zhdanov, Party boss of Leningrad and Chief of the State Defense Committee, decided
to try to evacuate one-fourth of the remaining population of the city over the ice
road, and Alexei Kosygin, then Deputy Chairman of the Council of Ministers of
the USSR, was put in charge of the operation. In four months, from January to
April 1942, under Nazi strafing and shelling, 514,069 people were evacuated —
primarily the old, invalids, women, and children. One was the mother of Anna
Zelenova. Anna and her mother were extraordinarily close and were never separated in their lifetimes except during the Blockade. From the beginning, Anna
herself had refused evacuation and continued to refuse to leave, writing in her
diary, "I am upset almost to tears. They are threatening to transfer me to work
in Moscow." Anna's mother also refused to leave and was persuaded only when
Anna declared that she would give up her own bread ration and die herself.

With the recapture of Tikhvin and the opening of the ice road, Hitler, enraged
that the first and most acute period of the battle for Leningrad had not had the
desired result, blamed his aristocratic Bavarian commander, von Leeb. Because
of von Leeb's religion (he was Catholic) and his lack of sufficient enthusiasm for
Nazi philosophy, Hitler had never trusted him. Now, ranting to his General Staff,
the Führer cried, "He is in his second childhood! He cannot grasp and carry out
my plan for the speedy capture of Leningrad. He is obviously senile — he has
lost his nerve. As a true Catholic he wants to pray not to fight!" At the end of
December 1941, von Leeb was relieved of command (officially announced at his
own request because of "illness") and in January 1942, the deeply committed
Nazi Colonel General von Küchler became commander of Army Group Nord.
But during his two years of command, von Küchler was no more successful in
conquering Leningrad than von Leeb had been, although, to maintain the Blockade, he sank ships bringing food to the city, dropped parachute mines of great
explosive force, and bombarded the city at long range with heavy caliber shells,
with no idea where they might fall.*

The steady stream of supplies that began to reach Leningrad, combined with
the lowering of the demands on available resources by both the evacuation and
the terrible death toll, made it possible for Leningrad to survive the next two
years. Yet despite all the heroic efforts of the Road of Life, only one-third of the

---

* Von Küchler's intention was to terrorize the population. Hitler promoted him to the rank of field marshal in
June 1942, but removed him from his post and retired him when the Blockade was broken. In 1948 he was
found guilty of crimes against humanity and sentenced to twenty years imprisonment. He served only eight
years in prison, however, released early because of illness and age.

supplies necessary for basic survival could reach the besieged city. Conditions in Leningrad remained desperate and the population at starvation levels until the siege was fully lifted twenty-four months later.

In the city, as the life of the body ebbed away, the spirit became more vital than ever before. On festival days the churches were full. Cultural and intellectual pursuits sustained the morale of the beleaguered city. Courageously, the orchestra of Radio Leningrad continued to play, the musicians often wrapped in sheepskin coats. Most of the theaters were evacuated, but the operetta stayed and performed. In December they gave *Rose Marie,* wearing felt boots and coats. Between acts many performers fainted from hunger. When there were air raids, which was often, an intermission would be called and the audience would go to shelters while the performers went up to the icy roof to stand guard. After a performance, the audience, too weak to applaud, would simply rise and stand silently for several minutes to show their gratitude. Scientists continued their research, poets read their verses regularly on the radio and were broadcast over loudspeakers set up in the street.* Painters continued to sketch and paint in the streets and in air-raid shelters and exhibited their paintings. At institutes, seminars were given on subjects as esoteric as the organization of vineyards in fifth-century Rome. These seminars absorbed people utterly; one historian recalled, "We gave reports that lasted for hours and listened more intently than I can ever remember doing since."

At the Hermitage, the fire warden's room became the pivot of academic life. Boris Piotrovsky, now director of the museum, observed, "Our scholarly exercises greatly eased our hardships, as those who had something to occupy their minds more easily bore the pangs of hunger." The director of the Hermitage, Iosif Orbieli, in 1941 organized a celebration for the five-hundredth anniversary of the fifteenth-century Uzbek poet Alisher Navoi, as well as one in honor of the eight-hundredth anniversary of the Azerbaijanian poet Nizama of Gianja. Some people were released from the front in order to attend the celebration, which went on despite the interruption of an air raid.

The iron rule of Anna and the group of curators at St. Isaac's was "Don't talk about food," which helped them to ward off the gastronomic hallucinations from

---

* At the height of the Blockade, Olga Bergholz, faint with hunger and cold, collapsed into the snow of a Leningrad street, ready to die where she fell as so many had done. At that moment she heard her own voice broadcast over the loudspeakers, reading to the populace. Aroused out of her stupor, she was able to climb out of the snowbank and continue on her way.

which many people suffered. Instead, they conducted "basement evenings" of art lectures and seminars, because, said Anna, "we knew that even under the conditions of the Blockade, people yearned for beauty." Marina Tikhmirova, a curator of Peterhof, was much in demand for lectures on ships of the Baltic Fleet. In the basement of St. Isaac's, curators from Gatchina, Pushkin, and Peterhof worked out detailed theses for future monographs on their museums. Anna wrote: "Problems of restoration already preoccupied me. It was difficult to guess the amount of destruction of our national treasurehouses but we knew of the Nazi intention to destroy them." In St. Isaac's, she began to work out the methods of restoration and the scholarly documentation that would eventually help to save the palace.

On the corner of the Nevsky and Sadovaya Street, one of the designated "danger corners" during shelling, stood the stately Saltykov-Shchedrin Library, which, with its nine million volumes and immense collection of manuscripts and first editions, proudly claimed to be, except for the British Museum, the largest library in Europe. During the entire Blockade, despite the shelling, the library never closed, not even during the worst days of the 1941/42 winter. The consuming aim of the chief librarian was to defend nine million volumes from the vile creatures who, for the first time in centuries, had made bonfires out of books.

The library staff managed to evacuate only a very small number of the most valuable things — about 360,000 items. They also carried masses of sand to the attics, decentralized the library, stored as much as they could in basements, bricked up and sandbagged the windows, secured water tanks, pumps, fire extinguishers, and organized a whole fire-fighting system. When all the glass panes had been shattered four times, they replaced them with plywood.

Before the war three thousand people a day came to their seven huge reading rooms. In late August 1941, the main reading room was closed and another, safer one opened on the ground floor with one hundred fifty seats. People who were very nervous could do their reading in air-raid shelters, for, as the chief librarian commented cooly, "not all people react the same way to bombing." In the basement the main catalogue was set up adjacent to a small public reading room.

The library was of enormous help during the Blockade. At first, people went and studied every conceivable source on sieges of towns. Later, when matches ran out, scientists and others went to the library and studied French, English, and German books one hundred to one hundred fifty years old on all the primitive methods of making matches. Thousands of questions were put to the librarians by both military and civil authorities, who asked how to make candles (librarians found recipes in eighteenth-century books), if there was any way of making yeasts, edible wood, artificial vitamins.

Day after day throughout the fall and winter, one or two hundred people, Anna Ivanovna among them, could be found sitting in fur hats and overcoats, huddled over books, reading by the light of small wick lamps. On January 26, 1942, the library lost all light and heat and had to close all the reading rooms, but readers were still permitted to use the director's room and the former dining room, which were heated by small temporary stoves. There were days when only five readers came.

For Anna, the library became a pillar of her existence, a place to which she could escape entirely into the study of Pavlovsk. She wrote: "Every night on my own, after my work in the museum section of St. Isaac's, I would go right to the archives, to the library. It is essential to collect, to study everything about Pavlovsk, everything about its creators — Cameron, Voronykhin, Gonzaga, Quarenghi, Rossi. If some terrible misfortune should happen at Pavlovsk, without these sources we would not be able to overcome it." She did not mention another worry — that the library itself, in the path of heavy shelling, could be destroyed at any time.

The distance from St. Isaac's to the public library is almost two miles. Anna trudged through the snow in the inky darkness. Along her way paralyzed trolley cars partially buried in snowdrifts stood like frozen behemoths. Everywhere around her were the little sleds of death, as people wearily dragged with their last strength the bodies of their loved ones toward the cemetery. Many simply gave up and sank into snowdrifts and eternal sleep.

At the library, wrapped in her coat and wearing a hat and gloves, Anna continued to work. "What a haven our library seemed to me up to the time of the war, so peaceful! No sirens, no worry. And now, the ink froze. I keep working on the material about Pavlovsk. At night I could see the silhouette in my dreams — phantasmagoric!"

Another day: "It became impossible to read, since the lenses of my glasses freeze up. There is a ringing in my ears. Everything darkens before my eyes."

"There was a demonic air assault. I was in the *Publichka** preparing a chapter about Pavlovsk for an anthology about the Leningrad outskirts." She also spent

---

* *Publichka* was the nickname for the Saltykov-Shchedrin Library.

time studying the development of social thought at the end of the eighteenth and beginning of the nineteenth centuries.

In peaceful days, there is a ritual, formal as a minuet, at the entrance to the library. Coats and hats are ceremonially taken by venerable old gentlemen and hung up, each in turn. There is no pushing; hurrying the ritual is unthinkable. But in 1942, Anna wrote, "The frost is severe. There is no longer any strict ceremony at the entrance to the library. Everyone goes in their coats, not even having the strength to shake the snow off their mittens. The librarians look like Dantesque shadows. Next to them are their pale, motionless, staring children."

Even when she was starving, Anna never gave up her trips, noting, "There is nothing left, except mustard and pepper. And from them one gets the most terrible pain in the stomach. Only the teapot can save one, but they have disappeared. Nevertheless, tomorrow I shall go to the library."

During the nine hundred days, Anna worked closely with the librarians and helped them to prepare over fifty textual and illustrated exhibitions. She also worked to organize an exhibition of original etchings, watercolors, posters, and photographic documents — "The Heroic Past and Present of Leningrad" — with materials provided by the library. In addition she organized more than fifty other exhibitions all over the city. In the Rossi Pavilion near the library she organized an exhibit for the hundred fiftieth anniversary of the Battle of Borodino, and one entitled "War in Children's Drawings." In August 1943, two years into the Blockade, when people were expending as little energy as possible and suffering from acute emaciation and exhaustion, Anna organized an exhibition at the library titled "Our Allies," about American soldiers and U.S. military aid to the Soviet Union, using individual newsreel frames, which she selected.

During the Blockade Anna was also appointed head of the Museum Department of the Office of Artistic Affairs of the Leningrad Executive Committee and took part in the inspection of all the museums of the city. The architect who headed the Government Agency for the Protection of Monuments (GIOP) asked her to join a group of architects who would establish the descriptions and measurements of museum-quality furniture and other artistic valuables that were in private homes, so that these could be given protected status. In the dark, frozen apartments of Leningrad, she made inventories of unique sets of furniture. Some prominent architects and sculptors had in their homes such treasures as original carved doors of Peter's time, fine porcelain, watercolors, and engravings. "These were sad visits," she wrote. "By the dim light of the *morgaski,* which we called the homemade wick lamps, the owners of these unique collections, wrapped in furs and rugs, exhausted and weak and many soon to be overcome by death, laid out their treasures before me. 'Write this down,' they would say, 'write everything down. Their place is in museums. For there will once again be a normal life and all of this will be needed by the people.'"

She had to warn them that once an object was recorded in the protected lists it could no longer be sold or traded for food. The reaction, she said, was, "What are you saying! Does one trade such a thing for bread? This is not simply a valuable object — it is history! Write it down!" In many apartments there was no one left to receive her.

All this she and her colleagues did on foot in the bitter winter cold. One night, she recounts, "From St. Isaac's I went with Irina Yanchenko to the Petrograd side. In the February snowstorm the wind sweeps you off your feet. We were engulfed by a snowdrift near the steps of Peter's house. We nevertheless took the opportunity to look it over and found it in good condition except for the shutters, which had been torn off by artillery blasts. . . . Three times I fell in the street. My weakness was great." On one such visit where there were many architectural drawings to be recorded, she was held up longer than usual. The local militiaman invited to be present at the session sat quietly on a couch near the door. As Anna was preparing to leave she went to wake him, only to find that he was dead.

For their work, Anna and this group were later awarded medals "For the Protection of Leningrad," although many who had earned them were no longer there to receive them.

As she did throughout her life, even during the Blockade Anna found the time and energy to keep a diary. Indefatigably, she wrote letters, answering everyone who wrote to her. Many wrote from the front asking, "What about our beloved Pavlovsk?" In her letters to her colleagues she shared her thoughts on the restoration of the palace, although she had no idea in what condition she would find it again, if it still existed at all.

With the coming of warmer weather, those who had survived that draconian winter came blinking out into the sun, bodies no more than skeletons, skin like parchment, walking unsteadily. The city was overflowing with corpses. They lay on the streets in the melting ice and snowdrifts, in the courtyards, cellars, and apartments, in hospitals and churches. The city and its people were filthy — there had been no baths, showers, or laundries since December. There was great concern about the possibility of epidemics, and it was essential to clean up the city as soon as possible. On March 8, Woman's Day, a traditional Soviet holiday, several thousand emaciated women came out and tackled the heaps of ice with shovels and picks. Through March and April three hundred thousand exhausted, starved people, the majority of them women, turned out to clean up the court-yards, sewers, and streets of the city.

Surprisingly, although there were some cases of cholera and typhus, no major epidemics of communicable diseases occurred. It was speculated that microbes could not live in the emaciated bodies. However, dystrophy and scurvy were rampant. People ate grass, nettles, and wild sorrel and planted cabbage gardens all over the city. Catherine the Great's Hanging Garden in the Hermitage, full of lilac and honeysuckle, was ripped out to make room for vegetables. Someone saw a man approach a tree, strip off the leaves, and shove them into his mouth. A professor invented a process for extracting vitamin C from pine needles, and schoolchildren went out to collect fresh pine branches. In every school canteen, office, and factory, there were buckets of this strange Leningrad vitamin drink, and people drank gallons to restore their malnourished bodies.

But the coming of spring brought to the museum workers another exhausting fight to protect their precious valuables against dampness and mildew. Winter had been hardest on people, but spring was hardest on objects of art, which, said one Hermitage curator, were "more susceptible to disease than living organisms." In St. Isaac's, the hoarfrost on the marble and granite walls melted, and streams trickled down the walls and along the floor. In April a frozen water main broke and water flooded almost all the sections of the cellar. Moisture settled on marble, mirrors, bronze. Molding cracked, gilding peeled. Once again everything had to be saved. Heavy, wet crates had to be dragged up from the cellar and all soaked things dried. In the Hermitage, the porcelain and crystal chandeliers, which had been resting in the cellar sand to protect them from artillery and bombing shocks, were found half submerged and floating in muck. Museum workers had to go into the dark cellars where water reached up to their knees, placing each foot down carefully so as not to step on the fragile china. Groping about, they tried to pluck out cups and dishes. Some of the plates floated on the surface, delicate vases jutted out of the water. Many, clogged with sand and filth, had simply sunk under the water to the floor. Many had come unglued. All had lost their inventory labels. The beautiful, fragile porcelain was laid to dry in the garden on the grass. Piece by piece many hundreds of chandelier crystals were cleaned off.

At St. Isaac's mold covered the Gobelins and the silk. Upholstery on couches and chairs was covered with a thick furry layer of mildew; the pieces looked as if they had been upholstered not in velvet and silk but in some hideous yellow-green sheepskin. Everything had to be aired. "Fifteen thousand three hundred articles have been dried," reads an entry in Anna's diary. As the days grew warmer and less humid, between bombing attacks and artillery barrages all the furniture was dragged out into the fresh air. Nestled between the huge granite monolith columns of red Finnish granite stood couches with rococo turquoise upholstery and Louis XVI tables on straight, delicate legs. Paintings were dried, turned with their backs toward the sun. Several rows of ropes were strung between the columns, and there bright widths of silks and embroidery were hung out, so that the open porticoes of the stern St. Isaac's Cathedral began to look like Neapolitan streets. But no one stopped to look at the incongruous sight. "In those days," said Anna, "the people of Leningrad were very anxious. If they were going anywhere, they were only hoping to get there alive." Everything was exposed to the fresh air for a few hours and then it all had to be dragged in again.

To dry out the cavernous cathedral, the huge bronze doors were flung open wide to the spring. But then such strong winds and gusty drafts blew that the cathedral seemed more like the prow of a fast-moving ship. Anna and her colleagues found that their crates, placed one on top of the other to save space, were hindering the circulation of dry air and thus threatening the interior of the cathedral itself. They had to move the crates and rearrange them again. Again, the work of hauling had to be done mostly by women much weakened by starvation. "Still," writes Anna, "we unloaded, moved, dragged things. This was our responsibility . . . and it never occurred to anyone that given the actual situation of the city on the front, the spending of one's energies moving crates from place to place for things which might not have anywhere to go after the war was a rather questionably useful activity. We were thoroughly convinced that we were protecting beauty which would be needed even more than before the war."

Spring brought to Anna a great personal sorrow. She had formed a close friendship with an eminent historian of Leningrad, Alexis Chernovsky, some years older than she and perhaps the only man she ever loved. This serious, bearded scholar was too reticent to declare his affection for her until the last day of his life. On April 27, 1942, he wrote, "I am weak. Soon I shall die. Darling Anna Ivanovna. You will stay my only and most beloved transmitter in the world. I kiss your tender hands. It is sad to leave this world. . . ." As he was dying, he dreamed of a new museum — a museum of the siege of Leningrad. After his death, Anna fulfilled his dream.

The Museum of the Defense of Leningrad, created during the last days of the Blockade, was destined to be living history of the wartime efforts of Leningrad.

Its organization was given to a historian from the Hermitage and an army major. Anna and a small group of curators were asked to plan the exhibitions and collect items for them. The creation of the museum was looked on as a military assignment, and the work began during the preparation for the great battle, which was finally to end the Blockade. Anna and her fellow curators worked around the clock in the Officers' Staff Building on the Liteiny Prospect. She recounts, "Not one museum worker had ever experienced anything like this. The collection of materials was conducted on the battlefield. With a roar, Soviet tanks advanced right to the museum in full speed." Victorious tanks had stars painted on their sides for every enemy tank destroyed. In the backs of trucks were heaps of automatic rifles and Nazi banners. Dumped on the floor of the Trophy Room of the new museum were heaps of punctured Nazi helmets and tattered banners with swastikas and eagles. Among the museum exhibits was a fiery map of Leningrad, lighting in red all the places hit by bombing, shelling, and incendiary bombs. One could step inside the cabin of a Soviet destroyer, gaze at exhibits of Blockade rations, at the wall of a Leningrad house shattered by bombshells. A room was full of portraits of war heroes.

The Blockade continued for another year and a half. There were to be two more winters before the end of the ordeal. Many more thousands were still to die, but nothing was as bad as that first winter. The fall of 1942 saw the worst periods of shelling, but the tide was slowly turning. On January 18, 1943, in a courageous offensive called "Operation Iskra" (Spark), Soviet forces captured the German fort at Schüsselburg, partially breaking the ring of siege around Leningrad. Two weeks later, in one of the crucial battles of the war, the Soviet army stopped the Nazi offensive at Stalingrad, fifteen hundred kilometers southwest of Leningrad, where the bulk of the German army's eastern flank was concentrated.*

Such was the fierce resistance of the Russians that the Nazis suffered more than 75 percent of their entire wartime losses on the eastern front, losing ten million men, 62,000 planes, 56,000 tanks and assault vehicles, and 180,000 guns and mortars.

In September of 1943, the Russians drew up plans to life the Blockade. Once again, Hitler miscalculated the tenacity of his adversaries. Thinking the Russians had shed too much blood in the Ukraine to be able to mount a new offensive before the spring of 1944, he transferred crack army units from Army Group

---

* The Battle of Stalingrad, the turning point of the war in the East, cost the Germans over 300,000 men, 750 airplanes, 1,550 tanks, 61,000 trucks, 8,000 guns and mortars, and vast quantities of other equipment.

Nord to Army Group Sud. But on January 14, 1944, the Russians launched a massive attack. Now, finally, they outnumbered the Germans by three to one in divisions and six to one in tanks, artillery, and aircraft. Their heavy artillery pounded the reinforced-steel and -concrete firing points on the heights at Pulkovo and Kolpino, which had tortured the city and been the backbone of the Nazi defenses. Within a week, the Germans began to disassemble their massive siege guns. Lacking reserves and maneuvering room, they began to fall back and were quickly exhausted in the winter conditions. From January 18 to March 1, the Russians retook Krasnoye Selo and began to encircle German units, which, despite heavy losses, had been forbidden to withdraw without personal approval from the Führer, who refused to give it.

On January 27, 1944, over the loudspeakers of the city, the citizens of Leningrad at last heard the long-awaited news: "Today the city of Leningrad has been fully liberated from the enemy blockade. . . . In the outcome of twelve days of fierce fighting, the troops of Leningrad have hurled the enemy back along the entire front to distances between sixty-five and one hundred kilometers away from the city." The Nazis had not conquered the city — it had conquered them.

At 8 that night, the multicolored glow of red, white, and blue rockets streaked the sky, illuminating the scarred and wounded buildings. Naval ships began to fire. An onlooker exclaimed, "It was as if the water of the Neva were rising fiery red!" A great thundering from a victory salute of twenty-four salvoes from 324 guns filled the air.

Halfway across the world in Siberia, someone excitedly brought the news of the end of the Blockade and the freeing of Peterhof to Anatoly Mikhailovich and the small group of curators in Novosibirsk. For the next two nights no one slept, waiting for the news that confirmed the freeing of Pavlovsk and Pushkin. Then there was a joyous celebration that lasted all night. In honor of the remarkable occasion, they permitted themselves something that they had never allowed themselves during the entire period of the evacuation. They unpacked Imperial crystal glasses with the coat of arms of Nicholas I's Peterhof dacha, Alexandria, designed by the poet Zhukovsky. Out came a bottle of red wine they had saved since 1941, and, sipping from the Tsar's glasses, they happily drank the long-awaited toast to the freeing of their palaces.

Russians are people of great emotion. Over and over their history has shown that when their emotions are involved they are capable of extraordinary feats. Leningrad is the greatest example of what Russians can do under stress for something they love. Because of their fierce love of their city, their capacity for patience, and their endurance, the people of Leningrad had proved, as did those of Stalingrad, that the determined resistance of a civilian population can defeat even a large and well-equipped army.

But they had paid a terrible price. The city was in ruins. Destroyed were 840 industrial plants, forty-four kilometers of water lines, and seventy-five kilometers of sewer lines. Seventy-five percent of the city's prewar industrial equipment was destroyed or evacuated. Factories hauled across Russia in wartime to the Urals and Siberia and the Chinese border are still operating there now. But the worst material damage was to housing: over three thousand apartment buildings had been burned or destroyed, seven thousand more were damaged, and nine thousand wooden houses dismantled. One hundred eighty-seven buildings out of three hundred classified as historical or architectural monuments had been destroyed or damaged.*

The population was down to only 639,000 — less than one-fourth what it had been on August 30, 1941. More people had died than have ever died in any military action in any modern city at any time — ten times as many as died in Hiroshima.† Much of the evacuated population would never return. Leningrad, which had traditionally been a male city, was left a city of women — a city with few fathers and even fewer grandfathers.‡ One Leningrad man, now in his forties, remembers that the most frightening thing about his childhood was seeing all the people without arms and legs wandering the streets. "There are not many now," he says, "because they all died very early."

No one will ever know exactly how many people died during the Blockade.§ In the mass grave at the Serafimov Cemetery there are three hundred thousand. At the Piskarevskoe Cemetery eight hundred thousand people lie in a common grave. Every May 9, Victory Day, thousands of people go to the cemetery, young and old, entire families. There, on the stark carpet of green grass, they lay flow-

---

* The Church of the Resurrection, also known as the Cathedral of the Blood, had been marked for destruction by Stalin on the eve of the war. Saved from demolition by the outbreak of hostilities, it survived the Blockade and is now being completely restored.

† The deaths at Hiroshima on August 6, 1945, were 78,150, with 13,983 missing and 37,426 wounded; the destruction of Warsaw left 300,000 dead. The total number of deaths in Leningrad and the surrounding suburbs, including both military and civilian casualties, are estimated to be between 1,300,000 and 1,500,000.

‡ In 1945, 76.4 percent of all Leningraders in traditionally male industries were female.

§ The Soviet Army newspaper *Red Star* admitted in 1964 that "No one knows exactly how many people died in Leningrad and in the Leningrad area." In the worst period of the Blockade — the winter of 1941/42 — thousands of corpses lay in the streets; so difficult was the task of gathering and burying them in the presence of intense cold and severe hunger, that many were buried, uncounted, in mass graves or were cremated. In addition, many records were destroyed by the Nazi shelling.

ers, sweets, cigarettes, and small pieces of bread. On a marble wall are engraved the words "No one has been forgotten. Nothing has been forgotten."

There was a final humiliation. After the war, to protect himself, Stalin minimized the death toll and heroism of the siege. Not until thirteen years later, in 1958, was the first official account of the Blockade published. Even today, much of what was written about the Blockade, including the research of scientists conducted during the siege, has not been printed. Nevertheless, Leningrad was given the title of "Hero City," and 470,000 people were awarded richly deserved medals. In 1944, even Stalin bowed to the will of the city, and many important streets were given back their historic pre-Revolutionary names.

Forty-four years later, in old apartments, traces of the war are still there: yellow stains on the floor from the makeshift *burzhuika* stoves, holes near the windows for blackout curtains, which, superstitiously, some people hang on to still, saying, "If I throw these out, war will begin." Everywhere in the city there are reminders. On the Anitchkov Bridge a shell hole has been left — beside it a plaque reading, "This is one of the 148,468 shells which hit Leningrad." On the Nevsky Prospect, near the Rossi Arch, a sign, freshly repainted each spring, reads: "Citizens, this side of the street is safest in case of shelling." Under it is a little shrine, where there are always mute offerings — a flower, a sprig of pine, a piece of bread. Despite the new blocks of housing that now reach beyond the defense lines, the Blockade left a scar on the soul of the city that can never be entirely healed. To know and understand Leningrad today, one must know the Blockade. There is no one in Leningrad who was not seared by it — virtually no family in the city that did not lose at least one and usually several members.

Among those who survived, an unbreakable civic pride and independence was forged. More than ever, Petersburg became a special city for special people — singled out by their common experience of suffering. Eighteenth-century Petersburg had been built by the sacrifice of thousands of lives — the beauty of the city is their monument. Two centuries later, the people of Leningrad paid with a million and a half lives to prevent this beauty from being conquered and destroyed. The continued life of the city, where "even in anguish one can live," is their common glory.

The Germans had declared, "Leningrad will be a desert." It is not. Because of the courage of its citizens, today the golden spires and domes of the noble Imperial city still gleam majestically under the midnight sun echoing the words of Pushkin:

PAVLOVSK

Stand fast City of Peter
And vaunt thy splendor
The very element shall surrender
And make peace with you at last.*

* "The Bronze Horseman."

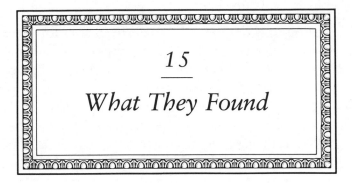

15
What They Found

"When Ivan comes home, everything will be empty."

— Nazi graffiti

PAVLOVSK WAS LIBERATED on January 24, 1944, by the Soviet Eighty-fifth Rifle Division. The core of this division had been formed from the People's Militia, those Minute Men of Leningrad who, when called to fight at the beginning of the Blockade, simply put on their overcoats and went to the defense of their city. By the end of the war, these divisions had been incorporated into the army and were included in the fighting strength of reserve units. One of the officers of the 110th Rifle Corps, part of the Eighty-fifth, recalled:

> That which I saw that day was horrible. The barbaric destruction was in no way demanded by military requirements. We interrogated prisoners and they told us that the destruction had been systematic, that the less that remained, the more we Russians would be punished. My scouts brought me to the headquarters of the 14th Rifle Regiment of the 225th German Division in the area between Antropshino and Novokakino [two to three kilometers from Pavlovsk]. This excellent fortification had several rooms. I walked in and it seemed that I had fallen into a wing of the palace: soft armchairs, a Gobelins tapestry hung on the wall. When they left, they cut a swastika out of the tapestry so it could not be repaired.
>
> Behind Pavlovsk they had a school for sabotage and there was also a building occupied by the Spanish, one of whom had been transmitting by radio to

our Intelligence until someone cut him off. There a group of Spanish were shot and a grave had been dug, flowers planted and the whole thing mined, so that when civilians returned, if they tried to plant or pick flowers, there would be an immediate explosion.

Clouds of smoke rising from the palace had been seen for three days. When the first soldiers of the Eighty-fifth arrived, flames were pouring from the windows of the library. As they watched, the ceiling and dome collapsed with a noise of thunder. "We saw that to extinguish the blaze would be impossible as the retreating German armies had blown up all the water mains." Russian troops tried as best they could to fight the fire with frozen dirt before they moved on.

Following immediately behind the Eighty-fifth, the second echelon of the Thirteenth Rifle Division fighting near Tosno was pursuing the Germans retreating from the Pulkovo Heights. As they passed through Pushkin, they came upon a huge German cemetery with birch crosses and latrines made of rare cupboards from the palace chopped in half. When they reached Pavlovsk, Major Esserman, then twenty-five, was called by two older officers to go with them to the palace. The three men ran into the inner courtyard. There, remembers Esserman, "all was silence except for a strange ominous snapping sound like that of an iced branch — yet there was no heavy frost that morning." Looking up, he saw that the crackling sound came from the palace itself. "The entire framework was burning, and even in daylight one could see bright tongues of fire licking up to the roof." Esserman turned to his companions, two older colonels whose bravery he greatly admired. Both were veterans of the Tsarist army and the First World War, decorated with the St. George Cross for their bravery in battle.* He was shocked to see these men openly weeping as they looked at the destroyed and burning palace. "I approached them and asked what was wrong. They answered that it would pass, and then turning away from each other and from me tried to control their tears." He did not learn until later that the officers, who had been joined in fighting by chance that day, were kinsmen; they had married sisters and in their youth before the Revolution had lived in Pavlovsk.

More than forty years later as he described that bitter January day, the memory of these brave men who had endured so much in battle weeping before the burning palace was still vivid:

---

* The decoration known as the St. George Cross, instituted by Catherine the Great on November 26, 1769, was the highest Russian military order. It was awarded for outstanding bravery and "encouragement of the art of war."

The palace had no doubt been burning for two or three days, for there was already soot around it and the framework was the last to burn. The Germans had splashed flammable liquid on all the walls, for everything was doused with it. They laid a special fuse cord 100 to 200 meters long, and as they retreated in the direction of Narva, lit it. We could see that they had meant to blow up the palace, for as we moved on to the left, we passed another place where there was an outside staircase. A quadrangle had been cleared in front of it, all the bushes cut down and the line of the fuse cord had burned a black streak in the snow. But the cord had been cut in time by those who had liberated the palace and so, although it had burned, there had been no explosion. Of course no one could take time to even try to extinguish the fire. The mains were blown and there was a war on. Above all it was necessary to pursue the retreating Nazis.

On February 1, 1944, eight days after the palace had been liberated and only five days after the official lifting of the Blockade, Anna Zelenova made her way back to Pavlovsk. In her memoirs of those days she wrote: "Immediately following the emancipation of the city outskirts from the Fascist occupation a group of artists and workers from the museum were sent to inspect the ruined palaces and parks near Leningrad. We left early, before dawn. We had to use a roundabout route as many of the direct roads were mined." Their first stop was Gatchina. There they found terrible destruction and a mocking sign scrawled on the naked walls: "When Ivan comes home, everything will be empty."

Reaching Pushkin, from a distance it seemed that the palaces were still standing — until they approached and saw that the buildings were only skeletons and utter desolation. In front of the Alexander Palace they found mounds of earth joined by two black thunderbolts of black metal; a swastika broken in two, the Nazi symbol of mourning. Anna wrote, "When I looked at this, I dreaded the trip to Pavlovsk."

But even her most terrible fears could not prepare her for the horrible reality she confronted when she reached her beloved Pavlovsk. In an account she later wrote, she described those terrible moments: "At the iron gates the driver asked, 'Which road shall I take?' Before the war this question would have been unnecessary. To the right was the town, to the left the park. But now there was no park on the left — over a mound one could see the silhouette of the palace." Nothing at all seemed to be left of the town. "I asked him to go straight. In less than a minute, the bus stopped, braking hard. The big bridge at the Marientalsky Pond in front of the palace was blown up."

The small group got out of their bus and stood on the edge of the steep bank of the Slavyanka. "Well," said one of the artists, "there is no way to go farther. Let's go back." But Anna Zelenova refused, exclaiming, "Go back! We must cross to the other shore," as she started to clamber down the bank.

The boulders were slippery and the remains of the exploded bridge dangerously untrustworthy. As she began leaping from one rock to another she suddenly felt a man strongly grasp her elbow. "Hold on to me," he said, "I'll jump first." Behind them the others called, "It's a bad idea! Come back! We must leave; we won't wait for you!" "Jump," said the firm voice of the person who had given her a hand. Her companion slipped and fell into the freezing water. Anna simply cried, "Hurry!"

"I ran past the Pavilion of the Three Graces and the servants wing of the palace," she continues, "noticing only the gaping holes of the windows. The sight was terrible." When she reached the courtyard in front of the main building she stopped short, appalled. The young director had come back only to find that she had the keys to a palace that no longer existed.

"The palace had been burning for ten days," she wrote.

> It was difficult to recognize the familiar silhouette of the building against the smoky sky, where the cupola rising above the colonnade had once been protruded what looked like a wide red pipe. Later I realized that this was the skeleton of the drum of the central Italian Hall. . . . and only the remains of several columns, like trees in a bombarded forest, leaning crazily in different directions. The roof was gone. On each expanse of wall over the windows was a tongue of soot. Nothing was left of the familiar symmetry of the wings of the building. The whole northern wall from the Throne Room was missing, from top to bottom. In its place only a wide red cascade of bricks stretching to the square.

Running to the central entrance, she climbed onto a mound of fallen roofing, still smoking from the fire, then, sinking up to her knees in ashes, she tried to get inside. Precariously she made her way across a charred beam into the Egyptian Vestibule. "I saw that the staircase leading to the upper halls was whole and only covered with collapsed roofing. Only a light cracking of decaying wooden beams broke the deathly silence. On a board hung on barbed wire was a sign in Gothic lettering, 'Achtung! Minen!'" At the feet of the huge scarred black statues were marble headstones, which had been packed by the Germans to be shipped out. Like a tear, from the ceiling a melted piece of lead fell on her camera. She kept it for the rest of her life.

Overleaf: Pil Tower, designed by Brenna in 1787; painted by Gonzaga
Above: Centaur Bridge

White birches

Statue of a nymph on the banks
of the Slavyanka

Wild irises

Monument to Maria Feodorovna's parents, by Ivan Martos, circa 1807

Signs of spring

The Great Circle: parterre designed by Brenna, 1799; sculpture of "Peace" by Pietro Baratta, early eighteenth century

Top of the Brenna Staircase: eighteenth-century Italian marble lion

The Old Sylvia, designed by Brenna, 1793–1796. Statue of Apollo Belvedere, eighteenth-century copy of Greek fourth century B.C.

Detail of the Black Bridge, first designed by Cameron, rebuilt by Brenna

The Visconti bridge, designed by Andrei Voronykhin, 1807

Statue of Paul I

Right: The Egyptian Vestibule, as it appeared in 1944

Bottom left: The Egyptian Vestibule today. Originally designed by Cameron, 1782. New statues executed after the fire of 1803 from designs of Voronykhin. Restored in 1963.

Bottom right: Arch of staircase leading from Vestibule: trompe l'oeil fresco by Giovanni Scotti, 1803; restored by Treskin, 1963

The State Bedroom today

The State Bedroom,
as it appeared in 1944

The Greek Hall, as it appeared in 1944

The Greek Hall today

View of Pavlovsk from the Linden Allée

As she continued her melancholy inspection, through one of the broken windows she saw that the ground floor of the North Wing had been converted into a stable with stalls for horses. Piles of manure and hay were heaped on the parquet floor. Turning a corner she found that Brenna's beautiful stone staircase of sixty-four steps down to the Slavyanka had been bombed. She tried to reach the Gonzaga Gallery, but there was no way to approach it. The walls of the Rossi Library were still burning. As she watched, beams cracked and fell before her eyes. "The frescoes are damaged!" she cried.

"They are no longer frescoes," said her companion angrily, his eyes full of grief.

Circumventing abandoned tanks and chains, they saw through the terraces the ruins of what had once been beautiful halls. Brokenhearted, Anna said quietly, "We must go, or they may leave without us."

"They won't go anywhere," gruffly answered the man who had joined her when no one else would — "I am the driver."

Vera Inber, a well-known Moscow poet who lived through the Blockade and recorded it in her book *Leningrad Diary*, was along that day to report the event. She writes, "The bridge over the Slavyanka River (as were all bridges in general) was blown up by the Germans. It was necessary to descend steep cliffs and cross the bleached logs. But a girl from Pavlovsk museum ran down and up the other side on the icy slope so quickly that the men barely kept up with her. She returned slowly, so pale that it was noticeable even in the frost. She told us that of the palace, only a 'box' remained, that is — its silhouette. Inside, only ruins."

After this first day, says Anna, "It was intolerable for me to wait for the next occasion for a trip to Pavlovsk." Since there was no transportation, a few days later she decided to go on foot. Although the distance to Pavlovsk from Leningrad is a little over twenty-six kilometers on the map, as the main roads were all still mined, there were no longer any straight routes from Pulkovo to Pavlovsk. Taking a great number of detours and circumventing mined areas, she was forced to take a roundabout way that increased the distance by several kilometers. "I saw everything along the way," she wrote, "the roads ground up by tanks, the snow black from explosions . . . tangled clumps of barbed wire, remains of combat equipment sticking out of snowdrifts, flocks of crows picking over dead bodies. As I came around a bend in the road I saw the motionless figure of a man, standing. As I came closer I saw that it was a Nazi who had met with a bullet as he tried to climb over a barbed-wire fence. He had died erect. His arms were lying on the wire and they were pointing toward Leningrad."

By the time she arrived at Pavlovsk darkness had already fallen. She was relieved to see a light in the window of a building that had once been the post office. The Executive Committee of the City Council of Pavlovsk, which consisted of two people, a president and a secretary, was using it as temporary quarters. The president was Alexandra Konstantinovna Ushakova, a former cleaning woman at the rest home at the palace. Anna remembered her well from the frantic days of the evacuation, when as the Germans were advancing on Pavlovsk the vigorous Ushakova had ridden about the park in a broken-down motorcycle, persistently urging Anna, "while there was still time," to allow her personally to chop down the trees of the palace *allée* to construct antitank barriers.

Jovially she greeted Anna, "Well, hello, Director of Burned Palace." To which Anna retorted quickly, "Hello to you, President of a City Council without a City."

"You are a fine girl for coming, Anushka," exclaimed Ushakova. "With you around we'll figure things out more easily. Some things we have to chop for firewood and some things will be listed under your preservation of monuments."

The next morning, before Anna had time to finish her tea, Ushakova shoved a thick sheet of paper under her nose. "Since you are working in art, you must make a sign for the City Council, because devil only knows where people will go if there is no sign!" So Anna carefully lettered the first Russian sign for the newly liberated Pavlovsk. Despite the fact that Anna protested that she was no doctor, Ushakova refused to let her leave until she had helped her prepare the medical papers on the safety of the drinking water of the surrounding wells for the Military Commission. "I'm no doctor either, Anyechka," she countered. "Just help me collect the water. Once they've requested an analysis, they won't leave us alone." Anna wrote:

> So as not to waste time arguing I followed her obediently. Washing out several bottles, we began visiting the wells and having collected a half a dozen samples we delivered them back to the office.
> "Now where will you send them for analysis?"
> "We're going to do it now," she answered calmly.
> Ushakova called her secretary, then placing a tin cup before each of us and filling the cups with a well sample, she gulped down the water. "Now we can light up a smoke. If our stomachs don't protest, we'll drink another."

They proceeded to test all the rest of the bottles in the same way. When they were through, Ushakova announced to her secretary, "Now write up a report.

The wells are analyzed. If nothing happens to us, send it to the Military Commission."

Then the energetic Ushakova suggested to Anna, "Let's go see the city, they say the Fritzes took a lot of things from the palace and dragged them to their quarters. At least you can recognize your things right away."

Of the thirty thousand prewar inhabitants of the formerly lovely town of Pavlovsk, only ten remained. All others had died, fled, or been carried away to slave labor. Only two hundred houses were left standing, and these were unfit for habitation. Tacked on to the few remaining buildings were crudely made German signs. From some inscriptions one could learn that certain houses had been used as centers for sorting those designated to be transported to Germany for slave labor.

Furniture, pianos, dishes, and clothing were strewn along empty, desolate streets. Despite the haste of the retreating Nazis, they had taken the time to mine some of the objects. On a low stone wall stood a new samovar; attached to it was a treacherous thin wire that led under the foundation of the barricade to an explosive. At the palace, on a pedestal near the Pavilion of the Three Graces, Anna saw an innocent-looking pair of new shoes; leading from them the same deadly telltale wire. Mined toys — dolls, rabbits, elephants, and automobiles that could attract the attention of children — were scattered about near houses.

The marvelous Pavlovsk park was totally devastated and honeycombed with mines. In a careful study of the park done by landscape architects only five years before the war, each tree in the park had been carefully counted. Then there had been 100,230. Now two-thirds of the park — seventy thousand trees — had been cut down by the German armies or hopelessly damaged by shelling and bombs. Gonzaga's beautiful White Birch Vale was gone. The centuries-old fir trees of the Old Sylvia had been felled and used for bunkers. The park was pitted with blast holes and over ten thousand craters. All the decorative bridges as well as the intricate drainage system designed in the eighteenth century, which kept all the paths dry even in the wettest weather, had been blown up. Eight hundred bunkers and fortifications of concrete and logs were scattered through what had once been the enchanted park. Cameron's graceful Temple of Friendship had been used as a shooting gallery, as had the priceless marble statues of the monument to Maria Feodorovna's parents. Krik, the romantic eighteenth-century wooden hunting lodge, scene of Maria Feodorovna's happy days as a bride, had been used as a pharmaceutical depot and then burned. Only two shattered walls were left standing. Krak, carefully preserved by Grand Duke Michael after his mother's death, the Constantine and Elizabeth dachas, and all the other pavilions of the park had met the same dismal fate. Nothing was left of them but ashes. The Rose Pavilion had been wiped off the face of the earth. The Germans had used its materials to construct an enormous dugout fortification in front of the lower gates. Burned, too, was the Voksal and the Philharmonic Hall with its incomparable acoustics, where Strauss had directed his waltzes and the music of Glinka and Stravinsky had delighted audiences.

Through the wintry days, Anna doggedly continued to go to Pavlovsk on foot. Sometimes dragging a sled behind her, she set off for the surrounding areas of Pyazelevo, Antropshino, and even Gatchina, hoping to find things from the palace looted by the Germans. Once, exhausted, she fell into the snow and nearly froze to death, saved in the nick of time by a local woman from Kolpino who happened to be passing by and was astonished to find the director of Pavlovsk in such a condition.

On each visit to the ruined palace she made notes of what she saw: "On the floor of the Egyptian Vestibule there had been torture. The floors were covered with blood. Stoves stood on the parquet floors without anything under them. Pipes were led through the windows, walls and mirrors knocked through." Holding a makeshift torch made of burning newspaper, avoiding the trip wires, she made her way down and through the cellars to see if the carefully camouflaged hiding place of the precious antique statues was still safe. To her immense joy, despite the determined search of the Gestapo, the bombs, and the fire, it was still intact.

As the first soldiers had observed, the palace had been purposely put to the torch by the retreating Nazis. A part of the floors of the choir stalls of the Egyptian Hall had survived, and traces of the flammable liquid poured on them were found. Bombs had been laid in various locations with the hope that they would explode from the fire; such bombs were discovered near the burial site of the statue of the Three Graces. Some of these bombs did explode and because of them, the chapel wing and a corner of the northern wing were destroyed.

Everything that could be taken away had been taken. The books of the Rossi Library sealed in the walls had been found and transported to Berlin. The rare photographic collection, which included twenty-five hundred glass negatives of the interiors of the palace taken in 1903, had also disappeared, along with the collections of cameos, coins, and butterflies. Gone or destroyed was all the furniture that had been left at the time of the evacuation. All the remaining porcelain disappeared without a trace, as well as a great portion of the paintings, including the abandoned Salvatore Rosa *A Shepherd and His Flock,* as well as the *Banishment of Eve,* and invaluable pastels. The life-sized portrait of Peter painted during his lifetime, which was fixed on the wall of Paul's Library, had been roughly cut from its frame. The splendid palace doors, which at the time of the evacuation had been removed from their hinges and placed along the side of the walls to protect them from shrapnel, had been dragged off, their bronze decorations and doorknobs pried off, then used as wooden beds in bunkers and officers' quarters. Most of the eighteenth- and nineteenth-century parquet floors had been ripped out for firewood; a few remaining pieces were found in unburned portions of the palace building near the stoves.

Upstairs, where the barracks had been, all sorts of foul writing and graffiti were found on the remaining walls. Done by officers and soldiers were drawings of naked girls and raised mugs. One depicted the Führer sending a weeping recruit to the eastern front, while an officer held a sword to his back. The German inscription read: "My homeland, my sorrow. Oh, to stay home!" Members of the Blue Division contributed drawings of Spanish Carmencitas with high combs and fans.

The southern wing had been converted into a military hospital. In the dumps were found cots, parts of medical instruments, dental instruments, chairs, X-ray caps, and surgical instruments. On a path leading to the front of the wing stood a large cylindrical stove with remains of amputated extremities scattered about it. Across from the entrance there was a tall shed filled to the top with packages of foul-smelling lice powder; on each package, the size of a man's hand, was a picture of a louse.

Anatoly Mikhailovich was called back from Siberia in early March 1944. It was not until a month or two later that he was able to conduct a careful examination of the palaces in Pushkin. "Travel out of the city even then was naturally still quite strictly controlled by pass, because the enemy could still make his way through. I went by military vehicle to Pushkin. It was an awful sight, with bodies and equipment still lying in the fields."

"The last palace of the last Tsar," the place where Anatoly Mikhailovich had been so happy, was no more. Quarenghi's splendid architecture was still standing; the Nazis had not had time to blow it up, but this palace too, had been burned. The grove of trees that, following Maria Feodorovna's example at Pavlovsk, had been planted by Nicholas II for each of his children had been felled. In the palace that Anatoly Mikhailovich had tended so lovingly, filth was everywhere. Everything inside had been destroyed, ransacked, and looted. As he passed through the empty soiled corridors, he meticulously noted everything he saw.

Ascending the stairs of the private entrance, he found that all the original doors were gone. In their place other makeshift, ill-fitting doors hung crazily askew on their hinges. With few exceptions the painted canvas walls had been ripped off, and the fine wood panels roughly ripped out with axes. Everywhere were piles of trash and hundreds of empty bottles, German and Spanish. Of Nicholas II's study, perfectly preserved up to the war down to the last inkwell, nothing was left except for the pediments over windows and doors. The fireplace was a pile of bricks; only the traces of panels were left on bare walls. A chain, all that was left of the chandelier, hung forlornly from the ceiling. Incongruously left on the wall was a lonely portrait of the last Tsar. A magnificent Mauritanian fireplace was smashed into little pieces — only a piece of its wide cornice was left. A horseshoe was nailed over the door of the dressing room of Nicholas II. ("Some luck," commented Anatoly Mikhailovich dryly.)

The main study, valued for its decoration of magnificent mahogany, was recognizable only by its dark blue walls. Everything else was destroyed: the Dutch tiles of the fireplace torn off, the marble columns robbed of their bronze capitals. Everything was defaced with Spanish graffiti. In the Jacaranda Room, of the woodwork only the doors and the upper portion of the fireplace survived; the wall paneling and wonderful veneer disappeared; one panel was later discovered in a restaurant in the town. The famous Mauve Boudoir of Empress Alexandra was burned. In place of the corner couch was a hole, above it only charred wooden beams. The beautiful painted frieze of irises hung in dirty twisted ribbons.

As Anatoly Mikhailovich walked along the corridor into the main halls, his steps echoed off empty walls. In the Corner Salon, where on the day war was declared he and his co-workers had worked so feverishly to pack the palace valuables, the ceiling had collapsed, the doors were gone, and on the floor were only the broken remains of the corner maple couch. In the center of the room lay a decapitated bust of Empress Alexandra done by the Russian sculptor Antokolsky. (Anatoly Mikhailovich later found the head thrown in a garbage pit.) In the library not a trace was left of the grand bookcases, five thousand volumes were gone, and only the pedestal of the evacuated bust of Peter the Great remained. Door panels had been battered with rifle butts, and all the walls covered in Spanish and German graffiti, even to life-sized images of horses.

Among the piles of trash Anatoly Mikhailovich found a porcelain vase with wolves, a piece that he had especially loved, smashed. Painstakingly he searched for the fragments in the filth. Later he carefully re-glued the vase, but to his sorrow one piece was missing and never found.

Outside in heaps under the windows he found various half-moldy remnants of the rooms: pieces of furniture and jacaranda doors and even broken pianos. In nearby bushes he discovered chairs from the palace salons, thrown out and left to rot. The Germans had drained the pond, and the muck was littered with more broken fragments. Along the banks of the pond they had constructed encampments made from broken bureaus of the palace library; restoring them, he saw, would be impossible. The invaders had fashioned a hitching post for horses from a large marble vase smashed into pieces. In the park in a bivouac he found Empress Alexandra's white writing table from the Mauve Boudoir. "Apparently the table did not fit through the door, so they broke off the legs." He kept the broken table "in memory," repaired the legs, and in his small apartment uses it now as his worktable. His archives had been scattered to the winds. He found a few stray pages in the mountains of trash outside — all that was left of all the work he had done as curator. In the decimated park, Catherine II's Chinese Theater, a jewel of architecture with interiors of rare lacquer, was, he said, "a big empty box without a cover." The interior had been completely incinerated, even the marble stairs blackened. Ironically, in the door left in the ruins hung a mass of burned and melted keys.

The frightened woman who had been summoned to the palace by the Nazis at the time of the invasion brought back the little vase and the veil of the Empress that the Nazi officer had allowed her to keep. Anatoly Mikhailovich returned it to her, saying sadly, "What is this veil for now? You guarded it, keep it for yourself in memory, because all of this was destroyed."

Everywhere — at Peterhof, Gatchina, Orienbaum — it was the same. Everything was gone. Everything had been destroyed and vandalized. In their vindictive rage, the Nazis had left nothing but ruins.

Yet despite the desolation and apparent hopelessness of what they saw all around them, Anna Ivanovna and Anatoly Mikhailovich were already obsessed with only one vision. The palaces would be restored. Their beauty would live again. On February 2, only one day after Anna had paled before the ruins of Pavlovsk, with the coolheaded determination and precision of thought that was so characteristic of her, she compiled the following orderly list of recommendations:

On the basis of my initial inspection of the Pavlovsk Palace-Museum Park and its pavilions . . . I believe it essential to conduct immediately the following measures for the preservation of the artistic valuables of Pavlovsk:

1. Immediately to clear the Palace-Museum of mines.

2. To establish a guard staff for the surveillance of the Palace-Museum, where, apart from the preserved precious architectural fragments of the building's trimming, those museum pieces of interior furniture which have survived (ancient sculpture, furniture, etc.) are located.

3. To establish a guard staff for the park and pavilions.

4. To organize emergency work for the tidying up of those still-intact sections of the museum where many valuables are buried under debris.

5. To equip the storage facilities where all the museum valuables of Pavlovsk which have survived are concentrated.

6. To conduct a precise determination of all the destruction caused by the Fascist barbarians to cultural-artistic valuables, for which is required: a) photographing; b) sketching.

7. To conduct a determination of the still-intact sections, details and separate articles of the Palace-Museum by means of photography, sketches, architectural measurements and scientific descriptions.

With the courage and stubborn determination that had sustained Leningrad through the Blockade, they began to confront the unconfrontable.

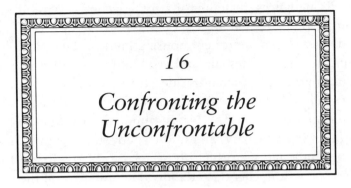

16

Confronting the
Unconfrontable

"Don't despair. The eyes are afraid
but the hands do — the skeleton of
the palace beckons."

— Mother of a girl minesweeper

FOR ZELENOVA AND KUCHUMOV, for the museum workers who had risked their lives protecting their treasures, who had suffered, worked, and dreamed of their palaces through the Blockade, there was never any question that the palace would be restored. Although when Anatoly Mikhailovich first saw Pavlovsk, he had the impression of a dead city: "Everything destroyed — the palace desecrated, the park dug up with bunkers, bivouacs, minefields. There were cities of German bunkers. It was a grievous sight." Yet he says, "Even in the worst moments, it never occurred to us to say, 'Well, this is doomed so forget it.' We had faith it could be restored."

Not everyone shared their indomitable belief. Others, when they first confronted the charred ruins, thought nothing could be salvaged. After her visit to the palaces with Zelenova, Vera Inber wrote: "Peterhof Palace is so badly damaged it will be beyond human effort to restore it." Looking at the same dismal ashes on January 27, 1944, Leningrad's mayor, Pyotr Popkov, who was within four years to vanish in new Party purges, exclaimed, "We will not rebuild it — we will level it all." The Tass correspondent who was with him disagreed, but argued only that the ruins should be preserved for all time as a monument to Nazi barbarism. The influential writer Ilya Ehrenburg expressed the opinion that Pavlovsk and Pushkin should be left in ruins, and urged that Leningrad be rebuilt as a new city. Some voices, including that of Vyacheslav Molotov, then foreign minister, thought that the buildings should simply be destroyed. Others urged that the sites be razed and apartment housing built in their place.*

One can understand the despair and resignation. Leningrad had been left a militarized encampment, the countryside strung with barbed wire and criss-crossed with trenches. Industry was decimated. Seven hundred and fifty thousand people were without housing. The Nazis, although in retreat, were still only a few hundred miles from the city, and in the south still occupied Soviet territory; restoring former Imperial palaces hardly seemed to be the first priority.

Yet such was the vision, energy, and individual initiative of the museum work-ers and architects, and so great the pride of the population of Leningrad in its history, that their faith did prevail. Within a few months after the lifting of the Blockade, restoration quickly gained recognition as a pressing national prior-ity — and this despite the fact that there were a daunting number of people to convince: not only the Leningrad Party and city authorities occupied with mu-nicipal priorities, but Moscow — and Stalin.

The architectural and artistic communities were the first to take aim at the problem. "Everyone was worried," said Kuchumov. Already in the spring of 1943, while the city was still under siege and being constantly shelled and bom-barded, Anna Zelenova had gone to the political officer of the Leningrad front. With the same determination with which she had confronted Borshchev, she demanded: "We strongly urge you to give the following order to all commanding officers: that the question of preservation of cultural, historical, and artistic mon-uments on the territory which the Red Army is protecting from the Fascist bar-barians is a question of national importance — a matter of honor for each soldier." Anna also asked that when they were recaptured, all outposts of mili-tary supply and transportation be removed from palace parks; she was so per-suasive that the headquarters of the Leningrad front found it impossible to deny her request.

Immediately after the lifting of the Blockade there were many impassioned meetings about what to do and how to do it. The newspapers and radio emo-

* Ironically, even today, Westerners often ask, "Why do you want all this beauty when you are short of housing?"

tionally described the condition of parks and palaces. Art and museum experts, architects, and city planners argued interminably about how to reconstruct the ruined palaces, about what to restore and what not to restore. With ever greater frequency and determination leaders of the culture departments of the city put before city Party officials the question of beginning.

On February 18, 1944, less than a month after the lifting of the Blockade, there was a meeting at the House of Architects on Herzen Street, by a strange coincidence Polovtsov's splendid former home. Both Kuchumov and Zelenova attended. The hall was packed. There, the distinguished architect, seventy-year-old Academician Aleksei Shchusev, three-time winner of the Stalin Prize, designer of the Lenin Mausoleum, and specialist on ancient Russian architecture, urged the group to opt for immediate reconstruction of the palaces, saying, "If we do not do this, we who know and remember these palaces in all their glory as they were, then the next generation will never be able to reconstruct them." His eloquent reminder that the human memory was essential — not only that of the head but of the heart — touched the group deeply. But Kuchumov and Zelenova, who were already convinced, knew they could not wait for the deliberations to finish. The pressing necessity was to preserve the opportunity itself, saving what had survived, protecting every original remaining detail, so that when the decisions were taken and the arguments resolved — as they never doubted — in the affirmative, the possibility of restoration would be there. The Nazis had been vanquished, but now there was another formidable enemy — nature. It was winter. The restorers would be working against time and the elements. At Pavlovsk, although the fire that had burned for more than ten days had badly damaged the interior decorations of the palace, it had not destroyed them altogether.

The roofs and ceilings had collapsed, bringing down with them all the fireplaces and tiled stoves of the palace, but the plasterwork on the walls and a portion of the frescoes had survived. Even the fire had been unable to destroy all the beauty of the architectural decor. But now, exposed to the elements, fragments of painting on the walls, bas-reliefs, molded ornaments, parts of cornices, pieces of *faux marbre* — the main elements of the palace decoration, which had burned and cracked from the heat of the fire — were peeling from the few remaining walls. The plaster was brittle and could not stand the weight of accumulated snow, which each day hastened its deterioration. Thawing snow turned to ice and fell to the ground, more each day, carrying with it precious remaining pieces of garlands and bas-reliefs. Frozen plaster crumbled into powder at a touch. Oil paint bubbled from frost and humidity, and winter winds blowing through the ruins of the palace further endangered the peeling frescoes. Somehow all this had to be protected, saved.

Saving the palace required money and, even more, materials and labor, and there was precious little of either. Russia was still at war, men still at the front. Yet acutely sensing the need for speed, those who were committed to saving their palaces went into action, and in those two first months a great many things happened.

Upon his return from Siberia, Anatoly Mikhailovich had been named Director of the Department of Museum Monuments of the Directorate of Artistic Affairs. In March 1944, a distinguished group of specialists from Moscow, led by Igor Grabar, Director of the Committee on Architecture of the Council of People's Commissars of the USSR and including Academician Arkady Mordvinov, Vice-President of the Academy of Architecture, and the writer Alexei Tolstoy, came to inspect the remains of the palaces. Anatoly Mikhailovich accompanied them. "They looked to see what had been left whole, what was left of windows, what was in dumps along the streets. Grabar afterward asked which halls, which palaces could be restored. Afterwards a big conference was held."

Local Party officials had made inquiries in Moscow about the possibility of doing at least some restoration. When they returned, Zhdanov asked, "How much did you ask for?" Rachinsky, the head of the Journalists Union, answered that twenty million was needed. Zhdanov's response was not encouraging. "Why so much?" he asked. "Our country is in ruins, many people are living in earthen huts. We do not understand why palaces and fountains are necessary. It is necessary to establish priorities, and we will allocate a small amount."

The Director of the Government Directorate of the Preservation of Monuments (GIOP),* Nikolai Nikolaievich Belekhov, an energetic man who actively supported the early efforts of restoration, ordered a survey of all the palaces. The finest photographer in Leningrad, Velichkov, whose photographs were used at the Nuremberg trials in 1945/46 to document the destruction of the palaces, photographed everything. Albums of his photographs bound in vellum were brought to the Secretariat of Stalin. Brusquely the Leningrad group was advised that Stalin would throw them out, along with their albums. Why did they bring these fragments? they were asked. He wouldn't give a cent. They were told, says Kuchumov, "You must show it in a way that will prove that they can be re-

---

* Gosudarstvennaya Inspektsiya po Okhrane Pamyatnikov Leningrada.

stored." So Velichkov went back and re-photographed everything, showing painting, plasterwork, and cornicing from other angles, trying to put the most hopeful light on the dismal ruins. This time the photographs were mounted on simple cardboard pages, tied with string — "Very serious, austere albums," says Kuchumov. These did reach Stalin, and these were the albums he looked at. Apparently he was convinced, and he gave an order to Zhdanov, for, continues Kuchumov, "One day, a car came for Rachinsky, which speedily delivered him to Peterhof, where Zhdanov appeared. He looked at the fountains and immediately asked how many millions of rubles were needed."

Thanks to all these efforts, within a very few weeks there was no more question about the principle of preserving the palaces. Anatoly Mikhailovich, who attended many of the meetings in the office of the Chief Architect of Leningrad, Nikolai Baranov, in late February and March, says, "It was already clear that it was necessary to preserve and restore the palaces. There were no suggestions that we build communities or apartment buildings."

At first it was not a full victory. Considering the wartime conditions and the shortages of building materials and manpower, it was not deemed possible to restore the structures of the palace buildings immediately, but a plan was adopted that provided for the careful conservation of the surviving ruins. And although the discussions continued about whether to rebuild them in their entirety, and upon what principles, the first, most immediate and essential step toward restoring the palaces had been won. And the government did give money. Since the war was far from over and many thousands of Russian towns and villages were in shambles, finding money for the palaces has to be counted as a great victory for the Leningrad spirit.*

Yet money alone was not enough, for, as Kuchumov explained, "After the liberation of Leningrad in 1944, money was designated for conservation, but there were not enough people or master craftsmen, and the money allocated by the government unfortunately was not used. Only fifty percent of the funds were spent, because the war was still going on — artisans, carvers, and sculptors were still at the front and many never returned."

In any case, before any other work could begin, the palace grounds and the palace itself, all honeycombed with mines, had to be cleared.† Starting in Feb-

---

* Only ten percent of the city budget in 1945 was devoted to restoring historic buildings. Between 1946 and 1948, the financial commitment for restoration rose from sixty million rubles to eighty-four million.

† At the Catherine Palace eleven huge high-explosive bombs were emplaced, with trip wires extending across the bottom of the Great Pond. What still remained of the palace was to fly up in the air and turn into a pile of debris.

ruary 1944, this dangerous task at Pavlovsk was done by girl minesweepers. The first step toward clearing the mines began when a field engineer cut through the barbed wire at the entrance to the Egyptian Vestibule and threw off the tin plate on which was written, *"Achtung! Minen!"*; the second, when the nails were removed from the trunk of a birch damaged by shrapnel on which a sign was posted, "Whoever enters this park will be shot."

These extraordinarily courageous girls, cut from the same heroic cloth as the young girls who had defused delayed-action bombs in Leningrad during the Blockade, were mostly teenagers, sixteen and seventeen years old. They would find the mines and then specialized sappers would clear them. When the spring came and the ground grew softer, they volunteered to do their work barefooted, because they could feel the mines better. According to the documents signed by the mine defusers and the Executive Council of the City of Pavlovsk, 240 mines and charges were removed from the cellars of the palace alone.

From this perilous work many did not return. Zelenova remembered that in the morning the girls would go out to work singing songs, and in the evening would return in silent formation, carrying a wounded or dead friend on a field stretcher. The initial mine-clearing took over three months. Mines were still being cleared three years later. There were so many thousands of mines in the park that not all of them were ever found, and even years later one would occasionally explode. There are still a few, now harmless, left in the ground today.

During those early months, Anna wrote, "Every day pieces of stucco molding fell at my feet, and sometimes on my head. Collecting them I headed for Leningrad to prove that we could not delay any longer, that the work of saving the molding had to be expanded immediately. Otherwise the authenticity of the restoration would disappear." Where was help to come for the colossal job of clearing the devastated park and shoring up the ruins of the palace?

She did not know herself to whom she could turn, or who had to be convinced, but as usual, the resourceful Anna found a way. One day as she was riding on the newly functioning trolleys of Leningrad she heard a fellow strap-hanger call her name. At first she did not recognize him, but then she remembered Robert Karlovich Taurit, a sculptor who before the war had been involved in restoration work at Pavlovsk.* She was delighted. "My dear," she said to him, "you are the one who can help." And she poured out her worries about the perishing molding. The sculptor, who was in uniform, sympathized and exclaimed, "If only I were

* Taurit later sculpted the monument to the Blockade dead at Piskarevskoe Cemetery.

free now!" and then, glancing uneasily at the other passengers as if he were afraid to expose a military secret, he explained that he was working with the Government Authority for Airport Construction (GUAS),* a military unit in charge of rebuilding the airport. But, he suggested helpfully, "We have construction sections. I'm in one of them. Maybe you could meet our superiors and request that they help you. Perhaps our brigade could be sent to you."

That was enough for Anna. Within the hour she was at the GUAS headquarters on Zagorodny Street. In her account of this episode she writes, "It would not be the truth to say that I simply and easily got to see the head of this respected establishment — but nevertheless I did. Instead of the elderly architect I imagined to be the head of the construction section, I was confronted with a young officer with a sharp profile."

The officer rose to shake her hand, crisply snapping out his name: "Captain Sapgir." He was distant and unwelcoming. "Where are you from?" he asked, glancing at his watch and then fixing her with what Anna described as "a very evil glance."

She started to explain that she was the Director of Pavlovsk Palace and Park and had come to tell him about the condition of the palace. The response was curt: "I doubt that you will soon be inviting our workers to an excursion at Pavlovsk."

Undaunted, Anna continued, "But that is precisely what I did come for, to invite you — that is, your workers — to Pavlovsk."

The captain, exasperated, pressed a button, which instantly summoned a flustered secretary, whom he reprimanded: "Before sending people in you could at least find out whether they are in the right place." While the secretary explained that she had done her job, and Anna begged him to hear her out, the captain rose and reached for his jacket. "I felt," she wrote, "that he would simply leave if I didn't tell him everything then and there." Hastily she explained, "Your sections have builders and sculptors. In Pavlovsk we need to have scaffolding erected. Your sculptors can strengthen the falling plaster and reform that which can't be left in place because of the fire in the museum . . . ."

"A fire in a palace . . . museum? What business is that of mine? Do you know what we are doing now? The reconstruction of military airports."

Still Anna insisted: "You have the worker strength for the palace, and you could —"

* GUAS stands for Gosudarstvennoe Upravlenie Aerodromnoe Stroitel'stvo.

"I can fulfill only what I have been entrusted to do."

Anna grew steely. "So you don't want to become involved?" she asked.

"The government has greater concerns," answered the captain.

"To whom can I make a complaint against you?" asked Anna, "Ispolkom? Gorkom?" *

"To Moscow, to Moscow, my little pigeon," said the captain patronizingly. "Our chiefs are there. We are military people, and," he added sarcastically, "I am sure you know who the Supreme Commander of the Armed Forces is."

"At that moment," continued Anna, "someone came into the room and my audience with the 'Armed Forces' was terminated."

But just as she was about to close the door behind her, Sapgir lightly threw out, "Tikhanovsky. That's who is our superior. Try to explain to him that you need us more than he does."

In her account of this exchange, Anna does not say what she did after that. But quite evidently within a few days she had managed to find the right man, for she ends her tale with this sentence: "And so, it was with such rejoicing in my soul that I again ascended that narrow staircase to Captain Sapgir, to place before him the paper which began the difficult matter of conserving the palace." On that official paper was written, "As a matter of exception, you are to begin work on the restoration of the interior decoration of the palace of Pavlovsk." †

While far to the west the war was still raging, the struggle of saving the palace began. With the single-minded devotion to Pavlovsk that characterized her whole life, thirty-one-year-old Anna threw herself into the direction of the gigantic enterprise of wresting the palace from the ashes. To her fell the responsibility of conducting the whole enterprise of finding funds, people, materials — no easy task in wartime. There was no palace — but she imagined it. There was not yet a plan — but the whole plan was already in her head. She forged new ground, developed new rules, and never forgot anyone who ever helped her — and, one must also suspect, anyone who opposed her. It was said of her that she had the tough-mindedness of a man and the diplomacy of a Jesuit. Formed by her tech-

---

* *Ispolkom* stands for *Ispolnitelny Komitet,* or Executive Committee. It is the executive body in charge of administering the day-to-day affairs (transportation, sanitation, etc.) of the city. *Gorkom* stands for *Gorodskoy Komitet,* or City Committee, and is the city's ruling Communist Party organization.

† Although at the time he treated her harshly, Sapgir later wrote, "I liked her face. In life we come across many beautiful female faces, but this one was unusual. The slightest movement of her radiant soul was instantly reflected on it and transformed it into an ineffable charm. Having once seen her face, I involuntarily began to search for this spiritual beauty in other faces as well."

nical training and German education at Peter Schule, she was a phenomenal organizer and administrator. She kept meticulous lists, made a master plan for each month, an individual plan for the tasks of each day.

In mid-September 1944, the Sapgir brigade came, and with them, Anna's friend Taurit. Under his supervision scaffolding was erected to shore up the remaining walls. Balancing on shaky ladders, sculptors and artists strengthened the artistic molding and frescoes that had survived. A special method of fixation of the remaining elements was devised. Before covering them with wooden boxes hung from above, plaster details were carefully soaked with a metal solution and, in parts, with vitriol. From the first application the plaster turned rust colored, and from the second green, but doing this permitted the casting of duplicates. The original castings were used to make molds. Everything that could not be removed was conserved on the spot. Details that could not be supported or that had already fallen were removed from the remains of charred walls or carefully picked out of heaps of coal and ashes and then taken to a special storeroom. This careful early conservation bore fruit later, for because of precipitation, the burned molding eventually crumbled and later was largely lost.

Sapgir's brigade was a help, but many more hands were needed. The available building specialists were occupied in the city, and to bring workers out from Leningrad was difficult, so Anna turned to the City Council of Pavlovsk, who, at the end of April, which in Pavlovsk can still be cold and snowy, sent the only workers available — a group of women. As during the evacuation, again it was women who did the first heavy work of taking away the log barriers that barred the first-floor windows, and of clearing the mountain of rubble around the palace. Once the mines had been removed, it was they who broke down the artful concealing wall and dug out the precious antique statues. Bent over the heaps of half-burned debris, up to their elbows in ashes and coals, the women sifted through it, carefully feeling each inch, collecting pieces of carved marble fireplaces, bronze ornaments, crumbled molded cornices and friezes, broken capitals of columns, and stone vases. They went on to sift the dumps in the park, mortally dangerous because of the ever-present threat of mines. Like archaeologists, they kept each fragment they found, even those of questionable origin, certain that every piece would be of help. Kuchumov remembers, "How happy they were when they found a broken table from a palace hall — from one of these we could later make forty like it."

In the cellars of St. Isaac's and during her freezing evenings in the library during the Blockade, Anna had carefully studied the methods of restoration used by other researchers before her, both foreign and Russian. But she never imagined the scope of the destruction she would find. No one had ever confronted such a massive task of restoration before, and entirely new methods had to be conceived. Now, using the methods she had developed as a base, she became the initiator and leader of the conservation work.

Every fragment of plaster was carefully gathered and placed on special cloths or plaster slabs, then put in storage, and there carefully sorted. Plaster fragments were then reinforced with vitriol and lacquer, marked, and coded. In most instances, plaster casts were then made of each individual detail — whether they were missing a small or a large piece. These elements of ornamental and sculptural decor were subsequently restored or turned into models from which new casts would be made to decorate the halls of the palace.

Working with Natalia Gromova, a senior museum researcher, Zelenova developed an entirely new system for coding the missing details, so they would not lose their historical "address" and could be returned to their proper place. Each hall had its own coding, its own designation; every room had its cipher, each wall its number. Zelenova did drawings of the elevations of the walls, fixing the position and number of each detail on each individual wall of each room. A folder in which all available prewar photographs were gathered was kept for every room; on them everything that had been destroyed and needed restoration or complete re-creation was scrupulously marked.

Fragments of paint remaining on the walls and ceilings were copied in color and traced. Tests were taken in layers from remaining wall paint. Two copies were made of all the molded decoration. After cleaning and restoration, one was used as a model for new casts, and the other, after being impregnated with binders, was kept as a standard for later restoration.

Soon at meetings about the restoration of the Leningrad palaces they were talking about the "Zelenovsky" method of research that facilitated the preparation for restoration. Anna's *Method of Scholarly Research for Restoration of Monuments of Architecture,* which she had worked out at Pavlovsk, was, in 1945, recommended by the Department of Culture of Leningrad for all the destroyed palaces outside Leningrad. It was also used by restorers in Poland, Bulgaria, and Hungary, who came to the Soviet Union to learn it.*

---

* The collection of the materials, the support and fixation system, the careful compilation and description of details, were all encompassed in what was called The Method. It included the entire sequence from covering and protecting remaining fragments to assembling restored segments on the walls.

This meticulous work, begun in 1944, was not completely finished until 1954, ten years later. By May 1945, according to an article written by Zelenova, over sixty thousand individual fragments had been "addressed."

In the storeroom, Natalia Gromova, a patient and painstaking scholarly researcher, collected and compiled every piece of information she could find. Voluminous research was needed; requests had to be put into the archives, prewar photographs found, as well as architectural drawings, measurements, and authentication of the architectural drafts of the original architects to complete an image of how the halls of the palace looked.

For all this early work Anna relied heavily on Gromova, her old friend and colleague Nikolai Weiss, as well as the park curator, Georgy Kurovsky, and his wife, Xenia. These colleagues made detailed reports about the halls of the palace and the park, and also helped dismantle the bunkers and protect the surviving park monuments.

It seemed that everything had to be done at once. With the coming of spring the work in the destroyed park became urgent. That park, of which Lunacharsky had written, "Pavlovsk Park possesses extraordinary charm. It should have special care, for each new cutting and each new planting may spoil the prospects created by the genius of Gonzaga, who arranged his trees as a painter his colors upon the canvas," now had to be virtually re-created. In order to save those that remained undamaged, it was vital to remove all the decaying and rotted trees, so that elements harmful to wood and the rot under the bark would not be transmitted to the healthy surviving trees. Trees damaged by shrapnel became diseased and dried up. They had to be chopped down and the stumps removed. Together with the Kurovskys, Zelenova worked out a method for research and restoration of the park. In determining which trees had been in each spot, the drawings and cases of documents *General Inventory of Pavlovsk Palace*, done by the great landscape architect-theoretician Tversky, which had been found by Anna and precipitously evacuated with the last load from the palace, made restoration possible. Now, all the plans of the park were speckled with special marks to show the destroyed trees. A mountain of documents and prewar photographs were studied in order to determine their species, and then in replanting, the rate of growth of each species had to be considered in order to restore the original conception of Gonzaga.

Although many of the *allées* of the park were impassable because of hidden mines, thirty-four thousand cubic meters of slashings had to somehow be removed, ten thousand craters filled in, seventy-four kilometers of canals dug out, eighty-two kilometers of *allés* and roads cleaned, and eight hundred bunkers and fortifications removed.

As the pace intensified, more and more hands were needed and found. The conservation work grew into an outpouring of popular effort. After the liberation, former residents and workers of Pavlovsk returned, some from labor camps, and offered their help. Despite the fact that their homes were destroyed and many lived in earthen huts, they set to work. Anna temporarily lodged many in the Spartan communal apartment where she and her mother lived at the palace, often turning over her bread ration to those who were doing the heaviest work, while she survived on cheap cigarettes. An entry in her journal of August 2, 1944, states simply, "Everyone ate berries from the park." While they all worked, her mother looked after the children in an informal kindergarten. The former parlormaid of Grand Duke Constantine, who had run off to join the partisans and managed to survive, came back to work on the restoration.

Some of the mothers of the girl minesweepers came out to join the effort, and one of them, looking at the ruined palace, said something that Anna remembered all her life: "Don't grieve. The eyes are afraid but the hands do — the skeleton of the palace beckons."

"In general," said Kuchumov, "everybody was mobilized — students, architects. They wrote and offered to do measurements, drawings, photographs." Many worked without pay. Whole groups of architectural students from Moscow came to Leningrad in 1944 to take measurements. Photographs of the time show them balancing on scaffoldings and crawling up into the remaining rafters in the upper stories. They took life-sized photographs in full detail of moldings and carvings that had remained intact, and these helped immeasurably with the later restoration. Artists came and sketched the ruins and the first stages of the restoration.

With their own hands, the population of Leningrad voted for the restoration. Thousands of people volunteered to work on Saturdays and Sundays,* sometimes as many as two thousand on a single day — citizens and workers from Leningrad factories and plants, military groups. In 1944, columns of German prisoners were also pressed into helping to clean the debris.

Beginning in 1944/45, all these volunteers managed to remove the thousands of stumps and damaged trees, and then to replant fifty thousand trees and bushes.

---

* These days, a Soviet tradition called *subbotniks* and *voskreseniks*.

Many a citizen of Leningrad has his own tree in the park today. Before the work was finally finished, many years later, every organization, establishment, school, and college of Leningrad had worked on the palace or the park.

The plans were studied and buried statues hauled out of their hiding places deep in the earth. Sometimes these excavations turned up surprises. When the statue of Peace was dug up, Anna found that the defiant inscription written in 1941 by an unknown worker — "We will come back and find you" — was still there. Anna's gamble had succeeded. All were found intact, including the white monolith marble sculpture of the Three Graces, which she had ordered buried at a depth of five meters, a formidable task for the women who did it. The statue was so heavy that it could not be hauled far and had to be interred in front of the pavilion next to a garden path. Such a deep excavation could not be entirely disguised. The Nazis dug down three meters, then, deciding that the Russians had fooled them, went no farther. Nevertheless, when they left, they mined the area. Of the remaining monuments and statues in the park, the only two that remained untouched and still in their places, presumably because of their German background, were the statues of Maria Feodorovna and of Paul, who continued, as he had during the entire occupation, to haughtily cast his stony eyes over all the events.*

The splendid *allée* of linden trees in front of the palace that turns to burnished gold in the fall had miraculously been spared, as the Nazis considered the trees too old and unfit to be used for building materials. The path of the Twelve Oaks had also survived, but for a more sinister reason. The Nazis had used these oaks for hanging partisans, and because of ancient Teutonic tradition, a place of executions could not be destroyed.

Anna was to hear a touching story about these trees. One day, an old gamekeeper from a nearby park appeared in her office. Placing a glass on the table, he said, "Anna Ivanovna — let's have one for the road. It seems my time has come." In what was to be his last conversation with her, he told her that after the Nazis had occupied the palace, they had announced the death of the Communist Zelenova. Not knowing that she had managed to escape, he and his fellow gamekeepers had risked German bullets and walked to Pavlovsk at night to look for her among the hanged and to bury her in Pavlovsk Park.

In retreat, the Nazis had blown up all the decorative bridges; Voronykhin's

---

* On the eve of the birthday of Pushkin, the day of the D-Day landing in Normandy, women at nearby Tsarskoe Selo began digging at the spot indicated in the plan for the burial of his statue; at a depth of approximately two meters they exposed the curly head of Pushkin. They wept with joy and threw wildflowers on the spot.

graceful Visconti Bridge, the most famous bridge in the park, named for the Italian master mason who constructed it, was mangled. Visconti had revetted his bridge with powdered limestone. All the decorative vases and lions' heads on the keystone arches were also made of the same stone. But the quarries had been worked out long ago. Where to get the material? Zelenova proposed that they exchange powdered granite for limestone. Divers working under the bridge were able to salvage several sections of the original grillwork.

Despite these painstaking efforts there were those who remained skeptical about whether a restoration could be done at all. The damage done to Leningrad by the Nazis was calculated at twenty billion rubles. A ruble can be replaced by another ruble, it was reasoned, but how were the works of human genius to be brought back to life? Some said that the palaces could never be the same — that they would be merely "stage sets"; "corpses could not be resurrected." Many specialists and leading intellectual figures, among them Academician Dmitry Likhachev, remained unconvinced that under contemporary conditions the palaces could be accurately reproduced in all their former beauty. It was believed impossible that modern man could duplicate eighteenth-century workmanship and quality. But one individual's impassioned words helped to influence the final outcome.

Early in 1945 the museum workers of Leningrad were called to a meeting to discuss the wartime damage of the palaces and monuments of art and the possible scope and difficulties of reconstruction. There, a distinguished professor of architecture, Andrei Andreivich Ol', was one of the speakers. He told the crowd that an international meeting of architects had been held in London and that the assembly had expressed sorrow at hearing the news of the destruction of the palaces of Petersburg, saying that "Mankind of the world has become poorer from the wasting of such monuments of civilization as Pushkin and Pavlovsk." Professor Ol' then bowed his head and asked the assembled crowd to observe a moment of silence in memory of the lost palaces.

The auditorium fell quiet — a silence abruptly broken by the sound of a hastily moved chair, and the heavy strides of soldiers' boots. A man in uniform walked up to the podium and, boldly shaking the hand of the startled professor, demanded rather than requested, "Allow me to say something on this matter." The flustered but proper professor turned to the chairman, saying, "With pleasure I offer the floor to our colleague, just returned from the front, the architect Feodor Feodorovich Oleinik."

The soldier then stretched his hands straight out to the audience and passionately exclaimed, "And what are these for?" And then, clenching his fists he beat on his temples. "And what is this for? What are hands and heads for? So that we could allow ourselves to become poorer? I don't believe that our people will permit us to leave Pushkin, Pavlovsk, Peterhof as ruined monuments to fascism on our land! In our country beauty was created — and the loss of this beauty, they say, makes the mankind of the world poorer. We must create it again! Our beautiful palaces are injured, they await us, specifically we, who know them to their last crumb, their last ion! I speak for myself." Then he continued, pulling a small notebook out of his chest pocket, "Here, while I was lying in the trenches between battles, I drew from memory what we are talking about. And this was on the front! Don't we have here in Leningrad hundreds of excellent architectural designs of our monuments? Is it only I who have the measurements of the burned cupola of Pavlovsk Palace? Don't we have thousands of photographs? And that which did survive — that is still alive. Wounded, but alive! Only we must absolutely not lose anything nor let it perish. We must save it, save it today and not wait for the end of the war! Let's roll up our sleeves, work, save that which is whole, and restore that which suffered and return to mankind of the whole world that which will make mankind richer! It is not the first time that we Russians have done this. Let us restore that which has disappeared!"

After this electrifying appeal, the auditorium exploded with applause. That evening, the energetic Nikolai Belekhov proposed that they intercede with the military command for the early demobilization of Oleinik so that he could devote himself entirely to the urgent task of conservation and head up a group of architects who would be responsible for beginning the plans for the restoration of Pavlovsk. Zelenova, who recorded this meeting, wrote, "The appearance of Oleinik was the first step in the restoration of Pavlovsk."

Zelenova had met Oleinik in 1938 when, under the guidance of an eminent professor, he and a group of graduate students worked at the palace restoring the frescoes of the Gonzaga Gallery. Oleinik was then preparing his thesis, "The Constructions of Pavlovsk Palace and the Frescoes of the Gonzaga Gallery." That same year, when he was in his early twenties, he co-authored an article titled "The Restoration of the Gonzaga Frescoes," which was published in the journal *Arkhitektura CCCP*. A talented artist and specialist in architectural monuments, Oleinik had measured and sketched the frescoes and the entire palace. The handsome dark-eyed young man was, according to Anna, "a merry, talkative fellow who stayed long after others had left, still working at the frescoes, removing the tracing cloth. While copying the frescoes he insisted on working in the early morning light 'so as not to lie in the color later.'"

Oleinik was first recalled from the front in the summer of 1944 to consult on the plans for the palace. In his eagerness to sketch the ruins he was almost inadvertently killed by the security guards that Anna had posted. An entry of August 2 in Zelenova's diary states laconically, "Tonight the artist F. F. Oleinik, having come to the palace at night 'to take the contours in the moonlight,' was almost shot."

When he was demobilized in 1945, he immediately began studying the decorative elements that had been preserved, and undertook the first reconstruction and restoration of the building. He used measurements that had been made of the exterior of the central body of the palace before the war, as well as those done by candidates for the Academy of Architects, which had also been preserved. At the Lenproekt Institute, under Oleinik's guidance, a group of architecture specialists, using both old and new measurements, began redrafting the palace façade and interiors. In the first years after the war, there was no one in Leningrad experienced in restoration on the scale that the seriously damaged palaces required. Oleinik was one of the first to venture into this area of monumental architectural restorations, and his contributions were enormous. Later, restorers of other palaces were to learn from his successes and mistakes.

In twenty-three months, from February 1944 to December 1945, an extraordinary amount of work had been done. The conservation was in full swing, mines had been cleared, trees planted, statues unearthed, thousands of fragments carefully stored and documented, all of this an astonishing accomplishment considering the conditions that prevailed in the city — no housing, and severe rationing. Like a phoenix, Pavlovsk had begun to rise from the ashes.

In April 1945, throwing themselves happily into each other's arms, Russians and Americans met at the Elbe and Berlin. On April 30, Hitler committed suicide, and on May 8, the war in Europe was over. The first atomic bomb was dropped on August 6, and by August 14, Japan surrendered. On November 25, the Nuremberg trials had begun. Peace had come again to the world at last.

At the end of that year there was a party at Pavlovsk for the children of the workers past and present. A Christmas tree was decorated, and, as there were still no men, again it was Anna who stepped in. She dressed up as Grandfather Frost for the children, and although there could be no gifts, somewhere she had managed to find some sweets.

17

The Search

"If you look, you will find everything."

— Anatoly Mikhailovich Kuchumov

*I*N EARLY FEBRUARY 1944, only three weeks after the lifting of the Blockade, Anatoly Mikhailovich was called back to Leningrad to testify to the Lensoviet about the condition of the treasures that had been evacuated under his care. He was able to report that all were safe, preserved in their entirety. He never went back to Siberia. The work of returning the convoy was left to others. Anna Mikhailovna, the Leningrad Philharmonic, and the 402 crates of Pavlovsk treasures came home to Leningrad on the same train some months later on December 18, 1944. Anatoly Mikhailovich was named both Chief of the Museum Section for the Directorate of Art Affairs of the Leningrad Soviet and Director of the Main Repository. Although it had been looted and severely damaged, the Alexander Palace, where the evacuation had begun for him, had not been entirely destroyed and was designated as the central repository for the returning treasures. At Pavlovsk, while Anna Ivanovna and her co-workers were beginning their conservation efforts, to Anatoly Mikhailovich fell the task of organizing all the repositories for the palaces.

But Kuchumov had another idea. During the impassioned meetings about the question of restoration, he had made up his mind. He would go look for the lost treasures.

The saga that unfolded over the next four years is a great art detective story. Inflamed by the love for art that had driven his life since childhood, Anatoly Mikhailovich began a search that was to take him all the way to Hitler's headquarters in Berlin. The fabled resourcefulness of the people of Mologa, all his talents — his extraordinary devotion, persistence, sharp eyes, and extraordinary memory — were to be put to the highest test. His experience in taking the inventory ("Everything passed through my hands, I touched everything") now was to become invaluable to his country. The man who blindfolded knew the place and personality of every object in every palace, who had played memory games with his colleagues, now set off over the war-devastated land.

He has never abandoned his search, pursuing it actively during the six years following the war and continuing it up to this day. His tenacity and heroic efforts have made it possible to restore Pavlovsk so that today it looks very much the way it did when Maria Feodorovna lived in it. Many other palaces of Leningrad have also greatly benefited from his work.

Sifting through the debris of war, often risking his life, he searched through German bunkers and fortifications, then in ever-widening circles, through destroyed and deserted villages and cities, where it was rare to meet a living soul. In the silence and desolation, relentlessly following the Nazis as they fled from towns and villages, he went looking for lost beauty — for fragments of furniture, a headless statue, a shard of glass.

Immediately after the lifting of the Blockade he began his search around Leningrad, roaming from site to site, giving museum workers advice as they sorted through the rubble. Marina Tikhmirova, a curator of Peterhof who spent the Blockade in St. Isaac's, remembers, "What we especially revered in him was his capacity to enumerate from memory all the objects in any given room in any of our palaces — to tell us which were preserved and when to search for something to compensate. Along with us, through the ruins he would go through all obstructions, advising, 'Don't ignore this piece. It seems we have here a piece of the chandelier of the Blue Salon. Don't let anyone take it away.'" He interrogated captured German prisoners.

"It was a big job," he explains in a typical understatement — another would have said impossible. "We tried to collect all the things stolen by the Fascists, beginning with the German encampments in the park, and all the way to Berlin, along the whole road. Had we not done that then, one wouldn't find these things now. Today they are still going around Berlin and other cities — that's their address now — but back then, the fresh tracks helped us, supported our efforts."

A great many things were found near the palace. There were often articles in Pavlovsk itself, simply thrown out on the lawn or along the road by the fleeing German armies. Many were abandoned in German encampments, fortifications, and bunkers. Fortifications of concrete and logs had been decorated with gilded cornicing, rare eighteenth-century fabrics ripped from chairs, gilded molding, carvings, panels of rosewood, decorations from the halls of the palace — even, in one case, an antique altar, which had been set up on a platform in front of one bunker. Priceless doors of various rare woods from the Agate Pavilion of the Catherine Palace had been chopped into firewood; some had been used as bridges across trenches.

"There were many things," remembered Anatoly Mikhailovich, "tables, wall mountings, chairs. Some things couldn't be brought through the doors so they sawed them in half, or cut off the legs of eighteenth-century tables and consoles. We still have these consoles. We saved them even though they are only pieces." Everything found was transferred to the repository in the Alexander Palace.

Throughout the devasted district Kuchumov gathered objects: eighteenth-century furniture designed by Rastrelli, couches made by the great French furniture masters, the brothers Jacob in Paris, for Catherine the Great.*

"Many encampments were mined, but we crawled into them. We saw the mines, because little wires would stick out, so we avoided them, careful not to step on them, not to disturb them. Anna Ivanovna and I went many times. Somehow, we weren't frightened, somehow we went courageously. Of course we walked carefully, first looking where we should step. In the Pil Tower there was an awful dump. We crossed the logs, crawled across the branches of the felled trees. When we emerged, we saw there was a wire strung and a board hung there with a leftover German sign, WARNING: MINES, but we came out safely on the other side. God, as they say, saved us — the ghosts of Paul and Maria Feodorovna preserved us so that we could restore the palace."

Once, in Peterhof, while Kuchumov was looking around a fortification, a sapper cried, "Watch out! There's a mine there!" It was too late, he had already stepped on it, but it did not go off "because," Anatoly Mikhailovich says chuckling, "I was too light. It was a large antitank mine. One had to weigh 250 kilograms."

---

* Chairs of this set were later found in East Prussia and other places. A Soviet general came across three in eastern Prussia, transported them to Kharkov, and wrote to Kuchumov. Today almost the entire set of furniture has been returned. Several of the chairs had been turned into stools by the Nazis who simply chopped off their legs.

He developed a pattern and a method, which he used everywhere he went. "When I got to a place I looked first for people. I asked, 'Which houses did the Germans occupy? Where did the generals, the colonels live?' Because they took the best things, I found things simply by following their tracks. Sculptures were most often found in the gardens of the houses where the generals and the bosses lived." In his neat hand he noted everything in the notebook he always carried with him. He began around Pavlovsk and Pushkin, then in an ever-widening circle scoured all the deserted villages in the surrounding area. The majority of them were empty. "I remember how terrible it was around Pavlovsk in the month of May 1944, the corpses had not yet been gathered, the snow had melted, and when the wind blew a horrible smell hit you in the mouth."

Kuchumov was told that the Nazis had built a prison camp in the Pokrovki Palace, designed by the nineteenth-century architect Bruillov for the aristocratic Samoilov family not far from Pavlovsk. He went on foot, only to find that everything had been burned. Two or three sheds remained, and there he found a few frames from the palace and the models of the façade of the Catherine Palace. These had been made by a young Russian sculptor before the war. The artist perished at the front, but the models he made were returned and used in the restoration and can be seen at the palace today.

In the cellars of Pokrovki the Germans had an officers' casino, and later a headquarters. When they retreated, they burned the palace, and it was there that much of the magnificent eighteenth-century art stolen from Pavlovsk was destroyed. Nevertheless, Anatoly Mikhailovich gathered the burnt slabs, pieces of marble, and broken porcelain he found.

In May 1944, he was in Antropshino, a tiny village some three kilometers from Pavlovsk. "It was deserted, so it was with joy that I found an old man to whom I could address questions. Old men always knew in which houses the Fascists had lived and where their headquarters were." Kuchumov had already searched some thirty houses. In one of them he had discovered two carved gilded tables from the Arabesque Hall of the Catherine Palace; in the untidy weed-filled garden of another, marble statues from the Gonzaga Gallery in Pavlovsk and stone cupids from the Catherine Palace. "The old man advised me to look into yet another hut. He told me there was some sort of a broken chair there — 'could be from some palace,' he said. I followed his advice, went in and up some creaking stairs to a dark attic. I found the chair immediately and was about to leave when in the garbage and refuse my foot hit something that felt like oilcloth." Rummaging in the mess, he came upon some crumpled canvases. When he unrolled one, he had found the famous life-size portrait of Peter the Great painted in his lifetime by the Saxon painter Tannauer, a unique work that had hung in Paul's Library in Pavlovsk. The painting had been roughly ripped out of its frame, fifteen centimeters were missing at the bottom. Peter's chest had been punctured with a knife, and an inscription in German crudely scratched into the canvas.

"At the last minute before leaving, some German cut it out and then rolled it up and threw it in the attic of the house where officers lived. What if we hadn't found it? What would be in its place today? Nothing. You couldn't find a portrait of the same size. It could not be evacuated because there was no container large enough for it — for the painting of Maria Feodorovna, one was found, but not for this." In the same garret he found another painting, of the Emperor Paul.

"Orienbaum, Peterhof. I walked tens of kilometers at a time." Every one of his forays yielded something. In one house in the Pavlovsk area he found a marble lion from the famous Brenna Staircase, in a hut some cast-iron vases from the incinerated Rose Pavilion.

Starting in the spring of 1944 and going on until 1947, Kuchumov began traveling farther and farther from Leningrad. "Why did I go?" he says. "I kept hearing stories. There was one museum person who had been in Riga during the occupation who said that the Germans had held an exhibition there. 'Go,' he said, 'go see if anything is left there.' The idea was mine. There was no Ministry of Culture then, only an organization called Kultursoviet. I would give them my request and they would say simply, 'Please go.'"

Armed only with an official letter that read: "Given to Comrade Kuchumov, A. M., to certify that he is in fact working to find museum valuables that were taken from the palace-museums of the environs of Leningrad by the German-Fascist thieves. We request that all civil authorities and military units situated in places where museum items may be located give their utmost cooperation to A. M. Kuchumov in receiving and hauling museum items, in providing transportation for trips to places that are located far from railroads, and transporting items. . . ." Carrying this letter he scoured the Baltic region, eastern Prussia, and finally Berlin itself.

He most often went alone, following the fleeing Nazis. "I walked, I took taxis, I hitchhiked; sometimes I found military cars. I used all forms of transportation in my search." Once he arrived at his destination he would again apply his method, always starting by searching for people and asking them for clues. "Then I would write down such and such a street or such and such a house — there one might find such and such a thing. There were no means of transportation.

When I could find some, I would go, but often by the time I arrived things were already gone. They had jumped to another place, with other admirers. I did almost everything on foot."

He went to Novgorod, to Pskov, and then Estonia.* "I got to Tartu, in 1944, only two days after the Germans had fled. In the Town Hall there was a large table, velvet chairs. On the table mugs of beer overturned, half-eaten sandwiches dropped on the floor. There was such a hurry to retreat they didn't even drink the beer." He examined every building and restaurant, cabin and hut, including, in all the towns of the Baltic that he visited, special brothels set up by the Nazis for local women. "I was in a building in Tartu and I saw a sign 'Women.' I was curious. When I opened the door I found a corridor, and a whole series of small rooms in which were only a bed, a couch, and a sign, 'Remember. The Enemy Listens.' So they were afraid — even there."

On September 22, 1944, he was called to Vyr, another Estonian city fifty-five kilometers from Tartu, and flown there from Leningrad in a specially assigned plane. A storehouse had been found. This time he had a companion, his old friend Vsevelod Veselovsky. They had first met as young men in 1930 and worked together at the Okhtinsky Chemical factory. Anatoly had become a museum worker and Vsevelod an architect. Wounded at the front, Vsevelod was demobilized and returned to Leningrad, where he found Kuchumov. In the storehouse in Vyr they discovered lacquered Japanese desks and chairs from the Catherine Palace, and walnut tables from Gatchina. Anatoly opened the desk drawers and found children's blankets and enameled dishes — all from the palace, and all labeled *"Oberst Dehle"* — the home of the colonel who had occupied the cottage and then fled.

"I don't speak Estonian," he recalls, "so I would just walk along the street, peering into houses. They are single storied there, so it was easy to do. Our documents gave us the right to inspect. Once, looking through the windows, I saw three young men sitting on a couch. I knocked, introduced myself, and explained that I wanted to examine the furniture. Then I threw myself under the table and looked for the palace inventory number. When I crawled out they looked at me as if I were a madman. They couldn't believe their table could be from a palace."

Anatoly Mikhailovich developed the habit of observing everything, seeing

---

* Ruled for centuries by their more powerful neighbors (including Russia from the end of the eighteenth century) the Baltic states — Estonia, Latvia, and Lithuania — gained independence after the Russian Revolution and the end of World War I. In 1940 they were overrun by Soviet forces and made republics of the Soviet Union.

everything, noticing everything. One day, he stopped at a local cafeteria for lunch. "We were not served for so long that I went to the manager to complain. Once I got there I forgot what I had come to say." There stood two magnificent mahogany cupboards, which he instantly recognized were from Gatchina. The manager of the cafeteria, a friendly woman, turned them over to him. He made the necessary notes and started back, but as he was passing the kitchen he noticed that a cook peeling potatoes was sitting on a seventeenth-century Venetian chair with a carved back. Next to her was another like it. Both were also from Gatchina. "Where did you get these?" he asked. "The Germans brought them," the cook answered indifferently, and then continued, "There are also two pots, we use them to make dough. Look under the staircase." There he found packing cases. The "pots"? — Japanese vases of the eighteenth century from the Chinese Hall of the Catherine Palace.

Trudging on the Estonian roads one day, he managed to hitch a ride with a passing military vehicle. Before he had even had time to strike up a conversation with the driver, he suddenly cried out, "Stop!" Startled, the driver asked, "What's the matter — mines?" But Anatoly Mikhailovich had already jumped out. In a ditch along the road lay a huge disorderly heap of marble busts, paintings, and books. "What are you planning to do, read?" shouted the driver impatiently. "I don't have time for this. My commander is waiting in Vyr." Suspiciously, the driver got out of his truck. Kuchumov was leafing through the books. He knew what he had found. In the ditch lay some four hundred volumes of fine nineteenth-century editions from his own Alexander Palace, fragments of the trim of Catherine's bedroom, done by Cameron, as well as four insets from the ceiling of the Arabesque Hall of the Catherine Palace, which subsequently made it possible to restore the whole ceiling.

What could be done with all this treasure on a deserted highway? Anatoly Mikhailovich tried to explain the value of his find. A little uncertainly, the driver agreed to help. Together they carried the old books with their fine bindings, the busts, the frames, and loaded them onto the truck. "For sure my bosses won't let me off today! How will I get a drink?" grumbled the driver as they drove off. Kuchumov reassured him that one day he would be happy to have done it.

From his searches in Vyr, Kuchumov managed to collect a full freight-car load. Collecting objects was one task, packing and shipping was another. "I made a circle around Vyr. While I looked, it was Vsevelod's job to organize transportation, to persuade railroad workers to give us cars." In those wartime days, railroad cars were almost nonexistent. There were no railroad stations, no warehouses — everything had been bombed or burned. "We deposited everything on what was left of the platform and then took turns watching it. He had the rank of lieutenant and wore a soldier's uniform. It was autumn. It was cold. So he said, 'All right, I will sit on the cupboard, and you cover me.' He sat, and I would go in the railroad man's sentry box and doze. Bombing started. He didn't leave the cupboard; he worried that the glass would break. And so we guarded it until morning, until they gave us a freight car, until the things left for Leningrad. Estonian comrades accompanied the things to Leningrad. I continued farther."

Kuchumov next went to Tallinn, a medieval city of ancient bastions, towers, and spires, located on a bay of the Gulf of Finland overlooking the sea, dominated by the fourteenth-century tower of St. Olaf's Church, which rose 135 meters into the sky.

On one of his methodical walks through the city streets, looking up at a second-floor window he spied the back of a gilded chair. Pondering which suite of furniture it could be from, he paced back and forth in front of the house several times. The city had been liberated on September 24, 1944, only a short time before, and it was still partly occupied by the Nazis. A suspicious sentinel stopped him and asked why he was taking such an interest in that particular house, which, it turned out, was a military headquarters of the Soviet Army. "I leave it to you to imagine my situation," he says. "As they were verifying my documents I explained that it was the chair that I was interested in. It was in a room occupied by one of the captains. The captain received me politely. I turned the chair over. It was a carved eighteenth-century velvet chair from the Crimson Drawing Room of Gatchina." As they talked, several other curious officers appeared. One of them remembered that he had seen several other such chairs. "But," he added, "the unit that was here before us took them away." The unit was some seven kilometers distant. No, he couldn't remember the name of the village. "But you'll surely find it — it's somewhere over there," he said, pointing. Kuchumov set out on foot. He found the unit, and among other things three more chairs, as well as two tables.

"In February of 1945 I went with Anatoly Alexandrovich Dmitriev, who was an engineer and wonderful with his hands, to check in Latvia. Someone had seen a sign in Riga, 'Treasures Saved from the Barbarism of the Bolsheviks' — the Germans had held an exhibition of seized objects. By the time we got there the exhibition had already been taken away. But we went to the museum anyway, to see if there was anything left."

The beautiful Baltic city of Riga, founded by the crusaders under Albert of

Bremen in 1200, was in ruins. There were few cities that held so fascinating a collection of architectural treasures in so small an area, but now the entire center of this city of ships and sailors, of narrow winding streets, steep red roofs, and crowstepped gables, was littered with bricks from collapsed houses. Destroyed were the thirteenth-century Church of St. Peter, with its fifteenth-century wooden spire, the highest of its kind in Europe, the Town Hall Square, and the old Town Hall. Destroyed too was the glory of the square, with its magnificent Dutch-Renaissance façade, the House of the Black Heads, a fifteenth-century order of unmarried merchants who had as their patron Saint Mauritius, a Moor. In this house there had once been a marvelous museum, with an exceptional collection of Swedish and Russian portraits of Gustavus Adolphus, Charles XII, Peter the Great, and his wife Catherine, done by the first Russian portraitists of the seventeenth century, as well as beautiful models of ships and a rich collection of silver. "All of this had been plundered," remembers Kuchumov. "The museum was burned along with the Town Hall and the famous Church of St. Peter."

Kuchumov and Dmitriev made their way to the fortress castle of the Teutonic Knights, first built in the thirteenth century. In the two wings of the castle were museums, and Kuchumov had information that there were valuables hidden in both. In stark contrast to all the destruction around it, this castle had not been touched by the Nazis. Loot, intended to be sent to Germany, had been brought to this place from Leningrad by the Nazi armies, and it was in this Prussian castle that he unexpectedly came upon one of his most valuable finds.

A Nazi sympathizer had been left as director. They were met suspiciously by the museum workers. When pressed, one of the workers admitted that the director "had some negatives." Kuchumov insisted on seeing them, and finally was given twenty-six drawers in which he found twenty-five hundred glass negatives of the interiors of Pavlovsk. These had been done by the famous Petersburg photographer Matveev at the request of Alexander Benois for the art journal *The Art Treasures of Russia* in 1900–1902.

"It was the first time that there had been permission to photograph the palace for publication. And like all good photographers, he had photographed everything: walls, frescoes, objects. A portion of these negatives had been preserved in Pavlovsk and had survived the Revolution. When I saw them, I was so happy, I literally jumped up and down. Because the evacuation had been so hurried, the museum workers at Pavlovsk had not been able to transport these extremely fragile glass negatives. These negatives, 18 by 24 centimeters, were a priceless find for curators and restorers, for if they had not been found much would have been done differently. I didn't know I was even looking for them. I found them accidentally, but when you look, you will find everything. The German staff of Rosenberg had given them to someone for a receipt. That person ran away with the Germans and left them behind. Thanks to these negatives, we were able to restore Pavlovsk. Artists did not have to ponder and guess."

In the same castle they found a great number of portraits, as well as many of the cameos that had been in the crate in the palace at the time the Nazis arrived. "They had been ordered especially from the artist Emaler Tennik, who worked as a jewel cutter for Catherine. There had been twelve thousand — we found some seven thousand, which is a lot, after all. Unfortunately the cases and boards on which they had been mounted were very much damaged — we restored them, but now there is still the enormous riddle of how to sort them according to the Hermitage collection."

Kuchumov spent three months in the castle in Riga. "By order of Rosenberg, who directed the seizing of objects, there were in the castle about five hundred very valuable portraits of the eighteenth and nineteenth century from Pavlovsk and Gatchina." He and his helper Dmitrievich sorted, made lists, numbered portraits. There were no typists, so they made an inventory by hand, no restorers, so they did preliminary restoring themselves. They found Jacob-Philippe Hackert's huge 2.5-by-4-meter painting, *The Chekmen Battle,* from Gatchina, broken in four pieces. When they unwrapped it, dried paint crumbled into their cupped hands. In the restorers' workshops they found some dried potter's glue. They warmed it, glued the painting with cigarette paper, then reinforced the painting's structure and rolled it onto a roller they had made themselves from plywood and boards. Paintings of the Russian nineteenth-century painters Kramskoy, Makovsky, Kustodiev, Dau, and Yarosenko lay about in piles. In the Museum of Latvian Art in another part of the city they found, among other items, paintings and icons stolen from the Peterhof Gothic Church.

In April 1945, Kuchumov sent back to Leningrad an entire sealed freight-car load of treasures, which included 463 paintings, 7,986 cameos, and the precious negatives. In 1945, from his searches in the Baltic region alone, he recovered twelve thousand objects for the palaces and museums of Russia — two thousand of these for Pavlovsk. Eventually he was to find more than three thousand of Pavlovsk's lost treasures.

The war ended in Russia on May 9, 1945. Known as "The Day of Victory," it is still celebrated as one of the greatest holidays in the Soviet Union. But Kuchumov did not stop. Now he went into the former enemy's territory, to

Königsberg in East Prussia.* "We went," he says, "because we had advice that a mass of things had been sent there, including the Amber Room panels.

"The city of Königsberg was in ruins, a terrible sight. In some districts of the city one could walk for several hours without meeting a single inhabitant."

A fortified city founded in the thirteenth century, Königsberg was the fortress stronghold of the formidable military Order of the Teutonic Knights, the seat of their Grand Masters, and in the fifteenth century of the dukes of Prussia. In the center of the city was the forbidding royal castle, a huge quadrangle with an extensive set of buildings and outbuildings, crowned by a hundred-meter-high tower that commanded the Pregel River and the surrounding countryside. There, Frederick I had been crowned King of Prussia in the eighteenth century — the arms of the Black Eagle were emblazoned on the church walls. Above the church was the Moscowitzer Saal, one of the largest halls in Germany. This historic seat of the Teutonic Knights had been a main repository of stolen art treasures for the Nazis until it was destroyed by English air raids in 1944.

"In that castle," remembered Kuchumov, "there had been a museum, and in that museum, many lost treasures of the palaces. When we arrived in the courtyard we found a number of pieces of broken furniture of the Catherine Palace piled in a heap. Proceeding through the burned rooms and half-collapsed arches, I got to the first floor. There was nothing there but a large heap of ashes. I was about to turn back when my foot hit something I recognized." Searching through the ashes, he found an embossed lock, which he immediately knew was from the famous Lyons Salon of the Catherine Palace. Looking further, he found five more — incontestable evidence that the doors and many other things had been there — but now were gone forever.

His careful search of the cellars, the vaults of the Imperial bank that adjoined the castle, the concrete bunkers along Langerai Street, and the bastions and towers of the castle and fortress, which spread over one-quarter of the city, turned up much valuable furniture.

Anatoly Mikhailovich went back to Königsberg several times. In March 1946, he and Stanislav Tronchinsky, Secretary of the Leningrad City Party and head of the Museum Section of the Cultural Administration of Leningrad, returned to conduct a detailed search of every remaining room, all the cellars, including the extensive wine cellars, which had once been the medieval torture rooms of the castle, and all the underground passages. In different parts of this huge burned

---

* Originally the Polish town of Krolewiec, this is today Kaliningrad in the USSR.

and heavily damaged castle they were able to find more fragments of palace furniture and broken Chinese and Japanese porcelain — but despite all their searches, not the Amber Room panels. "We were able to ascertain that the panels had indeed been there, in the sentry tower. Accompanied by soldiers, we searched all of many underground passages, which linked the castle and different parts of the city, but sadly, we were never able to find them. During the American and English air raids over the city, the Germans had brought the panels down and hidden them in the cellars. On August 30, 1944, the castle burned during a big air raid. The Amber Room was in one of the deep cellars, far underground. It did not suffer. The Nazis took them somewhere, but where?" There have been rumors that some of these cellars were flooded, and so perhaps the Amber Room has returned to the water from which it came. Its fate remains one of the great art mysteries of World War II.*

Although they never found the fabled amber panels, the search in Königsberg was far from fruitless. They did find more work of the brothers Jacob, and of Rastrelli, and also Voronykhin pieces from Pavlovsk. Another whole freight-car load was sent back to Leningrad.

Soviet soldiers found and returned many things. At Pavlovsk, veterans of those days remember that before the end of the war, in a German barracks, Soviet soldiers found a crate full of rare porcelain. They wrote to Anatoly Mikhailovich, who advised them to send their find to the central repository in Leningrad. In a month, the crate arrived. In it was carefully packed the famous Gurevsky service of more than a hundred pieces.† But what surprised the museum workers was that the return address was from somewhere in Siberia. The unit had been sent off to the Far East to join in the war against Japan, and they had taken the Tsar's service with them until they could find a secure place from which to send it.

In July 1945, six military trucks full of tired, cold, and wet soldiers arrived from Silesia. With them they brought two hundred fifty crates of museum valuables they had found in a German castle.

On April 4, 1946, an appeal from Kuchumov was published in the military journal *Vo Slavu Rodini* (For the Glory of the Motherland). Titled "Help Restore

---

*According to some accounts, it was buried in one of the salt mines and is still there. Other reports place it in a private castle in Saxony, or in an abandoned brewery in Königsberg. At one stage the Soviet Commission entertained the idea that it had been sunk while being shipped west via the Baltic; the Soviet government believed that it was being held by the West German government.

†This service, completed by the St. Petersburg Imperial Porcelain Factory in 1817, is remarkable for its decorations depicting the life of the people. The choice of such a subject matter was due to the recent Napoleonic invasion, which caused a tremendous growth of patriotic feeling among all strata of Russian society.

the Museums of Leningrad," the letter asked, "soldiers, sergeants and officers to advise us through the editors of locations where valuables of historical and artistic significance might be found, so that they may take their places again in our museums." This letter elicited many phone calls from former fighting men who had found pieces of old furniture, some of which turned out to be valuable.

By 1947 the Committee of Art of the Council of Ministers of the USSR had received an increasing number of documents that pointed to Berlin. Kuchumov was called to Moscow, and in October, along with three colleagues, took off from Sheremetyevo Airport for the German capital.

Berlin had been under steady bombing since 1943. From February 1 to April 21, 1945, it was bombed every night. The former business and government center of the city was in ruins. Anatoly Mikhailovich walked through huge devastated areas of demolished buildings. Poking around in the rubble, he picked up and kept as a souvenir a piece of what had once been Hitler's Chancellery.

The occupation forces had entered Berlin on July 4, 1945, and divided the twenty boroughs of the conquered city into four sectors — American, English, French, and Soviet — although there was movement among all sectors. The Soviets were located in the most heavily populated areas in the east and northeast, which included the central city, the central electric power plants, and the railroad stations.

Kuchumov searched all sectors. Although central Berlin had been destroyed, some of the extended city area was well preserved, including Karlshorst, where the Soviet headquarters were located. Soviet soldiers found many precious objects in Berlin in the most unexpected places. The archaeological collection of the Kerch Museum in the Crimea, thirteen crates' worth, was found in a cellar of a German castle. Many valuable paintings, both Western and Russian, were found in a damp warehouse, among them Argunov's *Portrait of an Unknown Lady in Blue,* which had been sent before the war by the Russian Museum in Leningrad to an exhibition in Alupka, Crimea. There, fallen into German hands, it had made the long trip to Berlin.

Many things turned up later. Himmler's hoard was found in a farmhouse in Westphalia not far from Wewelsburg Castle, the site of the S.S. school. Books from Kiev were found in Carinthia, Austria. More of the archeological collection from the Crimea was discovered in the 1980s in a Hamburg museum.

The Soviet administration maintained ties with the English, French, and American War Administrations, and when Russian valuables turned up they were delivered to a central location, a vast storage area called "Derutra," located in the eastern harbor of the river Spree. In gloomy one-story railroad warehouses, each almost a half a kilometer long, in total disorder, were piled masses of art valuables and treasures. Georgy Antipin, a museum curator who traveled with Kuchumov, recalled, "When we got to these places we couldn't believe our eyes. In a huge disorderly mess were piled framed paintings and rolled-up canvases, icons, wood and marble sculptures, manuscripts and books, parts of chandeliers, porcelain, tapestries, enameled objects, and much more. Hundreds, thousands of exhibits from the palaces of Pushkin, Pavlovsk, Minsk, Pskov, Novgorod, Kerch. Some of this property the Nazis had hidden there, but hadn't had time to drag or send anywhere because of the attack of the Soviet army." There were rare paintings and architectural details from the royal and patriarchal palaces in Novgorod, and the enormous chandelier of the Cathedral of St. Sophia, which had been destroyed by Nazi air attacks. "All of this had to be sorted out according to museum, packed, and sent back to the Soviet Union. We started working early in the morning and left late at night, with pains in our legs and backs." The Dutch tiles from the Catherine Palace alone filled thirty-five crates.

Originally, these valuables, which had been sent out of Russia by the Nazis, had been well packed in shavings and paper, then closed. But in the postwar period all the boxes had been opened and disemboweled by a wartime investigation committee before they ended up in the Soviet Zone. There were no lists or inventories, no way to determine what might have disappeared en route. Kuchumov relates, "We went to the English and to the American Zones. A great many things were proposed to us that had just been dumped in a heap, but I refused to accept them as they were. I insisted that they be packed properly, because the things had already suffered a great deal, and if we just took them as they were, could be lost completely. So the Soviet administration obtained a labor exchange and provided us with some hundred German civilians, the majority of them women, to help. Among them were even some quite wealthy people, owners of stores, for instance. Under my direction, they did the packing. I explained to them how important it was to handle these things carefully, what kind of paper to wrap them in.

"One day, I was searching for my steward, Paul, an industrious, hardworking German. Paul was the keeper of the keys. He would lock the doors to the storehouses at the end of the day and I would seal them. Adjoining the warehouses was a tall grain elevator. Some of its floors were filled with grain and several compartments had been kept for the storage of valuables. I went up several floors in the elevator looking for him. In one room I came upon a group of young men sweeping up grain and I saw that under the grain there was something that looked like a panel. I asked them what it was; they didn't know. I asked them to clear away the grain and pull out these screens. I saw wooden frames with numbers, and I understood that these were panels of parquet floor. This parquet turned out to be the priceless floor of the Lyons Hall in the Catherine Palace, made of rare wood and encrusted with Australian mother-of-pearl." Kuchumov had found the locks from the doors of this room in the Königsberg castle, and assumed that the floors had burned too.

"I always had with me a pocketful of photographs from all the palaces, so that I could show which things had been stolen from the palace. I quickly made a diagram, to see which panels were missing. We searched and found them in another place. In another room we found the parquet floor for the Gallery of Mirrors and the study of Catherine II." * Kuchumov thought he had collected all of the panels of this parquet in Berlin, but it was learned later that the most beautiful design of all, made from mother-of-pearl, had gone off to Novgorod. It was later found there along with some icons.

Kuchumov and Antipin combed the foundries. In one they found the huge bronze eighteenth-century statue of Hercules by Feodor Gordeyev that had adorned the staircase of the Cameron Gallery at the Catherine Palace, as well as the statue of Flora. "The Nazis had not yet managed to melt down Hercules, but he was badly burned. The Nazis would drag the heavy statues with tanks, simply throw a rope around the heads and pull. Hercules, strong man that he was, managed to stay whole, without damage, but poor Flora, as she was dragged, her head was bent down to her breast. Afterwards restorers sawed off the head, fixed the damaged place and cast it again so that now it is not noticeable, but it was difficult to do."

In the same foundry they found a huge three-meter-long early-eighteenth-century cannon with the Russian coat of arms, made in the reign of Empress Anna Ivanovna. "We did not know where it came from, but we knew we absolutely had to find a way to return it. We took it, but when we arrived in Pushkin, we almost had an unfortunate occurrence. The freight car on which were loaded Flora and Hercules started moving in the wrong direction and we had to go stop it. So we left the cannon in the station not knowing quite what to do with it. Then one day, when I was sitting on the commuter train to Leningrad, by chance I overheard two young men talking about how there was once in Russia a mar-

* This floor can now be seen exhibited in the Cameron Gallery at the Catherine Palace.

velous cannon which had been stolen by the Germans. I asked, 'Where was this cannon?' They said, 'In Smolensk.' So I wrote there, museum people came to check, and it was indeed the cannon from Smolensk. We returned it and it now stands on the main square, near a famous old church.

"We stayed in Berlin about two months. The general insisted that I stay and become their art expert, as they had none, but despite the fact that he offered really fantastic conditions — a car, a hotel apartment of three rooms, plus food — I was not attracted. I could not leave the palaces in Leningrad for a year. It was necessary to continue the search."

From Berlin, Kuchumov sent back eleven freight-car loads, which included twenty-five hundred crates of valuables to Pushkin. Eight loads went to Kiev, two to Minsk, and four to Novgorod, containing icons and decorations of the bombed Church of St. Sophia.*

After Berlin, Anatoly Mikhailovich never traveled abroad again, but at home he never stopped searching. Over the next fifteen years he kept looking everywhere in Leningrad and its environs for things that had left the palaces even before the Revolution, for things that had been given away or taken off to different places during the upheavals of the Revolution and Civil War.

He found rare pieces in the hospitals and hotels of the city, and kept an eye on old houses that were being renovated or rebuilt. "When my father worked in the Astoria and the Europe before the war, I often went to see him there and I noticed many pieces of furniture expropriated at the time of the Revolution from various palaces, the Sheremetyev, for instance. Afterwards, I don't know what happened to all this — perhaps it was destroyed during the Blockade. In 1932 I found much museum furniture in the Hotel Leningrad storerooms. Looking in this way many things turned up — just for Pavlovsk we found more than seven hundred objects: furniture, porcelain, vases, bronzes. In the Sverdlovsk Hospital X-ray room and reception rooms there was marvelous furniture of Karelian birch done by serf artists according to designs by the French master Perset Fontaine. Even if these things did not suit a historical interior, if we could not put any of it in the rooms of Paul and Maria Feodorovna, we could use it in our exhibitions." In many houses there were apartments of former aristocrats who had left, and simply abandoned their things. "I had plenty of work right here."

Occasionally things trickled back in surprising ways. "The Germans sent out a relatively small number of valuables under governmental supervision. Very few

---

* The Church of St. Sophia in Novgorod, bombed and destroyed by the Nazis, is today restored.

things went to the state in an organized way; the majority were simply stolen by generals and officers. Valuables were sold; they went to the French and to the Americans and then where afterwards? We do not know."

By chance one Soviet officer billeted with a German family saw on the table a large album bound in velvet, *Petersburg in the Reign of Nicholas I*. It had the seal of Pavlovsk. "He came here and returned it. And this was not the only thing returned in this way. In Czechoslovakia, a lady saw a book with the Pavlovsk seal in a bookstore. She bought it and sent it to us."

There were a few unexpected windfalls. In the 1960s, Kuchumov and a female museum co-worker saw the Soviet movie *War and Peace*. "We watched and dreamed. What wonderful furniture! She was able to make contact with the moviemakers. They had bought a lot of furniture in Moscow, from Moscow houses. She was able to show documentation that it belonged here, and we got a whole freight-car load of furniture free!"

In the 1970s Kuchumov received a crate that contained a splendid small carved round table from Pavlovsk. It was from a certain Feodor Ivanovich Yerofeyev — a Russian émigré living in Helsinki. He had seen the table with the inventory mark of Pavlovsk in an antique store, bought it, and decided to present it to the palace. When Kuchumov wrote to thank him, Yerofeyev came to Pavlovsk and Kuchumov took him to the room where his table stood. "We met as old friends," remembers Anatoly Mikhailovich. "He was not a bit like some of the rich tourists who come asking why we work so hard over the palaces of our former tsars, and even sometimes have offered us a few thousand dollars for a certain lacquered Roentgen chest of drawers. So I asked Yerofeyev why he had decided to give us this table, and added that, after all, if it had cost a lot of money surely we could pay him its worth. I will always remember his answer. He said simply, 'I am a Russian. I love Russian culture and I consider it my duty to return everything that belongs to Russia."

Anatoly Mikhailovich mourns not only for what was lost in the war, but before. "The tragedy is that the Soviet authorities started to liquidate Pavlovsk as a museum in 1929/30 and so many things were lost. Now, of course, it is a different time, much has been done, but it is distressing just the same that this happened. The palaces today are rebuilt, but it is hard to find furnishings — this is why I began to search not only here, but overseas."

Today, the Soviet Union is trying to recover historic art treasures of the national patrimony sold during Stalin's time, but because of this and the massive Nazi looting, many valuables from Pavlovsk and other palaces disappeared into the world's art market, surfacing from time to time. Many things are still most certainly tucked away in attics and homes in Germany and elsewhere. For years Kuchumov has been carefully collecting catalogues from auctions, clippings from newspapers and foreign journals about art sales abroad sent by foreign art dealers and museum curators who have volunteered their help.

In June 1971, an item in the *International Herald Tribune* noted that a Louis XVI writing table made by the German furniture maker Marten Carlin, which once stood in the bedroom of Maria Feodorovna at Pavlovsk, had been sold from the estate of Mrs. Anna Thomson Dodge, wife of the automobile magnate, to Habib Sadet, a Beirut-born private collector. The table had been bought by Lord Duveen from the Soviet authorities in 1930. Another news item reported that a cupboard with porcelain was sold from the collection of Mrs. Henry Ford II, but there was no information in the article of how it had reached her. Furniture with Pavlovsk inventory marks figure in collections in the United States, France, Italy, and Switzerland.

Marvin Ross, the late curator of the Hillwood Museum in Washington, was of special help to Kuchumov. The two museum curators became friends and corresponded for years. For Pavlovsk the single greatest loss of Stalin times were the four Gobelins given to Maria Feodorovna and Paul during their trip to France. For these, Anatoly Mikhailovich has never ceased to grieve. In 1971, Ross sent Kuchumov a photograph of Pavlovsk's precious Gobelins, which had found their way to an American art firm, then to Norton Simon in California. Later, for the relatively modest price of $190,000, Jean-Paul Getty bought them for his collection. Kuchumov was able to make contact with Getty's curator, and an exchange was agreed upon, but Getty died before it could be implemented, and the curator went back on his promise. Today the tapestries hang, out of their proper historical context, in an exhibit of Louis XVI furniture in the Getty Museum in Malibu, California.

When Juan Carlos, King of Spain, visited the Soviet Union a few years ago, Anatoly Mikhailovich sighed and said sadly, "Someone should have spoken to him. The Spaniards took a lot."

But when Anatoly Mikhailovich is gone, who will *know?* He says himself, "Today it is already over. There are no more such curators, it is another generation, and people have a different relationship to all these things. Today in the museums, people pass by and they don't even notice."

Now, forty-five years after he began his search, his body half paralyzed from a stroke, but his mind and memory still as alert as ever, he watches, remembers, and dreams. "If I were well today, I would continue looking. I say to the colleagues that not everything has been investigated, and that if they occupied themselves with this task today for Gatchina, a lot of things could still be found — and for Pavlovsk, too. By no means has everything been exhausted. So many things we found later; for example a Voronykhin chair from the boudoir of Maria Feodorovna in Pavlovsk, we found in 1945 in a burial vault in the Kazan Cemetery in Pushkin. The Nazis opened it, and some Fascist had made himself a cozy nest there. It is the only example we have, but we can make others according to it. We were able to finish the furniture of the Italian Hall — sixteen banquettes and two couches designed by Voronykhin — from fragments found around the palace. So much was stolen — things from Pavlovsk and Voronykhin could be in the home of some former German general or S.S. officer today — and no one would ever know or see it. You can never get everything back, but one must try. . . ."

THE DEBATE between those who believed that in the twentieth century it was possible to recapture an eighteenth-century image, and the doctrinaire "purists" with their credo "not a single stone that does not belong," was eventually won by those committed to full reconstitution of the palaces. "Not to do this," said Alexander Kedrinsky, the chief architect of the Catherine Palace, "meant that we might have ended up parting with our palaces and surrounding towns and villages."

But in a concession to the purists, who could be satisfied only with the original, every single step of the restoration had to find its proof in rigorous documentation. In the course of this process Leningrad developed the most exacting rules of restoration in the world. All designs had be approved by a committee of scholars, every surviving fragment located in its proper place with as much scientific exactitude as possible. Every decision had to endure scrutiny and questioning, be checked and rechecked by specialists and government cultural organizations. All work at Pavlovsk required the confirmation and sanction of the State Committee for the Preservation of Monuments (GIOP), organized in 1945 and first headed by Nikolai Belekhov. That year the city of Leningrad was divided up territorially by the Main Architectural Planning Directorate. This directorate, working as a team with GIOP, resolved all questions of construction and restoration throughout the city — treating it as a city of monuments. This early foresightedness and unified approach by the cultural authorities of Leningrad coupled with the tenacious devotion of its citizens to their cultural heritage had as its result that

Leningrad has been better able than Moscow and other cities in the Soviet Union to conserve its characteristic appearance and is today perhaps the best preserved eighteenth-century city in the world.

Leningrad was the first to venture into restoration in this massive and completely unprecedented way.* Sixty-two percent of Leningrad's historical buildings were damaged or destroyed, according to Alexander Kedrinsky. "There are five hundred palaces in the Leningrad area [this includes both aristocratic and Imperial residences]. We were deluged — there where we were, we started." There were no analogies in the world of art. Kedrinsky says, "Before the war, restoration was confined to conservation, the prevention of further deterioration and the restoration of small fragments. If before the war, we and Europe in general had developed the theory and practice of conservation that we now have today — things would have been better preserved and restoration would have required less reconstruction. Work would not have required the unbelievable amount of difficult research. We were the first to use the method of reconstitution. We had to put into action both theory and practice — that is the contribution of Leningrad."

Pavlovsk was the first experiment of this voyage into the unknown, and the experience gained there was used later in all other restorations. The first serious restoration work was begun by Zelenova there, the first specialized restoration workshop created at Pavlovsk by *Lenproekt*. Although in those early days work also went on at Peterhof, the decision to restore the gigantic Catherine Palace in Pushkin was postponed for many years because of the lack of materials and craftsmen needed to restore its massive baroque interior, which required a huge amount of gilding and carving and hundreds more measurements.

The task was so difficult and unprecedented that in twenty-five years of restoration, both designers and builders always remarked that it would have been a hundred times easier to start with an empty spot and rebuild entirely rather than having to resolve all the technical problems that arose from being concerned about not losing what had survived while re-creating that which had been lost.

Anna Zelenova, in her first comprehensive guidebook of Pavlovsk, made an allusion to the arguments against restoration, writing, "Several naysayers, people of little faith, believed that due to the scale of the destruction any attempts at restoration would be futile." Anna of course most firmly attested differently, for as she wrote:

* Warsaw and Dresden also carried out large post-war restoration projects; before beginning reconstruction they had to remove, respectively, twenty and eighteen million cubic meters of rubble.

In the course of a more thorough examination of the palace it became evident that although fire had greatly damaged the palace building and its decorative elements, the overall dimensions of the building with its architectural detail had fortunately escaped total destruction.

Elements of the interior which had been crafted of nonflammable materials had in part survived. Pavlovsk palace, built in the classical style, had interiors which were for the most part constructed of marble, plaster, stucco, partially gilded bronze, and even stained glass. There were a great amount of surviving fragments from the decor which could be utilized as original standards for copies of items which had been destroyed. There was not a single hall in which some traces of the former interior could not be found. Most frequently, items were found closer to the corners of the rooms; it was possible to see surviving pieces of carved cornices, and ornamental friezes.

On the wall, to the joy of the restorers, many fragments were also preserved; parts of framed wall, window and door panels. Most valuable of all that survived were the complicated series of frameworks for the carvings, bas-reliefs, medallions, and paintings. All of these had been damaged by fire, but they were originals and they gave the restorers the possibility of filling in the missing pieces. Also especially important was that the original designs and architectural drawings for the palace by Cameron, Brenna, Voronykhin, and Rossi were all preserved. These plans permitted the re-creation of the brilliant architecture. Taking into account all of these conditions, specialists came to the conclusions that the restoration of Pavlovsk was feasible."

It was precisely the "simplicity and nobility" so desired by Paul and Maria Feodorovna that one hundred fifty years later worked in Pavlovsk's favor, and, it was decided, made possible a more perfect and comprehensive restoration for a given expenditure. The fact that Pavlovsk was one of the best-documented houses of its date in the world was another invaluable advantage.* From the beginning, the palace's complicated building history had been recorded in extensive correspondence between owners, architects, and artists. The exceptional love it had inspired throughout its history, in both Tsarist owners and post-Revolutionary curators, played a vital role. The contributions of every epoch now became invaluable for its restoration, starting in Tsarist times with the precise and detailed inventory made by Maria Feodorovna in 1795, followed by the definitive book published on the occasion of the centenary of the palace by Grand Duke Constantine Nikolaievich in 1877, and the willingness of his son Grand

* Other palaces, such as the baroque Catherine Palace built earlier in the eighteenth century, were and still are hampered by lack of documentation.

Duke Constantine to have the palace extensively photographed for articles in the St. Petersburg art journal *The Treasures of Russia* in 1903. There was the courageous and timely intervention and work of Polovtsov at the time of the Revolution, and before the war the careful inventories done by Taleporovsky and later Kuchumov and others There were the invaluable original architects' sketches saved at the time of the evacuation, the twenty-five hundred Benois negatives recovered in the Prussian castle of Königsberg by Kuchumov, along with eleven thousand other photographs taken just before the war, found, and returned from Berlin. Finally, there was the miracle accomplished during the evacuation by Zelenova and her co-workers (thirteen thousand things saved at Pavlovsk versus only some two thousand of Pushkin's hundred thousand items), which meant that Pavlovsk's interiors could be restored largely as they had been. After the war, thanks to Zelenova's precise method of conservation of the precious remaining fragments, a method first used at Pavlovsk, work went faster there and available funds could be used more economically. Pavlovsk was the first palace to be restored, the first finished. It became the prototype for all other restorations that followed. Perhaps the most astonishing fact is that no formal decision officially to "restore" Pavlovsk was ever taken. Feeling their way, surmounting one obstacle at a time, the dedicated museum workers pressed on until "conservation" melted imperceptibly into complete "restoration."

On April 16, 1947, a methodology session was held, convening representatives of the palace museums, the municipal executive committee, and the Leningrad Inspectorate for the Protection of Monuments. The work at Pavlovsk was divided among various organizations, each responsible for certain aspects: *Lenproekt,* the Architectural Planning Commission of the Leningrad City Council under the direction of Oleinik, was to focus on planning and interiors; *Promzhilstroy* was to be responsible for the reconstruction of dome, ceilings, and overall structure, with *Facadremstroy* Trust as the main contractor all working with the scientific department of the palace.*

Starting in 1945, in a special studio created for Pavlovsk, Oleinik and his co-workers developed all the documentation for the restoration of the constructed elements of the palace.

---

* That year there was another wonderful sign of hope. The sculptor Vasily Simonov had taken two years to complete his re-creation of the huge statue of Samson from Peterhof. When it was finally cast in bronze and, on August 31, 1947, transported down the Nevsky Prospect on a special platform, people applauded and waved, hanging from their windows and cheering. The military saluted it as if it were a general, and many people wept with joy.

Oleinik was a purist, who over and over repeated: "Pay attention and do not use later details — only the original variant, only that done by Cameron, Brenna, Voronykhin, or Rossi." Of the dedicated Oleinik, Anna Zelenova wrote, "Huddled in a garret in one of the surviving houses on the grounds of Pavlovsk (the garret was warmer than other parts of the house where there were no windows or doors), he worked until midnight by the light of a carbide lamp on the first architectural drawings for the restoration of the palace. By day he did a lot of painting using a little pocket easel in a metal box." Oleinik's drawings were the most accurate in both color and precision, "tense and full of rage," says Zelenova, "no one could walk by them without stopping." They were later exhibited in Leningrad.

His first work in 1946 was the restoration of the cupola. Tracing the curved pieces of the cupola in full scale on the ground in front of a wing of the palace, he refused to allow a single piece to be raised to the roof until he was certain that all of the joints matched his design. Building materials were extremely scarce in those first years after the war, and when steel rails from the original Tsarskoe Selo Railroad were unexpectedly discovered in a storeroom, the decisive Anna ordered them to be used in the restoration. (There were a lot of questions afterwards, but the deed was done and the cupola more speedily rebuilt.) As a result of his earlier work at Pavlovsk, Oleinik knew the palace so well that when builders would ask him a question about how they could best connect a joint to a rafter, he would simply pull out his roll of architectural drawings and then, on the reverse side with a piece of charcoal, proceed to draw the joint from memory. He was never mistaken. By 1950 a forest of scaffolding enveloped the palace. Perched on top, workers began to re-create the molded plaster exterior decorations.

In 1946, in the first article published on the structural restoration, Oleinik explained the principles that guided his work: the restoration would adhere as closely to the original as possible and the only changes permitted would be in the modern materials used and the procedures to utilize these. For example, columns previously made of wood were now either poured concrete or constructed with iron bricks the same size and shape as the originals. The ceilings of the Italian and Greek Halls would be made of steel and concrete so that they would be durable and fireproof.

Sadly, in 1954, before he could finish his work, the passionate and talented Oleinik died prematurely, it was said as a result of wounds received at the front, perhaps also hastened from grief at the tragic death of his fifteen-year-old son, killed by a mine in Pavlovsk Park when returning home. According to Kedrinsky, "He died really when he learned that his son had been blown up."

After Oleinik's death the work at Pavlovsk was continued under the direction of Sophia Popova-Gunich, who had been his assistant. A woman of refined artistic taste who had expert knowledge of classical architecture, she re-created the Greek and Colonnade Halls, which had been destroyed by aerial attacks. Using the traces of the past, she found perfect proportions for these halls and their molded decoration, as close as humanly possible to the original appearance of the palace.

As this work was going forward at the palace, Anatoly Mikhailovich was relentlessly conducting his search for lost objects in Eastern Europe and Berlin, and when in Leningrad, supervising all the repositories occupied with the gigantic task of sorting everything that had been returned, preparing for the time when these objects would find their rightful home again.

All this activity somehow went on despite the fact that in a bizarre and sinister epilogue to the Blockade, in 1946 through 1948 the Leningrad Party was shaken by new purges. Andrei Zhdanov was called to Moscow and the Central Committee, and the mayor of Leningrad, Pyotr Popkov, took over his job as Party boss. Zhdanov proceeded to mount a vicious attack on his own city, including many of its leading literary figures, among them the poet Anna Akhmatova, whom he declared to be "half nun and half whore." In a public speech he declared, "All these palaces are gone forever."

Stalin, always suspicious of Leningrad, wanted to wipe out the memory of the siege entirely. This new purge, known as the "Leningrad Affair," was intended to silence all questions. Before it was over all the major figures of the siege had disappeared or were destroyed. Two thousand members of the Leningrad Party vanished. The Museum of the Defense in Leningrad, on which Anna had worked so hard in memory of her close friend Chernovsky — a museum that had fourteen rooms holding sixty thousand exhibits covering twenty-four thousand feet of floor space, and for which most of the artists of Leningrad had worked on dioramas and panoramas — was closed in 1949, and the director arrested. Many of its exhibits were dispersed, others were locked up and are still held secret. A new Museum of the History of Leningrad was opened in 1957, but many of the original exhibits were absent. The wartime notices — "This side of the street is safest in case of shelling" — were painted over. Yet somehow the restoration work at the palaces continued, although it did not get into full swing until after the death of Stalin in 1953.

At Pavlovsk, as director, the indefatigable Anna was in charge of the entire management, supervising everything that was happening. It was up to her to obtain funds and to find craftsmen and materials. Whatever was necessary for the restoration, whether a particular person or thing, she somehow managed to find it. She who had often given up her bread ration when there was nothing else now spared no efforts to get better food for her workers. In this she was very ingenious. From 1945 to 1948 the food situation in Leningrad was still extremely difficult, and it was almost impossible to get produce. Every citizen of Pavlovsk tried to obtain and keep a cow. The best place to graze them was in the palace park. Although it was in part still mined, in those hard days it was considered worth the risk. Townspeople went to Anna Zelenova for permission. She gave it, but as always, looking out first for her workers, entirely on her own, she leveled a tax: each cow owner had to give a liter of milk daily to the families of the construction workers with children. Although they protested and tried to resist, it was no use. As usual, when it came to Pavlovsk, Anna was adamant, and the children of her workers got their milk.

Like Maria Feodorovna before her, she adored children. She made paper planes and toys to amuse them, adopted the dogs of those who had to go back to the city in the fall. It was she who organized the first children's holiday at Pavlovsk after the war. Once, when the teacher of German in the local school left, Anna was asked to take over. At first she refused, but when one winter day the principal drove up in a sleigh, saying, "Get in, Anna Ivanovna, I want to show you the new school. It won't take long," she could not resist his invitation. He first led her through the newly painted halls and then opened a door into a classroom. "Children," he said, "here is your new teacher." Anna hung her coat on a chair and began the lesson. In the spring, when the good weather came, in a quiet corner of the park she would read poetry to young members of the Komsomol on Friday afternoons. A devoted member of the Party all her life, she organized the first May Day demonstration in the town after the war.

Despite all her work, she kept up her interest in literature and still managed to write many letters each day to different palaces and countries. She knew quantities of poetry by heart, and once, after giving a speech in Leningrad, returned to Pavlovsk with one of the city's war poets, Mikhail Dudin. Dudin began reciting, Anna continued, and together during the hour-long trip they went through the works of the Achmeist poets.* Whenever she read a literary magazine and

* Among the Achmeist poets were Sergei Gorodetsky, Mikhail Kuzmin, Nicholas Gumilev, Anna Akhmatova, and Osip Mandelstam.

discovered a fresh idea she would delightedly share her discovery with her colleagues, exclaiming, "Read this! Read it aloud! Good!" She took a great interest
in the theater, and at night wrote several scenarios about historic Pavlovsk celebrations. She was one of the first to create an independent theater in the town
after the war, for which she somehow made time.

For nine years, until her old illness, osseous tuberculosis, reached her eyes and
she was hardly able to see, she never took a vacation. She was then forced to
take several months off to recover in a sanatorium. During her "rest after the
battle," Anna Ivanovna wrote to one of her colleagues:

> I don't know if it was the doctors or the stubbornness of my spirit, but my
> eyesight was returned to me. The limits of reading and writing permitted to
> me are negligible (only 5 pages a day!). Of course I spent a whole year's worth
> in a month and this again took its toll on my eyes. This is my third month in
> a sanatorium. For the first time in years, I have the opportunity to think about
> things in peace. In our work, I think a certain "irresponsibility" or rather
> more precisely, a lack of too much rationalism, is needed — that which dries
> out our art and our work.

As a brilliant specialist, knowing two foreign languages, she was offered a post
at UNESCO, that of consultant and art historian in the restoration of monuments. It was a dazzling offer for a Soviet citizen of those days. She would have
worked in Paris, Geneva, New York, but she declined. Pavlovsk was her life, and
she could not leave it.

Although she had an apartment in town, she spent almost no time there, especially in the summer. Instead, at Pavlovsk, she and her mother shared a Spartan
one-room apartment virtually empty of furniture. She began work at dawn, and
especially loved, as the Empress Maria Feodorovna had done more than a
hundred years before her, to stroll alone in the park when the early rays of the
sun turned it into a magical place.

Anna always loved to stay up late talking. People came to see her day and
night. She never turned them away and they sometimes ended up staying with
her for weeks or even years at a time. Once she took in a young girl who was
studying at the conservatory and wanted to become a musicologist. Anna asked
her what she would like to write about, and the girl answered that she wanted
to do a book about Mozart. Zelenova told her that this was wonderful, but
Mozart lived through his notes and perhaps another book about Mozart was not
really necessary; people knew him through his music, they would play his music

and he would live on. But Gatchina, like Pavlovsk, had been destroyed, and if one took up this task it would take up a whole life. The girl changed her career and went to work on the restoration at Gatchina.

Anna interested herself passionately in the fate of those who turned to her for help, dictating petitions on their behalf and following up by going to the institutions where decisions were made. In true Russian style she thought little of money, and gave it away easily, very often finding herself short of funds for food before the end of the month.

She took the same maternal interest in her workers as Maria Feodorovna had in hers. In a special notebook, she wrote down the jokes of palace workers; when one was successful on an exam, she considered it a personal victory. When she received an allocation for Pavlovsk, she treated it as a holiday. A whole generation of workers grew up in Pavlovsk before her eyes.

For forty-nine years, she never stopped battling for her palace. Devoted member of the Party she was, but not subservient. She tells a story of how, during those early years of struggle to obtain funds for the palace, impatient with the tempo of affairs, she thought, "If the restoration of Pavlovsk were to go at that speed, it would take us a century." According to Anna's account, she then decided to take some time off and go to Moscow, determined to try to obtain additional allocations and the intensification of restoration efforts herself. She had very little money for the trip, and she stayed with friends who lived far from the center of the city. With barely enough change in her pocket for the subway, she went everywhere on foot and, sustained by her Blockade experience, allocated herself a cup of tea a day. As she later wrote, "An acquaintance of mine, an artist, had shot a rabbit in the Pavlovsk Park and gave me the fur. I had a muff made and felt myself almost fashionable — and my fingers didn't freeze." For almost a month she knocked on official bureaucratic doors tenaciously pursuing her goal. "Everyone was fed up with me. But I was nevertheless able to find some help for Pavlovsk. One night, at three o'clock in the morning, I was received in the Kremlin by Kliment Voroshilov.* He was then directing cultural questions. He listened to me carefully."

In the course of their conversation Voroshilov asked her who her parents were, and when she answered that her father was a metalworker and a Kronstadt sailor, Voroshilov answered, "Then I understand a great deal. Baltic sailor, re-

---

* Kliment Voroshilov helped organize the *Cheka,* the first Soviet secret police, in 1917. He was a military commander in both world wars, serving as commander in chief of the troops on the Leningrad front during World War II. He held numerous high governmental positions from the time of the Revolution.

spectable people. And you have a little bit of this. Good." Then he asked about Pavlovsk, saying that he had been in the palace in 1941 but that the situation at the front had prevented him from getting to know it. Anna showed him prewar pictures of the interiors and the landscaped park, as well as photos of the ruins. She explained their conservation efforts. Voroshilov paid close attention, read over all the documents, and then said, "I will put this before Joseph Vissarionovich. You prepare everything you have just told me." A few days later, Anna continues, "He advised me, 'I have good news. Your question regarding the restoration of Pavlovsk has been favorably resolved.'"

In her account of this episode, perhaps because of the time in which she wrote it, Anna leaves many details ambiguous, including the date. However, other evidence indicates that it perhaps occurred in 1947, for in a letter dated June 10, 1947, written by the Chief of GIOP, Nikolai Belekhov, to V. N. Makarov, Curator of Questions of the Protection of Monuments of the USSR Council of Ministers, Belekhov writes:

> I beseech you to help that heroic woman, the Director of Pavlovsk Palace Museum, A. I. Zelenova, who alone managed to secure the restoration of the Palace with her efforts in Moscow.
>
> Before her lies the resolution of complex and difficult questions in the Staff Committee, the Council of Ministers, etc. Your help will be greatly appreciated.

Later, in the 1950s, when the reconstruction of the palace building was in full swing, the chief of the *Facadremstroy* Trust, an old friend, warned her that the Pavlovsk façade might not be included in their next plan. Outraged, Anna, with what was described by a colleague as "a masculine cold-bloodedness and strategy," steamed to Moscow again and made the rounds of *Gosplan, Gostroy,* * the Ministry of Finance, and both national and regional ministries of culture, and absolutely insisted that it would be. Once again, she won.

Over the years Anna Zelenova turned out a whole stream of books, articles for magazines, and scholarly academic monographs about Pavlovsk. In her scholarly work her style of writing is exact, austere, self-effacing, never omitting praise of the Party, and usually referring to herself only in the third person. Of the famous restoring organization plan she devised, she says only, "The author of these lines took part in the creation of this method." She played a significant role in initiating the restoration of a number of other palaces, including the Catherine

* *Gosplan* is the State Planning Committee of the USSR; *Gostroy* is the State Committee for Building.

Palace and Peterhof. She particularly loved Gatchina and worked to see that it would one day be restored.* She applied great efforts to see that outside organizations that temporarily occupied the palaces would be sent elsewhere and that systematic restoration would begin.

The idea, born in Leningrad, was not only to preserve the palaces as memorials to the past, but more importantly as a living memory of the artistic work of the outstanding masters of art who had created them. But after the initial conservation work was completed, one of the questions to be resolved was to determine the period to which the now ruined palace interiors should be restored. Before the war all palaces had been kept in the state in which they were found at the time of the Revolution, with all the alterations that time and changing taste had imposed over the years. After the war, the guiding principle became that the monument was to be restored to the period of its greatest artistic importance or integrity, even when this entailed removal of later accretions — usually from the late eighteenth century. For Pavlovsk, that meant the time of Maria Feodorovna. To do this required scholarly research on a completely unprecedented scale, a time-consuming process sustained by the stoic patience that is the strength of Russia. But the greatest problem was where to find the expert craftsmen who could duplicate the work of the great artists and artisans of the eighteenth century, which the naysayers insisted could not be done.

"Before the war," says Kuchumov, "the palaces were in splendid condition and new craftsmen were not being trained. The small amount that was done was accomplished by older craftsmen." The Blockade and the war had greatly diminished this already small number of expert restorers, and there were not nearly enough for the monumental task at hand. Somehow a whole new group of restorers had to be trained in the exacting skills of the eighteenth century — some of them almost forgotten.

Yet even before the end of the war, in 1943, Leningrad had already begun. With the city starving and still encircled and the enemy only sixteen kilometers away from the center of the city, in a great leap of faith, a decision was made by the city authorities to create a school to prepare future craftsmen for the task of restoring the city when the victory came.

That fall, in Perm, Omsk, and Vologda, in the homes where evacuated children

---

* Five hundred rooms at Gatchina are being restored, although only a few have as yet been completed. Many items originally in Gatchina have been on loan to other palaces; at Pavlovsk these included lanterns and Gobelins tapestries similar to ones that once were part of the collection of Pavlovsk. Now Gatchina is claiming these loans back, causing distress in some cases.

had been placed, the word went out: an architecture-art school was to be created in Leningrad to prepare future restorers. Applicants had to be at least fifteen years old, have completed the seventh class, and, most important, be able to draw. Many applied; the most talented were chosen and sent by train back into the war-torn city. To reach Leningrad they had to cross devastated territory: empty towns in ashes, fields scarred by craters and bristling with fortifications. Approaching the city, sitting in frightened silence in unlighted cars because of the danger of artillery shelling, they passed through a zone only four kilometers from the front. Finally, on the morning of November 4, they reached the Moscow Station in Leningrad. There they were briefly greeted. Those who had parents were sent home, the others — over half — who were orphans, were sent to a dormitory. All were told to report at 8 A.M. the next day to what had been Zelenova's old school — Peter Schule on Sofia Perovskaya Street.

On November 15, the hundred teenagers who were to become the future restorers of the palaces gathered in an unheated auditorium where they sat wrapped in their coats, under a ceiling pockmarked with shell holes. They were told the citizens were already thinking of how to restore the city after the victory that would come, although the city was still under siege. However, before beginning their studies, they needed to attend to their own building, and so they were set to work repairing walls. Afterward, they were sent to eat in the dormitory that had been set up for them in a former Finnish church on a neighboring street. They received their bread ration and a list of tasks for the next day. Housed and clothed by the state, they were issued work smocks, boots, and their own uniform — cut-down soldiers' tunics and berets and three small metal initials, LKU,* which they pinned on their tunics or berets. Very soon everyone in the city came to know them, and to the people of Leningrad, astonished to learn of the creation of this new school under the conditions of the Blockade, the initials became a sign of hope.

Just as the school was forming its groups, a tragedy befell it. As they were lifting tables, stone, and marble from trucks to equip their new school, a Nazi shell hit. Four young people along with their teacher were killed outright, two others died of wounds, and several more were severely injured. The traces of the attack remained long visible on the walls of the school. Even now Anatoly Mikhailovich cannot speak of that day without tears.

It was not easy to find talented children, but in that third year of the Blockade,

---

* *Leningradskoe Khudozhestvenoe Uchilishe* — Leningrad Artistic School.

finding teachers who could instruct them, develop their artistic taste, give them an understanding of architecture and their professions, was even harder — harder in that beleaguered city, said the director Iosif Vaks, than finding jewels.

Yet one by one teachers were discovered: the best marble craftsman of the city was found working in an establishment that made shoe molds, an extraordinary metal embosser was working as an orderly in a hospital. One led to another, until all the groups were headed by master craftsmen who began passing on their experience to their new apprentices.*

A noted professor of architecture, Vladimir Pilyavsky, author of thirty-seven works on the subject, taught the children architecture. He took them to the Hermitage and the Ethnographic Museum. In the museum cellars, among the crates, the students drew porcelain, furniture, bronze, objects of stone and wood from life.

During their first year, a group of students from the school were called on to help restore the ceiling of the Maryinsky Theater under the direction of an elderly painter, Valentin Shcherbakov, a specialist in monumental painting. Half the theatrical paintings and virtually all of the ornamentation of the silver, gold, and blue theater, one of the loveliest in the world, had been damaged by shelling and had to be restored. Shcherbakov, a great teacher, able to inculcate both craft and courage in his charges, entrusted his students with the complicated and difficult work of repairing the monumental paintings of the theater ceiling. Bombs and artillery shelling had heavily damaged the colorful dome. The ceiling, made of many wooden squares, had broken through the canvas. In the blue sky of the huge painted ceiling, muses and cupids hung in shreds. Dampness and cold were finishing the job of destruction. The small group of teenagers climbed up on their sixty-foot-high scaffoldings, awed and frightened by what confronted them, but Shcherbakov gently and patiently guided them through their work, and under his direction the young students were able successfully to replaster the wooden foundation, glue the canvas back on it, and repaint the damaged section of the painting.

Another famous prewar professor of sculpture, Aleksei Bolshakov, taught the young people architectural molding. He took them through the war-torn city showing the examples of beautiful carving and molding in palaces and private homes and taught them about their origins.

---

* The first organizer of the restorers was the architect Anolik. He knew by heart all the names of the distinguished master craftsmen in Leningrad from before the war, and gathered them not only to work, but to train a new cadre of skilled craftsmen.

In the spring of 1944, Bolshakov took a group of thirty of his young charges to Pavlovsk to work on the destroyed molded decorations. Divided into two brigades, from the end of May to September 1944 they helped with the preservation and strengthening of the molding and trim in all the burned-out halls of the palace, as well as making molds in the palace workshop. One of these early students remembers, "We felt a great sense of responsibility in fulfilling this work, which took us three months. By the time we were through we left on the shelves hundreds of decorative details saved by our own hands. Practically the whole palace was roofless. Autumn was beginning, there was snow and rain, but when we returned to our dormitory at night, we felt almost professional and had a keen desire to learn, to master our craft." Oleinik also became a great teacher and mentor for the students of this first restoration school who trained at Pavlovsk and carried out much of the first molding work. He was extremely strict about accepting castings for moldings; any imprecision caught his eye immediately, so much so that "Oleinik would accept it" became the watchword and standard of quality in restoration work.

Among these original students were several who later became masters in their field and were to spend the next forty years in restoration work. One of them was Nadezhda Ode, who became one of Leningrad's most distinguished specialists in sculptured plaster molding. She says, "I remember our trip to Pavlovsk in the summer of 1944. Mines were everywhere, and the walls of the palace were about to collapse. With the aid of ropes, teenage boys climbed those seven-meter walls to the very top to remove the remains of plaster work. Today I am afraid even to look up so high."

Always the students were encouraged to study the technique of old artisans — not to copy their work blindly, but always to try to absorb the essence of their methods and their way of thinking. The students studied and relearned the secrets of many crafts and methods that were thought to have been lost.

After a year there were one hundred sixty people at the school. Teachers and pupils lived and worked as a family. For the more than half of the students who were orphans, the school and their dormitory became their only home and parent. After work and study they organized impromptu musical evenings and played the piano. There were dances, songs, and stories. They put on plays, which they directed, acted, and danced themselves.

By the end of 1945, they were delighted to receive the good news that they were considered so successful that the Soviet of People's Commissars of the USSR had decided to form a new and larger school, the Mukhina Leningrad Higher

Artistic Industry School,* formed on the basis of theirs, and they were given a larger building.

Within a few years a whole series of schools and workshops were organized in Leningrad. Another school was formed for the decorative arts alone — gilding, carving, metalsmithing — and made part of Mukhina. There was a mass of applicants. Young people were accepted from the age of fifteen for a program of three years, then put directly on the job for further training. Competition was stiff, exams extremely rigorous, and only the most talented were accepted. In addition to these schools, also under the guidance of elderly master craftsmen, a group of restoration workshops were created where apprentices learned directly on the job. These workshops were open to anyone through application or special selection, but apprentices not showing sufficient aptitude were quickly dropped.

As all these students and apprentices grew up and graduated, Leningrad was gradually provided with an entirely fresh crop of skilled craftsmen. Students from the first school fanned out all over the city and its environs, participating in the restoration of all the palaces and museums, including Elagin, Peterhof, Lomonosov, Pushkin, and Pavlovsk. Many received prizes and awards for their achievements. They, in turn, taught the next generation. Many of the original students who are still alive and officially in retirement continue to work today.

It was ten years before the painstaking process of documentation was completed. By then every wall of every room of Pavlovsk had been photographed, along with each of its architectural details — more than thirty thousand negatives and prints, added to and compared with the eleven thousand recovered photographs, which had been taken by the research department of the museum before the war. Hundreds of new measurements had been taken of each room, each wall, and each detail of decoration. To these were added all other prewar measurements of the palace, by both professional architects and students at architectural construction schools, that could be found. From many sources all kinds of visual materials had been collected: engravings, paintings, drawings of the eighteenth and nineteenth centuries as well as paintings by prewar artists. These helped not only to redefine the proportions but to verify the color, detail, and nuances of palace interiors. The most valuable and accurate information came from the archives of the palace itself. These had been thoroughly combed for documents relating to the construction and design of the palace and for illustrated alterations and additions made to the palace after its initial construction.

* Visoki Khudozhestvennoy Institut imenno Mukhina.

This permitted the various "layers" of construction to be identified and the restoration of the interiors closely to match the original appearance. In addition all books, articles, and extracts that described the art and architecture of Pavlovsk had been gathered and organized according to the appropriate interior of the palace. Only when all of these materials had been exhausted was a scientific summary of each hall compiled. These summaries gave a full picture of each element of architecture and decor, and they also included analyses of changes in the plans, information about materials that had been used in the construction, and details about the manner in which the work had been carried out. A research and development department at the museum had been established comprised of members of the museum council who worked in conjunction with GIOP.

In the park, work had been done to reinforce the riverbanks, clean out the park reservoirs, and restore the dams and bridges, including the beautiful Visconti and Centaur bridges. In 1950, after six years of tree planting, earth measurements, and canal clearing, a part of the park was once again opened to the public. By 1955, one year after Oleinik's death, the work on the façade had been accomplished, and the palace building was on its way to complete reconstruction.

Yet the colossal effort all this work had demanded was only half the task. Before it could come fully alive again there was the equally difficult problem of re-creating the interiors as they had been when Maria Feodorovna lived. This became another art mystery story in great part unraveled by that ingenious master art detective Anatoly Mikhailovich.

19

Beauty Will
Save the World

IN 1956, KUCHUMOV AND ZELENOVA joined forces, and for the first time since their youth began to work together again at Pavlovsk. Kuchumov was named Chief Curator. Working with a small staff of five women, including his wife, Anna Mikhailovna, he set to work directing and supervising the whole intricate puzzle of accurately re-creating the beauty of the interior decoration of the palace. As Chief Curator, he prepared the furniture, made assignments of what should go and stay, maintained contacts with sculptors, gilders, painters, carpenters, and mahogany workers. His little group did everything — even to sewing when it was necessary. As he says, "We were a collective, the collective wore a hat and that hat was me."

The proper place had to be found for each of the twelve thousand original objects that had been evacuated, plus the three thousand more that Kuchumov had found in his search. Removed from the palace, they were only separate and disconnected objects of applied art that could be displayed now and then. To restore their meaningful artistic image and that of their epoch, all surviving original articles had to find their way back to the place in the palace where they belonged. To this task, Anatoly Mikhailovich, who could recite the inventories of Pavlovsk, Gatchina, and the Catherine Palace as if they were multiplication tables, applied his phenomenal memory and talent for investigative research.

"Now for the first time in the history of the palace," says Kuchumov, "the question arose as to the genuine author of each palace interior. In order to rid the palace halls of everything incidental, it was necessary to identify all the later features brought by time, and by other architects who had changed the primary artistic design of the authors of the ensemble. All the archives from the first years of the construction of Pavlovsk had to be examined and reviewed. These included several thousand original records, tens of thousands of pages of documents, sometimes almost illegible, written in the cursive writing of the eighteenth century. Plans of the authors, drafts, old photographs had to be compared with documentary data taken from the archives."

In the process of this scrupulous investigation, much new material was discovered; this too was taken into consideration. A number of palace halls, where the decoration had been distorted or entirely destroyed in the nineteenth century, were restored in accordance with the original authors' designs. Maria Feodorovna's inventory and all the other inventories of the eighteenth and nineteenth centuries were studied. In case of loss, objects were replaced by similar ones from other palace collections that fit in character, time of creation, and style; lost and destroyed furniture had to be replaced by making copies from the specimens that had been saved.

Extracts from the archives permitted the identification and description of hundreds of names of master craftsmen, which had been preserved in agreements and notes from the eighteenth and nineteenth centuries, along with descriptions of their techniques and methods. In these old documents was much specific information about the furniture for each palace hall, as well as information about the craftsmen, the place the pieces had been made, how much they had cost, and how they were obtained for the palace.

As Kuchumov and his co-workers searched, Pavlovsk's history came alive again. "When we had to replace things," he says, "we went with things that had their own 'passport' so to speak. During the lifetime of Maria Feodorovna, objects rarely left Pavlovsk, but in the course of later years, with changing styles and reigns, things were moved." Through the dusty archives Kuchumov and his staff tracked objects as they were moved from one palace to another — gifts given by Alexander to his mother, malachite brought to Maria Feodorovna by Voronykhin, which she bought as presents for her son. A splendid large water pitcher and glass stand ordered by Alexander and made according to designs by Voronykhin had survived the war. It was discovered that a second, designed by Thomas Thonon, ended up in America and is now in the Corning Glass Museum in New York — bought in Denmark, where evidently it had been sent by Maria Feodorovna. A chest of drawers was found in the Puskhin Museum in Moscow. Many pieces that had been tucked away over the years in the vast storerooms and attics of the Winter Palace were discovered in today's Hermitage, among these a table made by Voronykhin given to Maria Feodorovna on her birthday, and the famous Berlin service given to Alexander by the King of Prussia, which he presented to his mother. In an old Hermitage inventory reports of furniture sent from Pavlovsk to Moscow were found, the furniture traced and returned to the palace.

As for the problem of reproducing furniture, "One had to uncover the expertise and trade secrets of old masters, to make thousands of tests to attain similarity with remaining specimens of the eighteenth century to re-create both color and manner of pattern," says Kuchumov. "Many first-class craftsmen had come to work in Russia. We studied their style and that of their contemporaries. Many valuable suggestions were gleaned from the work of English and French restorers."

Techniques that had almost disappeared were rediscovered and applied. In five halls of the palace, *scagliola* and *faux marbre*,* in a palette of different colors — mauve, green, rose — difficult to tell from the real, had been used extensively. Modern Russian craftsmen were able to duplicate it exactly. The almost forgotten technique of revetting† with artificial marble, generally used by invited Italian artisans, was revived and brilliantly mastered.

New techniques were developed and used in conjunction with the old. For their slow and painstaking work, gilders, taught by old artisans who had gilded the massive dome of St. Isaac's and worked in the palaces, still use fine brushes made of squirrel tails, blow on the ephemeral sheets of gold with their own breath, and smooth it with amber rods. A small piece of carving, approximately three feet long, takes a month or more to gild. The earlier technique of gilding was based on joiners glue, which with time cracked, leaving a network of fine lines on the gold layer. Today, according to Kedrinsky, "although the techniques of old artisans continue to serve us well, modern physics and chemistry help us in our work. Leningrad restorers now add new emulsions and a new substance to the primer, which ensure a long life to gilded articles." Kedrinsky helped to

* *Faux marbre* (false marble) is a technique whereby surfaces are painted to look like marble. It is often used in places where real marble would be expected — columns, floors, mantelpieces, etc. — and if done properly can be, at first glance, difficult to distinguish from the actual stone. A speckled base coat is applied, over which marblelike grains are painted. *Scagliola* is a material used since Roman times to imitate marble. It is composed of pulverized selenite, applied to a wet gesso ground, fixed under heat, then highly polished, and is used mainly for columns, pilasters, and other interior architectural features.
†Revetting is a facing of stone or other hard material over a less durable substance.

restore the decorative iron gates that lead into Pavlovsk. There the lions heads were made out of a synthetic material, which precisely duplicates bronze but is impervious to the elements.

To re-create the silk of the eighteenth century, a new factory was created in Moscow, famous in the years before the Revolution as a center for fine textiles. Specialists, working from fragments of original fabrics, determine the original weaving methods, thread counts, and dye colors. The silk is woven on restored eighteenth-century Jacquard-type looms, originally invented in France, which exactly reproduce the texture and quality of the original material.

For Pavlovsk, there was a serendipitous discovery when a cache of original material ordered by the Empress was unexpectedly found. Kuchumov tells the story: "In Maria Feodorovna's day, when the trimming of upholstery, curtains and furniture grew old, they were removed, placed in a trunk, and saved. During the war, one of these trunks was taken to St. Isaac's and after the war, when we were clearing everything away, we saw a trunk that contained what looked like torn rags. We began to check the documents and it turned out that among torn samples and fresh unused pieces were French silks that had been ordered in Lyons in 1782. You see, since Russia was far away, Maria Feodorovna, the mother of ten children and prudent mistress of a great house, always ordered materials in duplicate so that in case of accidents there would be enough for repairs." This original trimming and fabric were transferred to Moscow, and there new silk fabric was, and is still, being woven for the Halls of War and Peace, for Maria Feodorovna's Boudoir, and other rooms. Today, in some halls of the palace, original borders ordered by the Empress are placed on new silk, identical in color and quality to that of the eighteenth century. Throughout the palace the curtains and draperies have been rehung according to Maria Feodorovna's own sketches. So expertly have these fabrics been reproduced that when visiting French experts came to Pavlovsk, they could not believe that silk of such quality had been woven in our century.

An entire generation grew up with the restoration, and in the process a Russian school of twentieth-century master restorers was created. Many of these top restorers who first worked at Pavlovsk later went to other palaces: Irina Benois of the famous pre-Revolutionary Benois family of artists worked in the restoration of the Pavlovsk park pavilions, then went on to Peterhof to restore the Cottage and Alexandria dachas of Nicholas I; Alexander Kedrinsky, who worked on the decorative iron gates of the palace park, later became the Chief Architect of the

Catherine Palace and is now supervising the tremendously difficult job of restoring the Amber Room, which will be the crowning achievement of his life's work in that palace.

Among the craftsmen at Pavlovsk were some who could rival the original artists of earlier times. These craftsmen have been able not merely to duplicate, but to recapture, the nuances and spirit that the eighteenth-century artisan invested in his work. They learned to restore works of art in the same way as the original artisans would have done had these objects been destroyed in their lifetime. At Pavlovsk, a small number of craftsmen managed to accomplish miracles. Carvers, taken as young boys and learning from old masters, have done carving at both the Catherine Palace and Pavlovsk that would astonish Elizabeth or Maria Feodorovna. Using more than three hundred tools, ranging from a circular saw to a tiny chisel that fits into a manicure set, they turn wood into lace. Those who work in inlaid woods often make their own tools, embellished with wood inlaid decoration, that are works of art in themselves.

The carver Vsevolod Polyakin, a student at the first restorer school, has worked at Pavlovsk for over thirty years. His work has included the canopy for the formal bedchamber, the magnificent doors of the Greek Hall and the Hall of War, and the lamps of the chapel. Since the majority of trim and moldings were destroyed by the fire, the re-creation of the decorative carvings at Pavlovsk was extremely difficult. As a rule, Polyakin's carvings were based only on prewar photographs and stylistic analogies. He often made his basic measurements from the preliminary drawings of the original architects. Sometimes a sculptor would first fashion the molding, and then the gifted hands of Polyakin, using this model and constantly checking his work against prewar photos, would bring the wood to life. It was also Polyakin who began the re-creation of carved furniture decoration characteristic of the palace interior, copying from pieces that survived the war.

Anatoly Vinogradov, another carver also from the first school, has spent his whole life reproducing the carved decoration of Voronykhin furniture. His finished work is so expertly done that Zelenova herself was unable to distinguish an original Voronykhin stool from the one that Vinogradov made.

Valentina Soldatova, an extraordinarily gifted marble restorer, has also given nearly thirty years to Pavlovsk, restoring marble sculpture in the palace and park, as well as restoring other stone work, ivory, amber, and porcelain. Nadezhda Mal'tseva and Tamara Shabalkina, both also from the original children's restorer school, have worked all their lives at Pavlovsk. They re-created the bas-reliefs and sculptures throughout the palace and replaced the caryatids in the Little Lantern Room. Kuchumov remembers that when as young girls they first began work on these imposing caryatids, they were guided by an experienced and exacting sculptor named Igor Krestovsky. At first the old sculptor criticized their work so severely that the girls wept for two hours after his departure; but then they began redoing their work. He returned only to tell them that while things looked better, he was still not satisfied, and so they began again. They were forced to repeat the process many times. From the original group of students who came to work with Bolshakov at Pavlovsk in 1944, a great many talented modelers and sculptors emerged, among them Natalia Ode, who continues to work at the Catherine Palace today.*

Polovtsov observed that eighteenth-century Russians excelled in the art of making chandeliers and parquet floors. These traditional Russian talents of earlier days were to be again brilliantly demonstrated in our own day. Delicate chandeliers with hundreds of crystals were faultlessly reassembled and restored. In the Throne Room today hang four magnificent lanterns of crystal, ornamented with crystal lilies of the valley and green enamel leaves. These had been originally ordered from the firm of Johann Zeck for the Grand Hall of the Mikhailovsky Castle. As the craftsmen were making them, Paul was assassinated, and at Maria Feodorovna's request, the four lanterns were sent to Pavlovsk and hung in the Throne Room. Only one of these superb lanterns survived the war. The other three were duplicated in the Leningrad Glass Factory so perfectly that today even specialists at Pavlovsk find it difficult to identify the original.

After the fire of 1803, Voronykhin had not attempted to re-create the elaborate floors of many-colored woods created by eighteenth-century Russian master craftsmen. Yet these were reproduced in 1965 by Russian craftsmen. Using only a small chisel, a hammer, and a tiny saw, they have executed the complicated jigsaw puzzles of rich designs utilizing as many as fourteen different kinds of wood. In his research, Kuchumov discovered that after the fire, Maria Feodorovna had indeed ordered Voronykhin to restore the original ornate colored floors as quickly as possible, but, says Kuchumov, "taste had already changed to simpler, more geometric patterns rather than the flowery patterns of the eighteenth century, and Maria Feodorovna, in mourning over the death of her hus-

---

* The members of the U.S. Historic Preservation Team, in their 1975 report on their work in the Soviet Union, noted that individual Soviet craftsmen are always identified by name, stating that they found this approach "a refreshing change from the usual anonymity and lack of recognition of restoration craftsmanship in this country."

band, had concerns greater than her parquets, so she did not in the end insist. But we knew they were colored floors, so we thought, if we could find something, perhaps not exactly of the same design, but the same year . . ."

In his search of the archives he discovered that Catherine the Great had once ordered a palace on the Palace Square for her favorite, Lanskoy. Says Kuchumov: "As they were building the palace for him, he died, and the parquets were not put in place. Catherine ordered Cameron to use them, and although at first he did not wish to, he eventually put some of them in the Agate Pavilion and some in the Catherine Palace in the rooms of the new and last favorite, Zubov. Later, Alexander II occupied these rooms and by that time the parquet was covered with rugs, for these rich floors were no longer in style. No one even knew that there was a parquet floor under them. In the 1930s, in the process of fighting moths, we removed the rugs and discovered the parquet. When the Catherine Palace was burned during the war, this lower floor survived partially, but everything leaked and the parquet was terribly damaged. In 1944, when I returned, I asked that it be taken up and stored under the roof of the ruined Alexander Palace. Later we tried to use it but found that all the panels were rotted and molding. We discarded the base, made new underpanels, then glued the parquet panels onto them. Since a portion of the wood was destroyed, we needed to get new wood. Fortunately, the Vietnamese had sent a great deal of wood for the restoration of the Kremlin Palace parquet and we obtained some for Leningrad. So now we have eighteenth-century wood and Vietnamese wood together. This is the parquet that is now in the rooms of Pavlovsk. Another can be made in the future for the Greek and Italian Halls if some documentation can be found."

In examining the archives, he found that the Rossi Corner Drawing Room had been totally changed in the late nineteenth century. Thanks to the new documentation, it is now restored exactly as it was designed by Rossi, with lilac *faux marbre* walls, honey-colored Karelian birch furniture, and gilded carvings. In Moscow, after restorers were provided with Rossi's drawings and some of the original fabric, all the silk was rewoven. However, the original fireplace had disappeared. Kuchumov was able to replace it with one he accidentally discovered in a house on Petra Lavrova that had formerly belonged to the aristocratic Obelensky family. In this building, which was under renovation and in the process of being turned into a children's home, Kuchumov's sharp eyes spied a fireplace boarded up in a crate that turned out to be one made by the same craftsmen who had made a Rossi fireplace for the Michael Palace. He had it sent to Pavlovsk, where it completed the Corner Drawing Room restoration.

After the fire of 1803, Voronykhin took eleven fireplaces from Paul's Mikhai-lovsky Castle and had them put in Pavlovsk. Not a word could be found in the Pavlovsk archives about who had made these splendid fireplaces ornamented with lapis, malachite, and jasper. Although Kuchumov combed through a quan-tity of receipts of the eighteenth century, he was able to ascertain only that a peasant named Ivanov had been paid a certain amount of rubles for their delivery to the Mikhailovsky Castle. Who made them according to Brenna's designs? Where was the lapis lazuli brought from? Although all this still remains a his-torical mystery, the fireplaces were re-created in 1965 through 1967 as they were.

So expertly was all this work accomplished that Kuchumov delightedly re-counts the story that the current Duke of Bedford, when he visited the palace, at first refused to believe that Russians alone had done it. He was convinced that Belgian or Frenchmen must have helped. He asked to meet the craftsmen and tried to speak to them in foreign languages. Only when the Duke saw that the workmen understood and spoke only Russian was he convinced.*

Yet even all this correct replacement of the objects, repairing and re-creating the beautiful furniture, the chandeliers, and remarkable parquet floors could not bring back Pavlovsk. The palace had twenty rooms in which painting played a key role in the decoration of ceilings and walls, plus twenty more where it was necessary to re-create accurately paintings that were key to the harmony of the room. Where could artists be found who could subordinate their own individu-ality and re-create the work not of one but of several artists of the eighteenth century, each with his own style and method of working?

There was in fact only one, an artist whose whole life, like that of Zelenova and Kuchumov, seemed to have been preparing him for the unique work he was now to do.

Anatoly Treskin was a vigorous man, tall and handsome, with a shock of red-brown hair. Dressed for work in his high boots, beret tilted at an angle, he was a romantic figure. His grandfather, an Italian named Treskorni, had once been the chef of the aristocratic Shuvalov family, and he bequeathed to his grandson a warm Latin temperament and a lifelong love for fine sauces and cooking.

Coming into Treskin's spacious apartment on the top floor of an old building

---

* When the chief curator of the Louvre in Paris came to Pushkin, she told Kedrinsky, "At one time Russia invited artisans from Europe. Now it is time for us to invite artisans from Russia because we have no artisans like them."

overlooking the Nevsky Prospect was to step into the Petersburg past. Every wall had been decorated by him. Garlands of roses crept along the borders of the ceilings and baseboards, spilling over even into the kitchen. One wall of his bedroom was hung with icons, including a rare Rublev icon, a present from Countess Shuvalov to his grandfather on his wedding day. On the walls of the living room was his own work, landscapes and flowers, mingled with those of his wife, herself a gifted landscape painter. There were comfortable chairs, an old divan, a piano draped with a bright scarf; in one corner, a white marble nymph by the nineteenth-century sculptor Calvi, bought long ago at a Leningrad second-hand store. On the mantel an old French clock chimed away the hours in silvery tones. It was a warm place, an inviting place, where conversation was easy, the home of a sensual man who loved life — the home of an artist.

Treskin possessed what the Russians call "a wide soul." Always full of energy, he loved company. He could accept with spontaneous generosity a person he did not know and, says one of his friends, "sit and talk to him about everything." The door of his apartment was hospitably open to everyone all day and far into the night; his generous table, set with old porcelain, was ever ready to receive another guest. Treskin delighted in preparing food for his guests, and his culinary skills were as varied as his artistic talents. He collected old recipes and prided himself in producing tasty sauces of his own creation, jovially exclaiming, "People in the old days were no fools!"

Like Anatoly Kuchumov and Anna Zelenova, Treskin was a living link between the old world and the new. He was born on April 11, 1905, the year that Russia was involved in a disastrous war with Japan, the year that amid great rejoicing, an heir to the throne was born, a year of revolution, which ended with Nicholas II giving Russia its first constitution.

He drew his first watercolor at six during a family summer vacation, and his grandfather, praising him, predicted, "You are going to be an artist!" Yet he was given no formal training. He went to school on the Nevsky Prospect until 1918 when, during the Civil War, with Petrograd in turmoil and starving, his family fled to the Urals. It was an arduous journey that began on an open railroad car and ended on horseback in the tiny village of Staraya Zinovevka in the region of Simbirsk, a hamlet that had once been on one of the estates of Count Tolstoy. Like Kuchumov in his lost village gazing in wonder at half-destroyed estates, the remnants of the former world that had so precipitously disappeared were also to deeply affect thirteen-year-old Treskin. Although he had been born and had passed his early childhood in St. Petersburg, a city full of museums, surprisingly it was in this remote place in the Urals that he first saw a collection of art masterpieces by French, Dutch, and Italian painters. Fascinated, he stood for hours in front of these works, which had belonged to those who had lived in another era, and they awakened in him his vocation.

As the Civil War grew closer, his family fled again, this time to the city of Simbirsk, birthplace of Lenin. By the time Anatoly was sixteen, in 1921, he wanted only to draw, but since there were virtually no materials, he was forced to try his hand with stubs of pencils and charcoal from the stove. In the hills high above the Volga he ingeniously dug up colored clay and mixed it with sunflower oil to make a primitive paint. With these humble materials he painted his first pictures of the scenes around him. His father, a minor employee in a notary office, did not approve. Wanting his son to go into trade, in drunken rages he would often tear up and burn his son's work, but Anatoly's mother, an educated woman who spoke several languages, supported him. Although entirely self-taught, at sixteen he was hired in the Simbirsk carriage factory as an artist decorator. At eighteen, he had completed his first tempera mural for the factory workers' club and went on to do scenery for factory theater productions. At nineteen, the All-Russian Union of Metalworkers invited him to participate in an art exhibit, and from there he was selected to study art in a vocational art program for workers at the Academy of Art in what had become Leningrad.

This was the heyday of Socialist Realism — all other expressions, especially the abstract or the absurd, were prohibited. The result was that Treskin was trained as a classical artist, mastering principles and techniques that were later to prove invaluable to him. Teachers taught pupils the laws of composition and technical knowledge of color. Students were taught to draw from nature and work at still-life two or three hours every day. One of his professors, Vasily Kuchumov (no relation to Anatoly Mikhailovich), who knew and loved the French painters Watteau, Lancret, and Fragonard, took his students to the Hermitage every Sunday. There he turned his pupils' attention to color and composition, stressing the idea that every centimeter of a painting had to be artistically accountable.

Treskin was taught monumental painting under a great professor, Dmitry Kiplik, who also taught a theoretical course called "The Technology of Art." Under Kiplik's guidance, Treskin learned how to use colors and the chemical properties of pigments. Kiplik set his students to copying Old Masters, both foreign and Russian, a talent at which Treskin was to excel. At night, to support himself, Treskin worked in a bakery loading bread into trucks and drew posters for various organizations. As more and more of his assignments demanded composition, he began a lifelong habit of doing extensive research before embarking on any project.

He did so well that only a year after Treskin had arrived in Leningrad, Kiplik asked him to help restore the paintings done by the nineteenth-century Russian artist Andrei Ryabushkin in the Maly (Small) Concert Hall of the conservatory. (This work, which he did first at twenty, he repeated forty years later when the paintings perished during the Blockade.) While doing this work he met his future wife, whom he married eleven years later. They worked together on the mosaics of the Cathedral of the Blood and on the murals of the Kiev Railway Station in Leningrad, in Nizhny Novgorod, and in Moscow, where Treskin executed bands of blue mosaics for Lenin's Tomb. Later in Leningrad, Treskin restored paintings in the Shuvalov Palace, where his grandfather had once worked, as well as in the Yusupov and Stroganov palaces. In 1931, when he was twenty-seven, he was called to Pavlovsk to help restore the Gonzaga frescoes, never dreaming that one day he would re-create the paintings of the entire palace.

All his life, Treskin observed the admonition of Leonardo da Vinci: to be a good artist, never take a single day off from brush or pencil. After his work in the evenings, Treskin did pencil portraits of his family. On Sundays, sketchbook in hand, he would go to the country to work from nature. Many evenings he and his wife went to the Hermitage to sketch and copy Old Masters. On one occasion, they were so engrossed in their work that they missed the closing time and narrowly escaped being attacked by the watchdogs the guards set loose at night. Treskin loved this work, saying, "It is as if one were conversing privately with a great artist, coming to understand his innermost thoughts and intentions. And it is hardly as if one will begin to paint or draw worse because one has been copying the masters. One learns their technique, their style becomes familiar, and then there is the thrill of producing something so close to the original that it evokes almost the same feeling." He loved Titian and the Venetians for their extraordinary colors, and Leonardo for his humanism. He loved the Flemish painters, most of all Rubens, whose joy in the sensual pleasures of life was so close to his own nature. He could not have copied so accurately had he not learned from Kiplik the professional secrets of great artists of the past: that Titian tended to paint in silver and dark tones, while Rubens used much lighter tones. In time Treskin became so skilled that his copies often fooled experts and passed for the originals. This constant practice in copying artists of other centuries was to prove the invaluable training for the major work of his life — Pavlovsk.

In 1940, the Political Division of the Baltic Fleet invited Treskin to the island naval base of Hanko near Kronstadt in the Gulf of Finland, 230 kilometers from Leningrad. There, living in a picturesque cottage, he worked on theater decorations, painted murals for the Fleet Sailors' Club, designed posters and the set for Hanko's jazz ensemble, and taught the sailors drawing in the evening. On June 22, 1941, one of the first rounds of the war exploded on the roof of his cottage. Luckily he was out, but both a neighboring house and the square in front of it vanished. Hanko began a 165-day defense.

The base was bombed incessantly, as many as seven thousand rounds falling in a single day; Treskin remembers crawling on his hands and knees through broken glass to reach staff headquarters. He became a battalion artist, painting portraits of the military heroes of Hanko as well as a large martial mural that hangs today at the Kronstadt Naval Base. Treskin also entertained troops with his fine voice, singing Russian romances and arias from his favorite operas. Once, during an outdoor concert, he continued singing an aria from *Eugene Onegin* as German planes flew overhead and the courtyard emptied. Four months after the battle began, on November 5, 1941, the base was evacuated. Taking only two paintings with him, Treskin found his way back late at night to a dark, silent, and starving Leningrad.

Yet even during the Blockade he continued to paint. Working as a military artist for the Baltic fleet, he visited the front lines, drawing every day, and in 1944 was awarded the Order of the Red Banner for his outstanding bravery and service. The war decimated his family: his mother died during the Blockade, his sister, a ballerina, was killed on the Road of Life over Lake Ladoga, his brother died on the front.

After the war, as soon as he was demobilized, Treskin and his wife began to work at the Hermitage, restoring the interiors of the Winter Palace, which had been severely damaged by shelling and bombardment, By 1946 Treskin had become the leader of a small team of artist-restorers working in the museum. The work was unprecedented: for the first time, restorers faced not only the traditional requirements of restoration — cleaning away dirt and repairing — but the enormously difficult task of completely re-creating the work of great artists who had lived several centuries earlier.

They began in some of the less important galleries, restoring ceiling oil paintings. In one case, Treskin completed a previously unfinished decoration, and the directors were so impressed that he was asked by the chief of restoration at the museum to draw up a plan for the restoration of Rastrelli's ornate baroque Jordan Staircase in the Winter Palace. This magnificent eighteenth-century staircase, with its marble columns, gilded decoration, and painted ceiling over seventy feet high, had been almost completely destroyed by shelling. Treskin began by spending many days of study in the archives of the Hermitage, scrutinizing watercolors of the period as well as prewar photographs of the ceiling. After his sketches were approved, Treskin, perched on top of several stories of scaffolding, took precise measurements and then began to sketch. He and forty helpers removed centuries of dirt and rust from the iron ceiling, and attached a new canvas. Treskin then redid his original drawings full-size on large pieces of cardboard. The underside of these pieces, called *kartons* (cartoons), were thoroughly coated with natural pigments — red ochre or umber — and then applied to the newly painted white ceiling. The drawing on the underside was then carefully retraced by hand, leaving ochre or umber marks behind on the ceiling. From time to time, Treskin would have his workers remove the scaffolding to create a "window" so that he could glimpse the overall effect. Only after this careful preparatory work did they actually paint the ceiling. When they had finished, they went on to restore the gold leaf of the stairway moldings.

Treskin and his helpers restored twenty-one halls and galleries in the Hermitage. Then he worked restoring the Russian Museum, the Stroganov and Yusupov palaces, and the Marinsky (Kirov) Theater. He and his wife went to Novgorod to restore the famous Novgorod twelfth-century frescoes, and worked in both the St. Nicholas and St. Sophia cathedrals. He spent an entire year at the Catherine Palace in Pushkin. In 1954, as he was working there on the Upper Bath Pavilion, a woman entered and silently watched him for a long time. Finally she said, "I have known of you and appreciated your talent for some time. Come visit. Pavlovsk Palace awaits you." The woman was, of course, Anna Ivanovna Zelenova.

At Pavlovsk the re-creation of the paintings was perhaps the most complex and delicate task of the restoration. The painted ceilings and walls, components of a unified architectural conception, were essential to the original decoration. To make the task even more difficult, several different painters — Mettenleiter, the Scotti brothers, and Gonzaga — had accomplished the original work. Each of these artists had his own distinct style and technique. Said Anna Zelenova, "No artist wanted to take the responsibility for this incredibly complex and unusual work . . . but Treskin believed in his own strength and was able to see through the gaping holes in the floor, the dirt, and ruins to the future beauty."

From the beginning Anna believed in him completely and was to champion him against all those who doubted.

Treskin was fifty years old when he began the work for which his entire professional career had been preparing him, a work that was to be the crowning of his artistic life. He was to give the rest of his life to Pavlovsk and to re-create the paintings in forty rooms of the palace.

In 1955/56, to face the work ahead of him, Treskin needed all his imagination and energy. Although the reconstruction of the building was complete, nothing had yet been done on the interiors. There, desolation still reigned. A cold blue fog hung in the air of the damp halls. There were no floors; dust was everywhere. After a thorough study of the archives and records, he began to work in the Cavalier's Hall. Stretching his canvas on a subframe, inclined so that it did not point directly up at the ceiling, Treskin began his first painting, *The Miracle of St. Paul,* for the palace chapel (one of sixteen paintings he was eventually to re-create for the chapel). It was so cold that fingers and paint froze. The only available heat came from a small Blockade-type *burzhuika,* a wood-burning stove that wheezed and smoked. In order to provide sufficient heat, the stove had to be energetically stoked up all morning, and only then could the artists begin their work. Once, left unattended, it spewed out black soot, which covered the blue sky of a painting Treskin had just begun. The soot was carefully washed off, but the painting had to be entirely redone. In summer the temperature in the palace chapel remained fairly constant, but one day a window was opened and a gust of warm air caused condensation, which ruined the completed ceiling. The artists redid it. Despite all setbacks, Treskin's work of re-creation was so accurate that when the elderly artist Vladislav Izmailovich, who had restored the original ceiling in 1911, came to take a look, he assumed incorrectly that Treskin had used his sketches.

Kuchumov met Treskin in 1956. "At that time," he says, "all of the work at Pavlovsk proceeded jointly; we had daily meetings and consultations. Scaffolds were everywhere. Hardly a day went by that I did not scramble up one of them. Treskin was a diamond in the rough, an artist who had never completed the Academy, a master. He was invaluable to us at Pavlovsk because he was so intimately familiar with the style and techniques of the Old Masters. He tried to understand how they had worked — even to how they applied their primer.

"There is a great difference between Treskin's stroke and that of other restorers. For instance there were some at Pushkin who painted Alexander I's rooms

so far from the original that I made a report to the Monuments Protection Inspectorate and forced them to convene — as if we had the right to make corrections on the creations of great masters! Even in this case, when the original artist
was perhaps not so distinguished, he had created a room in a certain way and
so it must be again.

"Treskin drew flowers, especially roses, which are extremely difficult, so accurately that even a botanist could not find fault with the location of pistil or
stamen. He was wonderfully familiar with the technique of tonality — he could
sense it. From the beginning he believed in the possibility of the restoration of
the palace and its artistic treasures. This is a lot easier for us to talk about now
than it was then."

Treskin always worked quickly. He could, it was said, paint a setting sun in
twenty minutes. With a small band of six helpers he managed to re-create the
ceiling paintings at a surprisingly rapid rate — at first two or three a year, then
three or four. Each room presented a new challenge. In the Cavalier's Hall, because later restorations had distorted the original, he found a conflict between
Scotti's work and the actual dimensions of the room. Noticing that there was no
arch or canopy as there had been in the original Scotti sketches, Treskin corrected
this and then painted a lighter center with edges in darker tones, thus restoring
Scotti's original illusion. The molding, designed by Quarenghi, had been covered
with bronze gilt; soot had accumulated on the original plasterwork so that it was
unrecognizable. After skillful uncovering by Treskin, there was no doubt as to
the author.

The Rossi Library had been entirely destroyed by the fire. There were no prewar records that described the exact nature of the ceiling of the library — only
small photographs. Treskin studied the literature of the ancient philosophers and
thinkers to determine which should be represented in the library, finally deciding
on Plato, Aristotle, and Hippocrates. He then had to decide how to represent
them and settled on the technique of *grisaille*.*

In Maria Feodorovna's Boudoir, his research revealed that the walls had been
decorated with small landscapes representing the hours of the day. He repro-

---

* *Grisaille* enameling is a painting technique, used especially in wall and ceiling decoration, which achieves a
dramatic effect of light and shade and a profound sense of three-dimensionality. It was developed in the sixteenth century in France by the Limoges school of enamelers (as distinguished from the much older technique
of *grisaille,* employing only shades of gray). Pulverized white vitreous enamel is made into a paste by mixing
it with water, turpentine, oil of lavender or petroleum oil, and is then applied to a dark enamel ground. Lighter
areas of the design are thickly painted, while the gray areas are obtained by painting with thinner coats to
allow the dark background color to tone the white pigment.

duced the painted marble pilasters, which were copies of Raphael's in the Loggia of the Vatican, and the ceiling painting in distemper* from the sketches of Giovanni Scotti.

In the Family Study, Treskin re-created the ten muses on the ceiling, using scenes from vases in the Hermitage to reproduce the mythological scene. In Maria Feodorovna's bedroom, he reproduced on white marble the flower garlands originally created by Scotti. Throughout the palace he was able to understand and re-create the varied styles, including the visual illusion and perspective of the Upper Vestibule, originally painted by Scotti, which made the ceiling appear higher than it actually was. Despite the fact that Jacob Mettenleiter was a painter whose style Treskin personally found a bit saccharine, he nevertheless managed to duplicate Mettenleiter's brushstroke exactly.

He used oil and tempera on a great variety of surfaces: marble — both natural and artificial — canvas, silk, and glass. In the Third Anteroom, which leads into the Throne Room, the eighteenth-century wall panels had been decorated with panels made of a special type of blue glass. The secret of making this glass had been lost, but by ingeniously using normal glass painted under a cobalt light, Treskin managed to achieve the same effect.

The spectacular decoration of the State Bedroom with its walls of tempera-painted silk, originally done by Mettenleiter, caused him many problems — the paint repeatedly ran on the silk, and he was forced to do many experiments before finally being able to reproduce the exuberant eighteenth-century scenes of flowers, fruits, and birds. He decided to reproduce the bright, joyful colors of the original panels, a course the ever-vigilant overseeing committee of art first approved, then subsequently reversed, deciding they wanted more subdued colors.

Treskin was often impatient with what he felt was the excessive nagging by the flocks of "specialists" who constantly inspected and second-guessed his work, advising him at times to paint more simply in a planar, one-dimensional style in rooms that called for illusory, three-dimensional, monumental painting. Although he never lost his temper like Cameron and Gonzaga before him, he could be extremely stubborn when he was convinced his artistic principles were correct. In the case of the silk panels, he refused to budge and won his argument when

---

*Distemper is a crude form of tempera made either by mixing dry pigment into a paste with water, which is thinned with heated glue in working, or by adding pigment to whiting, a mixture of fine-ground chalk and size (a gelatinous glazing solution). It is used for stage scenery and full-size preparatory cartoons for murals and tapestries. When dry, its colors have the pale, mat, powdery quality of pastels, with a similar tendency to smudge.

he produced an original pillow, evacuated during the war, compared it to his own work, and convinced the experts that despite the bleeding of color and dirt that had occurred during the centuries the original colors had been as bright as his.

This master copier who could literally put himself in the skin and brain of an artist of another century explained his method in this way: "Re-creation is a very capricious process. One must be very careful, have a great deal of knowledge — know the epoch, the style, the time and other analogies where they exist. In the restoration of a statue, perhaps an arm or a leg has been preserved. If one is then able to re-create other parts from sketches or photographs, no one will notice the problems in the work; but if one does a tasteless copy which is not in the right style, which smacks of Picasso or Dufy for example, then it will turn out completely wrong. Restoration and re-creation are two completely different processes. When one faces, as we did, blank walls, and the work must be entirely redone, first one must carefully study all of the materials — scour the libraries for sketches and photographs. Then the artist must totally disengage himself from the modern world and become immersed in the qualities and the spirit of the master who created the work in bygone days. You must fully understand the artist's style and become imbued with it, forgetting your own personality completely for a time. One cannot allow oneself a single original brushstroke or it will be immediately noticed. In some situations I simply had to work intuitively."

Treskin needed all his remarkable intuition to overcome his most difficult problem and accomplish his most spectacular feat — the reconstruction, one hundred twenty-five years after Gonzaga's death, of a ceiling that had been erased not by the Nazis, but at least a hundred years before under unknown circumstances. This work was the re-creation of the monumental four-hundred-square-meter ceiling of Paul's Throne Room, for which only partial original sketches by Gonzaga existed. Prewar records of the condition of the palace showed this ceiling as plain white, and the rigorous standards of restoration established for the palace would admit no change unless other exact documentation could be found. Heated controversies ensued. A first controversial question was whether Gonzaga's plan had ever been executed. The conservative faction of specialists supposed either that for some unknown reason — perhaps Paul's death — the room had never been completed, or, that since Pavlovsk was a relatively unimportant Imperial dwelling, it had never been recorded. With no photographs or exact records to prove otherwise, this conservative viewpoint held that if one did not know exactly what to do, one should do nothing; lacking certain evidence, the ceiling should be left as it was before the war.

The opposing faction argued that, considering Paul's fierce desire for the throne and his efforts to impose his Imperial importance, it was extremely unlikely that he would have permitted the Throne Room to go unpainted, much less unrecorded, when all other rooms in the palace were decorated and meticulously documented. Such a major room, they insisted, could not have been left with undecorated ceilings; paintings along the lines of Gonzaga's sketches must have been made and later damaged and removed or painted over. They pointed to the fact that a document from 1818 was found that indicated that the ceiling of the Throne Room had been scraped, evidence that paintings had existed prior to 1818 that had been erased during the scraping process. These specialists insisted that there must be other, as yet undiscovered, documents that would support their view.

The crux of the controversy was what should be the guiding principle of the restoration. Was it to put the palaces back into the condition they were in immediately before the war? In this case, the Throne Room should have a plain white ceiling. Or was the goal to reconstitute each part of the palace as it was in its greatest period, when, as it did in this case, this would mean venturing into unknown and risky territory and cutting across the principles of meticulous objective research on which the restoration was based? Anna Zelenova decisively took the bolder path. She fiercely championed the idea of re-creating the ceiling and Treskin's ability to accomplish it.

In his preparation Treskin began by studying all of Gonzaga's plans and sketches at the Hermitage. He went to Archangelskoe, a former Yusupov estate outside Moscow, to see the Gonzaga stage decors preserved there. He spent time at the Suvorov Museum searching for an allegorical theme appropriate for the epoch of the ceiling. Then, working from the available original Gonzaga sketches, which covered only one-quarter of the ceiling, he developed a construction of what the ceiling might have been, a very remarkable *trompe l'oeil* painting that gave an illusion of a high dome reaching to an open sky.

At the end of his life, speaking of this controversial work in the Throne Room, Treskin said, "If it had not been for Zelenova, there would have been no sketches. She supported the idea, although many protested and were against it. The commission considered that it was important to preserve the historical, and since it was thought then that the ceiling had been unpainted before the war it should stay that way — that it was impossible to re-create Gonzaga's work, all the more so since sketches existed for only one-quarter of the ceiling. But she was very determined, a real director, the boss. She went to Moscow and proposed that if an artist could be found, he be allowed to try. I made some sketches that pleased them. She then went to the Deputy Minister of Culture, who at that time was also the president of the Academy of Art, and it was decided to go ahead and paint the ceiling. But for her, the Throne Room would not exist today."

Once his sketches were approved, Treskin and his small band of assistants worked for six months making the cartoons. Following the same procedure as for all the ceilings, these were done in full scale, with all colors, shadows, and shadings, indicating what the ceiling would look like when painted. These cartoons were attached to the ceiling, then the scaffolds pulled away so that the painters could look from the floor and make adjustments. The commission criticized and made suggestions. Then, piece by piece, very precise charcoal drawings were made. A tracing was then taken from the charcoal, and pinholes were made on the tracing. The tracing was then attached to the ceiling, and a wad of gauze with charcoal passed over the holes to mark the proper spots.

Said Treskin: "We painted for almost two years, plus eight months of preparation. We had to have our work finished by October of 1957, in time for the fortieth anniversary of the Soviet government, when the first halls were to be opened. We worked twelve-hour days, working the extra hours without pay, and then took cuts in our pay."

Zelenova's faith in the project and in Treskin turned out to be well founded. Within the last few years, new documents dating from the second half of the nineteenth century have been discovered that contain instructions to restore the ceiling of the Throne Room to its original condition. "Now," said Treskin with a smile, "they have found that there were indeed paintings on the ceilings after all — but we didn't know it then."

In the course of fifteen years of work on the ceilings of the palace, Treskin painted several hours a day with his head thrown back and right hand constantly raised. His hand would go numb and his shoulder muscles grew painfully tense. Workers much younger than he sometimes fainted, but not Treskin, who attributed his stamina to the fact that he always wore knee-high boots because these supported him well, and, he said, "I drink a little glass of spirits and put on my boots, never lacing them too tight, and I never suffer from blood pooling at my feet. I assert that is why I am a healthy man."

It was of course Treskin, who loved roses ("the flower of Venus, flower of love," he said) and painted them so perfectly, who was called on in 1 9 8 3 to begin sketches for the restoration of the Rose Pavilion. He managed to complete these and the cartoons. They were to be his last works.

During his entire working lifetime Treskin was never separated from his brush. Every morning, before breakfast, he would work for a time at his easel. Until the age of seventy-two he was full of energy, and only after seventy-five did he begin to decline. When he was eighty, suffering badly from arthritis, he fell ill. One day, an old friend arrived to find the artist in deep distress. That day he had finally understood that his illness was not temporary, as he had forced himself to believe up to that time. Sadly he said, "I now understand, my hand trembles. I can no longer paint." Then he wept.

Treskin died in 1 9 8 6 at eighty-one. The man who had begun his artistic life drawing with stubs of charcoal and paint made of clay had resurrected beauty all over his city. In his lifetime he had painted over three thousand square meters of ceilings; he once said that there was not a single restored building in Leningrad that he had not worked on. For his artistic achievements he had been named a Laureate of the State Prize of the USSR and had received a gold medal from the Academy of Art. It has been calculated that if all the drawings, sketches, and paintings he prepared for Pavlovsk were to be laid out in a line one meter wide, they would stretch for ten kilometers. His name is now as indelibly connected with the palace as those of the original creators; its reborn splendor is his best memorial.

In 1 9 5 7, thirteen years after the palace had been found in ruins, the first seven halls, which included the Cavalier's Hall and the Throne Room with Treskin's extraordinary *trompe l'oeil* ceiling, were opened to the public. At the ribbon-cutting ceremony, surrounded by their co-workers, a beaming and proud Anatoly Mikhailovich and Anna Ivanovna held a platter of bread and salt, the traditional Russian symbol of good fortune and welcome. In 1 9 5 8, four more halls, including the Picture Gallery, were finished. The following year, 1 9 6 0, eleven more rooms. Among these were all the private rooms, including the Pilaster Study as well as Voronykhin's masterpiece, the Little Lantern Room, with the tall caryatids that had been finally reworked to perfection by Shabalkina and Mal'tseva. Next, in 1 9 6 3, the Egyptian Vestibule, where Nazi tortures had taken place, and the main vestibules were unveiled, and in 1 9 6 5, the Italian Hall. By 1 9 6 7, the year I first saw the palace, six more main rooms were ready, including the gold and white Hall of Peace and the imposing Greek Hall with its green *scagliola* columns and magnificent fireplaces. To mark the event, Anna Zelenova composed a scenario for a historical theatrical production: *From a Tsar's Palace to a Soviet Museum.*

Twenty-six years after the war, on April 20, 1970, in honor of the hundredth anniversary of Lenin's birth, all the remaining eight rooms on the first floor were opened to the public: Maria Feodorovna's charming ballroom, the White Dining Room overlooking the Slavyanka, where the Nazis and Spaniards had stabled their horses, and the gilt and mauve Rossi Corner Salon, which had been re-created according to Kuchumov's research. For the first time, the income from tours was sufficient to cover the continuing expenses of restoration. That year, the sound of the harpsichord, the violin, and the harp were heard again in the Greek Hall with the beginning of regular concerts of the music of Pavlovsk, which have been conducted there ever since.

During those years all the central areas, the *allées,* and the circles of the park had been restored. Beginning in 1964, Gonzaga's original spatial composition of the park was re-created. Gromova, having carefully studied the history of the landscaping of the park, designed a restoration project for its *allées,* ponds, and little arched bridges. The birch-aspen forest, which had grown up in these areas, was cut out, uprooted, plowed, and replanted with four thousand pine seedlings, with the birch preserved as an enclave on the edge of the forest, a chorus around the conifers. Maria Feodorovna's Private Garden had been replanted and bloomed with lilacs, white roses, begonias, and ageratum. In 1974, the first exhibitions were held in the newly opened pavilions of the Pil Tower and the Temple of Friendship, which had been used as a shooting gallery by the occupying Nazis; by 1977 the Round Hall and the Music Pavilion were also restored. From 1966 to 1970, all the reservoirs of the park and the Slavyanka had been cleaned, the Visconti and Centaur bridges, as well as the Brenna Staircase with its bronze and marble lions, restored.

By 1977, a total of fifty halls of the palace had been opened to the public. Over ten million visitors from all over the world had come to see them. Among these were noted art specialists from many lands, and world figures, including, from the United States, President Nixon and Jacqueline Onassis. The stream of visitors continues; in 1988 there were close to two million: 1,703,264 Soviet citizens and 175,137 foreigners.

It is impossible to calculate the exact cost of the restoration. Zelenova in her guide to the palace writes, "Over a twenty-five-year period the cost of restoring the palace came to over three million rubles." To which she adds proudly, "This was a significantly smaller amount spent on restoration than on many similar projects." Kuchumov agrees, pointing out that "The Jubilee Palace of Sports in Leningrad cost nine million rubles. We spent only 3,330,000 rubles after the war to repair all the damages." But these figures do not include labor, nor the thousands of unpaid hours given by workers and public. Today, the original figure has been adjusted to over four and a half million rubles. Yet even this figure can only be an approximation, for as one specialist points out, "The four and a half million we talk of now is actually worth much more — back then our expenses were different; gold was cheaper as was molding work. Now the restoration of one of the large halls at the Catherine Palace could cost as much as the entire restoration at Pavlovsk. Over a thirty-year period (1945–1985), in Leningrad, four hundred million rubles was then spent on the restoration of historical and cultural monuments."

Estimating the cost of suites of furniture, sculpture, and objects of art lost or destroyed has been even more problematical. Says one museum specialist, "The magnificent Zech lanterns in the Throne Room, for instance, cost four thousand rubles in their own day — which is as much as they would cost now." Some years ago GIOP made an ingenious attempt at creative accounting to arrive at values. "They took a current price for an armchair — ten rubles — and then calculated that a chair from the eighteenth century was worth ten times more. Since these were museum items and part of an ensemble, the commission has worked out a special value for each piece. The lists which have been compiled, if one adds up all the palaces, add up to the sum of five billion rubles."

In 1977 Pavlovsk celebrated its two hundredth birthday. A hundred years earlier, to mark its centenary, a splendid book on the palace's history had been published by Maria Feodorovna's grandson, Grand Duke Constantine Nikolaievich. To mark its bicentenary, a ceremony was held in the restored palace, which included a tour of the reopened rooms, a concert, and a reception for the palace restorers. The room was packed. Those who attended said that as Anna Zelenova read a list she had carefully compiled of the names of all the individuals and organizations who had helped to bring her beloved palace alive again, her hands were shaking. Afterward, one old worker looking up at the restored palace said with pride, "I think the Tsar would be pleased."

In her guide to Pavlovsk, Anna, with some irony, writes, "It was then true, that much later, when work in the halls of the palace was finished, that many people suddenly grew wise to the growing interest in restoration and wanted to take part in the process — even artists from the capital began to take notice that the distance between Moscow and Leningrad no longer frightened them."

The small band of museum workers in Leningrad who, in an hour of national crisis, had acted independently to save and then rebuild their heritage, who had resurrected their palaces from oblivion through their dedication and self-sacrifice, had accomplished far more than merely re-creating buildings of mortar and brick. The restorations of Pavlovsk and other palaces have mirrored the commitment and fierce dedication of Russians to their culture. By proving that Russians could work to the highest and most exacting artistic standards, they restored Russian national pride and spirit.

Anna lived to see restoration become a great civic passion. The reconstruction of Pavlovsk and other palaces, spearheaded by architects and art specialists in Leningrad, set in motion what has today become a mass movement among all classes of Russian society to preserve its heritage. Among average Soviet citizens, including the young, the protection and restoration of favorite monuments has today become a personal mission for which they are prepared to sign petitions and even on occasion sit down in front of bulldozers. In a monolithic society that stifled personal expression, preservation became a powerful vehicle for voicing public feeling.

In 1965, the All-Russian Society for the Protection of Historic and Cultural Monuments was formed by a group of intellectuals and artists to protest the building of the Hotel Rossiya in Moscow, which was to have obliterated a number of historic churches. Today this society, to which anyone can belong by paying thirty kopecks, numbers more than thirty-six million members. The society now monitors development projects, gives classes, prints material, organizes demonstrations.* It has been granted legal authority by the Council of Ministers of the Russian Republic to pass on all planning and redevelopment projects bearing on preservation activity in the RFSR.

Commitment to preservation objectives now runs so deep that shared responsibilities of state and citizenry were embodied in Article 68 of the Soviet Constitution of 1977 — a body of legislation beginning in 1918 on nationalization and registration to recent policy decisions on protective zones regulating new construction around historic monuments and districts. Reconstructed palace ensembles fall under the legally defined category of "preservation region" (*zapovednik*),

---

* A few years ago the head of the Moscow restoration said that such is the passion for preserving the historic past that he "cannot touch a bridge now without a stream of letters."

assuring the integrity of the aesthetic blend of architectural and landscape environments. In 1983 Pavlovsk was the first to receive this designation and guards it jealously. Three years ago, workers and citizens launched a movement to alter the flight path of planes coming into the Leningrad airport only a few miles away; the planes, they said, were rattling the windows of the palaces. In 1986, under the sponsorship of Raisa Gorbacheva, the Soviet Cultural Fund was formed, one of whose goals is to support preservation efforts.

Shortly before her death, Anna Zelenova, musing on her life's work at Pavlovsk, said, "What is important is to help each person see beauty — so that for each individual the day does not disappear without a trace."

She died on the job on January 16, 1980, at age sixty-seven. As she was delivering a lecture at a Party meeting, in midsentence she uttered a cry and collapsed. Since her death, every year on her birthday her friends and co-workers gather at Pavlovsk to hear chamber music concerts and honor her memory.

Since his retirement as Chief Curator, Anatoly Mikhailovich Kuchumov has suffered two strokes and a heart attack, which have left him partially paralyzed. He has been forced to learn to write with his left hand, but still alert and energetic, he has completed several books and articles and at this date has just finished a definitive book on the Amber Room. He and Anna Mikhailovna celebrated their fiftieth wedding anniversary in 1986, and they live now in a small apartment in a retirement home in Pushkin. With great pride he says, "Pavlovsk was the first palace to take on the life of a museum. Our job was to bring it back after the terrible destruction and today the palace is almost exactly the way it was in the eighteenth century — a monument of architecture, a monument of art that is tied to the finest architects and artists. We are proud that we have passed something wonderful onto the following generations. But it is important that such a history should never be repeated."

In 1986 Kuchumov, along with five restorers, among them Alexander Kedrinsky and Natalia Ode, were awarded the Lenin Prize, their nation's most prestigious honor, for their accomplishments. The six gathered in Anatoly Mikhailovich's small apartment and celebrated the occasion with an evening of champagne and reminiscences.

It took less than three years to destroy the palace. The painstaking work of resurrecting it has taken forty-five years. To the restoration work, thousands of specialists in many disciplines — architects, chemists, biologists, draftsmen, architectural historians, physicists, engineers — have given all of their talent and energy and many years of their lives . . . and the work continues. Joined by a new generation, several of the original craftsmen of the restoration are still at work. Plans for the restorations of the Leningrad palaces extend well beyond the year 2000. At Pavlovsk, work is continuing on the further embellishment of the park and pavilions. The Rose Pavilion has been reconstructed and is in the process of full restoration. Hothouses have been rebuilt; flowers are blooming again. At the palace, museum workers dream of restoring the Voksal and of recovering their lost Gobelins, which hang on a museum wall in California.

Today, one can walk through the halls of the palace with Maria Feodorovna's 1795 inventory letter to her mother in hand and find the rooms exactly as she described them. Pavlovsk has been called the finest restoration in the world. The documentation of the entire project of restoring palace and park fills fifty volumes. In 1984, Leningrad was awarded the European Gold Medal for Achievement in the Preservation of Monuments of the Past.

Many times during the course of writing this book, awed by their achievement, I asked the restorers and craftsmen why they had attempted this monumental work. Kedrinsky said simply, "If people cannot see beauty they become monsters." He then added, "We like to believe that we have done this a little for you as well — that a part of Western civilization which was in the East should not perish forever."

But all those to whom I addressed the question, after thinking a moment, quietly responded with a single moving sentence of Dostoevsky: "Beauty will save the world."

Today, under the mother-of-pearl sky of the northern Russian countryside, the palace is set in a vast park full of silvery birches and dark firs. In the spring the tender green leaves and white blossoms of bird cherries cover the slopes. Thick bushes of lilacs perfume the air. In summer, luxuriant rolling meadows are sprinkled with fields of lavender and white wildflowers. Secret pools and lakes serenely disposed through the park reflect the passing clouds. In autumn among the dark green firs thousands of birch trees blaze yellow and the falling leaves turn the earth to amber. Then, rising like a dream at the end of an *allée* of burnished gold linden trees, the yellow and white colonnaded palace appears, blending the beauty of nature and art . . . a symbol of hope and of man's eternal quest for beauty, an oasis of serenity in a forever disordered world.

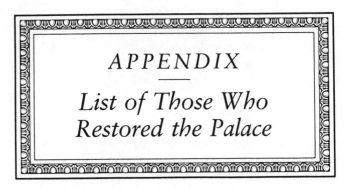

APPENDIX

List of Those Who Restored the Palace

Compiled by Anna I. Zelenova, April 13, 1970

SPECIAL SCIENTIFIC
RESTORATION AND REPAIR WORKSHOPS (STUDIOS)
LENINGRAD CITY SOVIET
SUBCONTRACTOR

Chief	S. I. Gaziyants
Site Supervisor	N. I. Medyntsev
Shop Supervisor	V. I. Mikheeva

"LENPROEKT" INSTITUTE,
MAIN APU OF THE LENINGRAD CITY SOVIET

Chief of the Design Studio	I. G. Kaptsyug
Architect (creator) of the Palace Restoration Plan	S. V. Popova-Gunich
Architects-Draftsmen	V. B. Mozhanskaya
	E. A. Sokolovsky
Builder	M. A. Yunoshev

GOVERNMENT INSPECTORATE
FOR THE PRESERVATION OF MONUMENTS,
MAIN APU OF THE LENINGRAD CITY SOVIET

Chief of GIOP	K. A. Pavlova
Inspectors	N. D. Kremshevskaya
	V. E. Tikhonova
Scientific Workers	L. A. Medersky
	Z. M. Skoblikova

PARTICIPANTS IN THE PALACE RESTORATION

300 workers from the Polufabrikat Factory worked on the façade
Special SMU of the Department of Culture, Leningrad City Soviet
LO of the Art Fund of the RSFSR
Sculpture Studio of the Academy of Artists
Scientific-Experimental Workshop of the Mukhina LVKhPU
"Monumental Sculpture" Factory
Leningrad Mirror Factory
The Hermitage
The Russian Museum
All museums of the Main Directorate of Culture
State Museum of Moscow in the Kremlin (Kremlin Museum)
State Historical Department in Moscow
Shusev Museum for Buildings and Architecture
Pushkin Museum for the Decorative Arts
Tretiakov Gallery
Pushkin Museum in Moscow
Novgorod Museum-Preserve
Kalinin Regional Museum
Archives of the Great October Socialist Revolution
State Archives of Film and Photographic Documents
Saltykova-Shchedrina State Public Library
Mosfilm
Leningrad Roentgenology Institute
Leningrad Hotel Trust
Lenfilm

    All the organizations, establishments, schools, and colleges of
    the city of Pavlovsk worked on the restoration of the palace.

LEADERS OF THE RESTORATION OF THE PAVLOVSK PALACE-MUSEUM

Ministry of Culture of the RSFSR
Executive Committee for Labor of the Leningrad Council of Deputies
Main Directorate of Culture of the Executive Committee of the Leningrad City Council

Head of the Central Board (Glavka)	A. Ia. Vitol
Deputy	A. M. Mukhin
Engineer	L. M. Aizin
Assistants	N. A. Iakovitsky
	I. D. Karpovich
	N. K. Kartseva

PUSHKIN REGIONAL COMMITTEE OF THE CPSS

First Secretary
G. M. Kamenev

PUSHKIN REGIONAL AND PAVLOVSK MUNICIPAL
EXECUTIVE COMMITTEES OF THE COUNCIL OF DEPUTIES FOR LABOR

M. V. Makarova
L. A. Zhuvalev

BOARD OF DIRECTORS OF THE PALACE-MUSEUM AND PARK

Director	A. I. Zelenova
Assistants	V. A. Belanina
	A. A. Avgustovskaya
	A. T. Kolynok
Head Preservationists	A. M. Kuchumov
	N. I. Gromova
	N. V. Veis
Architects	I. S. Skopich
	N. D. Shchetinin
	T. A. Akkerman
Scientific Workers	K. I. Kurovskaya
	K. P. Belavskaya
Superintendent of Work	N. I. Anufriev
	D. M. Trofimov
	V. I. Borusevich
Secretary of the Party Organization	L. A. Perlov
Chairman of the MK	A. I. Antonov

STATE AIRPORT CONSTRUCTION BRIGADE AND LENINGRAD
"GLAVGAZTOPSTROY"
(1944–1945)

Construction Site Supervisor	S. M. Sapgir
Engineer	A. M. Matveev
Work Supervisor	R. A. Vinkel

FIRST CONSTRUCTION DIRECTORATE
(General Contractors from 1954 on)

Director of the Trust	M. M. Antipov
Engineers	A. V. Dubitsky
	G. K. Lashchenko

Superintendent of Site Construction   M. B. Belenki
Superintendent of Construction within the Palace   O. O. Gendelman

VETERANS OF THE RESTORATION OF PAVLOVSK PALACE

ARTISTS
  Anatoly Vladimirovich Treskin
  Gegtor Antonovich Olshevsky
  Aleksandr Aleksandrovich Moroshkin
  Vasily Vasilevich Zverev
  Anatoly Ivanovich Burenin

HOUSEPAINTERS/WALLPAPERERS
  Maria Dmitrievna Biryukova
  Nina Dmitrievna Grechko
  Maria Vasilevna Kuzhelkova
  Anna Fominichna Ermolaeva
  Taisia Fedorovna Iudina

JOINERS
  Aleksei Ivanovich Efimov
  Georgy Antonovich Nikiforov
  Mikhail Markovich Kozlov
    (also a rare-wood worker)
  Aleksei Ivanovich Latus

CARVER
  Vsevolod Vladimirovich Polyakin

PLASTERERS
  Valentin Petrovich Kunygin
  Pavel Dmitrievich Ikonnikov
  Polina Andreevna Kasatkina
  Evgenia Matveevna Smirnova
  Maria Pavlovna Kostenko
    (also worked with synthetic marble)

MOLDING MODELERS
  Ivan Ivanovich Kalugin
  Nina Mikhailovna Relkina
  Iaroslav Aleksandrovich Smirnov
  Anatoly Aleksandrovich Chezlov

SCULPTORS
  Nadezhda Ivanovna Maltseva
  Tamara Petrovna Shabalkina

MARBLE WORKERS
  Pavel Dmitrievich Nikonorov
  Nikolai Fomich Varlamov

STONEMASON/BRICKLAYER
  Pyotr Ivanovich Vasilev

WELDER
  Shai Aizinovich Turetsky

CHAUFFEUR
  Leonid Ivanovich Bobrov

SPECIAL SCIENTIFIC RESTORATION WORKSHOP

GILDERS
  Galina Andreevna Maslova
  Vasily Petrovich Sokolov
  Vladimir Fedorovich Gorbachev

MASTER MARBLE WORKERS
  Nikolai Fomich Varlamov
  Vladimir Ivanovich Dvoretsky
  Mikhail Semenovich Plakov
  Konstantin Vasilevich Sobolev

MASTER METALSMITH
Mikhail Agapovich Ptashkin

WORKERS FROM THE PALACE AND PARK STAFF

G. B. Berlin	E. M. Kornilova	M. V. Romanov
E. I. Bogdonova	I. I. Kunavin	F. M. Romtsev
I. A. Borovikov	S. A. Kukushkina	G. B. Skerletova
Z. A. Veis	G. I. Kurovsky	T. M. Sokolova
M. I. Grigo	A. M. Kuchumova	I. A. Sokolova
N. G. Grekova	S. V. Lazareva	V. I. Soldatova
I. V. Grigoreva	D. A. lapshin	A. M. Stulova
V. F. Grigorev	P. A. maksimova	Kh. P. Suliaguna
M. V. Dergacheva	P. A. Malinin	M. M. Tazik
I. V. Ermolaev	I. A. Mamontov	A. G. Tretiakov
I. E. Ermolaeva	V. A. Mikhailov	A. A. Udalova
O. N. Iozef	M. K. Musatovna	I. V. Fedotov
A. K. Kirillov	M. I. Pavlova	E. T. filimonova
M. I. Kozlov	A. V. Pikalev	Z. E. Chezlova
M. P. Kozhevnikova	N. F. Rabin	B. . Iakolev
M. P. Kasatkin		

WORKERS FROM VARIOUS ORGANIZATIONS

A. P. Bobrin	V. A. Skorobogatko	F. F. Oleinik
N. I. Belekhov	I. M. Ustvolskaya	R. K. Taurit
V. S. Vishniakov	A. V. Pobedonostsev	O. N. Shilina
V. V. Kutuzov	A. G. Sukhotsky	V. I. Shevchenko
I. V. Krestovsky	A. P. Ramin	S. V. Korobkov

THE PAVLOVSK PALACE

— *Plans*

THE GROUND FLOOR

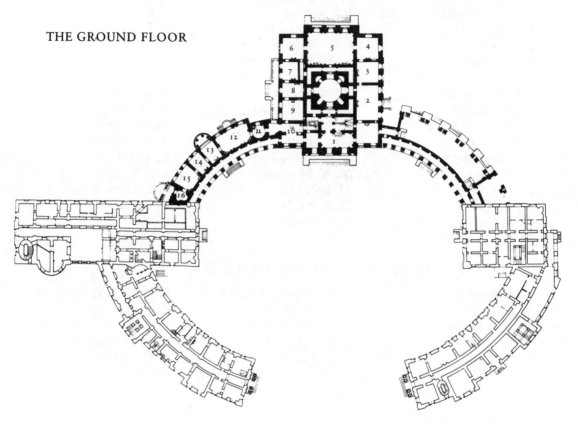

1 The Lower or Egyptian Vestibule

2 The Dancing Room

3 The Old Drawing Room

4 The Billiard Room

5 The Dining Room

6 The Corner Drawing Room

7 The New Study

8 The Family Sitting Room

9 The Crimson Room, or the Old Study

10 The Anteroom

11 The Round Room

12 The Pilaster Room

13 The Little Lantern

14 The Dressing Room

15 The Bedroom

16 The Oval Boudoir

THE FIRST FLOOR

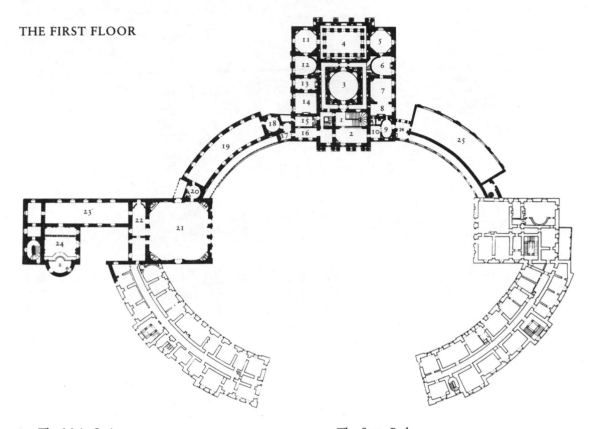

1 The Main Staircase
2 The Upper or State Vestibule
3 The Italian Hall
4 The Grecian Hall
5 The Hall of War
6 The Tapestry Room
7 The Library of Paul I
8 The Study
9 The Dressing Room of Paul I
10 The Secretary's Room
11 The Hall of Peace
12 The Library of the Empress Maria Feodorovna
13 The Boudoir

14 The State Bedroom
15 The Dressing Room
      of the Empress Maria Feodorovna
16 The Room for the Ladies-in-Waiting
17 The First Anteroom
18 The Second Anteroom
19 The Picture Gallery
20 The Third Anteroom
21 The Grand Hall
22 The Music Room
23 The Church Gallery
24 The Rossi Room
25 The Palace Library

Source Notes

CHAPTER 1: FIRST YEARS

The material concerning Sophia-Dorothea's background, childhood, and family is drawn from Shumigorskii, Oberkirch, and Grant. The description of Étupes also comes from Hayden. For details of Paul's "Instruction to Maria Feodorovna," and for an assessment of Paul's personality, see Ragsdale, *Tsar Paul,* and Morane. The material on Catherine is taken chiefly from Alexander and Anthony. Details concerning Pavlovsk Park and Palace are from many sources, chiefly Kuchumov, Kurbatov, Taleporovskii, and the various works by Zelenova. The material on Cameron is taken from Rae, Lukomskii, and Taleporovskii. Details of the beginnings of Pavlovsk Palace and Park are found in Kuchumov's works, as well as those by Kurbatov, Taleporovskii, and Zelenova. Much valuable material on the palace and its furnishings can also be found in *Les Tresors d'art en Russie.*

The statements attributed to Maria Feodorovna are taken from Oberkirch, pages 83 and 86, and Grant, page 43; Catherine's comments are found in *Lettres de Catherine II à Grimm,* pages 71–72 and 157–158, and Hodgetts, page 314; Paul's letters are contained in Shumigorskii, page 84.

CHAPTER 2: THE COUNT AND COUNTESS OF THE NORTH

The correspondence between Maria Feodorovna, her secretary Nikolai, and Kuchelbecker is taken from the Pavlovsk Palace Archives. For details on the Sèvres porcelain, see Ennes, "The Visit of the Comte and Comtesse du Nord to the Sèvres Manufactory." Details of Maria Feodorovna and Paul's grand tour are drawn from Oberkirch. For general information on items Paul and Maria Feodorovna acquired in France, see Polovtsoff and Svignine. The material on the Dairy is taken from Rae.

The observations of Baroness d'Oberkirch are drawn from Oberkirch, pages 147, 150, 156, 158, 177, 184, 217, and 223.

CHAPTER 3: THE PALACE IS BUILT

Details relating to Paul and Gatchina are drawn mainly from Ragsdale and Kobeko. The material on Maria Feodorovna comes from Shumigorskii. Paul's interest in the Knights of Malta is drawn from McGrew's article in Ragsdale, *Paul I*. For accounts of Paul's death, see Bruckner, Harcave, Vigée le Brun, and Waliszewski. The material concerning Brenna is found in Rae and Kuchumov, *Pavlovsk Palace and Park*. For information on artisans and applied arts see Solov'ev, Fersman, and Stemparzhetskii. See Kuchumov, *Russkoe Dekorativno-Prikladnoe Isskustvo*, for details of the Imperial Glass Factory and Pavlovsk bronze pieces, Chenevièvre for furniture, Verlet for French bronze pieces, *Art Objects in Steel by Tula Craftsmen* for a discussion of Tula steel, Fersman for stonework, Solov'ev for floors, and Shuiskii for material on serf artisans. Valuable material can also be found in *Les Tresors d'art en Russie*. Maria Feodorovna's inventory of Pavlovsk Palace can be found in *Tresors d'Art en Russie* and in *Pavlovsk: 1777–1877*.

CHAPTER 4: ANDREI VORONYKHIN

The material on Voronykhin is mainly drawn from Grimm, Panov, Shuiskii, and Terezhin. Also see *Mastera russkogo zodchestva* and "Ocherki ob istorii russkoi arkhitektury." For details concerning Romme, see de Vissac. For more information on the palace furniture, see Kuchumov, *Russkoe Dekorativno-Prikladnoe Isskustvo,* and Chenevièvre. Material concerning Napoleon's desire to marry Anna is drawn from Paleologue.

CHAPTER 5: GARDENS AND GONZAGA

Maria Feodorovna's letters to Kuchelbecker are found in the Pavlovsk Palace Archives and *Lettres de Mademoiselle de Nelidoff*. The material on Gonzaga is mainly drawn from Syrkina's excellent work *P'etro di Gottardo Gonzaga*, Efros, and from Gonzaga's monograph *La Musique*. Much of the information regarding the gardens is drawn from Taleporovskii, and especially Peter Hayden's articles; for the garden design also see Kuchumov's *Pavlovsk Palace and Park*. The description of Alexander's celebration at the Rose Pavilion comes from contemporary newspaper accounts of 1814; the arrival of Alexander was drawn from *Pavlovsk: 1777–1877*. The material on Pushkin was drawn from Troyat.

CHAPTER 6: LAST YEARS

The intimate details of the Imperial family's private life are taken from *Pavlovsk: 1777–1877*, which is based on material in the palace archives, and from Jackman's *Romanov Relations*. The information on Maria Feodorovna's good works is drawn from *Pavlovsk: 1777–1877*, Amburger, Svignine, and Granville. Maria Feodorovna's letters are in the Pavlovsk Palace Archives. The material on Pushkin is drawn from Troyat. For further details of John Quincy Adams's stay in Russia, see his *Memoirs*. The material on the Middletons is taken from the Middleton Plantation Archives; Mrs. Middleton's private journal is in the collection of the Charleston Historical Society.

CHAPTER 7: MUSICAL PAVLOVSK

Much of the material in this chapter is drawn from Rozanov's *Musikalnii Pavlovsk*. For additional general sources also see Sourbies's *Histoire de la Musique en Russie* and Garrard's *The Eighteenth Century in Russia*. Additional material was obtained from *Pavlovskii Muzykal'nii Vokzal'* and the Pavlovsk Palace Archives. For further information on the railroad to Pavlovsk, see *The Beginning of Russian Industrialization 1800–1860* by William L. Blackwell, and *Russian Economic Policy Under Nicholas I* by Walter McKenzie. The material on Gogol is taken from Troyat. The information on Glinka comes from his *Memoirs*. The material concerning the Tsarevich Alexis is taken from the author's interviews with Princess Vera of Russia.

CHAPTER 8: CALL ME COMMISSAR

For a full account of the Revolution, see Ulam's *The Bolsheviks* and Kerensky. Material on the life of the Romanov family at the time of the Revolution is taken from Robert Massie's *Nicholas and Alexandra* and Benckendorff's *Last Days at Tsarskoe Selo*. For additional information on Lunacharsky see Sheila Fitzpatrick's *The Commissariat of Enlightenment*. Lunacharsky's own views can be found in his essay "Pochemu my okhraniaem." For details of Lenin's attitude toward art, see Gorbunov's *Lenin on the Cultural Revolution*.

CHAPTER 9: TO THE LAST CHANDELIER

The material in this chapter is taken from Polovtsoff. For additional material on Kerensky, see Ulam's *The Bolsheviks*. Details of the death of the Imperial family are taken from Robert Massie's *Nicholas and Alexandra*.

CHAPTER 10: ANATOLY MIKHAILOVICH

The material on Stalin and collectivization is drawn from Ulam, *Stalin,* and Conquest, *The Great Terror.* The material on Anatoly Mikhailovich Kuchumov, and all quotes by him, are drawn from personal interviews with the author, recorded on tape in 1985–1986 and later transcribed.

CHAPTER 11: DESTROY ST. PETERSBURG!

Details of the beginning of the war are drawn from Salisbury's *The 900 Days,* Werth's *Leningrad* and *Russia at War,* and Ulam's *Stalin.* Information on the Amber Room is taken from interviews with Kuchumov and Kedrinsky, and archives at the Catherine Palace, Pushkin. Details of the evacuation of the Alexander Palace come from the author's personal interviews with Anatoly Kuchumov and from Telemakov's "Missia." The material on the Pavlovsk evacuation is drawn from Borshchev, Zelenova's article "Snariady," articles on Zelenova in the Soviet press, and from personal interviews given by Zelenova in connection with the documentary film by Irina Kalinina, *Reminiscence of Pavlovsk,* as well as the film script itself.

CHAPTER 12: "WE ARE BARBARIANS"

Material on the Nazis' arrival at Pavlovsk is taken from interviews with Anatoly Kuchumov and *Pravda* articles published in 1944. The material on the Spanish Blue Division is drawn from Kleinfeld and Tambs. The accounts of Nazi destruction are drawn from the testimony and documents of the Nuremberg trials, *Soviet Statements on Nazi Atrocities,* Soviet depositions deposited at Nuremberg, *Dokumenty obviniaiut,* Nikitin and Vagin, Dallin, and Quarrie, as well as contemporary Soviet newspaper articles. For further information on the Nazi theft of art, see Chamberlin's *Loot! The Heritage of Plunder,* Flanner's *Men and Monuments,* de Jaeger's *The Linz File,* and Roxan and Wanstall's *The Rape of Art.* The information on Hitler's final days comes from Speer.

CHAPTER 13: SIBERIA

The material in this chapter is drawn from the author's interviews with Kuchumov and Telemakov, and from Telemakov's articles in *Vpered.* The descriptions of Siberia come from Telemakov; the stories and incidents come from both men, who often describe the same event. The description of the city of Nizhny-Novgorod is taken from Proctor, *A Russian Journey,* as cited in Suzanne Massie's *Land of the Firebird.*

CHAPTER 14: THE SIEGE

Much material on Leningrad and the Blockade is drawn from Salisbury's valuable *The 900 Days*. Material and details of the siege are also drawn from *Saved for Humanity*, Pavlov, Werth, Fadeyev, Adamovich and Granin, Goure, Tikhinov, and memoirs of Skrjabina and Inber, and Zelenova's personal diary and her article "Vozrozhdenie."

CHAPTER 15: WHAT THEY FOUND

The account of the recapture of Pavlovsk and its condition are taken from an account in *Pamiat'* and the author's personal interviews with participating Soviet military officers. The descriptions of the palace in 1944 are taken from the eyewitness accounts of Vera Inber, Zelenova's personal journal, and her article "Vozrozhdenie"; additional material is found in the Pavlovsk Palace photographic archives. The material on the condition of the Alexander Palace is drawn from Kuchumov's personal journal written in 1944.

CHAPTER 16: CONFRONTING THE UNCONFRONTABLE

The material in this chapter is drawn from the published works and personal journals of Anatoly Kuchumov and Anna Zelenova, as well as interviews by the author with Kuchumov. Also, many valuable details and accounts of this period are drawn from Telemakov. Material on the reactions of city authorities is also drawn from Salisbury.

CHAPTER 17: THE SEARCH

The majority of the material in this chapter is taken from the author's interviews with Anatoly Kuchumov. Also see Telemakov's "Missia osobogo naznacheniia."

CHAPTER 18: WE WILL RESTORE

Much of the material in this chapter comes from the author's interviews with Kuchumov and Kedrinsky, and from Kedrinsky's *Letopis'*. Much valuable material, including details of the children's restorer school, is drawn from Telemakov, *Vozrozhdeniia krasoty*. Structural details of the restoration of the palace are in Oleinik's "*Vosstanovlenie Pavlovskogo Dvortsa*." Material on Zelenova's activities is drawn from Zelenova's interviews with Kalinina for her film. The account of Zelenova's interview with Voroshilov is from her article "Vozrozhdenie"; some details on Zelenova's personal life and habits come from Elkina. Accounts of the work done to restore the park come from the author's interviews with Marina Flit, the Pavlovsk Park Curator, and senior curators of Pavlovsk. For further details of the Leningrad Plot, see Ulam's *Stalin* and Salisbury.

CHAPTER 19: BEAUTY WILL SAVE THE WORLD

The material on restoration work at the palace is drawn from the author's personal interviews with Kuchumov and his article "*Vozrozhdenyi iz ruin.*" Material on the work of the Pavlovsk craftsmen is taken from Pavlovsk Palace Archives. For an American estimate of the restoration work in the Soviet Union and details of workmanship see *Enhancement of the Urban Environment* and Lynn Scheib's thesis. The material on Treskin comes from personal interviews with him by the author, from Telemakov's book *Vozrozhdeniia krasoti,* and from the author's interviews with the deputy curator of Gatchina. Statistics on visitors come from materials in the Pavlovsk library. Information on the cost of restoration is taken from GIOP statistics. See the December 24, 1977, issue of *Vpered,* honoring the two hundredth anniversary of Pavlovsk, for a chronology of the reopening of palace rooms to the public.

Bibliography

I. PAVLOVSK

Arkhangelskaya, N. E. *Pavlovsk*. Leningrad: Leningradskoe Otdelenie, 1936.

Hayden, Peter. "The Empress Maria Feodorovna as a Gardener," in *Study Group on Eighteenth-Century Russia Newsletter*, vol. 15 (1987), pp. 16–17.

———. "Imperial Culture at Pavlovsk," in *Country Life*, vol. 181, no. 24 (June 11, 1987), pp. 118–119.

———. "Pavlovsk," in *The Garden: Journal of the Royal Horticultural Society*, vol. 107 (June 1982), pp. 219–224.

Ivanova, O. A. *Pavlovskii Park*. Leningrad: Lenizdat, 1956.

Kuchumov, A. M. *Pavlovsk Palace and Park* (translated from the Russian by V. Travlinsky and J. Hine). Leningrad: Aurora Art Publishers, 1975.

———. *Pavlovsk: Putevoditel*. Leningrad: Lenizdat, 1980.

Kurbatov, V. *Pavlovsk: ocherk-putevoditel'*. St. Petersburg, 1912.

———. "Khudozhestvennye vesti." Doklad V. Ia. Kurbatova ob istorii zastroiki Pavlovska. Speech, 1911.

Lukomskii, G. *Pavlovsk i Gatchina*, St. Petersburg, 1922.

"Nazvaniia komnat Pavlovskogo dvortsa po opisi 1849," in *Khudozhestvennye sokrovishcha Rossii*, nos. 9–12 (1903), pp. 419–420.

Pavlovsk: Ocherki i opisanie 1777–1877. Sostavleno po porucheniyu Ego Imperatorskago Vysochestva Gosudarya Velikago Kniazia Konstantina Nikolaevicha, St. Petersburg: 1877.

Pavlovsk. Vidy parka/fotoal'bom. Avtor teksta A. I. Zelenova. Foto S. P. Ivanova. Moscow: Izogiz, 1956.

Pavlovskii Muzykal'nii vokzal'. *Istoricheskii ocherk', 1838–1912.* Sostavil' N. F. Findeizen'. St. Petersburg, 1912.

Rozanov, A. S. *Musikalnyi Pavlovsk.* Leningrad: Izdatel'stvo "Musika," 1978.

Taleporovskii, V. N. *Pavlovskii Park.* St. Petersburg: Izdanie Brokgauz-Efron, 1923.

Ukazatel' Pavlovska i ego dostoprimechatel'nostei. St. Petersburg, 1843.

Uspenskii, A. I. *Pavlovskie dvortsy i dvortsovyi park.* 3rd edition. Moscow: Obrazovanie, 1914.

Veis, N. V., Gromova, N. I., Zelenova, A. N., *Pavlovsk.* Moscow: Iskusstvo, 1952.

Zelenova, Anna Ivanova. *Dvorets v Pavlovske.* Leningrad: Lenizdat, 1978.

———. "Pavlovsk," in *Putevoditel' po Leningrady.* Leningrad, 1957.

———. "Pavlovskii dvortsovo-parkovoi ansambl" in *Vozrozhdenie: Vosponimaniia ocherki i dokumenty o vosstanovlenii Leningrada.* Leningrad, 1977.

———. *Pavlovsky Park.* Leningrad: Lenizdat, 1958.

Zemtsov, S. M. *Pavlovsk.* Moscow: Izdatelstvo Akademy Arkhitektury SSSR, 1947.

II. ART AND ARCHITECTURE

"A. N. Voronikhin" in *Ezhegodnik obshchestva arkhitektorov-khudozhnikov* (St. Petersburg), vypusk 9 (1914), pp. 5–24.

"A. N. Voronikhin v otsenke sovremennikov (k 125-letniu so dnia smerti)," in *Arkhitektura SSSR,* no. 4 (1939), pp. 74–76.

"Andrei Mikiforovich Voronikhin (Biografiia)" in *Khudozhestvennaia Gazeta,* no. 6 (1837), pp. 100–104.

"Andrei Nikiforovich Voronikhin. Nekrolog," in *Syn otechestva,* no. 12 (1814), pp. 231–236.

Arts Council of Great Britain. *Charles Cameron c. 1740–1812: Architectural drawings and photographs from the Hermitage Collection, Leningrad and Architectural Museum, Moscow.* London: The Arts Council, 1967/68.

Bartenev, I. N., and Batatkova, V. N. *Russkii inter'er XIX veka.* Leningrad: Khudozhnik RSFSR, 1984.

Bartoshevich, K. K. "Kabinet 'fonarik' " (v Pavlovskom dvortse 1807–1808, arkhitektor Voronikhin). Iz otchetnykh rabot aspirantov VAA po izucheniiu pamiatnikov v russkoi klassicheskoi arkhitekture Leningrada i Moskvy. LMS, nos. 2 and 14 (1936).

Bozherianov, I. "Andrei Nikiforovich Voronikhin," in *Sever,* no. 6 (1889), pp. 116–117.

Chenevièvre, Antoine. *Russian Furniture: The Golden Age, 1780–1840.* New York: Vendome Press, 1988.

Efros, A. M. "Gonzago v Pavlovske," in *Mastera raznykh epokh,* Moscow: Sovetskii khudozhnik, 1979, pp. 69–109.

———. "Zhivopis' Gonzaga v Pavlovske," in *Pamiatniki isskustva, razrushennye nemetskimi zakhavatchikami v SSSR.* Moscow, 1948, pp. 337–360.

Fersman, A. E. *Ocherki po istorii kamnia.* 2 vols. Moscow: Akademiia Nauk SSSR, 1954–1961.

Fomin, I. "Voronikhin, Andrei Nikiforovich," in *Istoricheskaia vystavka arkitektury* [catalogue]. St. Petersburg, 1914, pp. 46–47.

Gonzaga, P'etro di Gottardo. *La Musique des Yeux et L'Optique Theatral.* St. Petersburg: A. Pluchart, 1807.

Grabar', I. E. *Istoriia russkogo iskusstva,* vol. 3. Moscow: I. Knebel', 1912.

Grimm, G. G. "A. N. Voronikhin (Biograficheskii ocherk)," in *Trudy Gosudarstvennogo Ermitazha,* no. 3 (1959), pp. 170–187.

———. Arkhitektor Voronikhin. Leningrad: Gosudarstvennoe izdatel'stvo literatury po stroitel'stvu, arkhitekture i stroitel'nym materialam, 1963.

Hunt, Ino Leland. *Giovanni Paisiello: His Life as an Opera Composer.* New York: National Opera Association, 1975.

Il'in, M. A. "A. N. Voronikhin," in *Istoriia russkogo iskusstva,* vol. 8, book 1. Moscow: Akademiia Nauk SSSR, 1963.

Jacob, Heinrich. *Johann Strauss: Father and Son.* New York: Greystone Press, 1940.

Kennet, Audrey. *The Palaces of Leningrad.* New York: G. P. Putnam's Sons, 1973.

Krutetskii, A., and Lundberg, E. "Andrei Nikiforovich Voronikhin. Materialy k biografii," in *Arkhitektura SSSR,* no. 5 (1937), pp. 41–50.

Kuchumov, A. M. "Printsipy dekorativnogo resheniia inter'era v tvorchestve arkhitektora V. Brenny." Tezisy dokl. nauchy. sessii Gosudarstvennogo Ermitazha. "Arkhitekturnoe i dekorativnoe reshenie russkogo inter'era XVIII–ser. XIX v." Leningrad, 1968, pp. 10–11.

———. *Russkoe Dekorativno-Prikladnoe Isskustvo v sobranii Pavlovskogo dvortsamuzeia.* Leningrad: Khudozhnik RSFSR, 1981.

Kurbatov, V. Ia. *Sady i parki.* St. Petersburg: M. O. Vol'f, 1916.

Lanseré, Nikolai. *Arkhitektor Charl'z Kameron: sbornik statei* . . . Moscow: Gosudarstvennoe izdatel'stvo, 1924.

Lisovskii, V. G. *Andrei Voronikhin.* Leningrad: Lenizdat, 1971.

Lukomskii, Georges. *Charles Cameron (1780–1812): An Illustrated Monograph on his Life and Work in Russia, particularly at Tsarskoe Selo and Pavlovsk, in Architecture, Interior Decoration, Furniture Design and Landscape Gardening.* Adapted into English and edited by Nicholas de Gren. London: Nicholson and Watson — The Commodore Press, 1943.

Neshchataeva, N. "Gonzagina Galeriia," in *Neva,* no. 6 (1967), pp. 219–220.

"Ocherki ob istorii russkoi-arkhitektury," in *Zodchii,* no. 35 (1906), pp. 27–29.

Panov, V. A. *Arkhitektor A. N. Voronikhin: ocherk zhizni i tvorchestva.* Moscow: Izdatel'stvo Vsesoiuznoi Akademii Arkhitektura, 1937.

Rae, Isobel. *Charles Cameron: Architect to the Court of Russia.* London: Elek Books, 1971.

Russkaia mebel' v Gosudarstvennom Ermitazhe. Leningrad: Khudozhnik RSFSR, 1973.

Sapozhnikova, T. "Kameron v Pavlovske," in *Sredi kollektsionerov,* no. 5 (1923), pp. 30–35.

Shuiskii, V. "Genii iz grafskikh krepostnykh," in *Neva,* no. 10 (1984), pp. 197–202.

Solov'ev, A. K. *Russkii Khudozhestvennye Parket.* Moscow: Iskusstvo, 1953.

Soubies, Albert. *Histoire de la Musique en Russie.* Paris: Société Française d'Editions d'Art, 1898.

Stemparzhetskii, A. G. "O primenenii dekorativnykh tkanei v inter'ere Pavlovskogo Dvortsa-Muzeia," in *Izvestiia vysshikh uchebnykh zavedenii Ministerstva Vysshego Obrazovaniia SSSR: Stroitel'stvo i arkhitektura,* no. 10 (1958).

Svignine, Paul. *Description des objets les plus remarquables de St. Petersbourg.* St. Petersburg, 1816.

Syrkina, Flora Iakovlevna. *Petro di Gottardo Gonzaga 1751–1831.* Moscow: Iskusstvo, 1974.

Taleporovskii, V. N. "Arkhitekturnyi Ansambl'Pavlovskogo Dvortsa," in *Pamiatniki is-skustva, razrushennye fashistami,* pp. 305–335.

———. *Charles Cameron.* Moscow: Vsesoiuznaia Akademiia Arkhitektury, 1939.

———. "Kameron v Pavlovske," in Lansere's *Arkhitektor Charl'z Kameron* (op. cit.), pp. 45–71.

Taranovskaia, M. Z. *Karl Rossi: Arkhitektor, gradostroitel', khudozhnik.* Leningrad: Stroizdat, Leningradskoe otdelenie, 1980.

Terezhin, A. S. *Arkhitektor Andrei Voronikhin.* Perm: Permskoe Izdatel'stvo, 1968.

Les Tresors d'art en Russie. Khudozhestvennye sokrovishcha Rossii, izdanie Imperator-skago obshchestva pooshchreniia khudozhestv . . . . Vols. 1–7. St. Petersburg, 1901–1907.

Uspenskii, A. I. *Materialy dlia opisaniia khudozhestvennykh sokrovisch Pavlovska.* St. Petersburg, 1903.

"V imperatorskom Spb. obshchestve arkhitektorov," in *Zodchii,* vol. 43, no. 11 (1914), pp. 123–124.

Verlet, Pierre. *Les Bronzes Dorés Français du XIIIe Siècle.* Paris: Picard Editeur, 1987.

Voronikhin, N. N. "Andrei Nikiforovich Voronikhin," in *Russkaia Starina,* vol. 44, no. 10 (1884), pp. 195–198.

———. "Po povodu nekotorykh versii ob A. N. Voronikhine," in *Arkhitekturnoe nas-ledstvo,* no. 9 (1959), pp. 73–78.

Wechsberg, Joseph. *The Waltz Emperors.* New York: Putnam, 1973.

Zemtsov, S. "Andrei Nikiforovich Voronikhin (k 200-letniu so dnia rozhdeniia)," in *Arkhitektura SSSR,* no. 12, (1959), pp. 45–46.

III. THE ROMANOVS

Alexander, John T. *Catherine the Great: Life and Legend.* Oxford: Oxford University Press, 1989.

Almedingen, E. M. *The Empress Alexandra 1872–1918: A Study.* London: Hutchinson, 1961.

Anthony, Katherine. *Catherine the Great.* Garden City, NY: Garden City Publishing Company, 1925.

Bibliotheque Slave Elzevirienne, XIV Correspondance de sa Majeste L'Imperatrice Marie Feodorowna avec Mademoiselle de Nelidoff sa Demoiselle D'Honneur (1797–1801): Lettres de Mademoiselle de Nelidoff au Prince A. B. Kourakine. Publiée par La Princesse Lise Troubetzkoi. Paris: Ernest Leroux, 1896.

Bruckner, Alexander. *Smert'Pavla Pervago. Professora Shimana i professora Bricknera. Perevod s nemetskago* . . . Moscow: "Obrazovanie," 1909.

de Choiseul-Gouffier, Madame La Comtesse. *Historical Memoirs of the Emperor Alexander I and the Court of Russia,* London: Kegan, Paul, Trench, Trubner and Co., Ltd., 1904.

Ennes, Pierre. "The Visit of the Comte and Comtesse du Nord to the Sèvres Manufactory," in *Apollo* (March 1989), pp. 150–156.

Grant, Mrs. Colquoun. *A Mother of Czars: A Sketch of the Life of Maria Feodorowna, Wife of Paul I and Mother of Alexander I and Nicholas I.* London: John Murray, 1905.

Harcave, Sidney. *Years of the Golden Cockerel: The Last Romanov Tsars, 1814–1917.* New York: Macmillan Company, 1968.

Hodgetts, E. A. Brayley. *Life of Catherine the Great of Russia.* London: Methuen and Co., 1914.

Jackman, S. W., editor. *Romanov Relations: The Private Correspondence of Tsars Alexander I, Nicholas I and the Grand Dukes Constantine and Michael with their sister Queen Anna Pavlovna 1817–1855.* London: Macmillan and Company, 1969.

Kobeko, Dimitri. *La Jeunesse d'un Tsar: Paul Ier et Catherine II (Tire du russe par Dimitri de Benckendorff).* Second edition. Paris: Michel Levy Frères, 1896.

———. *Tsesarevich Pavel Petrovich, 1754–1796.* St. Petersburg, 1882.

Lettres de Catherine II à Grimm. Sbornik Imperatorskago Russkago Istoriisskago Obshchestva. Vol. 23. St. Petersburg, 1878.

Morane, Pierre. *Paul Ier de Russie avant l'avenement 1754–1796.* Paris: Librairir Plon, Plon-Nourrit et Cie, 1907.

Neledinskii-Meletskii, Prince Obolenskii. *Khronika Nedavnei Stariny iz Arkhiva Kniazia Obolenskago-Neledinskago-Meletskago.* St. Petersburg, 1876.

Paleologue, Maurice. *The Enigmatic Czar: The Life of Alexander I of Russia.* Translated from the French by Edwin and Willa Muir. London: Hamish Hamilton, 1938.

Palmer, Alan. *Tsar of War and Peace.* London: Weidenfeld and Nicolson, 1974.

Ragsdale, Hugh, editor. *Paul I: A Reassessment of his Life and Reign.* UCIS series in Russian and East European studies; 2. Pittsburgh: UCIS, University of Pittsburgh, 1979.

———. *Tsar Paul and the Question of Madness.* New York: Greenwood Press, 1988.

Shilder, N. K. *Imperator Pavel Pervyi: Istoriko-Biograficheskii ocherk*. St. Petersburg: Izdanie A. S. Suvorina, 1901.

Shumigorskii, E. S. *Imperatritsa Mariia Feodorovna (1759–1828): Eia Biografia*. St. Petersburg: I. N. Skorokhodov, 1892.

Squire, P. S. *The Third Department: The Establishment and Practices of the Political Police in the Russia of Nicholas I*. Cambridge: Cambridge University Press, 1968.

Strakhovsky, Leonid I. *Alexander I of Russia: The Man who Defeated Napoleon*. New York: W. W. Norton, 1947.

Vissac, Marc de. *Romme le Montagnard*. Clermont-Ferrand: Dilhan-Vives, Libraire-Editeur, 1883.

Waliszewski, K. *Paul the First of Russia, the Son of Catherine the Great*. London: W. Heinemann, 1913.

———. *The Story of a Throne: Catherine II of Russia*. London: W. Heinemann, 1895.

———. *Syn' Velikoi Ekateriny: Imperator Pavel I, ego zhizn' tsarstvovanie i smert', 1754–1801*. St. Petersburg: Izdanie A. S. Suvorina-Novoe Vremia, 1914.

IV. MEMOIRS

Adams, John Quincy. *Memoirs of John Quincy Adams: Comprising portions of his diary from 1795 to 1848*. Vol. 2. Edited by Charles Francis Adams. Philadelphia: J. B. Lippincott and Co., 1874.

Benckendorff, Count Paul. *Last Days of Tsarskoe Selo*. London: William Heinemann, Ltd., 1927.

Buchanan, Meriel. *Recollections of Imperial Russia*. London: Hutchinson and Company, 1923.

Chernay, Father Alexey. *Russian Odyssey: The Life-path of an Exile*. Roodepoort, South Africa, 1981.

d'Arpentigny, Casimir S. *Voyage en Pologne et en Russia, par un prisoner de guerre de la garnison de Dantzick, 1813 et 1814*. Paris: Ambrose Dupont et Cie, 1828.

Davies, E. C. *A Wayfarer in Estonia, Latvia and Lithuania*. New York: Robert M. McBride and Co., 1938.

Fleming, Thomas. *The Man from Monticello: An Intimate Life of Thomas Jefferson*. New York: William Morrow and Co., 1969.

Franklin, Benjamin. *Autobiographical Writings*. Carl van Doren, editor. New York: Viking Press, 1945.

Garrett, Wendell D. *Thomas Jefferson Redivivus*. Barre, MA: Barre Publishers, 1971.

Glinka, Mikhail Ivanovich. *Memoirs*. Translated from the Russian by Richard B. Mudge. Norman, OK: University of Oklahoma Press, 1963.

Granville, A. B. *St. Petersburgh: A Journal of Travels to and from that Capital*. Vol. 2. Second edition. London: Henry Colburn, 1829.

Jefferson at Monticello. Edited with an introduction by James A. Bear, Jr. Charlottesville, VA: University Press of Virginia, 1967.

Kerensky, Aleksandr Fyodorovich. *The Catastrophe: Kerensky's own story of the Russian Revolution.* New York: Kraus Reprint Co., 1971.

Masson, Charles François Philibert. *Secret Memoirs of the Court of St. Petersburg* (translated from the French). London: H. S. Nichols and Co., 1895.

Nerhood, Harry. *To Russia and Return. An Annotated Bibliography of Travelers' English-Language Accounts of Russia from the Ninth Century to the Present.* Columbus, OH: Ohio State University Press, 1968.

D'Oberkirch, Baronne Henriette-Louise. *Memoires de la Baronne D'Oberkirch sur la cour de Louis XVI et la société française avant 1789.* Paris: Mercure de France, 1970.

Van Doren, Carl, editor. *Benjamin Franklin's Autobiographical Writings.* New York: Viking Press, 1945.

Vigée le Brun, Madame Elisabeth. *Souvenirs.* Paris: C. Charpentier Ed., 1882.

"Vospominanie o Pavlovske." Film, Irina Kalinina, director. Leningradskaia studia dokumental'nykh fil'mov, 1983.

V. REVOLUTION, WAR, AND BLOCKADE

Adamovich, Alex, and Granin, Daniil. *A Book of the Blockade.* Moscow: Raduga Publishers, 1983.

Bartov, Omer. *The Eastern Front, 1941–45, German Troops and the Barbarisation of Warfare.* London: Macmillan, in association with St. Anthony's College, Oxford, 1985.

Borshchev, S. N. *Ot Nevy do Elbe.* Leningrad: Lenizdat, 1978.

Chamberlin, Russell. *Loot! The Heritage of Plunder.* London: Thames and Hudson, 1983.

Conquest, Robert. *The Great Terror.* London: Macmillan and Co., 1968.

Cooper, Matthew. *Nazi War Against Soviet Partisans, 1941–44.* New York: Stein and Day, 1979.

Dallin, Alexander. *German Rule in Russia, 1941–1945.* Boulder, CO: Westview Press, 1981.

Dokumenty obviniaiut: sbornik dokumentov o chudovishchnykh zverstvakh germanskikh vlastie na vremenno zakhvachennykh imi sovetskikh territoriiakh. Vypusk I i II. Moscow: "Ogiz," 1945.

Fadeyev, A. *Leningrad in the Days of the Blockade.* Translated from the Russian by R. D. Charques. London: Hutchinson and Company, 1946.

Fitzpatrick, Sheila. *The Comissariat of Enlightenment.* Cambridge: Cambridge University Press, 1970.

Flanner, Janet. *Men and Monuments.* New York: Harper and Brothers, 1957.

Gorbunov, V. I. *Lenin on the Cultural Revolution.* Moscow: Novosti Press Agency, 1980.

Goure, Leon. *The Siege of Leningrad.* Stanford, CA: Stanford University Press, 1962.

Howe, Thomas Carr, Jr. *Salt Mines and Castles.* New York: Bobbs Merrill Co., 1946.

Inber, Vera. *Leningrad Diary.* Translated by Serge M. Wolff and Rachel Grieve. London: Hutchinson and Company, 1971.

International Military Tribunal. *Trial of the Major War Criminals before the International Military Tribunal. Nuremberg: 14 Nov 1945–1 Oct 1946.* Nuremberg, Germany, 1947.

de Jaeger, Charles. *The Linz File: Hitler's Plunder of Europe's Art.* Exeter, England: Webb and Bower, 1981.

Kleinfeld, Gerald R., and Tambs, Lewis A. *Hitler's Spanish Legion: The Blue Division in Russia.* Carbondale, IL: Southern Illinois University Press, 1979.

Landwehr, Richard. *Lions of Flanders: Flemish Volunteers of the Waffen SS 1941–1945.* Silver Spring, MD: Bibliophile Legion Books, 1983.

Luknitskii, Pavel. *Skvoz' vsiu blokadu.* Leningrad: Lenizdat, 1964.

Mihan, George. *Looted Treasure: Germany's Raid on Art.* London: Alliance Press Ltd., 1944.

Nikitin, M. N., and Vagin, P. I. *The Crimes of the German Fascists in the Leningrad Region: Materials and Documents.* London: Hutchinson and Co., 1946.

Pamiat': Pisma o voine i blokade. A. K. Varsobin, editor: Leningrad: Lenizdat, 1985.

Pavlov, Dmitri V. *Leningrad 1941: The Blockade.* Chicago: University of Chicago Press, 1965.

Piliavskii, V. "Vandalizm nemetsko-fashistskikh zakhvatchikov v prigorodakh Leningrada," in *Arkhitektura SSSR.* Vypusk 7 (1944), pp. 35–38.

Polovtsoff, Alexander. *Les Tresors d'Art en Russie sous le regime Bolsheviste.* Paris: J. Pavlovsky and Co., 1919.

Quarrie, Bruce. *Waffen SS in Russia.* Cambridge: Patrick Stephens, 1978.

Roxan, David and Wanstall, Ken. *The Rape of Art. The Story of Hitler's Plunder of the Great Masterpieces of Europe.* New York: Coward-McCann, 1964.

Salisbury, Harrison E. *The 900 Days: The Siege of Leningrad.* New York: Harper and Row, 1969.

Seydewitz, Ruth. *Dama s Gornastaem.* Moscow: Progress, 1966.

Skrjabina, Elena. *Siege and Survival: The Odyssey of a Leningrader.* Translated by Norman Luxenberg. Carbondale, IL: Southern Illinois University Press, 1971.

Soviet Government Statements on Nazi Atrocities. London: Hutchinson and Co., Ltd., 1946.

Speer, Albert. *Inside the Third Reich.* New York: Macmillan, 1970.

Tikhonov, Nikolai. *The Defence of Leningrad.* London: Hutchinson and Co., Ltd., 1943.

Trevor-Roper, H. R. *Hitler's Secret Conversations: 1941–1944.* New York: Farrar, Straus and Young, 1953.

Ulam, Adam B. *The Bolsheviks.* New York: Macmillan Co., 1965.

————. *Stalin*. Boston: Beacon Press, 1987.

Wechsberg, Joseph. *In Leningrad*. Garden City, NY: Doubleday, 1977.

Werth, Alexander. *Leningrad*. London: Hamish Hamilton, 1944.

————. *Russia at War, 1941–1945*. New York: Carroll & Graf Publishers, 1964.

VI. RESTORATION AND CONSERVATION

Barr, Cleeve, editor. *Bulletin of the Architecture and Planning Group November 1948*. London: Society for Cultural Relations with the U.S.S.R., 1948.

Belyakova, Alla. "Beauty Reborn," in *Soviet Life*, no. 1 (Jan. 1987), pp. 55–65.

"Blagoustroistvo Pavlovskogo parka," in *Stroitel'stvo i arkhitektura Leningrada*, no. 3 (1964), p. 37.

Bulychev, K. "Pavlovsk — a remarkable feat of restoration," in *Soviet Union*, no. 10 (1971), pp. 49–50.

Central Committee Resolution and Zhdanov's Speech on the Journals "Zvezda" and "Leningrad." Translated into English by Felicity Ashbee and Irina Tidmarsh. Royal Oak, MI: Strathcona Publishing, 1978.

Daniloff, Ruth. "Restoring a Russian Heritage turns out to be a Byzantine task," in *Smithsonian*, no. 13 (March 1983), pp. 64–72.

Desiatnikov, Vladimir. "Preserving the Past," in *Soviet Life*, no. 3 (March 1978), pp. 33–36.

Elkina, A. "Na vysokom vzlete," in *Neva*, no. 5 (1980), pp. 159–161.

Enhancement of the Urban Environment: A Report of the US–USSR. Joint Working Group, May 25–June 14, 1974. Washington, D.C.: U.S. Historic Preservation Team, 1975.

Fitch, James Marston. *Historic Preservation: Curatorial Management of the Built World*. New York: McGraw-Hill, 1982.

Haight, Amanda. *Anna Akhmatova: A Poetic Pilgrimage*. New York: Oxford University Press, 1976.

Harris, Dale. "Paradox in Russia: Why are the Soviets Restoring a Splendid Czarist Palace?," in *Connoisseur*, no. 214 (March 1984), pp. 96–102.

Ianpol'skii, N., and Oleinik, F. "Vosstanovlenie fresok Gonzaga," in *Arkhitektura SSSR*, no. 12 (1938), pp. 73–76.

Ilyin, Oleg. "The Catherine Palace: A Miracle of Restoration," in *Soviet Life*, no. 2 (Feb. 1978), pp. 49–52.

Jackson-Stops, Gervase. "The Palace of Pavlovsk, Leningrad," in *Country Life*, no. 15 (Oct. 30, 1975), pp. 1142–1145, and no. 16 (Nov. 6, 1975), pp. 1222–1225.

Kedrinskii, A. A., et. al. *Letopis' vozrozhdeniia: vosstanovlenie pamiatnikov arkhitektury Leningrada i prigorodov, razrushenykh v gody Velikoi Otechestvennoi Voiny ne-metskofashistkimi zakhvatchkami*. Leningrad: Izdatel'stvo Literatury po stroitel'stvu, 1971.

Kovalenko, N. "Izuverov ne proshchaiut!," in *Sovetskaia Kul'tura,* no. 738, (March 1965), pp. 25–30.

Kuchumov, A. M. "Vozrozhdenyi iz ruin," in *Khudozhnik* (1970), pp. 33–38.

Lunacharskii, A. V. "Pochemu my okhraniaem dvortsy Romanovykh — putevye vpechatleniia," in *Ob izobrazitel'nom iskusstve.* Vol. II. Moscow: Sovetskii khudozhnik, 1967.

———. *Stat'i ob iskusstve.* Moscow-Leningrad: Gosudarstvennoe izdanie "Iskusstvo," 1941.

Mikhailov, A. "Vladelets Pavlovskogo dvortsy," in *Otchizna,* no. 6 (1978), pp. 21–24.

Okhrana i restavratsiia pamiatnikov arkhitektury Leningrada. Leningrad: Lenizdat, 1981.

Oleinik, F. F. "Restavratsiia fresok Gonzago," in *Arkhitektura Leningrada,* no. 5 (1938), p. 53–54.

———. "Vosstanovlenie Pavlovskogo Dvortsa," in *Arkhitektura i stroitel'stvo Leningrada* (Nov. 1946), pp. 36–[39].

Orbeli, I. A. "My byli ne odni," in *Podvig Veka.* Leningrad: Lenizdat, 1969, pp. 31–34.

Pamiatniki arkhitektury prigorodov Leningrada. Leningrad: Stroizdat, Leningradskoe otdelenie, 1985.

Pamiatniki zodchestva, razrushennye ili povrezhdennye nemetskimi zakhvatchikami: dokumenty i materialy. Vypusk I. Moscow: Gosudarstvennoe arkhitekturnoe izdatel'stvo Akademii Arkhitektury SSSR, 1942.

Papernaia, Nina, editor. *Podvig Veka: Khudozhniki, skul'ptory, arkhitektory, iskusstvovedy v gody velikoi otechestvennoi voiny i blokady Leningrada.* Leningrad: Lenizdat, 1969.

Rozadeev, B. A. "Vozvrashchenie k zhizni," in *Stroitel'stvo i arkhitektura Leningrada,* no. 5 (1970), pp 13–17.

Saved for Humanity: The Hermitage during the Siege of Leningrad. Leningrad: Aurora Art Publishers, 1985.

Scheib, Lynn. "No Longer a Memory: The Restoration of Pavlovsk Palace." Unpublished master's thesis, University of Maryland, 1985.

Shvidkovsky, Oleg A. "The Historical Characteristics of the Russian Architectural Heritage and the Problems of its Relation to Modern City Planning Practice," in *Journal of the Society of Architectural Historians,* no. 38 (May 1979), pp. 147–51.

Society for Cultural Relations with the USSR. Soviet Reconstruction Series, no. 2 (1944).

"Soviet Reconstruction Series," Arthur Ling, editor. Nos. 1–17 (1944–Aug. 1948). London: Society for Cultural Relations with the U.S.S.R., 1944–1948.

Staleva, Tamara. "Ot imeni chelovechestva," in *Sel'skaia Molodezh',* vol. 12 (1977), pp. 11–14.

Telemakov, V. "Missia osobogo naznacheniia," in *Vpered,* nos. 43–47 (April 10–April 22, 1982). Also printed in *Neva*'Izdatel'stvo "Khudozhestvennaya Literatura." Leningrad, 1985, pp. 136–143.

————. *Prekrasnomu zhit' vechno.* Leningrad: Lenizdat, 1981.

————. "Tak vossozdaiutsia shedevry," in *Stroitel'stvo i arkhitektura Leningrada,* no. 12 (1977), pp. 32–35.

————. *Vozrozhdeniia krasoty.* Leningrad: Lenizdat, 1972.

Tikhomirova, Marina Aleksandrovna. *Pamiatniki. Liudi. Sobytie Leningrad.* Moscow: Khudozhnik RSFSR, 1984.

————. "Podvigu podobno," in *Zvezda,* no. 2 (1972), pp. 166–175.

The U.S.S.R. in Reconstruction: A Collection of Essays. New York: American Russian Institute, 1944.

Voronin, M. *Rebuilding the Liberated Areas of the Soviet Union.* London: Hutchinson and Co., 1946.

Vosstanovlenie pamiatnikov kul'tury: (problemy restavtatsii). D. S. Likhachev, editor. Moscow: Isskustvo, 1981.

Williams, Vivian C. "Beautiful Ghosts from the Past: the Paradox of Leningrad's Revival," in Smithsonian, no. 3 (May 1972), pp. 66–72.

Zelenova, A. I. "Snariady rvutsja v Pavloske," in *Podvig Veka.* Leningrad: Lenizdat, 1969.

————. "Vozrozhdenie," in *Podvig veka.* Leningrad: Lenizdat, 1969.

Zvereva, M. "Vozrozhdennoe shedevry (o nauchno-dokumental'nom fil'me "Vozrozhdenie," posviashch. vosstanovleniiu dvortsa i muzeia v Pavlovske)," in *Znaniesila,* no. 6 (1968), p. 34–35.

VII. GENERAL

Amburger, Erik. *Geschichte der Behördenorganisation Russlands von Peter dem Grossen Bis 1917.* Leiden: E. J. Brill, 1966.

Baedeker, Karl. *Northern Germany as far as the Bavarian and Austrian Frontiers: Handbook for Travellers.* Leipzig: Karl Baedecker, Publisher, 1904.

————. *Russia with Teheran, Port Arthur and Peking: Handbook for Travellers.* Leipzig: Karl Baedecker, Publisher, 1914.

Clark, Kenneth. *Civilisation: A Personal View.* New York: Harper and Row, 1969.

Dostoevsky, Fyodor. *The Idiot.* Translated from the Russian by Constance Garnett. London: Heinemann Ltd., 1969.

Fitzpatrick, Sheila, ed. *Cultural Revolution in Russia, 1928–1931.* Bloomington: Indiana University Press, 1984.

Garrard, J. E., ed. *The Eighteenth Century in Russia.* Oxford: Clarendon Press, 1973.

Murray's Handbook: Russia, Poland and Finland. London: John Murray, Albemarle Street, 1868.

Pares, Bernard. *A History of Russia.* New York: Alfred A. Knopf, 1944.

Pavlovsk Palace Archives

Pushkin, A. S. *Mednyi Vsadnik.* Leningrad: Nauka, 1978.

Troyat, Henri. *Divided Soul: The Life of Gogol.* Translated from the French by Nancy
        Amphoux. New York: Doubleday and Co., 1973.
————. *Pushkin.* Translated from the French by Nancy Amphoux. New York: Double-
        day and Co., 1970.
Turgenev, Ivan. *A Sportsman's Sketches.* Vols. 1 and 2. London: William Heinemann,
        1902.

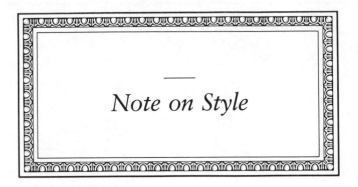

Note on Style

THERE IS NO UNIVERSALLY ACCEPTED METHOD of transliteration. I have in general followed the Library of Congress method with certain exceptions: for instance "y" for final "ii" and "oy" for "oi," "yu" and "ya" for Russian Ю and Я . Soft and hard signs are omitted. I have also made several other exceptions in order to make the text as clear as possible to a lay reader. These exceptions are especially evident when the names of persons are so well known and accepted in one spelling that to change them would only serve to confuse: for instance "Tchaikovsky" and not "Chaikovsky."

All tsars and members of the Imperial family have been rendered in English form; otherwise all first names have been rendered in the Russian fashion.

The old Russian name Feodor, by the end of the nineteenth century generally spelled Fyodor, was retained in the case of the patronymics of the tsarinas, i.e., Maria Feodorovna.

The bibliography is transliterated in standard Library of Congress style.

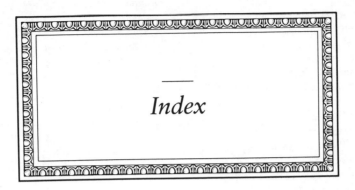

Index